Studies of Economic Growth in Industrialized Countries

Japanese Economic Growth

Studies of Economic Growth in
Industrialized Countries

MOSES ABRAMOVITZ & SIMON KUZNETS, EDITORS

Japanese Economic Growth

TREND ACCELERATION IN THE TWENTIETH CENTURY

Kazushi Ohkawa & Henry Rosovsky

Stanford University Press, Stanford, California   1973
London: Oxford University Press

Stanford University Press
Stanford, California
London: Oxford University Press
© 1973 by the Board of Trustees of the
Leland Stanford Junior University
Printed in the United States of America
Stanford ISBN 0-8047-0833-9
Oxford ISBN 0-19-690408-0
LC 72-97203

FOR NITZA AND SACHIKO

かたかくた人はいふとも
　　　　織りつがむ
我が織物の
　　白麻衣

万葉書末尽七・二九八

People may say this or that,
but I will go on weaving
the white hempen robe
on my loom.

Manyōshū, Poem no. 1298

Preface

International cooperation is always difficult and time-consuming; sometimes it is also pleasurable. The writing of *Japanese Economic Growth* partakes of all these characteristics. We began in 1961, expecting to complete our task in two or three years. Instead, distance, data revision, administrative duties, university turmoil—and perhaps our own sluggishness—extended completion for a decade.

In this long period we have accumulated a formidable list of obligations that can only partially be acknowledged in a brief preface. To Professors Simon Kuznets and Moses Abramovitz we owe our greatest debt: both read the manuscript more than once and provided extended critical comments. Our feelings of *giri* (obligation) are very great.

Many other individuals assisted at various stages of the research. In Japan, we are especially grateful to Tsutomu Noda and Yō Ōtani of the Economic Planning Agency, and Nobukiyō Takamatsu and Shigeru Ishiwata for their help at Hitotsubashi University. Eiko Nozawa also gave generous help to her father. In the United States, we were assisted by Ichirou Inukai, Arlon Tussing, Peter Heller, and two uncomplaining secretaries: Penny Gustavson and Sharon Zanowiak.

We were also aided by a variety of institutions. The main financing for travel and research was provided by the Ford Foundation and the Social Science Research Council. We are especially indebted to Messrs. John Everton (formerly at Ford) and the late Paul Webbink (SSRC) for their patience and kindness. At Harvard University, the East Asia Research Center and the Yenching Institute gave frequent and generous support. The Institute of Economic Research of Hitotsubashi University also supplied unstinting and continual help. In 1964, the Rockefeller Foundation made us welcome at its Bellagio facilities—a stay that both of us recall with great pleasure.

A special word of thanks is due the Columbia-Harvard-Yale Japan Economics Seminar that has met once a month since 1965. From time to time we had the opportunity to present parts of this volume to this expert audience, and their comments were most rewarding.

We wish to express our gratitude to Professor Shūjirō Sawada for contributing his beautiful calligraphy, and to Professor Donald H. Shively for his translation of the Manyōshū poem.

We also thank the following individuals and publishers for granting permission to reprint portions of previously published materials: The University of Chicago Press (K. Ohkawa and H. Rosovsky, "The Indigenous Components in the Modern Japanese Economy," *Economic Development and Cultural Change*, April 1961); Richard D. Irwin, Inc. (K. Ohkawa and H. Rosovsky, "Postwar Growth in Historical Perspective: A Second Look," in L. Klein and K. Ohkawa, eds., *Economic Growth: The Japanese Experience Since the Meiji Era*, Homewood, Ill., 1968); A. J. Youngson (Henry Rosovsky, "What Are the Lessons of Japanese Economic History?," in A. J. Youngson, ed., *Economic Development in the Long Run*, London, 1972); The Japan Society (Henry Rosovsky, "Japan's Economic Future: An Overview," in Jerome B. Cohen, ed., *Pacific Partnership: United States–Japan Trade*, New York, 1972).

Finally, there are two remaining constituencies whose support we can never hope to acknowledge adequately. First, there is the large group of Japanese scholars who have worked with great skill and diligence to improve the quantitative basis of Japanese economic growth. Without their results our analysis would have been impossible. Second, our task would have been nearly impossible—certainly far less pleasant—without the good-natured support of our wives, to whom this book is dedicated.

By way of conclusion, a word of friendly advice to prospective readers. Many chapters in this book are full of numbers and tables, and not everyone's taste for this type of evidence is equally refined: some readers demand it, others would like to know that it is available without having to suffer through it. For this latter category, one may suggest that they confine themselves to Chapters 1 (historical introduction), 2 (long swings, trend acceleration, and a preview of findings), 8 (the economics of trend acceleration), and 9 (beyond measurement). We do not recommend this, but the last decade of joint work has taught us to be realists.

Kazushi Ohkawa
Henry Rosovsky

Tokyo and Cambridge, Mass.
October 1972

Contents

Figures

Tables

BASIC STATISTICAL TABLES

Abbreviations and Notation

The most frequently used sources for this study are fully described in the introduction to the Basic Statistical Tables at the end of the book. In the footnotes and table notes, the following abbreviations are used.

- BST Basic Statistical Tables
- KTH *Kōgyō tōkei-hyō* (Census of Manufacturing)
- NIS Annual Reports on National Income Statistics
- IR Interim Report of the Statistical Research Association
- SRA Statistical Research Association volumes of long-term economic statistics
- LTES Estimates of Long-Term Economic Statistics of Japan Since 1868
- WS Unpublished work sheets

The following abbreviations and notation are used in the text and the tables with the meaning given here, except where there is an explicit indication to the contrary.

A Agriculture, forestry, and fisheries
B Arable land
C Construction; consumption
C_p Personal consumption
F Facilitating industries
G Rates of growth
GC Government consumption
GDP Gross domestic product
GNE Gross national expenditure
GNP Gross national product
I Investment
K Capital
L Labor
M Imports; manufacturing and mining
MP Marginal product of labor
NDP Net domestic product

NNP Net national product
P General prices
R Residual
r Rate of return on capital
S Services
$\overline{W}$ Weight or sectoral share of output
w Wage rate
w_a Agricultural wages
w_m Wages in manufacturing
w_n Wages in nonagriculture
X Exports
Y Output
α Relative income shares of capital
β Relative income shares of labor
ρ Rate of utilization

Japanese Economic Growth

CHAPTER ONE

A Historical Introduction

OVERVIEW

The purpose of this book is to explain the growth of the Japanese economy during the twentieth century, with special emphasis placed on the years after World War II. It represents an attempt to fit Japan's experience into an historical growth model of the type familiar to economists.

In this first chapter we begin with a brief historical introduction designed to show what position Japan had reached when the twentieth century started. This will establish the "initial conditions." Chapter 2 establishes the basic pattern of twentieth-century growth with an analysis of long swings and trend acceleration in private capital formation and a variety of other aggregate economic measures. It also contains a preview of the explanation, i.e. a brief statement of major conclusions elaborated in later chapters. Chapter 3 introduces an aggregate production function restricted to private nonagriculture and measures the crude and refined input of capital and labor to arrive at crude and successively refined residuals. These residuals are considered at sectoral levels in Chapter 4 where specific industries are analyzed together with the effects of intersectoral shifts, the role of agriculture, and some general considerations concerning technological progress. Chapter 5 studies the demand and supply for labor, with special emphasis on the notion of "flexible supply" from 1900 through the 1960's. The role of aggregate demand, in a gross national expenditure or resource allocation framework, is treated in Chapter 6, which also contains an analysis of savings. Chapter 7 is devoted to the impact of the foreign sector on Japanese growth, including exports, imports, the balance of payments, and resource constraints. The first seven chapters conclude the part of the book focusing on empirical results; the last two chapters are both theoretical and speculative. Chapter 8 presents the outlines of a historical model designed to explain long swings and trend acceleration in this century. The concluding Chapter 9 focuses on institutional innovation and Japan's rising social capability to import advanced technology; it also casts a look at Japan's economic future.

THE PREMODERN BACKGROUND

No country in the history of the world has risen to international prominence as quickly as Japan. One hundred years ago, this insignificant kingdom located in a remote corner of east Asia was of little interest to those concerned with global political or economic affairs. At that time the European powers occupied center-stage, and the United States was just emerging as a major contestant for world power. In Asia—if Russia is considered a European country—only India and China were relatively well-known, but neither one of these vast countries had an effective voice in international affairs. India was a colony and China mattered only in the sense that her population and resources appeared attractive to countries with commercial and/or colonial ambitions. This was the situation a century ago, and in most ways this description retains its validity until the beginning of the twentieth century.

Today the scene is radically different. Europe's role has been relatively diminished, and colonialism is largely a matter of the past. Russia and the United States have assumed the position of superpowers; China's voice appears to be stronger; most African and Asian countries are independent. But Japan has changed most of all: at present it is one of the major industrial powers of the world. The size of its gross national product exceeds that of all countries except the Soviet Union and the United States. Japan leads the world in shipbuilding, and is second in steel production. Japanese goods of high and sophisticated value-added content—automobiles, cameras, computers, etc.—are consumed in large quantities throughout the world. In fact, today the Japanese are considered serious competitors at nearly all levels and types of economic activity, and it took Japan much less than a hundred years to achieve this astonishing transformation.

It must be self-evident that Japan's transformation or modernization was not confined to economics alone. One can no longer call the Japanese remote or of little concern to the rest of the world. In nearly all facets of current life, ranging from mutual security arrangements to architecture and religion, the Japanese occupy positions of world importance. Perhaps this is especially true because Japan is an Asian and nonwhite country: as of now, Japan is the only country of non-European origin to have achieved full modernization.

The economic transformation of Japan has been the most celebrated aspect of its modern history. As we shall demonstrate, especially for the past sixty years or so, this transformation can be conceived in terms of a series of growth phases or developmental "waves" consisting of a spurt and followed by a period of less rapid growth. The greatest growth spurt began after the destruction of World War II and the ensuing years of reconstruction and rehabilitation. Frequently this spurt has been called Japan's "economic miracle," which started in 1952–54 and may be ending in the early 1970's. However, there were earlier spurts and earlier waves of growth. During the 1930's the Japanese economy developed at a most impressive pace, which was abruptly interrupted by the events leading to World War II. Similarly, the years between the end of the Russo-Japanese War (1905) and the end of World War I (1918) witnessed very rapid development, followed by much slower growth during the 1920's. These three spurts as well as the in-between years will be fully studied in later chapters because they all illustrate a similar developmental pattern: growth based on the ever more speedy absorption of modern Western technology. In this process, changes in the rate of *private* investment were especially crucial.

There was, however, one critical phase of modern economic growth that does not fit into the twentieth-century pattern based on the absorption of Western technology. This is the development of the economy during the years of the Meiji era, roughly from the 1860's until the outbreak of the Russo-Japanese War.[1] Although we shall not be concerned primarily with this period of "initial" modern economic growth, some background is needed so as to place the later events in proper historical perspective. To appreciate fully how Japan developed since the early 1900's, it is necessary to describe the economic conditions pertaining at that time. One also has to understand what economic forces created these conditions. In short, we must provide a brief review of Meiji economic history and perhaps even a review of some of its antecedents.

Where should one begin? The temptation in a review of this type is go back further and further, to become a victim of what Marc Bloch once referred to as the historian's "obsession with origins." The problem can be made clearer by considering the significance of "A.D. 1868" or "Meiji 1." On one side, before 1868, lies the "traditional" or "feudal" rule of the Tokugawa when from the economic point of view it was rather difficult to distinguish Japan from other backward countries in Asia.

[1] The Meiji era actually began in 1868 and ended in 1912, but from an economic point of view, dating based on the reign of an Emperor is meaningless.

On the other side of 1868 lies the modern era ushered in by the Restoration of the Meiji Emperor, who fronted for a new government dedicated to, among other things, economic growth. These statements are not necessarily incorrect, but they are highly oversimplified. Neither Tokugawa (1603–1868) nor Meiji Japan can be compartmentalized so easily.

Japan was ruled by the Tokugawa family for over two hundred years. These were rich, eventful years from the cultural, economic, and social point of view, and it is impossible to give an adequate overview of this period in a few lines. Yet, in considering Japanese economic growth in *this* century, is there anything that needs to be said about the Tokugawa shogunate? The answer is yes, because although Japan remained in a state of relative economic backwardness under Tokugawa rule, its condition, even prior to the Restoration, must not be confused with that of those countries where economic and other types of backwardness were closely combined.[2] And this situation was a most important asset for future economic development.

That Japan was operating with a relatively backward economy during the seventeenth, eighteenth, and most of the nineteenth century is not at all difficult to ascertain, even though quantitative evidence is sparse and of poor quality. To begin with, we know that the overwhelming majority of the population at this time were peasants of a rather common Asian type. Their output constituted the major proportion of total product. These peasants cultivated small and often irrigated plots (average size perhaps slightly less than one hectare), and many of them must have been living on the border of subsistence at least during the first half of this period. Production techniques varied region by region, with the southwest generally ahead of the northeast. Broadly speaking, agricultural technology was traditional, and yields were well below their potential level even in terms of existing practices. Very little capital equipment was employed by the peasants; the use of organic fertilizers was highly restricted (chemical fertilizers were unknown), and scientific practices such as seed selection and optimum sowing dates were largely unknown. Double-cropping was also employed at well below optimal levels. These observations can be put in general terms. Agricultural technology falls into three clear types: biological, chemical, and mechanical. The Tokugawa years contained some biological advances, and the Meiji era led to considerable biological and chemical innovations. Significant mechanical improvements, such as the use of machinery, did not occur until after World War II.

To cite solid figures for these assertions is nearly impossible, but

[2] This undoubtedly was the case in much of Africa and in some parts of Asia.

reasonable guesses are not out of the question. Toward the end of Tokugawa rule, i.e. in the middle of the nineteenth century, roughly 80 percent of the people were officially classified as peasants. Not all those designated "peasants" in the official class structure actually engaged in farming. Some worked in crafts and trade, and lived (sometimes illegally) in cities. But most of the peasants must have engaged mainly in cultivation of the soil, and certainly the Tokugawa regime was anxious to see this situation maintained, since taxation of the peasantry was its main source of income. So perhaps the figure of 80 percent exaggerates the rural nature of Tokugawa Japan. However, even scaling it down to 75 or 70 percent does not change the picture of a society in which the average inhabitant was an Asian peasant. And the presumption is that in a society of this type the level of income per capita, *an average concept*, is low. Of course "low" implies a comparative standard, and to cite actual numbers (usually supplied in U.S. dollars) would only confuse the issue. Following the reasoning of Simon Kuznets, we can simply say that, other things being equal, the greater the proportion of total gainfully employed population in agriculture, the lower the level of income per capita.

When one turns to the nonagricultural sectors of the Tokugawa economy, it becomes obvious that other things were, in fact, equal. Nonagricultural production consisted of crafts and services. Craft output frequently combined beauty and usefulness; services often were most sophisticated. Nevertheless, these sectors were untouched by the liberating forces of the industrial revolution, which made men more productive. Machinery was not in use except in the most unusual circumstances; units of production were small; steam power had not been introduced. In essence, agriculture and nonagriculture resembled one another: both used labor intensive methods that depended for gains in productivity on the skills of the individual worker. Fixed capital was only a minor element in the production function.

There is no more revealing evidence concerning Tokugawa Japan than its demographic balance and international contacts. To begin with the latter, we must recall the famous "closing of the country" decree issued by the third shogun of the Tokugawa line. The reasons for this drastic step, taken in 1637, are not entirely clear to this day. Some scholars believe that Shogun Iemitsu feared internal strife fomented by *rōnin* (masterless samurai), and closed the country to prevent these malcontents from securing outside help. Others espouse the more likely explanation that an external threat was the main cause. According to this view, Iemitsu understood the danger of Western expansionism, specifically of the sword following the cross, in the Philippines and China.

He feared that Japan's turn was coming. Whatever the shogun's motives, "closing of the country" (*sakoku*) has to be taken quite literally: no Japanese was permitted to leave Japan, and if someone succeeded and returned, he was to be put to death. Foreigners were not allowed to visit or to reside in Japan. Only two minor exceptions were made: the Dutch and the Chinese retained extremely limited trading rights at Nagasaki. In order to take advantage of these, however, Dutch and Chinese traders lived as virtual prisoners in the far south of the country. The sakoku decrees remained in effect for well over two hundred years. They were fully lifted only in the 1860's, when the Tokugawa had reached the last tottering years of what had been an illustrious reign. By then, isolation had become a deeply ingrained tradition, and objection to its abandonment was strong even in the second half of the nineteenth century. Now, however, outside pressure from the major Western powers could no longer be resisted. Commodore Perry and his ships made their point in an unmistakable manner.

What were the consequences of long and self-imposed isolation? These are difficult to trace unambiguously; yet there is little reason to believe that sakoku had only negative effects. To be isolated from empire-building Europeans may have been advantageous; to be left alone may have created sources of inner strength. All of this is possible, but from the economic point of view, a closed country also meant a necessary condition of relative backwardness, not so obviously in the seventeenth century when the policy was begun but very obviously by the time the nineteenth century opened. In the intervening years the Western world—more precisely Great Britain—had given birth to the industrial revolution. From then on the absence of international contacts meant the availability of only second-best technology and organization, and this remains true today.

Japan's demographic balance before the Meiji Restoration is equally revealing. The first real population census took place only in 1920, but experts agree on the broad magnitudes of earlier figures. In the 1860's total population was around 30 million. At the start of the Tokugawa era population is estimated to have been approximately 20 to 25 million. These figures convert into low rates of natural increase typical of less-developed areas before the introduction of modern medical advances. Students of Japanese demography have pointed to another phenomenon of equally great interest: between the late seventeenth or early eighteenth century and the 1840's, for roughly 150 years, the population remained stable; growth began again in the 1840's. The reasons for stability are again not entirely clear, but it has frequently been asserted that infanticide (*mabiki*) was an important means of achieving a zero growth rate. In general, we think that population at this time was a representative variable for the entire economy: change took place, but its pace was slow.

What has been said up to now is only half the story. Though unable to avail itself at that time of modern technology and most scientific advances, Japan nevertheless was a vigorous, advanced, and effective traditional society. In many ways it was more advanced than many countries in Africa or Latin America today. This deserves special stress, because there is no denying that we tend inevitably to associate low income per capita with poor organization, corruption, lethargy, and undernourishment. And this gives a false picture of Japan before the Restoration.

A few illustrative details should be helpful. The pre-Restoration governmental structure was effective at both central and local levels. The capital and the major cities were under direct Tokugawa control. Local authority was in the hands of Tokugawa vassals. The entire country was divided into about 200 "baronies" or fiefs, each headed by a lord or *daimyō*. A daimyo was responsible for the affairs of his fief, but he was also closely watched by the central authorities, and with sufficient cause his office could be taken away. In return for exercising local authority, daimyo received the rights to an income stream originating in their fiefs; its most important form was the privilege to levy a yearly harvest tax with which they supported themselves and their retainers. Tokugawa administration has frequently been described as "centralized feudalism," and this is quite accurate. As shogun, the head of the House of Tokugawa was the leading lord of the land: he was the largest individual fiefholder and his revenues and number of retainers exceeded those of all other lords. At the same time, all other lords were, directly or indirectly, vassals of the Tokugawa; this was the "centralized" part of the feudalism.

The road system of pre-modern Japan was very much in keeping with the centralized nature of government. Major arteries crisscrossed the country, and both goods and people moved relatively rapidly by nineteenth-century standards. A special word must be added about the institution of *sankin kōtai* (alternate residence), since it has often been linked to the quality of the roads. According to this Tokugawa regulation, the lords had to alternate their place of residence between the national capital (Edo, since renamed Tokyo) and their local capital. Wives and children of lords had to remain in Edo all of the time. Normally, the lord and selected retainers spent one year in the capital and one year in the provinces. The idea behind this regulation was simple: hostage families encouraged the lord's good behavior, and his frequent absences in Edo prevented the creation of a rival and local power base. The resulting movements of people, sometimes in the colorful daimyo processions so well depicted by Hiroshige, no doubt contributed in the development of everything connected with travel: roads, inns, restaurants, etc.

Government and roads are part of a broader picture of competence and efficiency. Much of this can be seen by focusing briefly on some of the items used in everyday life under the Tokugawa. Housing was usually well-designed and well-engineered, and satisfied the people's needs. The same can be said of clothing. Indigenous dress was beautiful, functional, and specifically designed to fit harmoniously into the traditional way of doing things. Japanese cuisine performed equally well. It was nutritional, attractive, and somewhat bland; these were exactly the most desired characteristics. Of course the point is not at all that the average Japanese in (say) 1850 was adequately fed, housed, and dressed. Probably this was not true. But the point is that the means of satisfying these wants were available within the traditional society; indeed, when a wider choice became available, traditional methods often continued to be preferred.

To give a more complete picture of Tokugawa life, other points should also be stressed: the vigor of urban culture in the large cities (Edo, Kyoto, and Osaka were among the largest cities in the world at that time); the high average standards of education ensuring that approximately 40 to 50 percent of all males benefited from some formal schooling; the official class structure of *bushi* (samurai), farmers, and merchants, which was conservative in intent but did supply the country with a group of leaders largely of samurai and "gentry" farmer background. None of these points can be treated in detail, but they all add up to an important premise: in Tokugawa Japan the gap between economic and "other" backwardness was unusually large, and this made the prospect of modern economic growth all the more promising. This gap between the technology actually applied and the capability of borrowing and absorbing more advanced methods based on a well-functioning sociopolitical infrastructure deserves particular stress because it has been a fundamental factor in Japan's success not only in the nineteenth century but until the present time. We will frequently have occasion to return to this theme.

THE MEIJI RESTORATION

The term *Meiji Restoration* refers to January 1868, when the last Tokugawa shogun "voluntarily" surrendered power and turned the task of governing back to the Imperial family, and specifically to the young Emperor Meiji. Without a doubt this was an epochal event in Japanese history, and it can stand comparison with many other great dates in national histories, such as 1066 and 1776. The Restoration was so crucial that many volumes have been devoted to its interpretation, and there are available any number of social, political, and cultural interpretations. In the general study of "modernization"—today such a very popular subject—the Meiji Restoration is one of the most important and favored examples. Our own focus, however, must be quite narrow. We will confine ourselves to outlining the main economic trends from the 1860's to the turn of the century as necessary background information.

Why did a restoration occur and why did it occur in 1868? These are questions that undoubtedly will never be answered with precision. Students of the period have suggested many reasons for this change of government: a renewed foreign threat that made continued isolation unviable and called instead for modernization; the presence of a group of discontented lower-ranking samurai from outlying domains who saw their own opportunities for advancement blocked and who wanted power and glory for themselves; a secular economic deterioration as a result of rising expenditures by the Tokugawa (and other domains) without further means of increasing revenues. All of these and others contain much truth, and it is not really necessary for us to delve into this subject more deeply. The main point is that Japanese modernization—economic, political, and social—began, at least symbolically, in 1868, when Emperor Meiji was "restored" to the throne.

A few years ago it would have been a relatively easy task to present a simple account of major economic trends in Meiji Japan. Now it has become somewhat less simple in view of recent controversies and revisions, but the main features of the era continue to stand out in an unmistakable manner. In considering this period of somewhat over 30 years, it is best to divide it into two segments: the years of "transition" from 1868 to perhaps 1885, and the years of "initial" modern economic growth, beginning in the middle of the 1880's and ending with the turn of the century. Let us look at each of these segments in turn.

The years of transition, during which the initial shock of Western contact was absorbed, were necessarily confused, full of false starts and experimentation. They were more important as years of institutional reform spearheaded by the government than as years of rapid economic growth. (Indeed, the available quantitative information is such that it is most difficult to establish aggregate economic growth rates before the middle of the 1880's.)

TABLE 1.1
Structure of the Meiji Economy

Category	1934–36 prices (Million yen)		Current prices (Percent)	
	1887	1902	1887	1902
Output by industry:				
Agriculture, forestry & fisheries	1,604	2,044	41.1%	40.3%
Manufacturing & mining	316	672	13.6	16.6
Facilitating industries: transportation, communication, public utilities	44	146	2.6	3.9
Construction	93	192	3.6	4.0
Services, all other industries	2,068	2,752	39.1	35.2
Net domestic product	4,125	5,806	100.0[a]	100.0[b]
Resource allocation by use:				
Personal consumption	3,737	5,440	80.3	77.7
Govt. current expenditure	291	719	7.2	10.3
Gross fixed capital formation	383	679	13.5	13.6
Exports of goods & services & factor income received from abroad	91	325	6.5	12.2
Imports of goods & services & factor income paid abroad	178	631	7.4	13.8
Gross national expenditure	4,330	6,650	100.0[c]	100.0[d]
	Numbers (Thousands)		Proportions (Percent)	
	1887	1902	1887	1902
Gainfully occupied population:				
Agriculture, forestry & fisheries	16,533	16,265	73.1%	65.9%
Manufacturing & mining; facilitating industries—transportation, communication, public utilities; construction	2,909	4,263	12.9	17.3
Services, all other industries	3,161	4,162	14.0	16.8
Total gainfully occupied population	22,603	24,690	100.0	100.0

Source: Calculated from series contained in LTES, vol. 1.
Note: All figures are five-year averages centered on the years shown.
[a]¥754 million.   [b]¥2,280 million.   [c]¥850 million.   [d]¥2,754 million.

A brief look at the major reforms should make their significance obvious. Between 1869 and 1871, for example, the government entirely revamped the old feudal class structure. The official categories of court noble, warrior, peasant, merchant, and outcast were abolished and restructured into two new classes—a small nobility and everyone else. By 1876 the government had also succeeded in pensioning off all the former members of the warrior class—previously they had received stipends from the Tokugawa or from their domain—at a cost of over 200 million yen. During this time also the new government abolished previously existing barriers to internal travel and opened the ports to external visitors. Of great importance was the agricultural reform that occupied the new leaders during most of the 1870's. The land was formally turned over to the peasants (in feudal times ownership had been officially in the hands of the Emperor), but they were now required to pay a heavy land tax to the central and local government. This tax was placed on the assessed valuation of the land (and not as in the past on the harvest) and was levied at nationally uniform levels. Currency and banking reforms also occupied the Meiji oligarchy in this period. It introduced order into the system of coinage, and by the end of the 1880's it had succeeded in creating a central bank (the Bank of Japan) and in establishing regulations for a growing private banking system. Other well-known activities of the public sector might also be mentioned for this period: the establishment of model factories, the hiring of foreign experts, and the dispatch of students abroad. All of these activities taken together added up to a most active period of institutional innovation.

During this transition the Japanese economy underwent severe fluctuations. Until 1876 the situation remained relatively calm, but from then on there occurred some "great shocks" in the form of a severe inflation lasting until 1881, followed by a harsh deflation ending only in 1885. The causes of these events are intricate and need not detain us for long. Briefly, throughout the transition years the government lacked sufficient revenue even for its ordinary needs. In the latter half of the 1870's, however, these needs were much magnified by the desire to pension off the warrior class and by the outbreak of the Satsuma rebellion. The government and the bank turned to the printing press, and the resulting inflation, beneficial to no one but the farmers, endangered the stability of the new leadership. Its revenues, especially those relating to the land tax, were fixed and were being diminished in real terms by rising prices. Economic order was restored by Finance Minister Matsukata, but it required four years of severe and officially sponsored deflation.[3]

Modern economic growth in Japan began during the next subperiod, that is to say, sometime after the middle of the 1880's, and Table 1.1 provides a broad overview of change in the structure of the Meiji economy. Clearly Japanese industrialization was not in any sense an accomplished fact by the time the twentieth century had started, but some very significant steps had been taken in the right direction. The 15 years following the Matsukata deflation represented a period of virtually

[3] See Henry Rosovsky, "Japan's Transition to Modern Economic Growth, 1868–1885," in Henry Rosovsky, ed., *Industrialization in Two Systems* (New York, 1966).

uninterrupted development of modern industry. Silk and cotton spinning were the main achievements of the private sector, while road building, railroads, and general public works were carried out and encouraged by the government.

THE INITIAL PHASE OF MODERN ECONOMIC GROWTH

From our perspective the most noteworthy element in initial economic growth is its dynamics. The Japanese economy following the Restoration and to this day contains a number of rather well-defined sectors. Usually these have been labeled "modern" and "traditional," and sometimes we have added the category "hybrid." There is nothing new or surprising about these categories; they are part of all dual economy analyses. The characteristics of the sectors are equally known, and they pertain as well to other countries. Modern sectors rely on imported Western technology and organization and employ methods of relatively high capital intensity. By contrast, traditional production relies on more indigenous technology and organization, and on relatively low levels of capital intensity. Hybrid sectors fall in between, combining (say) modern techniques and traditional organization. The Asian peasant cultivating his small field with hand tools is a clear example of the traditional economy. The large cotton-spinning establishment with its machines and wage workers is a clear example of the modern sector.

All of this is familiar to students of economic development just as is the fact that modern economic growth is a process by which traditional ways of doing things gradually yield to modern ways. What is perhaps less familiar is the vividness of the contrast between modern and traditional in the Japanese setting. There the traditional economy often has a quaint and, at least for Westerners, exotic appearance—one need only think of the wonderful Japanese crafts and their range of unusual services—and therefore the dichotomy is more readily identifiable. But in terms of economic analysis this added bit of color makes little difference.

Four simple propositions apply to modern economic growth in its initial phase. First, in the absence of large capital imports, the initial establishment and subsequent development of the modern economy depended on the accelerated growth of the traditional economy—and also to some extent on the accelerated growth of the hybrid economy. Second, the traditional economy was capable of producing such accelerated growth. Third, the growth potential of the traditional economy was limited. When its growth rate began to decline, approximately at the time of World War I, the initial phase of modern economic growth came to an end. And last, by the time the initial phase came to an end, the dependence of the modern on the traditional economy greatly decreased, although it had not disappeared.

These propositions can be further summarized: the opportunities of initial economic modernization hinged on the more rapid growth of peasant agriculture, because this produced the needed surpluses for development (public revenues, private investment funds, foreign exchange, and labor force). When traditional agriculture faltered, a different model came into play.

How valid is this scheme? The major problem undoubtedly relates to the rate of growth of traditional agriculture during the Meiji era. Earlier we have said that at one time it would have been easy to outline the main economic trends. If this is no longer so, it is due to a lively controversy concerning Meiji agricultural growth. This is not the place to cover this dispute in detail: it has been done in many places elsewhere and all we need to do here is to state our conclusions.[4]

Many authorities seem to agree that Japanese agriculture during the relevant years (from the 1870's to the 1900's) grew at about 1.7 percent per year. Some would place this figure slightly lower, some very much lower, and some may select slightly higher figures; 1.7 percent seems to us an acceptable modal value. If this rate is approximately correct, it follows that the Meiji era witnessed a marked acceleration over the older Tokugawa values, for no one has ever suggested that before the 1870's growth was of this magnitude. Undoubtedly Tokugawa agricultural output grew much more slowly than Meiji agricultural output, no matter what the actual rate may have been.

Various reasons can account for the acceleration of agricultural output in Meiji Japan. Of undoubted importance were the improvements and diffusion of indigenous techniques partly achieved by individual farmers and their organizations, and partly the result of government sponsorship and research. For example, these activities led to improved seed selection and a wider and more rational use of fertilizer. The improved incentive structure for landowners must also be taken into account. In Tokugawa Japan, the peasant paid a heavy harvest tax, which fluctuated considerably from year to year and frequently depended on the specific short-term financial needs of the lords. Thus there was no guarantee that the agriculturist would be able to retain any of the increased output. In Meiji Japan, the situation was entirely different, since the land

<hr>

[4] See Henry Rosovsky, "Rumbles in the Rice Fields," *Journal of Asian Studies*, 27, no. 2 (1968).

tax was based on the value of land, and it was pretty well known that the assessments would remain fairly stable. Another element in explaining output acceleration is connected with the regional structure of the pre-modern Japanese economy. The agricultural economy of Tokugawa Japan—especially with respect to levels of productivity—was not at all uniform. Areas of relatively high and low productivity existed, and only in part could this be explained by differing qualities of soil or geography. In very broad terms agriculture was more backward in northeastern Japan than in southwestern Japan. The Restoration provided an opportunity for exploiting these productivity gaps. Before the 1860's the transfer of know-how and technology had been impeded by Tokugawa theory and practice; now it became an aim of the Meiji government to spread useful knowledge throughout the entire country.

This type of expansion, however, had limited possibilities. Output grew in Meiji agriculture owing to the employment of techniques based on increased labor input combined with improvements in conventional inputs—seed, fertilizers, etc. All these were highly divisible and suited to the peasant unit of production. But this could not go on indefinitely. Eventually, when these types of improvements had been fully exploited, maintaining the growth rate would have required major capital and land improvements. These did not come in significant amounts until after World War II, and therefore shortly after 1914 the rate of growth of Japanese agriculture started to stagnate.

Why was the situation in agriculture and other sectors in similar positions so crucial? This is easy to see when we consider the needs of modern economic growth. Fundamentally it is an issue of raising surpluses in an economy dominated by traditional occupations. In the beginning the productivity levels of these occupations were low, but by raising them they could generate the necessary surpluses with which to begin industrialization. And given the traditional techniques, this could be accomplished without heavy expenditures on fixed investment.

After all, what were the needs of modern economic growth at a time when reinvestment by a small modern industry was tiny? How were they met? First of all, Japan needed a growing food supply for a larger population in which the standards of diet were rising. Importing food was relatively expensive and diverted funds from productive investment possibilities. In large measure the increased food supplies were provided by the peasantry. Second, the new government required a rising flow of revenues for social overhead and other investment purposes as well as for administrative modernization. Again the traditional economy played a key role here through land tax revenue and as a source of indirect taxation. Third, foreign exchange was a vital need for importing modern producer durables and to acquire the services of foreign experts. The Meiji economy secured this exchange largely through the export of tea and silk, both products closely linked to traditional agriculture. Finally, the Japanese economy needed to effect a labor transfer so as to provide the workers for the expanding modern sectors. These workers came almost entirely from rural areas, and this transfer did not adversely affect the rate of growth of agricultural output.

Having outlined the mechanism of Meiji economic growth, let us now examine the character of pre-twentieth century capital inputs. We can accomplish this most easily by attempting to sharpen the contrasts between the nineteenth and twentieth centuries.

By 1900, the proportion of gross fixed domestic investment to gross national product in Japan had reached 13.3 percent, by no means an insignificant level.[5] Yet the share of modern industry in the economy was very modest. Factory output accounted for some 6 percent of net domestic product, and the definition of a factory—establishments with five or more employees—meant that a great deal of handicraft production was included. We know that factory output grew rapidly during the 30 years before 1900—in 1885 the proportion had been approximately 4 percent— but we also know that it continued to increase, reaching levels of over 30 percent after World War II. By 1905 factory gross output accounted for 47 percent of total manufacturing gross output.

The output stream emanating from these factories underwent a considerable change during the Meiji era. In 1868, 66 percent of gross output came from food processing and kindred activities, and 28 percent from textile manufacturing, which was dominated by the silk industry. By 1905 the share of food processing had dropped to 39 percent, textiles had risen to 38 percent, with cotton becoming more important, and chemicals, metals, and machines accounted for 23 percent. However, it should be added that the representative units were small. At the turn of the century, when factory employment was 24 percent of manufacturing and 3 percent of total employment, 68 percent of the workers in food processing were engaged in establishments with fewer than 50 employees; for textiles and heavy industry this proportion stood at 37 percent and 43 percent, respectively.

[5] Since Japan's foreign borrowings were very limited except in times of war—the biggest foreign loans of the Meiji era ocurred in 1905 and amounted to ¥592 million or 18 percent of GNP—capital formation was largely financed by domestic savings. Consequently, the investment proportion must have been close to the savings ratio.

Once more, a glance at future developments can indicate the magnitude of change to come. Whereas Meiji industrial output was dominated by food processing and textiles produced by rather small units, twentieth-century production, certainly by the 1930's, was dominated by heavier industry and larger units. For example, at the end of the 1930's, chemicals, metals, and machines accounted for about 70 percent of gross industrial output, and nearly 50 percent of the labor force in these industries was working in large factories.

The early and limited industrialization of Meiji Japan was supported by a specific pattern of capital formation (see Figure 2.4, p. 34). This pattern can best be described as follows: public investment generally exceeded the level of private productive investment; investment in construction outweighed investment in producers' durable equipment; and most of the investment represented the application of "traditional" techniques and therefore did not embody imported technological progress. Let us briefly discuss each one of these characteristics.

Government investments generally exceeded those of the private sector until World War I: in 1884 they were 66 percent and in 1901 54 percent of the total. This was undoubtedly due to a combination of two factors. First of all, the government was very active in improving the quantity and quality of social overheads; it was also very active in raising Japan's military capability. Indeed, during the Meiji era one can account for well over half of central government capital formation by summing up expenditures on public works (especially railroads) and military investments. If one adds reconstruction expenditures related to recurring natural disasters such as earthquakes and typhoons, it is possible to account for over 70 percent of government investment expenditures.

The second explanation of the government's large share in total investment simply relates to the small absolute size of private industry. Private investments were gaining on those of the public sector, but during most of the Meiji period the types of industries that made extensive use of expensive capital equipment were still infants—though growing at a lusty pace.

At this time also, especially if we concentrate on productive investment (excluding military investments and residential dwellings), construction was the main form of national investment, usually accounting for well over 50 percent of gross domestic capital formation. This generalization is valid through the first decade of the twentieth century; sometime between 1911 and 1917 a sharp break occurred in the composition of domestic capital formation and from that time on private producers' durable equipment absorbed the greatest share of resources. For example, in 1917, 57 percent of gross domestic capital formation was taken up by private producers' durables. In 1911 the share had been 32 percent.

In large measure the leading role of construction was merely a reflection of the overall primacy of public investments and their nature at this time. Road building, port improvements, government buildings, etc. —all construction activities with high capital-output ratios—accounted for over two-thirds of public capital formation. Even in the private sector, investments were about equally divided between construction and durable equipment until the time of World War I, when the latter category suddenly assumed a new level of significance. Factory and commercial construction and also, before the nationalizations of the early twentieth century, private railroad construction represented expenditures that were nearly as great as those on machinery and equipment.

The last aspect of the Meiji investment pattern is, perhaps, the most unusual. In Japan at this time, capital goods were produced by two rather distinct methods: one can be called "traditional" and the other "modern." When it came to building railroads and water works, or the acquisition of producers' durables, modern and imported techniques were necessarily involved. Road beds had to be scientifically surveyed and graded; steam pumps and iron pipes were needed for water works; producers' durables meant machines activated by steam engines and later electricity. All these were "ways of doing things" largely unknown in Meiji Japan. But there was also another side to the coin. Traditional techniques could also create capital goods, as in the case of residential and commercial construction (largely wooden structures), or irrigation and land reclamation for agriculture, and even for road and bridge construction. In these instances, pre-Meiji techniques of a highly labor-intensive nature retained their usefulness and supported the modernization process. In the circumstances of the times, these techniques were especially "economical": they used labor, tools, and skills that were readily available; they did not require much capital or new skills that were relatively expensive.

According to this classification, in Meiji Japan roughly half of the capital goods were produced by traditional techniques.[6] This was a unique characteristic of early Japanese industrialization, because in post-Meiji years the proportion of traditional investments declined sharply

[6] See Henry Rosovsky, *Capital Formation in Japan, 1868–1940* (New York, 1961), pp. 16–19. These estimates have been revised, but the conclusions concerning traditional capital formation remain unaffected.

while, simultaneously, many of the older ways in (say) house and road building were abandoned in favor of imported methods.

Perhaps we can now summarize the situation obtaining in the last third of the nineteenth century. Initial modern economic growth was in large measure based on the achievements of a traditional economy. This was the first step toward the accomplishment of industrialization. It was now time to take the second and much bigger step—maybe one could call it the leap toward a semideveloped state—and for that we turn to an analysis of the period 1900 to the present.

CHAPTER TWO

The Contours of Modern Growth

INTRODUCTION

Japanese economic history in the twentieth century has many dimensions, since each decade contained events of considerable economic and social significance. The century began with Japan's astonishing victory over Russia in 1905. World War I (1914–18) brought a great economic boom as well as the famous Rice Riots. In the 1920's, Japan was struck by the Great Tokyo Earthquake—perhaps the worst natural disaster in its recorded history—and by slower growth and difficult competitive conditions abroad. Economic growth picked up speed again in the 1930's, but it was accompanied by the Great Depression, political instability, and eventually a military dictatorship and World War II. During the 1940's, following the defeat in 1945, Japan sank back to a much lower level of economic well-being, and the entire decade was an unhappy mixture of war and occupation. And then, what is now called the "economic miracle" began in the 1950's, culminating perhaps in the great payments surpluses of the late 1960's and the "Nixon shocks" of the early 1970's. Today, Japan appears to the world as a leading economic power exerting a disequilibrating influence owing to its somewhat unusual industrial structure. How to fit Japan smoothly into the world economy has become a major issue in international economic affairs.

There is no intention of analyzing these events in detail. Instead, we hope to provide historical continuity by taking a much more schematic look at Japan's growth experience in this century. We shall do this by studying the long-term movements of aggregate output and expenditure, their principal components, and movements of the population and labor force and its components. All this will entail an analysis of long swings and trend acceleration, two terms that will be fully explained in later sections. Chapter 2 concludes with a preview of findings—a brief statement of the major analytical themes that are also more fully explored in the rest of the volume.

One of the concerns of this volume is to "explain" Japan's economic performance since World War II. We therefore lead off with a brief review of the facts that stress the prewar and postwar economic similarities and contrasts.

Broadly speaking, Japanese economic development since 1945 has been dominated by three main influences. First came the effects of direct dislocation of economic activity, including large-scale capital destruction, associated with defeat inflicted by the Allies. This resulted in a period of conversion, recovery, and rehabilitation frequently assumed to have ended in 1952–54. A second influence relates to longer-lasting consequences of the war, particularly those associated with Japan's technological isolation between the late 1930's and early 1950's. It concerns primarily the opportunities for rapid technological progress. A third category must rather vaguely be called "new elements introduced into the Japanese economy by war and defeat." Here we have in mind certain increases in the social capacity of the nation to utilize the international backlog of technological progress. If, in fact, increased social capacity exists and can be identified, it could raise the long-run growth potential of the economy.

In studying the effects of Japan's technological isolation and what we believe to be a causally related investment boom, we will make use of the finding that Japanese growth has taken the form of recurrent waves of retardation and acceleration that we call "long swings." The very high rate of aggregate growth following the end of rehabilitation as well as the somewhat slower rates of growth of some components since 1962 seem to fit a possible long-swing hypothesis, and this framework also allows illuminating comparisons with similar expansions and contractions before World War II. Specific comparisons will be made with the 1910's and 1930's, when there was also considerable acceleration in the rates of growth of aggregate output. The long-swing framework has the additional advantage of providing a good method of observing changes in trends. Evidence will be provided to show that trend rates of growth, measured in a variety of ways, have been rising, and the significance of this acceleration for postwar growth must be taken into account.

Let us begin by looking at the long-range growth pattern of the Japanese economy in terms of gross national product. It appears in Figure 2.1, in constant prices, for the period 1887–1969, almost the entire span for which a quantitative record is available. The graph contains two series:

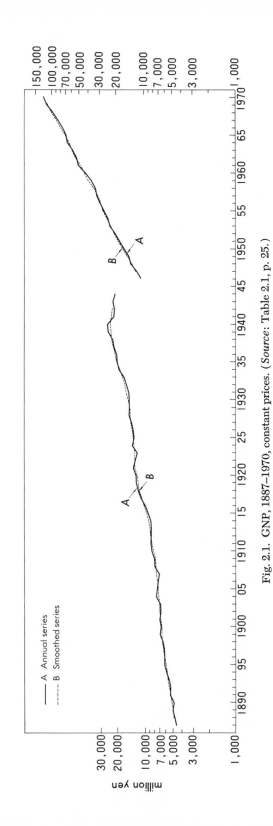

Fig. 2.1. GNP, 1887–1970, constant prices. (*Source*: Table 2.1, p. 25.)

one simply depicts the annual values, whereas the other shows annual values of GNP smoothed by a moving average the duration of which is approximately equal to the average length of the business cycle.[1]

Three observations are suggested by Figure 2.1.

1. Most obvious, perhaps, is the enormous and unprecedented dislocation caused by World War II. In 1946, for example, the level of GNP abruptly dropped to the 1917–18 level, and although doubts exist concerning the accuracy of statistical observations during the years 1946–50, there can be no question about the extent of economic disarrangement. A similar conclusion can be based on the observation that the prewar annual peak for GNP was reached in 1939, and was not attained again until 1954, although the quality of the statistics are doubtful especially for 1939–42, when military expenditures were very large.

2. A closer look, especially at the smoothed series, also indicates, in the long run, periods of faster and slower growth along the path of a rising secular trend. We consider these alternations to be long swings of the growth rate of total output (frequently referred to as Kuznets cycles), and we believe that the rapid postwar expansion, at least since 1954, is appropriately treated as a long-term upswing.

3. That the trend is rising has already been mentioned, but a comparison of the prewar trend and postwar growth also reveals a clear acceleration in the last decade and a half.

These observations lead to a number of interpretative questions. Has there been an "economic miracle"? Does the postwar acceleration of the GNP growth rate represent a radical shift in Japan's trend rate of growth? If the prewar trend between 1917 and 1937 (long-swing peaks) is extrapolated, the postwar GNP reaches the secular trend in only 1963. Is this what some observers have in mind when they attempt to explain postwar acceleration as a process of catching up with the historical growth trend?

These questions are too simple and it is our view that the postwar growth pattern is a mixture of elements only partially illustrated by these queries. Three things have to be considered: the influences of war dislocation and rehabilitation, of a long-swing expansion, and of the trend. In practice it is impossible to disentangle the weights of these influences in clear fashion. We shall, however, speculate about the relative importance of these separate elements in postwar growth, recognizing at all times that complicated interrelations must blur the analysis and qualify the answers.

[1] Seven years before World War II, and five years in the postwar period.

War Dislocation and Rehabilitation

We can most conveniently begin by stating our views concerning the direct effects of war and rehabilitation. Increasingly in the 1930's, and most especially from 1939 onward, the needs of war affected the normal functioning of the Japanese economy. Total defeat came in 1945, leaving the national economy in great disorder. Between 1945 and 1952–54, Japan's economy was most heavily influenced by reconstruction and rehabilitation. During these years abnormal growth factors outweighed the normal. This situation changed after 1952–54, although some consequences of the defeat in World War II and its aftermath are still felt by the Japanese economy. Can these views be substantiated?

Both quantitative and qualitative evidence supports a 1952–54 demarcation. The 1939 prewar peak level of GNP was for the first time surpassed in 1954, and the same is true for GNP per capita. The aggregate capital-output ratio also rose to more usual values in 1953, indicating the end of a period in which previously existing excess capacity played a major role. Furthermore, the occupation ended in 1952 and Japan began once more to run its own affairs, both as a nation and as an economy. More confirmation of the demarcation can be found by looking again at Figure 2.1. Movements of the postwar growth rate are clear: a decline from the very high levels of the early postwar years reaching a turning point near 1954; after that the rate of growth accelerates. Our interpretation of this is that the high rates of the immediate afterwar years were heavily influenced by recovery factors that tended to fade away in the middle 1950's. The subsequent growth spurt must therefore be attributed to "new" factors having an existence relatively independent of direct war dislocation.

There are possible objections to the 1952–54 demarcation, and it may be said with some justice that our reasoning is too mechanical. Certain legacies of war dislocation and rehabilitation are still present in the Japanese economy. Some war-created shortages still plague Japan; excellent examples are residential housing and social overhead capital. War-induced demographic factors are still significant. Also, advances in science and technology that were developed during the war, combined with simultaneous manpower training, are still relevant in understanding post-1952–54 rapid growth. It is also possible that the decline of the rates of growth near the turning point were caused by factors other than the exhaustion of war recovery: for example, the end of the Korean war may have been involved. We have no particular quarrel with these doubts, some of which we share, but still believe that 1954 is the most appropriate year with which to begin the analysis of "normal" postwar growth. It represents a clustering of forces pointing to a reestablished normal economic situation.

Long Swings of Aggregate Product

The pattern of historical long-swing fluctuations is shown in Figure 2.2. In this graph, measurement is based on the smoothed GNP series, and two kinds of growth rates are shown: year-to-year percentage changes, and the intercyclical average rates of change.[2] Both methods bring out the swings with clarity, but an unambiguous selection of peaks and troughs is not a simple matter. Our selection of long-swing peak and trough years depends on two principles: a trough year (or better "band of years," since each year stands for the center of a moving average) must precede a sharp and sustained increase in the average annual rates of growth; if a period of rapid growth is characterized by a plateau during which the rate of growth maintains a high level, the end of the plateau is selected as the peak. As explained below in the section on investment, the actual dating of peaks and troughs is based on fluctuations of *private capital formation* and *not* on fluctuations of output.

Between 1901 and 1969, the real GNP of Japan grew at about 4.68 percent per year, while GNP per capita expanded at 3.44 percent and population at 1.24 percent. However, as Figure 2.2 suggests, and Table 2.1 confirms, this growth was not at all of even intensity. Both versions of GNP and GNP per capita growth rates[3] show systematic expansions and contractions within the demarcated long-swing phases. The figure makes possible the historical comparison of four long-swing expansions: 1888–97, 1901–17, 1931–37, and 1956–62. Although the dating of prewar swings is intuitively reasonable from the historical point of view, a word of explanation has to be added concerning the postwar period. We shall assume that 1956 represents a very special kind of long-swing trough, and that the years of rapid growth that follow form the first postwar upswing. The justification for this is the economic abnormalities associated with rehabilitation and reconstruction, lasting at least until 1954, and therefore affecting the moving averages until 1956. At present, in

---

[2] "Year-to-year" changes are percentage changes between successive annual values of the seven-year moving average. "Intercyclical average rates of growth" are growth rates between seven-year averages displaced six years. That is, the intercyclical growth rate centered on, say, 1895 is a growth rate calculated from the average of 1889–95 to the average of 1895–1901.

[3] Panel A is a "bridge" calculation between peaks and troughs; Panel B is the average value of the annual growth rates during an expansion or a contraction. The results are nearly identical.

TABLE 2.1

GNP and GNP per Capita: Average Annual Rates
of Growth During Long Swings

(Smoothed series, constant prices; *percent*)

Period	Panel A[a]			Panel B[b]		
	GNP	GNP per capita[c]	Total population	GNP	GNP per capita[c]	Total population
(1) 1897 (peak) – 1901 (trough)	1.96%	0.86%	1.10%	2.17%	0.99%	1.18%
(2) 1901 (T) – 1917 (P)	2.88	1.64	1.24	2.87	1.66	1.21
(2′) 1912 – 1917	4.56	3.28	1.28	4.35	3.09	1.26
(3) 1917 (P) – 1931 (T)	2.75	1.42	1.33	2.97	1.64	1.33
(4) 1931 (T) – 1937 (P)	5.71	4.31	1.40	5.91	4.48	1.43
(5) 1937 (P) – 1956 (T)	1.83	0.53	1.30	1.83	0.53	1.30
(6) 1956 (T) – 1962 (P)	10.72	9.69	1.03	10.42	9.48	0.93
(7) 1962 – 1969	11.91	10.90	1.01	11.00	9.94	1.06

Source: For the period 1905–69, GNP and population from BST. 7 and BST. 15. For earlier years see LTES, vol. 1.

Note: All series smoothed by a seven-year moving average before World War II, and by a five-year moving average thereafter, except for 1969, which represents a three-year centered average. Prewar data in 1934–36 prices. Postwar data in lines (5) and (6) in 1960 prices, line (7) in 1965 prices. Line (7) has been tentatively converted to 1960 prices by using the aggregate deflator. The values for 1937 (1934–36 prices) and 1956 (1960 prices) have been linked using the aggregate deflator for GNE. It was 321.6 in 1955 (1934–36 = 1). See LTES, vol. 8 (Prices), p. 134.

[a] Average compound growth rates between successive trough and peak years of the smoothed series.

[b] Simple average of individual annual growth rates during demarcated periods. (Because of lack of data for 1945 and the overall poor reliability of statistics in this time span, line (5) uses only the method of panel A.)

[c] GNP – total population = GNP per capita.

terms of an investment periodization, 1962 seems a good choice for the first postwar long-swing peak, although it is much too early for a definitive opinion. That is why line (7) of Table 2.1 has been added without peak and trough identifications, because we are not yet certain whether these years will eventually be considered a continued postwar expansion or the first contraction after World War II.[4] Of course, the period 1937–56 is also affected by World War II. There was very little secular growth between these two dates, and those years witnessed a decline occasioned by the war with a trough in 1946–47, followed by the abnormally high postwar recovery rates.

[4] Readers will undoubtedly notice a certain inconsistency in our treatment of the 1960's. Sometimes the period 1962–69 is included; sometimes we stop in 1962; and mostly we stop in 1964. Unfortunately this is unavoidable, since the period in question is recent from the perspective of historical analysis, and therefore no firm conclusions can be reached; and data problems are equally severe because we have always worked with moving averages so that 1962 includes estimates for 1964, 1964 includes values for 1966, and 1969 requires information for 1971. In many cases the required information is simply not available. In general, the analysis will conclude in 1964 for smoothed series so as to include a portion of the investment downswing beginning in 1962. When necessary for clarity it will be extended if possible. In Chapter 9 the history of the last half of the 1960's will be discussed again.

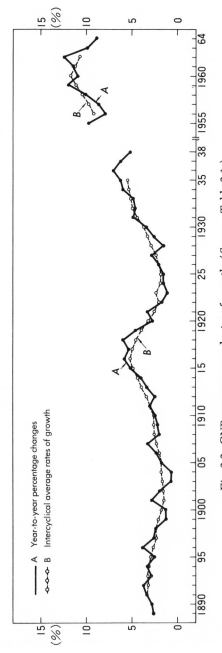

Fig. 2.2. GNP, average annual rates of growth. (*Source:* Table 2.1.)

A few specific comments must be added concerning the findings in Table 2.1. Upswings have become progressively higher for both GNP and GNP per capita, rising, respectively, from 2.87 and 1.66 percent per year in 1901–17 to 10.42 and 9.39 percent per year in 1956–62. Furthermore, the aggregate and per capita series move in a very similar manner because population growth was relatively slow and quite steady. The range of population growth was between 1.01 (1962–69) and 1.40 (1931–37) percent per year since the turn of the century, rates reminiscent of Western European rather than Asian experience.

Finally, a word about the shape of Japanese output swings. Usually, economic fluctuations are visualized as "triangular" with a movement toward a peak, immediately followed by a descent toward a trough. However, the long swings of output in Japan appear to be rather more "rectangular," with peak periods lasting for a number of years and forming a plateau. This plateau combined with a rising trend is an important element in producing the upward historical drift of growth rates. The rectangularity is not very obvious in Figure 2.2, because the observed swings are neither simple nor uniform. But as Table 2.2 demonstrates, Japanese long swings do indicate higher average growth rates for upswings and lower rates for downswings, and this implies a plateau during expansions and a rectangular pattern. Why the shape was, in fact, "rectangular" will be examined in our model.

Trend Acceleration

There are many ways to measure a trend rate of growth, and some can give misleading results. If the growth rate of real GNP in Japan is calculated between 1901 and 1937, the result is an average annual rate of increase of 3.75 percent, and a comparison of this prewar trend with postwar values—1955–69, 10.37 percent per year—may lead to overemphasis on economic miracles and sharp breaks with the past. But this type of trend measure seems inappropriate when long swings are present. In that case, complete swings are preferable as the unit of trend measurement. Panel I, Table 2.2, estimates trend growth between average levels of long-swing expansions and contractions; Panel II measures growth between successive peaks and troughs; and Panel III compares average growth rates during whole long swings. In general, all three methods give consistent and similar results.

We interpret Table 2.2 as indicating that the measured trend rates of growth rise for GNP and GNP per capita in the twentieth century; and this is what we call trend acceleration. To some extent this is already obvious in Figure 2.1, since the slope of the GNP series becomes steeper

TABLE 2.2
GNP and GNP per Capita: Average Annual Trend
Rates of Growth
(Smoothed series, constant prices; *percent*)

Period	GNP	GNP per capita	Total population
I. Between average levels[a]			
(1) 1897–1901 to 1901–1917	2.24%	1.04%	1.20%
(2) 1901–1917 to 1917–1931	3.25	2.04	1.21
(3) 1917–1931 to 1931–1937	3.66	2.21	1.45
(4) 1931–1937 to 1937–1956	2.70	1.48	1.22
(5) 1937–1956 to 1956–1962	5.14	3.89	1.25
II. Between peak and trough years[b]			
A. Peak to peak			
(1) 1897 (P) – 1917 (P)	2.61	1.40	1.21
(2) 1917 (P) – 1937 (P)	3.67	2.36	1.31
(3) 1937 (P) – 1962 (P)	5.41	4.16	1.25
(3′) 1937 (P) – 1964	6.43	5.23	1.20
B. Trough to trough			
(4) 1901 (T) – 1931 (T)	2.97	1.71	1.26
(5) 1931 (T) – 1956 (T)	2.65	1.43	1.22
III. Long-swing average growth rates[c]			
A. Peak to peak			
(1) 1887 (P) – 1917 (P)	2.73	1.52	1.21
(2) 1917 (P) – 1937 (P)	3.68	2.33	1.35
(3) 1937 (P) – 1962 (P)	3.64	2.41	1.23
(3′) 1937 (P) – 1964	4.14	2.93	1.21
B. Trough to trough			
(4) 1901 (T) – 1931 (T)	2.92	1.64	1.28
(5) 1931 (T) – 1956 (T)	2.66	1.33	1.33

Source: See Table 2.1.
   Note: For smoothing procedures, prices, and derivation of per capita figures, see notes to Table 2.1.
   [a] Compound rates of growth between average levels for indicated periods.
   [b] Average compound growth rates between successive troughs and peaks.
   [c] Average of annual growth rates during whole swings.

on a semilog chart. It is equally obvious when the various early and late trend measures are compared. For example, GNP rising at 2.24 percent per year in Panel I, line (1), and 5.14 percent in line (5). However, our concept of trend acceleration also includes the notion of gradual increases in secular rates of growth during the entire period, and this requires a more detailed analysis of the results.

Starting with Panel I, the three average-contraction-to-average-expansion measures (lines 1, 3, and 5) show strong trend acceleration: 2.24–3.66–5.14. This is not so for the two average-expansion-to-average-contraction measures (lines 2 and 4): 3:25–2.70. The exception clearly originates in the collapse of the economy in World War II and the very low values for 1937–56.

Similar exceptions exist in Panels II and III, although they are somewhat less evident. The peak-to-peak measure for 1937–62 (IIA, line 3) shows some acceleration, but the trough-to-trough measure for 1931–56 (IIB, line 5) does not produce the anticipated acceleration. And the same is true of lines (3) and (5) in Panel III. The absence of a rise in the interval ending in 1956 has already been explained in the preceding paragraph. But why only a moderate increase for 1937–62? Because in many ways the depressing effect of World War II continued into the early 1960's, something that is frequently forgotten. When the time span is extended from 1962 to 1964 (lines IIA and IIIA 3′), acceleration becomes stronger. It would appear even more strongly if the analysis was extended to more recent years.

The major point is that it took the Japanese economy until the beginning of the 1960's to reach output levels projected by a prewar trend line. That is one way of measuring the economic cost of the war and the achievement of recovery. Figure 2.3 gives a schematic presentation of the situation. Line (g) is a smoothed picture of actual postwar output growth, and line (t) is a peak-to-peak trend. Points P_1 and P_2 are the prewar peaks of 1917 and 1937. P_3 is the tentative postwar peak of 1962, selected in terms of the movement of private investment. T_3 indicates the point where the level of GNP is equal to that of the prewar peak P_2,

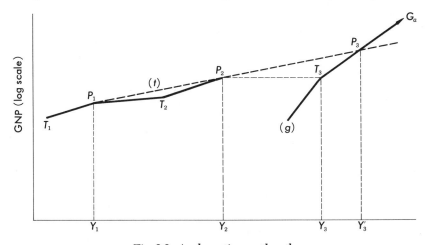

Fig. 2.3. A schematic growth path.

approximately 1954. It took Japan about 17 years to reach once more the peak output level of 1937, and that is the way "recovery" is normally defined. Yet the time span from Y_3 to Y_3' (growth path T_3P_3) lasted another eight years, and this period must be considered part of the "catching-up with oneself" process. Looked at in this fashion, the post-war recovery lasted a full 25 years. Reasons for the lack of acceleration have also been clarified. P_2 and P_3 lie on a trend line of unchanging slope; once we go beyond 1962 and add the portion P_3G_a, trend acceleration reappears in full force.

We conclude that the statistical findings confirm trend acceleration when the effects of World War II have been taken into account.

PERIODIZATION AND CAPITAL FORMATION

For those concerned with long-term economic change, periodization is a difficult though familiar necessity. Historical experience is complicated and diverse; to consider it systematically requires the formulation of comprehensible analytical units.

The actual scheme used throughout the remainder of our study has already been introduced, since many measures of Japan's economic performance were supplied, usually as rates of growth for year periods of unequal length. These measures gave evidence for the existence of alternating periods of more and less rapid economic development, and it should be clear that the duration of these periods — whether when growth was more or less rapid — places them outside the limits of ordinary business cycles.[5] What follows is an explanation of how these periods were selected.

As the primary indicator of periodization we have used the rate of growth of *private nonagricultural gross domestic fixed capital formation*, excluding residential construction ($\Delta I/I$). It is a choice with a number of justifications. Most important, our model will make investment, and especially private investment, a key dynamic element for economic growth. And second, the amplitude of private $\Delta I/I$ moves with great clarity.

Quantitative analysis of Japanese capital formation covers a period of nearly 90 years, from the present back to the 1880's. For this long period, the pattern has been remarkably stable. It consists of a steeply rising trend combined with wavelike movements of the growth rate. An investment wave or long swing consists of a period of relatively rapid

[5] In fact, the measurements are all based on seven-year (prewar) or five-year (postwar) moving averages, the purpose being to eliminate so far as possible business cycle fluctuations.

growth of capital formation followed by a number of years of lower growth. This can be observed in Figure 2.4, and we shall look at the private sector for the purpose of dating long swings in the rate of growth of capital formation.

Taking the broadest possible time span, it is possible to speak of three and one-half swings. The first consists of very high growth rates until the middle of the 1890's, followed by about six years of much slower capital formation. A second upswing begins somewhat hesitantly during the Russo-Japanese War, falters a bit between 1909 and 1912, but then the expansion carries through World War I. The latter half of this swing comprises the rather low investment growth rates prevailing during the entire 1920's. Then, beginning in the 1930's, and until the impact of the coming war made itself felt directly, a sharp investment spurt is in evidence. This has to be considered a "half-swing" because the period between the late 1930's and early 1950's, some 15 years, includes the destructive effects of World War II, the occupation, and the initial rehabilitation of Japan's economy. Normal economic analysis for this time span would make little sense; statistics are much less reliable, and a great variety of distortions effectively prevents the fitting of these years into a consideration of long-run development. However, after World War II the familiar pattern appears again. Private investment expands at near-record rates somewhat beyond the 1950's; this upsurge is followed by considerably slower investment growth through 1966, when our data run out.

Although a general identification of these long investment swings is a pretty simple matter, the selection of actual turning points (peaks and troughs) is inevitably more complicated and more debatable. Leaving aside the economic history of the nineteenth century, we have chosen the following dating:

	Trough	Peak	Trough
Swing I	1901	1917	1931
Swing II	1931	1937	
Swing III	1956	1962	1966

Perhaps some of these dates could be shifted one year in either direction, but this would not affect the conclusions. In any event, peaks and troughs are based on moving averages, and each individual year stands for a centered point of a band of seven (prewar) or five (postwar) years. What should be unambiguous, especially after an inspection of Table 2.3, is that before and after each turning point (T or P) the annual rates of growth of private investment maintain, for a long time, quite different levels.

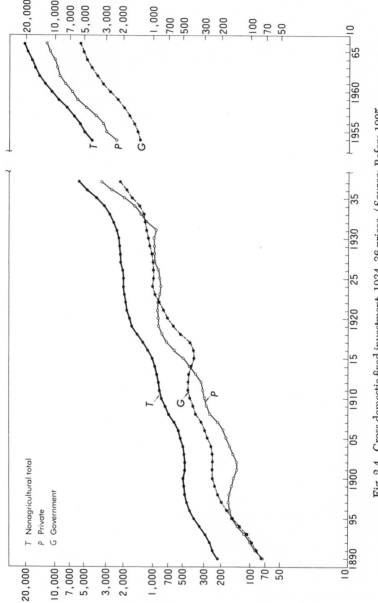

Fig. 2.4. Gross domestic fixed investment, 1934–36 prices. (*Source:* Before 1905, LTES, vol. 1; since 1905, BST.8 and BST.9.)

TABLE 2.3
*Private Nonagricultural Investment: Annual Rates of Growth
in Constant Prices*

Year	Percent	Year	Percent	Year	Percent
1901	−7.2%(T)	1918	8.9%	1935	20.3%
1902	2.7	1919	6.3	1936	31.4
1903	14.5	1920	−0.4	1937	20.2 (P)
1904	9.8	1921	−2.5		
1905	12.0	1922	−8.5		
1906	9.7	1923	−9.5		
1907	14.0	1924	−9.8	1956	12.1 (T)
1908	19.3	1925	−4.2	1957	15.1
1909	6.1	1926	1.2	1958	25.3
1910	5.4	1927	8.0	1959	26.4
1911	6.1	1928	−2.1	1960	18.6
1912	2.6	1929	−4.7	1961	17.6
1913	9.1	1930	−2.0	1962	18.3 (P)
1914	18.9	1931	5.0 (T)	1963	9.0
1915	24.0	1932	12.0	1964	6.0
1916	23.9	1933	11.4	1965	11.4
1917	19.3 (P)	1934	13.9	1966	16.0

Source: BST. 9, except for 1901–4 from WS, section I.
Note: Investment in residential construction is excluded. Growth rates are based on series smoothed by a seven-year moving average before World War II, and by a five-year moving average after World War II. Prices before World War II are 1934–36 prices, and after World War II are 1960 prices.

Let us, however, make note of three specific problems of interpretation relating to the selection of turning points.

First, in our periodization, 1901–17 is treated as a single upswing even though the smoothed growth rate of private capital formation falters from 1909 to 1912. Had World War I not provided a strong stimulus to entrepreneurs during the decade following 1910—and we must always keep in mind that these are time series smoothed by a seven-year moving average—it is entirely possible that 1909–12 would have developed into a full-fledged downswing. As it is, we prefer to consider the period as a unified step forward containing a small stumble.

Second, the postwar investment spurt is dated as beginning in 1956. This decision contains a measure of arbitrariness and, as explained earlier, is related to the aftermath of defeat in World War II.

Last, a word about the 1966 turning point. A new investment spurt may have begun at that time. Alternatively, one may eventually wish to treat 1962–66 as a "stumble" analogous to the earlier experience of 1909–12. In any event, the data are as yet too sparse for making a long-range historical judgment.

Individual private investment spurts can be observed in Table 2.4, column *PCF*. What is perhaps most noticeable is the rising vigor of these spurts in the twentieth century: 6.26 percent per year for 1901–17, 11.42 for 1931–37, and 16.93 for 1956–62.

THE CHANGING STRUCTURE OF THE ECONOMY

Tables 2.4 through 2.7 complete the broad picture of twentieth-century growth within the long-swing framework. All these tables deal with different sectoral breakdowns of the economy, and we can begin with the components of gross national expenditure in Table 2.4. Of course private capital formation (*PCF*) conforms extremely well to the long-swing movements, since it was used as the main dating base. The other components of GNP, with the exception of total capital formation (*GFCF*), conform only in some cases, and quite frequently indicate movements in the opposite direction. In other words, the long swing in Japan is particularly closely associated with private investment and aggregate output and expenditures.

Major sectors of output also have had very different growth patterns and swing associations, all of which underline the differences between agriculture and nonagriculture. As Table 2.5 shows, agriculture lagged behind nonagriculture by a growing margin. The trend growth of primary production is low and uneven; for secondary and tertiary produc-

TABLE 2.4

Average Annual Rates of Growth of Gross National Product Components
(Smoothed series, constant prices; *percent*)

Long swings[a]	GNP	PC	GC	GFCF	PCF	GCF	X	M
(1) 1897 (P) – 1901 (T)	2.18%	1.67%	6.98%	1.46%	-0.91%	7.10%	10.80%	5.19%
(2) 1901 (T) – 1917 (P)	2.87	2.72	3.45	5.34	6.26	3.26	9.43	2.87
(3) 1917 (P) – 1931 (T)	2.97	3.01	5.27	3.20	0.86	7.85	4.80	5.81
(4) 1931 (T) – 1937 (P)	5.91	2.36	11.23	10.56	11.42	9.56	10.40	4.35
(5) 1937 (P) – 1956 (T)[b]	1.83	0.89	-1.44	-0.03	0.88	-2.76	-5.03	-3.86
(6) 1956 (T) – 1962 (P)	10.42	8.77	4.98	16.33	16.93	14.72	12.51	14.38
(6') 1962 (P) – 1964[c]	9.77	9.76	6.70	12.34	12.22	12.70	15.16	13.28

Source: 1905–64 from BST. 6; earlier years from LTES, vol. 1.
  Notation:
    GNP, Gross national product.
    PC, Personal consumption.
    GC, Government current expenditures.
    GFCF, Gross fixed capital formation (*PCF* + *GCF*); since inventory changes are not available for prewar
        years, they have been entirely omitted.
    PCF, Gross private capital formation (including residential construction).
    GCF, Gross government capital formation (military investment is included prewar and excluded postwar).
    X,   Exports of goods and services (including factor payments).
    M,   Imports of goods and services (including factor payments).
    [a] Simple average of individual annual growth rates during demarcated periods.
    [b] For this period, prewar and postwar entries have been linked with individual price indexes (1934–36 prices
prewar, and 1960 prices postwar). These indexes are of rather doubtful accuracy, and therefore their use has been
restricted to 1937–56.
    [c] Line (6') added to show beginning of investment downswing.

TABLE 2.5
Average Annual Rates of Output Growth by Major Sectors
(Smoothed series, constant prices; *percent*)

Period	Agriculture	Other industries	Services	Nonagri-culture
I. Long swings[a]				
(1) 1897 (P) - 1901 (T)	1.88%	5.60%	0.95%	2.14%
(2) 1901 (T) - 1917 (P)	1.40	6.28	3.94	4.68
(3) 1917 (P) - 1931 (T)	0.91	5.89	1.86	3.58
(4) 1931 (T) - 1937 (P)	1.18	7.23	3.75	5.66
(5) 1937 (P) - 1956 (T)[b]	1.78	1.54	1.66	1.59
(6) 1956 (T) - 1962 (P)	3.20	15.47	10.71	13.41
(7) 1962 (P) - 1964	-0.13	13.52	11.40	12.57
II. Trend rates[c]				
A. Peak to peak				
(1) 1897 (P) - 1917 (P)	1.49	6.15	3.26	4.17
(2) 1917 (P) - 1937 (P)	1.00	6.29	2.43	4.21
(3) 1937 (P) - 1962 (P)	2.12	4.81	3.83	4.43
(3') 1937 (P) - 1964	1.95	5.53	4.37	5.02
B. Trough to trough				
(4) 1901 (T) - 1931 (T)	1.17	6.10	2.96	4.16
(5) 1931 (T) - 1956 (T)	1.62	3.02	1.87	2.64

Source: Since 1905, BST.4, with capital depreciation allowances especially estimated for this table. (Sectoral output deflators are not available in the official national income statistics, and therefore no estimates are given after 1964, when our estimates end.) For 1897–1904, see LTES, vol. 1.

Note: Agriculture includes forestry and fisheries. For other industries (manufacturing and mining plus facilitating industries–transportation, communication, public utilities–plus construction), see Table 1.1.

[a] Simple average of individual annual growth rates during demarcated periods.

[b] Estimated as a bridge calculation between 1937 and 1956.

[c] Average compound rates between successive peaks and troughs.

TABLE 2.6
Average Annual Rates of Growth of Labor Force
During Long Swings
(Smoothed series; *percent*)

Period[a]	Total labor force[b]	Agriculture	Other industries	Services	Non-agriculture
(1) 1897 (P) - 1901 (T)	0.53%	0.00%	1.63%	1.83%	1.72%
(2) 1901 (T) - 1917 (P)	0.53	-0.36	2.07	2.03	2.04
(3) 1917 (P) - 1931 (T)	0.81	-0.32	2.27	1.89	2.16
(4) 1931 (T) - 1937 (P)	1.08	0.23	2.20	2.15	2.17
(5) 1937 (P) - 1956 (T)	1.47	0.38	1.78	2.47	2.21
(6) 1956 (T) - 1962 (P)	1.52	-2.58	4.45	3.08	3.76
(7) 1962 (P) - 1969	1.60	-3.76	3.49	3.52	3.50

Source: From 1905, BST.5. Before 1905 from LTES, vol. 1.

Note: See Table 2.5 Note.

[a] Simple average of individual annual growth rates during demarcated periods.

[b] See Table 5.2 and pp. 124–25 for an explanation of the concept.

TABLE 2.7
Long-Term Changes in Key Ratios: Agriculture and Nonagriculture

Year	K/Y			K/L			Y/L		
	Total	Nonagri.	Agri.	Total	Nonagri.	Agri.	Total	Nonagri.	Agri.
Prewar, 1934–36 yen									
1897 (P)	1.56	1.27	2.00	353	592	240	231	464	120
1901 (T)	1.62	1.44	1.92	393	675	250	243	466	129
1917 (P)	1.82	1.76	2.02	735	1,252	346	404	711	171
1931 (T)	2.25	2.22	2.40	1,205	1,922	478	534	863	199
1937 (P)	2.09	2.05	2.39	1,439	2,201	516	850	1,069	229
Postwar:									
1934–36 yen[a]									
1956 (T)	2.43	2.27	3.43	1,673	2,117	950	684	930	276
1962 (P)	2.06	1.87	3.85	2,625	3,125	1,447	1,271	1,661	379
1964	2.10	1.91	4.29	3,171	3,693	1,742	1,391	1,933	405
1960 hundred yen									
1956 (T)	2.91	2.78	3.55	724	916	411	2,480	3,293	1,155
1962 (P)	2.46	2.29	3.98	1,136	1,352	626	4,607	5,880	1,584
1964	2.51	2.33	4.44	1,372	1,598	754	5,044	6,846	1,695

Source: From 1905, BST.16 (Capital), BST.15 (Labor), BST.2 and BST.4 (Output). Before 1905, from LTES, vol. 1.
Note: Five-year averages centered on indicated year.
Notation: K, Gross fixed capital stock (excluding residential construction). L, Labor force. Y, Output (gross of depreciation).
[a] Tentative linkage.

tion it is high and accelerating. In addition, nonagriculture and its components—industries and services—fit the long-swing pattern quite well; this is not at all true of agriculture.

The contrast between agriculture and nonagriculture is further elaborated in Table 2.6 containing comparative growth rates of the labor force in different sectors between 1897 and 1969. While industry and services (last three columns) are gaining workers at fairly steady rates, and at rates well in excess of the expansion of the total labor force, agricultural labor force growth rates are *negative* or close to zero during the entire period of analysis. The sharp increase in total and nonagricultural labor force following World War II should be noted; the participation of agriculture in this process is in the form of large declines in its work force.

Last, let us look at the sectoral key ratios—K/Y, K/L, and Y/L—of Table 2.7. Once again, the contrast between these two sectors is apparent. Throughout the period they exhibit two different levels of capital intensity (K/L), with the higher level always prevailing in nonagriculture. The relative gap in capital intensities widens in the prewar period from $(K/L_{NA}/K/L_A)$ 2.47 in 1897 to 4.27 in 1937. In the postwar years, the gap continues to exist, although it has gotten slightly smaller, having dropped from 2.23 in 1956 to 2.12 in 1964 (in 1960 prices).

A similar long-term gap pertains to (partial) labor productivity (Y/L), and, of course, nonagriculture again outperforms agriculture. In this case, however, the gap $(Y/L_{NA}/Y/L_A)$ not only widens in prewar times from 3.87 in 1897 to 4.67 in 1937, but also widens in recent years from 2.78 in 1956 to 4.05 in 1964 (in 1960 prices).[6]

The historical experience of sectoral K/L and Y/L are brought together in the capital-output ratios of Table 2.7. Initially K/Y is lower in nonagriculture, but beginning in (say) the 1920's, the two sectors indicate similar levels. After the war, the capital-output ratio of agriculture is higher and rising; in nonagriculture it is lower and falling. In other words, we may suggest in a very preliminary way that capital in agriculture has been used less efficiently than in nonagriculture, especially after World War II. Reasons for this will be explored in later chapters.

The Differential Structure

The type of sectoral growth outlined in the preceding sections has, during the course of this century, produced a specific form of dual economy characterized by different productivity levels for the modern and traditional sectors in terms of product per worker. Modern growth in modern sectors has been accompanied by increases in labor productivity owing to technological progress and capital accumulation. The productivity levels of traditional sectors have also risen, through traditional technological progress or by means of progress induced by the modern sector. In general, however, the possibilities of traditional productivity increases would appear to be much more limited, and as time passes, they have fallen behind the modern sectors. Changes in these sectoral productivity and wage levels, particularly the rate of growth of the differentials, was one of the basic elements of structural change in Japan. From about World War I until the 1960's, and perhaps even now, these differentials have grown wider, and it is this growing gap that we shall call the differential structure.[7]

A more analytical and quantitative treatment of the differential structure and its consequences will appear beginning with Chapter 5, but it is useful to make a few introductory remarks here.

As a group, modern and traditional sectors can be considered in two

---

[6] A tentative conversion—see Table 2.7—of postwar figures into prewar price valuations indicates that the pattern described in the text has not been significantly affected by changes in relative prices.

[7] We use this term to emphasize the *growing* gap, since the more usual term "dual structure" merely implies a gap without specifying its growth in any direction.

rather different ways. No doubt the basic division lies between agriculture and manufacturing, and if the purpose is to measure broad aspects of the differential structure, one is almost forced to concentrate on this particular definition. And indeed, the results are rather clear: manufacturing or factory production, on the average, was, of course, the leader of economic modernization, and quickly left behind the large numbers of workers who continued to make their living as small farmers, employing on the whole traditional techniques. Throughout the period of analysis, especially before World War II, the numbers of those left behind was never insignificant.

Although not shown here, there is another way of looking at the modern-traditional division *within* the nonagricultural sector, and it lies in the size structure of industry. Small-scale industry is a weighty employer in all industrial categories, and especially so in food-processing and textiles. Naturally, small-scale industry (and services) has a very different appearance from the perspective of productivity. Those activities in which small units are numerous, as in food and certain textiles, have lower-than-national-average levels of labor productivity. A most revealing specific example can be taken from "midget enterprises" in the year 1957, when 54 percent of all industrial establishments employed between one and three workers; these units accounted for about 9 percent of the industrial labor force; and for about 2 percent of the industrial ouput.

A strong relation exists between the concept of "traditional" and small-scale industry. These two categories are nearly the sole producers of a wide range of traditional commodities, as, for example, pottery, fishing nets, lacquer ware, and roof tile, and many of these items are still important in daily life. In many of these activities, economies of scale are low. Of course, small enterprises in Japan make an extremely wide variety of things, many of which are modern, such as toys, light bulbs, and bicycles. Nevertheless, the tie to the traditional economy remains strong. Unpaid family workers and especially female labor continue to be used at far more than average levels, and whenever possible the skilled or semiskilled hand is used in preference to the machine. Readily available cheap labor is the oxygen of the small enterpriser: it permits him to operate. Lack of sophisticated modern technology at prices he can afford means lower levels of productivity, lower wages, and, at least for workers, a difficult existence, especially compared with those fortunate enough to find work in large enterprises.

Obviously this particular economic structure has had a strong effect on all of Japan's modern economic and general history. The differential structure affected the price of labor and thereby the price of all output;

it influenced the choice of technology; it even played a role in creating the militaristic era of the 1930's. All these, as well as some other facets of this matter, will be discussed below.

A PREVIEW OF THE EXPLANATION

By now the reader has been supplied with both historical background and a broad quantitative picture of Japanese economic development since the 1880's. Before beginning the analysis of individual aspects of growth, it may be helpful to provide a preview of the explanatory mechanism that will be dealt with in much greater detail in Chapter 8, when we turn to our model. This study addresses itself to three central themes.

1. Why has long-term Japanese growth been so rapid, and more particularly, why has the pace of growth been rising during the twentieth century?

2. Why has the post–World War II rate of growth been so much higher than earlier? (Can it last?) Despite the rising pace of growth throughout this century, the years following the war represent a sharp break, and this also has to be explained.

3. Why has Japanese growth taken the form of marked spurts (upswings), followed by periods of relatively slower growth, and why have these spurts lasted a long time?

In attempting to answer these questions we shall make frequent use of four concepts and four preliminary assumptions. The first concept is that of the long swing, already shown to be a very general phenomenon in the Japanese economy, especially in terms of rates of growth. The second concept is that of the private nonagricultural investment spurt, and refers to the periods of especially rapid private investment growth associated with long-swing expansions. The third concept is trend acceleration, and is intended to describe the extensive and gradual quickening of most Japanese indicators within the long-swing framework in the last 70 years. The fourth concept is the differential structure and refers to the growing labor productivity and wage gaps between the modern and traditional sectors of the Japanese economy.

Next, a brief statement of the four preliminary assumptions applying to the entire period of analysis—1900 to the present. First, we assume the existence of a gap between technology actually applied in Japan and the increasing capability of borrowing and absorbing more advanced methods based on a well-functioning sociopolitical infrastructure.[8] Second, we assume that autonomous investment based on bor-

---

[8] Another type of gap is the consequence of Japan's isolation in the 1930's and 1940's. It deserves special consideration in interpreting post–World War II acceleration.

rowed technology is the major driving force of Japanese economic growth. Third, we assume that to explain Japan's particular pattern of growth requires use of a two-sector model that includes the categories "modern" and "traditional." And finally, we assume that Japan's extraordinary postwar performance is linked to the development and strengthening of forces already in operation before the war. To that extent, it is meaningful to speak of Japan's postwar growth as a reflection of "trend acceleration" and to regard it, therefore, as an integral part of her entire historical experience.

Now, we can turn to a brief summary of the explanatory mechanism for Japan's growth pattern in the twentieth century. Modern technology is associated with the employment of capital equipment and structure of new design. It also involves larger amounts of capital per man than the traditional technology did. Furthermore, the capital-labor proportion of modern techniques is relatively rigid, whereas that of traditional techniques is somewhat more flexible. These characteristics imply a close connection between the volume of gross investment and the growth rate of capital stock on the one hand, and the growth rate of labor productivity on the other. To put it another way, the pace of transfer of labor from traditional to modern sectors is constrained by the volume of investment and the growth rate of the capital stock. Given the gap mentioned in the first assumption above, additional capital applied to transferring a worker to the modern sector results in a notable increase in productivity. By contrast, workers who cannot be absorbed into modern industry for lack of capital *can* be and are absorbed into the traditional sectors at lower levels of productivity.

In Japan, the technology gap took the form of a dualistic structure of industry and the labor market. There were marked differentials in productivity and wage rates. The productivity differentials reflected the scarcity of capital and the different capital intensities prevailing in modern and traditional sectors, and the wage differentials rested on the peculiar Japanese labor market institutions (permanent employment, seniority payments, etc.) that kept modern sector wages high in the face of surplus labor. This combination of conditions produced a flexible labor supply response to increases in demand for labor, and hence underlay a wage lag with respect to labor productivity that was itself the condition for high profits and a high investment and savings rate.

The average investment and savings ratio was high in Japan, and the various characteristics of Japanese society that define its capability to exploit modern technology meant that a large part of capital formation went to modern sectors. The high capital formation and savings rate depended on a number of major factors. First, additional capital, applied in modern sectors, meant rapid output growth. Additional output produced a high share of capital (profits) in income because the characteristics of the Japanese labor market, notably surplus labor in traditional sectors and "lifetime commitment," caused wages to lag behind productivity. Given the expectation of high profits, unincorporated private enterprises and corporations enjoying profits saved and invested a large proportion of their own, as well as borrowed, income. Household savings from income were also, in general, large because consumption patterns remained conservative, and consumption increases lagged behind the growth rate of disposable income.

Economic modernization in Japan required not only a high capital formation ratio, but also a large expansion of exports. The need to export was reinforced by Japan's limitations of raw material endowment and dependence on foreign suppliers for modern equipment, which kept the propensity to import high and therefore required a large volume of exports to finance the growth of imports. The ability to generate the necessary export volume on the basis of traditional products proved limited; but rapid increases in modern sector labor productivity combined with lagging wage rates gave Japan an expanding comparative advantage in modern sector products, and permitted rapid import substitution. Hence, both the problems of saturating the home market and the import-finance requirements of modernization could be met.

The elements sketched above also provide most of what is needed to explain why growth took the form of sustained spurts and long swings. Given the occurrence (for any reason) of an interruption to growth, one can postulate that the unexploited pool of highly productive modern technology becomes larger. Renewed investments, therefore, produce an acceleration of productivity and output growth. This is especially rapid because labor comes to be used less intensively, even in the modern sector, when the growth rate of demand falls off. Return to normal intensity of use implies higher productivity growth. Flexible labor-force response means lagging wages and vaulting increases in the rate of return on capital. Hence, rapid expansion of saving and investment. And since there are large pools of surplus labor, the process can go on for a long period of time.

The usual problem of financing growing imports, which constrained output spurts in other countries, was also solved for long periods because Japanese productivity and labor market conditions produced improvement in Japanese competitiveness in export markets (not as fast in spurts as in retardation, but fast enough to avoid balance-of-payments crises for long periods). One must recognize, of course, the special help to exports from world market conditions during World War I.

Next, let us very briefly consider trend acceleration. Unlike spurts and long swings, the trend is necessarily an abstraction. We propose to consider it as a "normal or equilibrium" growth path running through the periods of maximum potential growth (spurts) and ensuing adjustment years (downswings). In this normal long-term growth path the expected and steady rates of return on capital are such as to lead to an ever-rising proportion of capital formation. A growing capital formation proportion is also associated with trend rates of increase in capital per worker and in total factor productivity (the residual). The link between more capital per worker and a larger residual is one of the basic relationships underlying trend acceleration. However, the phenomenon of trend acceleration cannot be explained in terms of single causes. Therefore we shall introduce a number of other factors coalescing around the concept of Japan's rising social capability to import technological progress. Specifically, rising income, savings, learning by doing, and institutional innovation will be seen as interacting positively with the basic link between rising capital per worker and a larger residual.

The elements outlined above also provide a framework of argument accounting for the especially rapid growth after World War II. The war and its aftermath produced a long interruption of normal Japanese private sector investment, and hence an especially large gap or pool of untapped modern technology. This was further enlarged by the acceleration of productivity growth in industrialized countries generally.

As a consequence of war and of the rehabilitation period, there was also a buildup in the pool of underemployed population in the rural and other traditional sectors. Rapid productivity growth in agriculture and other traditional sectors in the postwar period also fed the pool of surplus labor. Hence, though transfer to modern sectors had been going on for decades, a large pool of surplus labor existed at least until the beginning of the 1960's and permitted postwar Japanese growth to continue on the basis of the flexible labor response process.

Given a flexible labor response and therefore a wage lag, and an especially large increase in output associated with increase in capital, the rise in profits and savings was very large. This increase in savings was further supported by the decline in absorption of income and output by government, especially for military purposes.

The increase in output associated with investment growth was large, not only because of the enlarged technology gap but also because the capital stock was depleted and so a given volume of investment meant a more rapid growth of capital stock.

The expansion of exports was very rapid because of the combination of extraordinarily rapid productivity growth with flexible supplies of labor. The scale requirements of modern technology were aided by the export expansion, and also because in the postwar period Japanese incomes were now sufficiently high to produce a large growing home market for modern products.

CHAPTER THREE

Factor Inputs and Aggregate Productivity

The next two chapters are closely related and begin the more detailed analysis of Japanese economic growth. Both are concerned with the relation between factor inputs — labor, capital, and "nonconventional" items — and output. And this, of course, includes a consideration of "residuals" or "total factor productivity." In studying the growth of productivity we intend to follow a by now conventional approach that is capable of quantifying and separating two components. One of these components is the contribution to productivity growth made by factor inputs (primarily labor and capital). The other arises because productivity or output growth frequently exceeds additions of inputs, giving rise to an unexplained increment, the so-called "residual." As discussed below, this approach necessarily entails some restrictive assumptions. Despite these restrictions, we believe that this is a most convenient method for clarifying the pattern of productivity growth in Japan.[1]

Chapter 3 concentrates on factor inputs and the aggregate residual in the private nonagricultural sector. (Unless otherwise specified, all calculations pertain to this sector.) One of our basic assumptions has been that a two-sector approach is necessary to analyze the historical experience of Japan, and that is why agriculture receives separate treatment in Chapter 4. Here we will concentrate on capital and labor, and on the refinements of these inputs, moving from a crude to an adjusted nonagricultural aggregate residual.

---

[1] In recent years other productivity measurements of this type have been calculated for Japan, but they are generally confined to the postwar period. For example, see R. F. Kosobud, "Measured Productivity Change in the Economy of Japan, 1952–1968," in R. F. Kosobud and R. Minami, eds., *Econometric Studies of the Contemporary Economy of Japan* (Chicago, forthcoming), and H. Kanamori, "Nihon keizai no seichō wa naze takai ka" (What Makes Japan's Economic Growth Rate High?), *Keizai bunseki*, no. 31 (Sept. 1970). Despite some technical differences in approach, these results coincide broadly with our own.

Then Chapter 4 adds an analysis of residuals in specific industries and considers the effects of labor reallocation between sectors and the connection between residuals and technological progress. It also attempts to provide a general interpretation of what the movements of the residual have meant in Japanese development. This is also discussed again in Chapter 8 (the model) and Chapter 9 (Beyond Measurement).

THE CRUDE RESIDUAL

The actual measurement of the residual is based on this simple formula:

$$G_Y = G_R + \alpha G_K + \beta G_L, \qquad (\alpha + \beta = 1) \qquad (1)$$

or

$$G_R = \alpha(G_Y - G_K) + \beta(G_Y - G_L) \qquad (1')$$

In these equations, Y = output, K = capital, L = labor, R = residual, α = relative income share of capital, β = relative income share of labor, and G = rate of growth.[2]

For the initial approximation of aggregate G_R, Y is taken as gross of capital depreciation (i.e. gross domestic product, GDP, of the private nonagricultural sector), K as gross capital stock at the midpoint of each year (reproducible fixed capital excluding residential buildings), and L as the number of the labor force employed; α and β are also used gross of capital depreciation and correspond to the gross concept of Y.[3]

The procedure of estimating equations (1) and/or (1') entails four steps. First, annual series of Y, K, L, α, and β are smoothed by a seven-year (prewar) and five-year (postwar) moving average. Second, annual rates of growth, based on the smoothed series, are obtained for Y, K, and L. Third, the annual values of α and β are then used to obtain yearly values of αG_K, βG_L, and G_R. And finally, these annual figures are averaged to obtain values for the demarcated phases of long swings outlined in Chapter 2.

One last word of caution. The three assumptions contained in footnote 2 have not yet been empirically verified. Consequently, these computations yield only a first approximation. In Chapter 4 we will have an

[2] In estimating the residual, we will initially assume the existence of three conditions in the Japanese economy: nearly competitive determination of factor prices, constant returns to scale, and disembodied technological progress and Hicksian neutrality.

[3] For a detailed explanation of definitions, coverage, and estimation of K, see the section on "capital stock" below. Prewar labor statistics have certain peculiarities; these are more fully surveyed in Chapter 5. For a detailed report on the estimation of α and β, see Appendix Note.

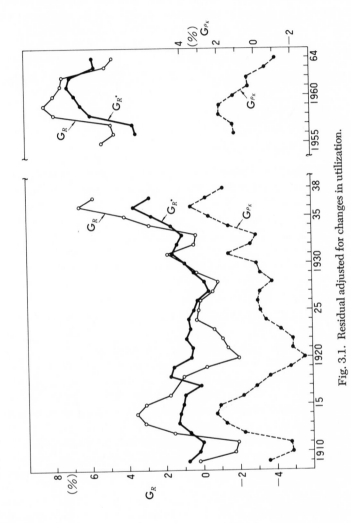

Fig. 3.1. Residual adjusted for changes in utilization.

TABLE 3.1
TABLE 3.1
Average Annual Growth Rates of Residuals and Related Terms:
Nonagriculture, 1908–64
(Percent)

Term	1908-17	1912-18	1917-31	1931-38	1955-61	1962-64
G_Y	5.07%	6.75%	3.12%	6.73%	13.04%	12.71%
G_K	6.46	6.85	5.24	4.60	9.54	12.73
G_L	2.19	2.70	1.99	1.91	4.87	4.29
$G_Y - G_L$	2.88	4.04	1.13	4.82	8.17	8.42
$G_Y - G_K$	-1.39	-0.11	-2.12	2.13	3.50	0.02
$G_K - G_L$	4.27	4.15	3.25	2.69	4.67	8.44
α	45.4	47.5	37.8	37.1	29.0	33.3
β	54.6	52.5	62.2	62.9	71.0	66.7
αG_K	2.95	3.28	2.08	1.73	2.82	4.24
βG_L	1.18	1.41	1.22	1.19	3.46	2.86
G_I	4.12	4.69	3.30	2.92	6.28	7.10
G_I/G_Y	81.30	69.50	105.80	43.40	48.20	55.90
G_R	0.95	2.05	-0.18	3.81	6.75	5.61

Source: Y from BST.4, K from BST.16, L from BST.15, α and β from BST.17.
Note: Averages of annual figures calculated from smoothed series for demarcated periods.
Notation: Y, output; K, capital; L, labor; R, residual; α, relative income share of capital; β, relative income share of labor; and G, rate of growth.

opportunity to examine the validity of the three conditions in somewhat greater detail.

Table 3.1, encompassing the entire period of analysis, is intended to provide the broadest overview of crude residual growth rates. (The annual results are also graphed in Figure 3.1.) Terms and data used in this table have nearly all been explained earlier. Nevertheless, it is useful to define briefly some of the relations that will recur frequently:

αG_K = contribution of the growth rate of gross capital stock to the growth rate of output

βG_L = contribution of the growth rate of the labor force employed to the growth rate of output

G_I = growth rate of total input contribution = $\alpha G_K + \beta G_L$

G_R = growth rate of residual = $G_Y - G_I$

G_I/G_Y = proportion of explained output growth.

Two things stand out about the growth rates of residuals. One is that the residual has grown much more rapidly since World War II. The prewar range was between 0.18 and 3.81 percent per year; postwar, the range lay between 5.61 and 6.75. The other finding is that growth rates of residuals are highly correlated with the investment-output periodization. Residual growth was more rapid in 1908–17 and 1931–38 than in 1917–31; it was also more rapid in 1955–61 than in 1962–64.

The proportion of explained output growth varied widely. Until the 1930's, at least 70 percent of the increases in output can be directly explained by the marginal contributions of capital and labor, with the contribution of capital invariably exceeding that of labor. Since then, the explained part of output growth has generally been below 50 percent.

Why does a residual exist at all, and why has its importance increased in Japan during this century? At this crude stage of measurement, many possibilities come to mind. Both capital and labor can vary in their rate of utilization, and this may alter the relation between input and output. Quality improvements in both factors could have the same effect. The same is true of factor reallocation from (say) small unincorporated enterprises to larger corporate units, or more generally from less to more productive uses. Economies of scale could also exert a similar influence. If all these elements are properly taken into account—a nearly impossible task—and if the residual has not been entirely eliminated, it is then acceptable to label the remainder as technological and organizational progress *and* "unknown factors." (The residual has sometimes been referred to as a measure of our ignorance!) Most of these factors will be discussed in this and the following chapter, and an interpretation of the residual in Japanese growth will have to be postponed to the end of Chapter 4.

ADJUSTED RESIDUALS

The Rate of Utilization

Capital utilization. Among the input adjustments that are required, taking the rate of capital utilization into account is most important. That the rate of utilization exhibited large historical variations is to be expected, if only because of the large swings of capital formation that persisted despite the elimination of business cycles. Yet, to measure utilization with any degree of precision is extremely difficult.[4] We shall

---

[4] The Ministry of International Trade and Industry publishes a capital utilization index (*kadōritsu*) but it is restricted to postwar manufacturing. In addition, the Economic Research Institute of the Economic Planning Agency and Kōnosuke Odaka have made long-term indexes beginning in 1905; however, they are not suitable for our purposes because of their heavy reliance on manufacturing. See Japan, Economic Planning Agency, Economic Research Institute, *Nibumon seichō moderu ni yoru senzai seichōryoku no sokutei* (Measurement of Growth Potentials by Two-Sector Models), Study Series no. 23 (March 1971), and K. Odaka, "Senzen Nihon keizai ni okeru kadōritsu no sokutei" (Estimates of Utilization Rates in Prewar Japan), *Keizai kenkyū*, vol. 23, no. 3 (July 1972).

have to proceed with the help of some very bold assumptions: that K/Y at long-swing peak years represents the "true" capital-output ratio at capacity output; that these full capacity values of K/Y can be linearly interpolated for each year between peaks.[5] That changes in demand and in the rate of capital utilization had considerable effect can be seen in Figure 3.1.

Working hours and work intensity. Just as with capital, it is possible to use a given employed labor force at different degrees of input effort. Working hours can be raised or lowered, and the intensity of work during each hour can change in the short or long run. Working hours can be measured fairly easily; the intensity of work is beyond aggregate quantification.

A considerable practical difficulty, however, is the fact that pre–World War II working-hour statistics are extremely limited, and therefore not usable for present purposes.[6] In the postwar period, reliable data become available for all industries. These are used as a five-year moving average to indicate the rate of utilization of labor (ρ_L), and its rate of change ($G_{\rho L}$) is derived by a method similar to that previously employed for capital.[7]

---

[5] The actual steps of the calculation are as follows. First, K/Y in a peak year, e.g. 1917, is taken as output at 100 percent utilization of capacity, or K/Y^*. Then the values between K/Y^* in 1917 and 1938 are determined by interpolation, yielding K/Y^* for all intermediate years. Finally, for every year there exists an actual K/Y, and the relation between it and the interpolated value gives the rate of utilization of capital.

$$\rho = Y/Y^* = Y/K \div Y^* / K \quad \text{and} \quad G_{\rho K} = G_{Y/Y^*}$$

[6] Statistics for working hours per day and working days per month are available in Japan, Statistical Bureau of the Prime Minister's Office, *Chingin maigetsu chōsa* (Monthly Survey of Wages), 1923–40; and Bank of Japan, *Rōdō tōkei* (Labor Statistics), 1923–39. These sources have slightly different coverage and survey methods, and indicate the following results for selected years:

| Year | Maigetsu chōsa | | | Rōdō tōkei | | |
	Hrs/day (1)	Days/mo (2)	Hrs/mo (1)×(2) (3)	Hrs/day (1)	Days/mo (2)	Hrs/mo (1)×(2) (3)
1923	9.28	27.5	260.3	10.09	26.7	271.0
1927	9.24	26.9	253.0	9.51	26.8	264.0
1931	9.05	26.5	293.7	9.33	26.5	253.1
1935	9.17	26.9	250.1	9.51	27.0	266.0
1939	9.17	26.9	250.1	9.57	27.1	269.0

In the opinion of most experts, these figures are not reliable enough to indicate change in *actual* working hours. They pertain rather to *kitei rōdō jikan* (regular or standard working hours), and the information concerning days is believed to be the more reliable series. In addition, the coverage of these series concentrates heavily on manufacturing.

[7] Japan, Ministry of Labor, *Maigetsu kinrō chōsa* (Monthly Labor Survey) supplies actual average working hours per worker per month in all nonagricultural in-

TABLE 3.2
*Average Annual Rates of Growth of the Residual
Adjusted for Capital and Labor Utilization*
(Percent)

Term	1909–17	1912–18	1918–31	1932–38	1956–61	1962–64
1. $\alpha G_{\rho K}$	0.27%	0.65%	−0.39%	1.03%	0.49%	−0.47%
2. $\beta G_{\rho L}$	0.16	0.38	−0.33	0.84	0.22	−0.50
3. (1)+(2)	0.43	1.03	−0.72	1.87	0.71	−0.97
4. G_R^*	0.52	1.02	0.54	1.94	6.04	6.58

Notation: See p. 47.

In studying the relation between $G_{\rho L}$ and $G_{\rho K}$ for 1953–65, we find that $G_{\rho L}$ appears to be 0.3–0.4 of $G_{\rho K}$. This relation has been used for estimating the prewar values of $G_{\rho L}$. Actually, 0.5 was employed on the assumption that the prewar coefficient must have been higher than values for the 1950's and 1960's. Two principal reasons may be cited. First, the prewar proportion of temporary and underemployed workers was much higher. Second, the statistics of "gainfully employed population," a concept in use before World War II, did not exclude those unemployed for shorter periods, and hence are probably less sensitive than postwar labor force statistics as indicators of changes in employment.

The residuals adjusted for capital and labor utilization are finally derived with the formula

$$G_R^* = G_R - (\alpha G_{\rho K} + \beta G_{\rho L}) = G_R - \varepsilon G_{\rho K}$$

where $\varepsilon = \alpha + 0.5\beta$. Annual values of G_R^* are shown in Figure 3.1, and the same numbers demarcated in long-swing phases are given in Table 3.2.

It has to be admitted that, owing to data constraints, these are only rough approximations for the impact of changes in utilization. However, if the adjustments are at all valid, one can now observe that G_R^* fluctuates much less than G_R; furthermore, G_R^* always lies below G_R in upswings and above G_R in downswings. One can conclude that residual growth is dampened when utilization is taken into account, but the residual does not disappear and its general historical time path has not been altered.

---

dustries. The results are as follows for selected years (average monthly hours are in crude annual figures; the average annual growth rate is calculated from a smoothed series):

Year	Ave. hrs/mo	G_{ρ_L}
1955	194.8	0.94
1958	198.0	0.82
1961	202.7	−0.10
1964	192.9	−0.82

TABLE 3.3
Indexes of Labor Input
(1954 = 100)

Year	N	H	S	E
1953	98.6	97.1	96.6	96.4
1954	100.0	100.0	100.0	100.0
1955	103.2	102.2	101.7	101.6
1956	105.2	105.9	106.2	106.0
1957	107.8	110.0	110.0	110.2
1958	108.3	111.0	111.6	111.4
1959	109.5	112.4	112.9	113.2
1960	111.9	114.9	115.7	116.8
1961	113.1	116.7	117.1	118.3
1962	114.6	116.7	119.0	120.3
1963	115.7	116.5	119.4	120.4

Source: Prime Minister's Office, Bureau of Statistics, *Rōdō ryoku chōsa* (Labor Force Survey); Japan, Ministry of Labor, *Shūgyō kōzō kihonchōsa* (Basic Survey of Employment Structure); Ministry of Education, *Gakkō kihonchōsa* (Basic Survey of Schools).

Notation: N is index based on total employed labor force. H is N adjusted for man-hours worked. S is H adjusted for sex and age composition of labor force. E is S adjusted for level of education of labor force.

The Quality of Labor

It seems inherently plausible that if inputs were adjusted for improvements in quality, labor's contribution to output growth would be raised. Denison's stimulating research has lent strong support to this view, especially in the United States. Japan is famous for its high average levels of education, and it might be expected that in Japan also a quality adjustment will significantly affect measured labor input. And yet this is not the case after World War II for reasons that will be explained in this section.

Quality is usually defined in terms of sex, age, and education. With these concepts, male workers are of higher quality than female workers, middle-aged workers are more qualified than the young (and very old), and the greater the level of education, the higher the quality of workers. It must then be assumed that these differentials are competitively evaluated by the labor market, so that higher levels of quality are reflected in higher wage rates.

Postwar. Effects of changing quality in labor input in postwar Japan can be studied in Table 3.3. Adjustments for sex, age, and education result in only minor modifications as we move from index N (the crudest formulation) through index E (the most "sophisticated" formulation).[8] Indexes E and S do not rise much more rapidly than N and H; therefore,

[8] According to T. Watanabe, the labor quality index rose at 1 percent per year for male and 0.3 percent for female workers. See "Improvement of Labor Quality and Economic Growth—Japan's Postwar Experience," *Economic Development and Cultural Change*, vol. 21, no. 1 (October 1972).

taking these variables into account leaves residual growth rates more or less the same, as shown in the following average annual rates of growth: quality adjustment for 1952–55 was .01, for 1955–61 it was .36, and for 1961–63 it was .43.

Measured changes in quality are the result of variations in labor force composition (age, sex, and education) and weights (wage differentials). Let us look briefly at each of these items, beginning with the postwar sex composition. As shown in the *Labor Force Survey*, the proportion of males and females in the employed labor force remained quite stable (Japan, Statistics Bureau, Prime Minister's Office, *Rōdōryoku chōsa kaisan hōkoku* [1957], pp. 34–38, for 1952 and 1955, and *ibid.* [1971], pp. 36–44, for 1961 and 1965):

Year	Total male	Primary	Non-primary	Total female	Primary	Non-primary
1952	60.1%	50.0%	68.1%	39.9%	50.0%	31.9%
1955	58.6	48.7	64.9	41.4	51.3	35.1
1961	59.5	46.9	64.9	40.5	53.1	35.1
1965	60.3	48.4	64.9	39.7	51.6	35.3

Because of lower female wages, a slight increase in the proportion of females until 1955 had a depressing effect on quality. The reverse was true after 1955, but in general the changes were insignificant.

The average age of the labor force was also quite stable after World War II, as indicated in the census figures:

	1950	1955	1960
Total	31.8	34.7	35.2
Male	32.5	35.5	35.8
Female	30.9	33.7	34.2

Between 1950 and 1955 the rate of age increase was relatively rapid, but since then it has become very gradual. The impact on quality must have been small.

Sex and age are demographic characteristics, and one would expect these to have only a limited impact in the short run. Levels of education, on the other hand, can be expected to change more rapidly in a shorter period of time. It is here that we must look for the major force underlying increases in quality. Evidence presented in Table 3.4 shows that during 1950–62 the average education level of the employed labor force (*shūgyōsha*) rose by .5 year for males and by .6 year for females. This is similar to the rates of increase in France and the United Kingdom, though well below the performance of Italy and the United States.[9]

---

[9] There may be some difference in educational definition between Japan and other countries, but the comparison of rates of increase should be safe enough. Note that in both 1950 and 1962 Japan ranks immediately behind the United States in average level of education.

TABLE 3.4
Average Years of Education, Japan and Selected Countries, 1950-62

Country	1950		1962		Increases, 1950-62	
	Male	Female	Male	Female	Male	Female
Japan[a]	9.5	8.7	10.0	9.3	0.50	0.60
United States	9.68	10.01	10.68	11.08	1.00	1.07
France	8.09	7.89	8.65	8.51	0.56	0.62
West Germany	7.93	7.95	8.24	8.19	0.31	0.24
United Kingdom	9.16	9.43	9.71	9.86	0.55	0.43
Italy	4.23	3.89	5.10	4.88	0.87	0.99

Source: Japan from decennial censuses. Other countries from E. F. Denison, assisted by J. P. Poullier, *Why Growth Rates Differ: Postwar Experience in Nine Western Countries* (Washington, D.C., 1967), Tables 8-12, p. 107, and Appendix F.
   [a] Japanese results are for 1950 and 1960.

The degree to which compositional changes in the labor force affect measured quality increases (or decreases) is determined by the weights —in this instance, the relative wage structure stratified by quality differentials. These can be examined in Table 3.5.[10] There is no doubt about the relatively low wages received by female workers. With a completed compulsory education and in the prime of life, women earned only about half as much as men. Even highly educated women of suitable working age did not reach the wage levels of adult males with a middle school education. These findings do not appear to be peculiar to Japan. E. F. Denison, in his study of the United States, observed very similar male-female differentials.[11] In any event, the sex composition of the labor force did not change enough to affect labor input significantly.

Age differences produce a wide range of wage rates in Japan, and this is a reflection of a strong *nenkō-joretsu* or seniority system.[12] Any one of the columns in Table 3.5 reveals the upward pull on wages exercised by age, especially for male high school, junior college, and university gradu-

[10] These weights were used to calculate the labor input indexes. Watanabe, in *Sūryo keizai bunseki* (Quantitative Economic Analysis; Tokyo, 1970), chap. 5, using similar materials and procedures, has calculated wage differentials for 1954, 1961, and 1964. His results are, broadly speaking, in keeping with our own conclusions.
   The wage differentials due to level of education may also include certain "innate" differences in people unrelated to schooling. See E. F. Denison, assisted by J. P. Poullier, *Why Growth Rates Differ: Postwar Experience in Nine Western Countries* (Washington, D.C., 1967), p. 83. We have made no adjustments for lack of data. Therefore our quality adjustments include the effects of both education and "innate" elements.
[11] *The Sources of Economic Growth in the United States and the Alternatives Before Us* (Supplementary Paper no. 13, Committee for Economic Development, New York, 1962).
[12] This system has especially intrigued foreign students of the Japanese economy. For example, see James C. Abegglen, *The Japanese Factory* (Glencoe, Ill., 1958).

TABLE 3.5
Postwar Wage Differentials by Sex, Age, and Education, 1954

Group	Compulsory middle school (1)	High school (2)	Junior college (3)	University (4)
Males:				
20 and under	41.4	48.8	–	–
20–40	100.0	108.6	130.7	140.2
40 and over	128.2	166.1	211.5	255.0
Females:				
20 and under	36.6	41.7	–	–
20–40	51.0	65.0	85.9	86.6
40 and over	48.4	75.0	86.7	99.3

Source: Japan, Ministry of Labor, *Kojinbetsu chingin chōsa* (Survey of Wages by Individual Workers; 1954).
Note: Based on a sample survey of 2,500 persons working in establishments employing ten or more workers. Excludes agriculture, forestry, fisheries, and services. Category (1) includes prewar primary school; category (2) includes prewar middle school. Males age 20–40 = 100.

ates. But again one must recall that the age composition of the labor force has remained rather stable in the postwar period, so that the effects of seniority on the quality index could not have been large.

Educational wage differentials are by far the most interesting aspect of measured quality change. It may be true that sex and age wage differentials are as large in Japan as elsewhere—or larger—although this problem has not been investigated in detail. On the other hand, it is certainly true that wage differentials with respect to education have been *smaller* in postwar Japan than in the United States and northwestern Europe. Denison cites the following differentials for 1949 (wages of workers with eight years of elementary education equals 100):[13]

Country	High school 1–3 years	High school 4 years	College 1–3 years	College 4 years & over
United States	109	124	139	181
Northwestern Europe	122	139	152	194

These findings are comparable with those in Table 3.5,[14] even though our results, which separate sex, age, and education, are almost too detailed. Similarly detailed figures were not uncovered for the United States or Europe. Nevertheless, a number of things about the situation in Japan become obvious. In the age range 20–40 for men—this being the bulk of the labor force—the educational differential of 40 percent between minimum and maximum schooling is conspicuous by its small-

[13] *Why Growth Rates Differ*, Tables 8.2 and 8.3, pp. 83–85.

[14] Category 3 (junior college) corresponds to 1–3 years of college, and category 4 (university) corresponds to 4 or more years of college. Compulsory middle school corresponds to 8 years of elementary education.

ness.[15] For a single figure (including men and women of all ages in the labor force) expressing wage differentials in postwar Japan due to education, one can use Watanabe's results. He found, for 1954–64, an average university–middle school differential of 155, and this is considerably below the corresponding American and European figures. The larger Western returns to education certainly affect measures of quality change. When Western weights (wage differentials) are substituted for Japanese weights and applied to Japanese levels of education, labor input is raised by 7.2 percent in 1955 and 6.8 percent in 1961.

It is tempting to speculate a bit about the significance of the last observations. One thing is clear: in Japan, high-quality labor is available at relatively low prices, and this undoubtedly increases the country's capability to absorb new methods from abroad. As we will say later, this situation raises Japan's "social capability" to import technological progress. But why should educated labor be so poorly evaluated by the market? Is there intellectual underemployment that permits entrepreneurs to exploit educated workers? Perhaps this is true in some cases, but our inclination is to argue a rather different line. Compared with the United States or Western Europe, where the education payoff is high, the qualified Japanese worker is surrounded by a much lower level of capital intensity. He is therefore less productive, and the market places a correct evaluation on this fact. This is not an unfavorable situation for future growth since the workers in question are fully able to take advantage of more sophisticated capital equipment; however, in the process wages and differentials will almost certainly rise.

Prewar. Prewar changes in measured labor quality raised the contribution of this input more than in the recent past. Why this was so, and the data supporting this conclusion, require separate treatment. As earlier, three characteristics of the labor force need to be examined: age, sex, and education.

Variations in the age and sex composition of the labor force can have had only a very slight effect on the rates of growth of adjusted labor input. As we already demonstrated for the years following World War II, compositional and demographic variables change slowly relative to rates of growth of employed labor, and therefore the impact of these forces is limited. This was true also for the period 1900–1940, although the data for substantiating this conclusion are necessarily rather limited. Data on wage differentials classified by age and sex begin only in 1924 and are confined to factories and mines. A close analysis of this information

---

[15] For workers over 40 the differentials are much larger, but this must be ascribed to seniority rather than to education.

shows that an index of labor input adjusted for age and sex grows at about the same rate as the crude labor input index. We know of no reason to assume that things were radically different between 1900 and 1924.

The role of education gives a somewhat different picture. Any attempt to gauge the effect of education on labor input also creates considerable statistical difficulties, but with generous allowance for error they can be overcome. Two major items of information are necessary: a time series of the stock of labor force classified by levels of educational achievement and wage differentials classified in the same way.

Our estimate of the first item is presented in Table 3.6. This table shows the changing educational levels of the working age population (ages 15–64) from 1905 to 1940; direct information concerning the gainfully occupied population is not available, but we can safely assume that

TABLE 3.6

Composition of Working Age Population by Education Level, 1900–1940

(Percent)

	Males			Females		
Year	Compulsory education not completed (1)	Compulsory education completed (2)	Education beyond primary (3)	Compulsory education not completed (1)	Compulsory education completed (2)	Education beyond primary (3)
1900	80.1%	19.6%	0.1%	96.5%	3.5%	–
1905	70.2	28.9	0.8	87.8	11.9	0.3%
1910	59.4	38.6	2.0	77.3	22.0	0.6
1915	49.4	46.4	4.2	68.1	30.4	1.5
1920	40.8	50.9	8.3	60.0	37.2	2.8
1925	32.1	53.7	14.2	51.0	43.2	5.8
1930	24.4	56.5	19.1	41.8	48.7	9.5
1935	18.2	58.5	23.3	33.7	53.6	12.7
1940	13.7	59.4	26.9	26.0	56.8	17.2

Source: LTES, vol. 2, forthcoming.

Note: This table entails extensive computations.

1. Method of calculation. We begin with the age group 15–19 in 1905, and for this group estimated the total number in categories (2) and (3). Category (1) is obtained as a residual. Next, we assume that death rates and effects of migration are identical for the three groups, and apply these rates, supplied by K. Akasaka, to subsequent years. This procedure is repeated at five-year intervals from 1905 to 1940, and the table shows results of summations.

2. Problems of classification. Two major problems need to be mentioned. First, the number of years of compulsory primary education rose from four years in 1890 to six years in 1908, where it remained for the rest of the period. This one-time change should not cause any major distortions. Second, and more serious, is the fact that throughout this period there existed many specialized schools—vocational institutions are a good example— and their classification necessarily involves a good many arbitrary decisions. For example, we classified graduates of the *kōtō shōgaku* (higher elementary school) under (2). An equally good case could be made for classifying these pupils in category (3).

3. Coverage. Almost all public and private schools under the jurisdiction of the Ministry of Education are included in the survey. This includes the large majority of Japanese pupils. However, those pupils under the jurisdiction of other ministries—railways, communications, agriculture and commerce, and army and navy—are not included. The total number of graduates from these specialized schools is quite small, but it increases over time.

the educational characteristics of the working age and gainfully occupied population are very similar. Furthermore, we are only concerned with nonagriculture, whereas these data apply to the entire population; but we believe that this will not affect the computations significantly. In general, we feel that the results of this table probably err on the side of conservatism; if anything they may tend to understate the rates of change.[16]

In the early twentieth century approximately 70 percent of the men and 88 percent of the women of working age had not completed compulsory education. Perhaps this finding will cause some astonishment, because Japanese levels of education as far back as the middle of the nineteenth century have been judged "relatively high." Actually, the numbers presented above do not necessarily contradict the traditional evaluation. People placed in category (1), with less than a compulsory primary education, need not all be totally uneducated or illiterate. Especially during the starting years of this century, significant numbers who did not graduate from primary schools had received traditional educations, for example, in *terakoya* (temple schools). Furthermore, we can well imagine a high dropout rate persisting in a society that remained predominantly rural until at least the Russo-Japanese War. R. P. Dore's guess is that at the time of the Restoration in 1868, 40 to 50 percent of all Japanese boys and perhaps 15 percent of the girls were "getting some formal schooling outside their homes."[17] Both his guess and our estimates are plausible. More relevant to present problems is the dramatic transformation of education levels between 1905 and 1940. By 1935 well over half the males and females of working age had finished their required primary schooling; indeed this was already true for men in 1920. During the 1920's, even those with some more advanced education were beginning to form a visible part of the population most engaged in productive activities. Obviously those changes in the educational composition of the population were more drastic prewar than postwar, partly because the base year position was more primitive and there was more room for improvement, and partly because we are considering a longer time period.

Educational wage differentials are the second major requirement of the analysis, but these are not available for the years before World War II in any usable form, with one exception, a survey of gainfully occupied

---

[16] Possible reasons for a downward bias are omitted schools and general lengthening of period of attendance in certain schools without change in school designation. We are especially conscious of the difficulties involved in distinguishing between categories (2) and (3) in Table 3.6. For a fuller explanation see the table note.

[17] See *Education in Tokugawa Japan* (Berkeley, Calif., 1965), Appendix I.

TABLE 3.7
*Average Annual Increases in Prewar
Labor Quality Indexes*

Period	Male	Female	Weighted total[a]	Average annual rates of increase *(percent)*
1901-5	3.89	3.14	3.63	0.71%
1906-10	2.86	2.05	2.58	0.52
1911-15	3.14	1.68	2.63	0.53
1916-20	3.65	1.76	2.99	0.59
1921-25	3.95	2.59	3.48	0.68
1926-30	4.27	2.44	3.63	0.71
1931-35	1.67	2.00	1.79	0.56
1936-40	2.07	2.21	2.12	0.42

[a] Males 65; females 35. (This is an approximation, since no sex breakdown is available for the private non-agricultural sector.)

population published by the City of Tokyo in 1935. This survey covers the period 1932–34. Taking the wage of category (2) males as 100, we derived the following standardized wage differentials: male—(1) 80, (2) 100, (3) 135; female—(1) 50, (2) 60, (3) 72.[18] By combining the composition statistics of Table 3.6 with these wage differentials, we derive the entries of Table 3.7, which show the growth of prewar labor quality. These results (weighted distribution) have been used to arrive at the average annual rates of increase of labor quality (G_{QL}) for the time spans demarcated in Table 3.1. Taking the entire period 1908–64, they look like this:

	1908–17	1912–18	1918–31	1932–38	1955–61	1962–64
G_{QL}	.56%	.58%	.66%	.49%	.36%	.43%
βG_{QL}	.30	.37	.42	.32	.26	.29

Most noticeable is the greater improvement of quality before the war. Still, these adjustments do not affect the residual in any major way.

The Quality of Capital

Capital stock. Despite its many controversial aspects with regard to concepts, evaluation, coverage, etc., the use of reproducible capital stock data (excluding residences and inventories) in constant prices is an indispensable requirement of empirical analysis. Without measures of capital stock (K), it is impossible either to approximate residuals within an aggregate production-function framework (the present task) or to estimate rates of capital return (a future task).

[18] The Tokyo Survey gives 90 for category (1) males and 54 for category (1) females. Slight downward adjustments have been made to take into account wage differentials related to age. The categories are the same as in Table 3.6.

TABLE 3.8
Average Annual Rates of Growth of
Gross Capital Stock
(Percent)

Period	Private non-primary sector	Government	Total
1908–17	6.46%	6.87%	2.66%
1917–31	5.14	6.10	3.30
1931–37	4.39	4.64	3.13
1956–62	10.89	9.02	8.17
1962–64	13.03	12.02	10.26

Source: BST.16.
   Note: Rate of growth is based on smoothed series. The total includes primary sector and residential buildings.

Denison recently stated a pragmatic and acceptable standpoint of evaluation: "The value, in base period prices, of the stock of durable capital goods (before allowance for capital consumption) measures the amount it would have cost in the base period to produce the actual stock of capital goods existing in the given year (not its equivalent in ability to contribute to production)."[19] This statement accords with our view of evaluation, and the raw series used here have been treated by this method. Nevertheless, the data are crude, especially when compared to the sophisticated concepts implied by an aggregate capital stock series. We restrict ourselves to "gross" ("sudden death" assumption) rather than "net" series, because the gross concept suits our analytical purposes better and because it is not possible to measure depreciation corresponding to changes in productive capacity with any degree of precision. (Either formulation requires compromises.) Adequate information concerning age structure, retirement, and types of capital stock is also beyond reach for long-term analysis. Perfect consistency between investment and capital stock data cannot be expected.

With all of these warnings and disclaimers, let us now look at the Japanese experience, as seen in Table 3.8. Average annual rates of gross capital stock accelerated very markedly after World War II in both the private and the public sector. However, unlike capital formation, neither sector indicates clear growth spurts. The low rates of private capital accumulation in the 1930's are most responsible for creating the contrast with the pattern of capital formation.

These differences are accounted for by the changing industrial composition of the capital stock, shown in Tables 3.9 and 3.10. A division exists, and the dividing point is World War II. Before that time, capital

[19] *Why Growth Rates Differ*, p. 134.

TABLE 3.9
Average Annual Rates of Capital Stock Growth
(Smoothed series, private nonagriculture; *percent*)

Period	Manufacturing	Facilitating industries	Construction	Services
1908–17	6.93%	8.60%	7.41%	3.94%
1917–31	3.34	6.79	5.52	3.54
1931–37	8.72	3.15	9.74	3.45
1956–62	13.59	12.15	21.41	6.71
1962–64	14.66	11.74	21.14	10.82

Source: BST.16.

TABLE 3.10
Industrial Distribution of Capital Stock
(Smoothed series, private nonagriculture; *percent*)

Year	Manufacturing	Facilitating industries	Construction	Services	Total
1908	19.0%	36.7%	2.2%	42.1%	100.0%
1917	19.9	43.9	2.3	33.9	100.0
1931	15.5	54.6	2.5	27.4	100.0
1937	19.8	50.8	3.3	26.1	100.0
1956	39.0	18.5	1.5	41.0	100.0
1962	45.1	19.8	2.6	32.5	100.0
1964	46.4	19.4	3.0	31.2	100.0

Source: BST.16.

stock was largely in the hands of facilitating industries and the commerce and service sectors. Together, these sectors made up about 80 percent of the total. Since then, manufacturing has assumed an increasingly dominant place. These changing weights, together with sectoral growth rates, put the aggregate fluctuations of capital stock into better perspective.

Capital stock in manufacturing, as well as in the less important construction industry, did in fact grow in a manner reminiscent of private capital formation, with spurts and retardations at the expected times. On the other hand, facilitating industries were out of step with the suggested periodization especially in the 1930's, while capital stock in commerce and services grew at a low and steady rate before the war and then began to expand at a rising pace. We can, therefore, speak of spurts of capital accumulation, but they should be considered as sectoral rather than aggregate phenomena. For example, during the 1930's aggregates grew slowly because there was no rapid expansion of facilitating industries at a time when their weight was still great. But in the 1930's there certainly were impressive growth spurts in manufacturing and construction capital stock accumulation.

The two accepted categories of capital stock—producers' durables and nonresidential buildings and other structures—have very different life spans, and that is why the distribution by type varies considerably depending on whether stock or flow measures are examined. Before the 1950's, information for types and age structure is poor. Such studies as have been attempted indicate speedy relative gains for producers' durable equipment: 25.4 percent of the total in 1905; 43.0 percent in 1919; 43.6 percent in 1931; and 45.1 percent in 1937. The comparatively large proportion of capital stock devoted to durable equipment is no doubt a distinct feature of Japan's investment process. Two factors should be considered in this connection: capital stock was quickly put into a more productive (low capital-output ratio) form, and the quality of structures remained cheap and minimal and therefore did not make major claims on the resources of the country.

In recent years, many details have become available concerning both types and age structure of the capital stock.[20] An important feature of the postwar scene has been the rapidly changing composition of capital stock, which may lead to misreadings if the focus is exclusively on the totals. The relevant figures for observing these changes are supplied in Table 3.11. One can observe a decline in the proportion of buildings, and quite sharp increases in structures other than buildings, machinery, and vehicles. To put it in slightly different terms, after World War II the share of producers' durables has again risen.

Table 3.12 shows the average age of capital stock according to the same classification and years. The most important feature of change is

---

[20] Two versions exist of age structure and composition calculations, both based on unpublished data made available to us by the Economic Planning Agency. One is called the perpetual inventory (*PI*) method, and the other a benchmark year(*BY*) calculation. It is extremely difficult to make a choice between *PI* and *BY*. Both series contain problematical elements. *PI* adopted the official estimates of war damage (cited below, p. 62), and we believe these to be overestimates. This series also had to rely on prewar capital formation series, which probably are underestimates. *BY*, on the other hand, is based on the national wealth survey of 1955, and for that year its estimate of capital stock is some 60 percent above *PI* results. One important reason for this is that in Japan, as elsewhere, service lives are often longer than the formal calculations stipulate, and this is especially true of buildings. This explains some of the discrepancy, and also the fact that the differences in average ages of buildings is particularly large for *PI* and *BY*, and why it is much higher in the latter series. Last, it should be kept in mind that the two series become more similar during recent years, because since 1955 they both rely on the same capital formation series.

TABLE 3.11
Composition of Gross Capital Stock by Type of Capital Goods
for Selected Years, 1953–64: Private Sector
(Percent)

Year	Buildings (1)	Structures other than (1) (2)	Machinery (3)	Ships (4)	Vehicles (5)	Furniture, fixtures & tools (6)	Total (7)
1953	58.4%	8.4%	19.2%	4.1%	3.6%	6.3%	100.0%
1955	55.5	8.7	20.3	4.8	3.6	7.1	100.0
1961	43.3	10.1	29.8	5.8	4.6	6.4	100.0
1964	37.7	10.0	33.7	5.7	5.6	7.3	100.0

Source: The original data are from Japan, Economic Planning Agency, Economic Research Institute, "Taipubetsu shihon suttokku suikei" (Estimates of Private Capital Stock by Type of Capital Goods; mimeo., November 1967).
    Note: Benchmark year method based on EPA, Shōwa 30-nen kokufū chōsa hōkoku (National Wealth Survey for 1955; 1958).

a decline in the average age of capital stock, which starts in 1955. In general, it seems clear that the average age of capital stock is low in Japan when compared with the industrialized countries of the West. Comparable data indicate for Germany an aggregate average of 25.0 years in 1950 and 21.8 years in 1960; for the United States 15.6 years in 1950 and 14.7 years in 1960.[21] For this period, the Japanese average ages are 11.66 in 1953 and 11.05 in 1960. Comparisons of this type are very much affected by service life assumptions, but a low average age for Japanese capital stock is a reasonable result. Three main reasons can be cited: the extent of war destruction coupled with a rapid recovery;[22] the great capital formation spurt from 1955 to 1961; and the larger relative proportion of producers' durables or, what amounts to the same thing, the smaller relative proportion in buildings.

Table 3.13 deals with the sectoral patterns of change during the postwar period. They show changes in average age by type of capital good, with a positive number indicating an increase in average age and a negative number a decline. The rather clear aggregate pattern—a decrease in average age beginning in 1955–56 and a deceleration in the

[21] Denison, Why Growth Rates Differ, p. 147.
[22] According to the Economic Stabilization Board's official Taiheiyō sensō niyoru waga kuni no higai sōgō hōkoku-sho (Report on Damage of the Pacific War; 1949), the following percent of gross capital stock was destroyed in 1945:

	Direct damage	Indirect damage	Total
Structures (including bulidings)	18.8%	5.7%	24.5%
Producers' durables	20.1	14.2	34.3
Ships	71.9	8.7	80.6
Vehicles & other transport equipment	12.5	9.4	21.9

TABLE 3.12
Average Age of Capital Stock by Type of Capital Goods, 1953–64:
All Private Industries

Year	Buildings (1)	Structures other than (1) (2)	Machinery (3)	Ships (4)	Vehicles (5)	Furniture, fixtures & tools (6)	Total[a] (7)
1953	15.60	13.32	5.14	2.11	2.67	4.13	11.66
1954	16.27	13.59	5.26	3.12	1.97	5.17	11.99
1955	16.97	13.58	5.52	4.17	2.39	5.93	12.43
1956	17.10	12.17	5.43	4.61	2.73	6.50	12.30
1957	17.26	11.34	5.13	4.86	3.05	6.69	12.07
1958	17.47	10.54	4.92	5.19	3.39	6.96	11.87
1959	17.66	9.25	4.73	5.61	3.47	7.24	11.56
1960	17.52	8.56	4.51	6.05	3.43	7.33	11.05
1961	17.27	7.69	4.21	6.24	3.40	6.94	10.47
1962	17.03	7.29	4.04	6.38	3.45	6.52	9.98
1963	16.63	6.74	4.01	6.64	3.47	6.23	9.53
1964	16.27	6.46	4.02	6.68	3.61	6.06	9.38

Source: See Table 3.11.
Note: Assumed service lives: buildings (1) and structures other than buildings (2), 35 years; machinery (3), 15 years; ships (4), 9 years; vehicles (5), 5 years; furniture, fixtures, and tools (6), 9 years.
[a] The total is a weighted average of items (1) through (6). Weights are the shares of gross capital stock during each year.

pace of decrease after 1961—is the result of a quite different sectoral pattern. Buildings (1) and furniture, fixtures, and tools (6) rose in average age until 1959–60 and then began to decrease. Machinery (3) and structures (2) started to decrease vigorously in 1955–56, and just as in the case of the aggregates, decreases slowed down in the 1960's. Finally, ships (4) and vehicles (5) have continued to rise in average age throughout the period, although the pace of increase appears to be slackening in recent years.

Postwar changes in quality. Any student of industrialization knows that the quality of capital is capable of rapid upgrading. However, as we have already seen when dealing with labor, quality concepts are difficult things, and especially in the case of capital they can at best represent only a very simplified version of reality.

In dealing with these questions, we shall go through three steps: first, an explanation of our own concepts for measuring changes in capital quality; second, an analysis of our own results; and third, a brief comparison of our method with alternative methods.

The measure to be used here relies on the widely held assumption that quality is inversely related to the average age of capital stock. The lower the age of capital stock, the more productive the stock can be;

TABLE 3.13
Changes in the Average Age of Private Capital Stock by Type, 1953–64
(Years)

Year	Buildings (1)	Structures other than (1) (2)	Machinery (3)	Ships (4)	Vehicles (5)	Furniture, fixtures & tools (6)	Total (7)
1953–54	.67	.27	.12	1.00	−.70	1.00	.33
1955	.70	−.01	.26	1.00	.42	.76	.44
1956	.13	−.41	−.09	.44	.34	.57	−.13
1957	.16	−.83	−.30	.25	.32	.19	−.23
1958	.21	−.80	−.21	.33	.34	.27	−.20
1959	.19	−1.00	−.19	.42	.08	.28	−.31
1960	−.14	−.69	−.22	.44	.04	.09	−.51
1961	−.25	−.87	−.30	.19	.03	−.39	−.58
1962	−.24	−.40	−.17	.14	.05	−.42	−.49
1963	−.35	−.55	−.03	.26	.02	−.29	−.45
1964	−.41	−.28	.01	.04	.14	−.17	−.15

Note: Calculated from Table 3.12, benchmark year method data.

what is new is always superior as far as capital is concerned—this must, in general, be true for our measures to be valid.

To give a numerical expression to this assumption is not difficult. We shall take the changes in the ratio of average age of different categories of capital stock, and assume that the reciprocal of average age is a direct indicator of changing capital quality. Two illustrative calculations should make the procedures clear. First, from 1960 to 1961, the average age of machinery declined from 4.51 to 4.21 years. Taking the age of 1960 as 100, the ratio 4.51/4.21 gives a reciprocal value of 107.12. This is taken as the increase in capital quality for 1960–61. And second, during the same period, the average age of buildings declined from 17.52 to 17.27 years, an absolute decline similar to that of machinery. But the ratio of the reciprocals—17.52/17.27—gives an index of only 101.44, which represents a much smaller increase in quality. These indexes for each of six categories of capital goods are then aggregated into a weighted average, with the weights being the shares of each type of capital good during a particular year. This method has one important advantage: variations in age are related to average age by categories of capital stock, so that a similar absolute change is related to the age structure of a particular category.

It should be stressed that the capital quality index derived by the method described above is analogous to the previously derived labor quality index. In measuring differences and changes in labor quality, we relied on wage differentials (associated with levels of education) and

TABLE 3.14

Average Annual Rates of Change in the Indicators
of Capital Quality, 1953–64

(Percent)

Period	Buildings (1)	Structures other than (1) (2)	Machinery (3)	Ships (4)	Vehicles (5)	Furniture, fixtures & tools (6)	Total (7)
1953–55	−4.17%	−0.96%	−0.11%			−5.70%	−3.15%
1955–61	0.29	9.93	3.42	−6.06%	−13.85%	−0.39	2.68
(1955–58)	−3.70	8.81	1.54				1.55
(1958–61)	0.39	11.17	5.33				4.27
1961–64	2.01	5.98	1.55	−2.25	−1.98	−4.42	3.71

Source: See Tables 3.12 and 3.13.

assumed that these were proportional to the marginal product of labor (nonagriculture only). The problem becomes somewhat more complicated for capital. A most logical parallel indicator for capital quality is the rate of return, which can be assumed to bear some relation to the marginal productivity of that factor. However, the rate of return cannot be used because it is not available for different types of capital goods, and we believe that a reasonable amount of disaggregation is necessary. We need another indicator of capital productivity and therefore have adopted the average age of capital stock.[23] The underlying assumption remains as stated previously, that age by type of capital good is inversely proportional to the marginal product of that capital good. Note also that the aggregation procedures for capital and labor are similar. For labor the weights were the proportion of workers in the various education-wage categories. For capital the weights are the proportions of types of capital goods within total stock.[24]

Table 3.14 contains the quality adjustments. It shows the average annual rates of growth of the quality indexes based on sectoral reciprocal

[23] One of our friendly critics has raised a question concerning our method of estimating the quality of capital and the usual procedures of estimating net capital stock. The question is a reasonable one because the method used by us may be regarded as a measure of the rate of change in the relation of net depreciated value to gross value of capital according to a specific formula in which depreciation cumulates in proportion to age. The method adopted here aggregates units of capital stock according to their base-period prices without allowance for differences in quality (per yen of base-period price) at time of installation. Therefore, the result can be looked at as one way of accounting for depreciation over time. We chose our method so as to give a relatively heavy weight to a year's change in average age in the case of a relatively young capital stock such as Japan possessed. Our purpose is not to account for accumulated capital depreciation.

[24] Our method may give the impression that we adopt an embodiment hypothesis. This is not the case. See "A methodological note," p. 66.

ratios and aggregated every year by sectoral weights. Postwar quality improvement of capital was not a negligible factor.[25]

A *methodological note.* Labor quality has been adjusted so as to measure more accurately this factor's input effects or contributions to output. Capital quality adjustments are basically similar. Both share the characteristic of concerning "attached" qualities such as education, sex, and age, and should be kept conceptually separate from "unattached" qualities, which can be altered only through changing factor combinations. A good example would be the reallocation or shift of factors: both capital and labor of the same "attached" quality can, under some circumstances, increase their contributions to output—raise their marginal products—by shifting from one sector of the economy to another. This kind of improvement is obviously quite different from the "attached" adjustments discussed above.[26]

"Attached" quality is not the same thing as what is usually meant by embodiment, and thus far we have been careful to avoid those difficult terms—embodied and disembodied technological progress. Many different definitions exist for these terms, and in our work we have not found the embodiment distinctions especially useful. However, in order to make clear what we are *not* doing, a few words should be added concerning this range of issues.

There are two main approaches for measuring changes in capital quality. One approach generally uses the rate of return as an index of capital quality and the other subscribes to the embodiment hypothesis. These are very different ways of viewing the problem. In the former case, the purpose is simply to take into account the diversity of the capital input, which consists of many types of goods of differing productivities, and to develop an input measure that is a weighted average of these types. Our method, although necessarily relying on a vintage procedure, is of this kind.

The embodiment hypothesis raises a much broader issue. It is not merely concerned with changes in quality, but makes the upgrading of capital quality identical to the sum total of technological progress. We reject this view as too restrictive, and instead we shall analyze techno-

---

[25] As previously mentioned, there exist two estimates of capital age structure (perpetual inventory and benchmark year), and as in the past, we have shown the latter in Table 3.14. The quality change indicator by perpetual inventory rises at 5.73 percent per year for 1955–61, and is almost identical to the benchmark year results after that period. In the final adjusted residual calculations, benchmark and perpetual inventory measures have been averaged for both 1955–61 and 1962–64.

[26] See Chapter 4 for further discussion of shift or reallocation effects.

logical progress in terms of "backlog-inflow" combined with "social capability."[27]

Prewar changes in quality. Vintage data are not available before World War II, and any attempt to take changes in capital quality into account needs to be a very crude approximation. For the postwar period, one can derive a rough elasticity of capital improvement with respect to capital stock (rate of change in average age/rate of capital stock growth): .42 for 1955–61 and .20 for 1961–63. These elasticities are applied to the prewar growth of capital stock but in reduced form, since the proportion of durable equipment was lower at that time.[28] With this undoubtedly oversimplified method, using the above-mentioned elasticities for the postwar period, the following annual rates of increase of capital quality are derived:

	1908–17	1912–18	1918–31	1932–38	1955–61	1962–64
G_{QK}	0.97%	1.35%	0.70%	1.29%	4.21%	3.57%
αG_{QK}	0.44	0.46	0.25	0.46	1.22	1.19

THE UNEXPLAINED RESIDUAL

Most of the adjustment procedures have now been completed, and an overview is provided in Table 3.15. Long swings that have provided the framework of this analysis combine the effects of supply and demand. Changes in the rate of utilization of existing capacity are, as we have seen, a demand effect of considerable importance. On the other hand, the growth of factor inputs suggests that the supply side or productive capacity has also contributed to the amplitude of long swings. At this stage one can perhaps offer the following additional summation: the quality of capital throughout improved more than measured increases in the quality of labor; the rate of utilization had a powerful effect on the level of inputs; the adjusted or unexplained residual (G_R^*) hardly grew at all before World War II, although it should be stressed that its growth did not entirely disappear; the sharp dichotomy. between the prewar and postwar periods is reinforced, since even after all the adjustments have been made, residual growth has been rapid in the 1950's and 1960's.

In terms of adjusted inputs, the growth rate of capital has also been two to three times higher than that of labor throughout the entire period. And historically the relative contribution of capital to output growth has exceeded that of labor. But the percentage contribution of capital has

[27] See Chapters 4, 8, and 9.
[28] The elasticities applied were .15 for 1908–17, .21 for 1912–18, .13 for 1918–31, and .28 for 1932–38.

TABLE 3.15
Adjusted Factor Inputs and the Adjusted Residual:
Average Annual Rates of Growth
(Percent)

Factor	1908–17	(1912–18)	1917–31	1931–38	1955–61	1962–64
G_{QK}	0.97%	1.35%	0.70%	1.29%	4.21%	3.57%
G_{QL}	0.56	0.58	0.66	0.49	0.36	0.43
αG_{QK}	0.44	0.46	0.25	0.46	1.22	1.19
βG_{QL}	0.30	0.37	0.42	0.32	0.26	0.29
G_Q	0.74	0.83	0.67	0.78	1.48	1.48
$G_{\rho K}$	0.51	1.26	−1.12	2.71	1.66	−1.42
$G_{\rho L}$	0.26	0.63	−0.56	1.86	0.37	−0.72
$\alpha G_{\rho K}$	0.27	0.65	−0.39	1.03	0.49	−0.47
$\beta G_{\rho L}$	0.16	0.38	−0.33	0.84	0.22	−0.50
G_ρ	0.43	1.03	−0.72	1.87	0.71	−0.97
$G_Q + G_\rho$	1.17	1.86	−0.05	2.65	2.19	0.51
(G_R)	0.95	2.05	−0.18	3.81	6.75	5.61
$G_R{}^*$	−0.22	0.19	−0.13	1.16	4.56	5.10
Rates of Growth of Adjusted Factor Input						
Capital	7.94	9.46	4.82	8.60	15.41	14.88
Labor	3.01	3.91	2.09	4.26	5.60	4.00
Percentage Contribution of Adjusted Factor Input to G_Y						
Capital	72.2	62.1	62.2	47.8	34.7	38.9
Labor	32.3	32.0	42.0	34.9	30.2	28.6
Sum	104.5	94.1	104.2	82.7	64.9	67.5

Notation:
  G_{QK} = rate of growth of capital quality.
  G_{QL} = rate of growth of labor quality.
  G_Q = $\alpha G_{QK} + \beta G_{QL}$.
  G_ρ = $\alpha G_{\rho K} + \beta G_{\rho L}$.
  $G_R{}^*$ = residual after adjustment = $G_R - G_Q - G_\rho$.

declined steadily since the beginning of the century while that of labor
has remained much steadier; consequently the relative contributions of
capital and labor appear much more similar at present.

A cautionary note can stand repetition. These residuals, crude and
adjusted, are first approximations, and should be interpreted with care
and prudence. Estimates of the rate of utilization are particularly weak
for prewar years. To the extent that we have overestimated fluctuations
of utilization (ρ), we have also underestimated the growth of the adjusted residual ($G_R{}^*$). This possibility must be kept in mind.

More generally, the purpose of measurements of this type is not to
give a single estimate of factor productivity at the aggregate level. In-

stead, in estimating crude and adjusted residuals, we have attempted, insofar as possible, to explain the "contribution" of various factors. The crude residual or unadjusted total productivity is an initial approximation of the historical path of aggregate productivity in relation to conventional factor inputs. It shows in rather simple terms what actually happened during the process of Japanese economic growth. The ensuing adjustments consider rates of utilization and the quality of inputs (reallocation effects and scale economies are treated in Chapter 4), and they necessarily involve a number of restrictive assumptions. We readily admit that the adjustment measures and concepts are rough, and yet they do supply additional information and therefore allow a more refined analysis to be made of aggregate productivity change for the private nonagricultural sector.

CHAPTER FOUR

Sectoral Growth Patterns and Intersectoral Relations

SECTORAL PATTERNS OF PRODUCTIVITY AND RESIDUAL GROWTH

The historical performance of aggregate residual growth in the private nonagricultural sector—very slow expansion before World War II and very rapid expansion during the past 20 years—is not necessarily favorable for the preview presented in Chapter 2. There we stressed gradual trend acceleration, and waves of technological progress during all upswings. We postulated a "unity" for the entire period of analysis, 1900–1965, whereas the aggregate residuals instead suggest that two radically different models are required to explain the situation before and after the 1950's.

In fact, the problem is not the conceptual framework of Chapter 2, which is, we believe, valid. The difficulty lies in the nature of all aggregate measures: they obscure structural changes and sectoral differences, and these have been prominent in Japan as in all other rapidly developing economies. An approximation of their extent can be read off Table 4.1. During the twentieth century, there was a significant change in the relative labor productivity levels of manufacturing: in 1908–17, 40.0 percent of the labor force produced 22.3 percent of nonagricultural output; in 1961–64, 39.3 percent of the labor force accounted for 47.4 percent of output. At the same time, the decline of relative productivity in commerce and services was marked. Around World War I, approximately 47 percent of the nonagricultural labor force found employment in this sector, and it produced 68 percent of output. Currently, these ratios are, respectively, 44.8 percent and 37.6 percent.[1] One must also

---

[1] The service sector contains many different activities, including wholesale and retail trade, banking, insurance, and real estate. (In the present figures, government services have been excluded.) An output breakdown for these subsectors does not exist before World War II. According to the 1920 census, the gainfully occupied workers in the service sector were 66.1 percent in wholesale and retail trade, and

TABLE 4.1

Sectoral Distribution of Output, Labor, and Capital: Private Nonagriculture

(Smoothed series, constant prices; *percent*)

Period	Manufacturing	Facilitating industries	Construction	Services	Total
Output					
1908-17	22.3%	7.6%	2.1%	68.0%	100.0%
1917-31	28.4	11.4	2.4	57.8	100.0
1931-37	37.1	11.6	3.0	48.3	100.0
1955-61	44.4	8.3	5.8	41.5	100.0
1961-64	47.4	8.8	6.2	37.6	100.0
Labor					
1908-17	40.0	6.3	7.1	46.6	100.0
1917-31	42.2	5.8	6.6	45.4	100.0
1931-37	44.7	5.1	6.2	44.0	100.0
1955-61	39.0	5.8	9.1	46.1	100.0
1961-64	39.3	6.1	9.8	44.8	100.0
Capital					
1908-17	19.5	41.3	2.3	36.9	100.0
1917-31	16.9	51.1	2.4	29.6	100.0
1931-37	17.9	52.5	3.0	26.6	100.0
1955-61	42.0	19.2	2.0	36.8	100.0
1961-64	45.5	19.6	2.7	32.2	100.0

Source: BST.4, BST.15, and BST.16. These tables give sectoral output, labor, and capital, from which private sector figures are derived.

Note: Percentages calculated by averaging the weights at the first and last year of each interval. Prewar figures at 1934-36 prices; postwar at 1960 prices.

observe that the level of relative capital intensity in facilitating industries was extraordinarily high before World War II. These activities regularly contained around half the capital stock of the country, while employing only about 5 percent of the workers. A structural change occurred beginning in the 1950's, when the relative capital share of manufacturing displaced the previous position of the facilitating sector. Relative capital-output ratios have also altered materially in this time span. They were very high for facilitating industries until the 1930's—half of

29.0 percent in non–wholesale and retail trade services, with the remainder classified as "other." Among the service workers at that time, 42.2 percent were classified as proprietors (*gyōshu*), whereas only an average of 23.1 percent were so designated in manufacturing, facilitating industries, and construction. The large majority of service proprietors were owners of traditional unincorporated enterprises. Only agriculture had a higher proportion of such individuals.

It is widely recognized that to estimate output and input for services is most difficult. Even the concepts are unclear. These deficiencies are especially serious in Japan, and the data for the service sector certainly are of relatively low reliability. Nevertheless they are all we have, and they give the best available picture of this large and important activity.

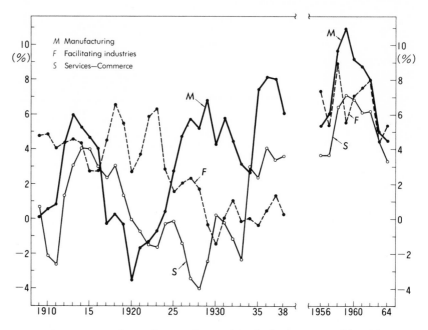

Fig. 4.1. Annual growth rates of sectoral residuals. (*Source*: Table 4.2.)

the capital stock and around 10 percent of output—and then declined to
more moderate levels. Presently the aggregate capital-output ratio is
dominated by the much lower levels prevailing in manufacturing, and
it is clear that the time path of this ratio, described in Figure 3.1, most
of all reflects the changing weight of manufacturing and facilitating
industries.

All these findings suggest that in this century the Japanese economy
contained sectors using different techniques and organizations, and presumably also diverse forms and opportunities for technological progress.
One way of bringing these differences to the surface is the analysis of
sectoral factor inputs and residuals contained in Table 4.2 and Figure
4.1.[2] Keeping in mind the severe limitations of conclusions based on
crude residuals, sectoral patterns do emerge with great clarity.

In manufacturing, the magnitude of G_R is considerable and its trend
has been rising, and each investment spurt brought forth a higher rate

---

[2] The computations are the same as those of Table 3.1. Residual growth rates
are *crude* because sectoral information necessary for adjustment is not available.

Difficulties encountered in estimating changes in the rate of utilization have been
described in Chapter 3; see especially pp. 48–50. Using Odaka's index of utilization for manufacturing (changing weights, see p. 48), the effects of taking this

TABLE 4.2
Average Annual Growth Rates of Crude Sectoral Residuals
(Percent)

Category		1908-17	1912-18	1917-31	1931-38	1955-61	1962-64
	M	2.38%	3.48%	2.21%	5.65%	7.89%	5.49%
	F	4.09	4.09	2.67	0.95	7.63	5.76
G_R	C	−1.47	−1.84	3.30	6.25	5.99	7.35
	S	1.26	2.84	−0.84	2.46	5.37	4.92
Manufacturing							
$G_Y - G_L$		4.57	5.01	2.76	8.46	10.49	9.97
$G_Y - G_K$		0.28	2.16	1.69	2.32	3.79	−0.72
$G_K - G_L$		4.29	2.85	1.07	6.14	6.70	10.69
Facilitating industries							
$G_Y - G_L$		7.74	7.40	5.46	2.50	10.26	8.23
$G_Y - G_K$		0.81	1.40	−0.33	−0.89	3.76	2.66
$G_K - G_L$		6.93	6.00	5.78	3.40	6.50	5.57
Construction							
$G_Y - G_L$		0.50	−0.13	4.33	8.63	7.40	10.39
$G_Y - G_K$		−5.40	−4.84	0.23	−0.95	−3.85	−6.29
$G_K - G_L$		5.90	4.71	4.10	9.52	11.24	16.68
Services—Commerce							
$G_Y - G_L$		2.23	3.86	−0.35	3.20	5.73	6.22
$G_Y - G_K$		−0.31	1.32	−2.03	−0.61	4.25	0.34
$G_K - G_L$		2.53	2.54	1.68	2.58	1.48	5.88

Source: Original data on Y (output) from BST. 4, on L (labor) from BST.15, and on K (capital) from BST.16.

of increase: from 2.4 percent to 5.7 percent to 7.9 percent. Except for the first spurt in this century, the residual grew more rapidly in manufacturing than in any other sector, implying high and rising rates of technological progress for the affected industries. The annual entries of Figure 4.1 show a very steep decline of G_R for manufacturing toward the end of World War I. This must have been related to the shock created by the end of the war when demand fell as a result of collapsing foreign markets. The upturn in the 1920's and the high level of the late 1920's is somewhat more puzzling especially because of the low levels of $G_K - G_L$ at that time: 1.07 percent per year. We think that a number of factors may be involved. A partial explanation may be a rise in the

factor into account were approximated for the G_R (manufacturing) results of Table 4.2. In general, the changes are very minor except for 1917–31—a period of excess capacity—for which the value of G_R^* becomes 4.3. (G_R for manufacturing in the table is 2.2.) Thus, taking utilization into account would support the rising trend of residual growth in manufacturing.

Sectoral relative income shares are also unavailable for prewar years, and have been approximated on the basis of postwar information. See Appendix Note.

rate of utilization that was due to expansion of textile exports. In addition, the category "manufacturing" is still very broad. Some industries, notably the cotton industry, certainly raised their levels of capital intensity particularly in the second half of the 1920's. By 1930, 23 percent of the looms in integrated spinning-weaving mills were automatic, placing Japan well ahead of Italy, France, Germany, and Great Britain. This had not been the situation in 1920.[3] Furthermore, the policy of "rationalization" in many instances involved *organizational* changes that would not have required raises in capital intensity. In cotton production, as examples, one can mention time-and-motion studies, scientific cotton blending, and the activities of the Bōseki Rengōkai (All-Japan Cotton Spinners' Association).

Residual growth patterns in the other sectors are quite obvious, and will not require extended comment. Facilitating industries had the highest G_R's until the 1920's, and after a long hiatus are again in second position at present. Residual growth in the construction industry is most difficult to explain: decline during the great spurt of World War I, increases in the 1920's and 1930's, and rapid growth in the 1950's and 1960's. Until the last few decades, improvements in technology played only a small role in this sector, and it is probably safe to assume that other factors determined the fluctuations: government policies and greater than average "errors of measurement" may have been important. For commerce and services, the long-lasting negative values during the 1920's and 1930's are particularly striking. No doubt fluctuations in aggregate demand, rather than technological progress, were a major element in creating this pattern—a subject that will be explored more thoroughly immediately below. Of course, the maintenance of negative values for a lengthy period creates conceptual problems: how could the entrepreneurs remain in business? The answer is to be found in the heterogeneous composition of this group. Modern commerce and services would, under these circumstances, find themselves in great difficulties. But traditional units remained numerous, and continued to exist by underpaying the factors of production—including the entrepreneurs themselves.

The Role of Demand

Attempting to gauge the historical influence of demand alterations is not new to this analysis. The earlier discussion made the rate of utilization (ρ) a most significant part of the crude residual. Now we intend to demonstrate that the demand effect is related to the industrial struc-

[3] Teijirō Uyeda, *The Small Industries of Japan* (Shanghai, 1938), p. 75.

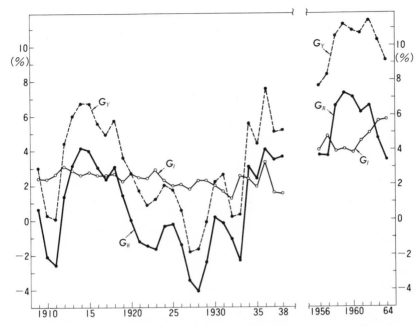

Fig. 4.2. The service sector: relations between factor inputs and unadjusted residual. (*Source*: Table 4.2.)

ture, and that it has been particularly powerful in some sectors. No better example exists for Japan than the historical experience of services-commerce (S).

Figure 4.2 contains three annual (smoothed) series for the service sector: G_Y, G_R, and G_I, for the period 1909 to 1964. There is no difficulty in summarizing these movements: G_R and G_Y fluctuate in close association, while G_I pursues its independent path: flat before the war, and some rise beginning in 1960. In other words, fluctuations in commerce-service growth of total inputs appear to have absolutely no relation to movements of income and the residual. Rather, it is G_Y and G_R that are related.

We surmise that for this sector the residual reflects mainly changes in demand affecting the rate of growth of aggregate output and utilization. Construction has had a rather similar experience, but it was emphatically not the case in manufacturing and facilitating industries, in which G_I and G_R are quite well associated. In general, therefore, it can be said that the effect of ρ, and demand, differs among sectors: its influence is largest in commerce-services and smallest in manufacturing.

With this information it is now possible to place the aggregate mea-

TABLE 4.3
Average Annual Growth Rates of Weighted Sectoral Residuals
(Percent)

Category	1908–17	1917–31	1931–38	1955–61	1962–64
Manufacturing	0.53%	0.63%	2.10%	3.50%	2.60%
Facilitating industries	0.31	0.30	0.11	0.63	0.51
Construction	−0.03	0.08	0.19	0.35	0.46
Services	0.86	−0.49	1.19	2.23	1.85
All sectors	1.67	0.52	3.59	6.71	5.42
Nonservices	0.81	1.01	2.40	4.48	3.57

Note: For method of calculation see Table 3.1. Weights are average output proportions during demarcated periods.

sure in some perspective. World War II remains as a major dividing line, but it must be carefully qualified. Until the end of the 1930's, sectoral G_R's had a tendency to cancel each other, and this was particularly true in the interplay between manufacturing and facilitating industries. As a consequence, the aggregate residual does not well represent reality. The postwar performance is unique in that all sectoral residuals move similarly; manufacturing is the leader, but all others are close behind. For this reason, there exist the distinct prewar and postwar levels of aggregate residual growth. To put it differently, postwar economic growth, if agriculture is excluded, has created a sectoral productivity balance that in earlier times was absent. The unity of which we spoke earlier is still present, except that technological progress was sectoral in the past and has now become general.

Finally, let us consider the relations between the present findings and the crude aggregate residuals of Chapter 3. This can be done with the weighted sectoral G_R's of Table 4.3.[4] Most of what emerges is relatively self-evident, but once again, the peculiar position of services is underlined. In the postwar period, the G_R of services is 33–34 percent of the total; during the two prewar upswings it weighed in at 51 and 33 percent; and in 1917–31 the negative rate of growth of the service residual also had a considerable effect. Clearly, the aggregate, especially before World War II, has been very much influenced by the wide fluctuations of residual growth in service sectors. And we may safely assume that these movements were closely related to changes in demand. In contrast, the sum of non-service residuals expands along a more stable path; presumably different forces are at work.

[4] The sum of weighted sectoral figures cannot be identical to the direct aggregate measure because of structural changes. These have to be neglected in the table, and the comparison is therefore only approximate.

The Relationship Between Residuals and Economies of Scale

That the residual contains a variety of factors is generally accepted. Of the ones listed at the beginning of Chapter 3, there remains one item not yet discussed: the difficult concept of economies of scale. It lends itself particularly well to sectoral analysis, since scale effects do not apply with equal force to all kinds of economic activities.

On the one hand, it is our view that economies of scale must have been an important factor in the creation of residuals. On the other hand, we know of no easy or accurate way to quantify this factor. From the (sectoral) macroeconomic point of view, economies of scale can be defined as the response of productivity growth to increases in demand or to a larger market.[5] This is difficult to convert into an empirical measure, because ideally it would be desirable to isolate the influence of demand on supply and to leave out all other elements that might have affected supply-production, such as technological and organizational progress, government policies, and institutions. All that can be done is to relate productivity growth to output growth taken as an independent variable in different sectors. Since, in fact, this type of long-term analysis does indicate distinct patterns, we can hope that, *ceteris paribus*, some aspects of scale economies will have been revealed.[6]

Figures 4.3 and 4.4 provide illustrations of the two distinct patterns. In manufacturing, the relationship between G_Y and $G_Y - G_L$ is linear and fits the entire period of analysis. We will interpret this to mean that

[5] Equations (1) and (1′) (p. 45) used, as a first approximation, the assumption of constant returns to scale. Increasing returns to scale certainly may have existed in some sectors of the Japanese economy, in which case $\alpha + \beta > 1$, and the residuals of Chapters 3 and 4 must be overestimated. This possibility is particularly strong for manufacturing. It is, however, extremely difficult either to identify increasing returns to scale empirically or to take them into account when measuring residuals.

The economies of scale defined in the text are not the same as increasing returns to scale. In the latter, scale is defined by the size of factor inputs on the supply-production side. Our definition makes scale relevant to the size of the market in an aggregate sense. No evidence can be cited for claiming that in Japanese economic development these two scale concepts have been closely associated, though this is not an unlikely supposition.

[6] The computation is $G_y = a + b\,G_Y$, where G_y is the rate of growth of labor productivity. $G_Y - G_L$ is used as an approximation for G_y. In this connection, see Nicholas Kaldor, *Causes of the Slow Rate of Economic Growth of the United Kingdom: An Inaugural Lecture* (Cambridge, Eng., 1966), and especially the author's discussion of the "Verdoorn Law."

For a faster expansion of the market to lead to more rapid productivity, it must affect the production organization process through (say) accelerating the division of labor in a classical sense, and/or result in greater organizational specialization (including, for example, the spread of subcontracting). At the present stage of our knowledge we are unfortunately unable to establish the links.

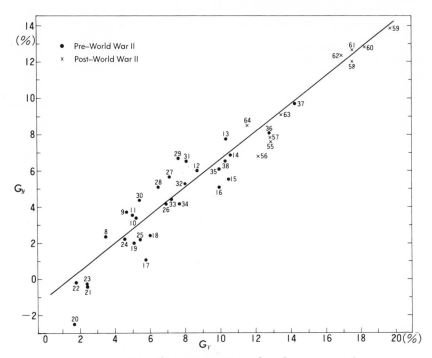

Fig. 4.3. Manufacturing: output and productivity growth.

manufacturing adapted smoothly and profitably to increases in demand, and that there is a strong presumption for the presence of scale economies. The position of manufacturing, however, is unique: all other sectors have periods of linear relationships between output and productivity, but during the past 60 years these have shifted *to the right* one or two times.[7] For example, commerce-services had one pattern for 1912–38, followed by a shift for the period 1955–64. We interpret these shifts to the right as "resistance points" to market expansion, and as evidence for the presumption of a lower level of scale economies. Thus, in the service sector, postwar output has grown more rapidly, but this has had a smaller than expected impact on productivity, as indicated by the trend of earlier years. Shifts to the right took place in the other sectors on the following dates: facilitating industries, 1908–14 → 1915–64; construction, 1908–38 → 1955–64. Agriculture shifted to the left, indicating the increased presumption of scale economies, as follows: 1908–57 → 1958–64.

[7] The only exception was the postwar shift of agriculture to the left.

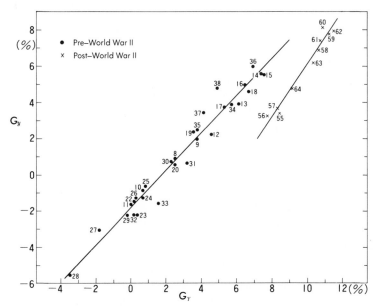

Fig. 4.4. Services: output and productivity growth.

Let us now try to summarize this evidence with a view to saying something about the influence of economies of scale in the various sectors. The critical aspect must be looked for in the shift pattern. It is entirely absent in manufacturing, and that is the strongest case for assuming that scale economies played a highly positive role. Next, there are the facilitating industries in which the shift came very early, before World War I, and since then the relation has been steady in periods when output has expanded at unprecedented rates. Both manufacturing and facilitating industries really belong in one category as economic activities in which economies of scale have probably been considerable. In construction and services there were also long periods in which output and productivity growth were closely matched.[8] However, these came before

[8] Regression parameters for these sectors are as follows:

Sector	a	b	$\bar{R}^2$	Period
Manufacturing	−1.345	0.786	0.936	1908–64
	(0.341)	(0.033)		
Facilitating industries	0.866	0.578	0.885	1913–64
	(0.384)	(0.036)		
Construction	−1.433	0.977	0.941	1908–38
	(0.291)	(0.045)		
Services	−1.831	1.024	0.968	1908–38
	(0.137)	(0.033)		

Obviously these calculations are very approximate, and serious identification problems may be present. The existence of negative intersects are a case in point, since

the enormous postwar expansion of output. When faced with the recent explosion of demand, these sectors "shifted to the right," indicating a weaker capacity to face market enlargement or a lower level of economies of scale.

Our conclusions have to remain in this rather unsatisfactory state. Historically, manufacturing and facilitating industries have shown a better capacity to adapt to market enlargement than construction and services. And we believe that this capacity is closely linked to the possibilities of taking advantage of scale economies. If so, manufacturing and facilitating residuals especially reflect these forces. A more precise statement does not seem possible at this time.

THE GROWTH OF FACTORY PRODUCTION

The sectoral analysis in the preceding section emphasized the impact of commerce-services and manufacturing in determining the historical time path of residuals. Given the state of statistical information, we cannot elaborate the analysis of service activities. We can, however, provide a better understanding of manufacturing by studying the growth of factory production during the usual long-term interval.

In 1900 the proportion of private factory output must have been well under 6 percent of national product; if government factories were included, the proportion would still remain considerably below 10 percent. Therefore one should not, as has sometimes been done, exaggerate the significance of modern industries or modern industrial organization during the initial years of modern economic growth. By contrast, during this century, factory production acquired a much greater role and

---

they would seem to indicate that productivity growth would have been zero or less in the absence of growth in demand. Negative intersects cannot be present if scale economies alone affect the variables treated here; some other systematic effects may have influenced these time series. However, we stress that our emphasis is primarily on the shift pattern.

There may be some questions owing to the fact that the elasticities of construction and services are higher than those of manufacturing and facilitating industries. We do not believe that this is illogical. The higher elasticities are due, we think, to greater changes in the rate of utilization, although this cannot be tested with the available data. They relate to demand changes under existing productive capacity, rather than to the structure of production. More important are the shifts to the right, which do pertain to the production structure of each sector.

The case of agriculture is exceptional because its postwar shift *to the left* resulted from decreases in its labor force, as is obvious from the equation:

$$G_y = 0.130 \ + \ 1.151 G_Y (\bar{R}^2 = 0.935)$$
$$(0.141) \quad (0.053)$$

Loss of labor was not true of any other sector.

TABLE 4.4
The Growth of Factory Production
(Prewar, million yen at 1934-36 prices; postwar, billion yen at 1960 prices)

Year	Factory output (1)	Manufac- turing output (2)	Factory/ manufac- turing (1) ÷ (2) (3)	Manufac- turing net output (4)	NDP (5)	Manufactur- ing net output/NDP (4) ÷ (5) (6)	Factory/ NDP (3) x (6) (7)
1890	413	1,311	31.5%				
1895	746	1,812	41.2				
1900	972	2,086	46.6				
1905	1,021	2,163	47.2	754	5,780	13.0%	6.1%
1909	1,268	2,742	46.2	890	7,037	12.6	5.8
1914	1,859	3,533	52.6	1,282	7,927	16.2	8.5
1919	3,697	6,100	60.6	2,035	11,638	17.5	10.6
1925	4,594	7,043	65.2	2,189	12,908	17.0	11.1
1931	6,926	9,466	73.2	3,497	13,586	25.7	18.8
1937	12,854	17,320	74.2	5,280	19,510	27.1	20.1
1940	16,784	20,210	83.1	8,706	24,604	35.4	29.4
1953	5,602	6,078	92.2	1,999	7,072	28.3	26.1
1958	9,951	10,431	95.4	3,227	10,950	29.5	28.1
1961	18,753	19,853	94.5	5,817	16,018	36.3	34.3
1965	29,371	30,321	96.9	8,899	22,968	38.8	37.6

Source: Prewar. (1) K. Ohkawa and others, The Growth Rate of the Japanese Economy Since 1878 (Tokyo, 1957), pp. 79-80. Deflator, LTES, vol. 8, pp. 192-93. (2) LTES, vol. 10, pp. 144-47 (Series A). (4) BST. 4 (mining is included). (5) BST.4. Postwar. (1) Annual issues of Kōgyō tōkei-hyō (Census of Manufactures, or KTH). Deflator, WS, section P. (2) Japan, Economic Planning Agency, Economic Research Institute, Keizai bunseki (Economic Analysis), no. 27 (1969), pp. 44-45. (4) NIS (1970), pp. 306-7. Deflator same as in (1). (5) BST. 4.

reached a level of over 30 percent of aggregate output in the 1930's, and again at the end of the 1950's. See Table 4.4.[9]

Historical Changes in Industrial Structure

That factory output grew rapidly is, once again, an entirely expected finding. Much the same observation applies to the changing output stream emanating from these factories. Three quite distinct types of industries, which we shall label Groups I, II, and III, are involved. Group I industries are dominated by food processing and kindred activities. These are forms of production whose traditional character has remained pronounced, and whose techniques are generally of low capital

[9] These statistics are not uniformly available for all these categories. Factory output net of intermediate goods appears in the official Kōgyō tōkei-hyō (Census of Manufactures, or KTH) only since 1957. Prewar estimates of manufacturing net of intermediate goods are not readily available; M. Shinohara, LTES, vol. 10, gives only output gross of intermediate goods. Manufacturing output net of intermediate goods (column 4) is our own estimate and begins in 1905. (See BST.3 and BST.4.)

intensity. Group II industries represent textile products, and contain the first modern industry, cotton. Group III production largely consists of chemicals, metals, and machines. Generally these activities are of a "heavier," more modern character and are representative of what might perhaps be called "post-textile" technology.[10] The trends represented in Table 4.5 are clear. In 1868 (not shown in the table) output gross of intermediate goods was, very roughly, 66 percent in Group I and 28 percent in Group II. Group III did not really exist. By 1886 (not shown in the table) gross output was, still very roughly, 53 percent in Group I, 39 percent in Group II, and 8 percent in Group III. Since those early years, the pattern has changed only slightly. The share of Group I industries has remained remarkably steady. Group II increased its share through World War I and has since declined almost continuously. Group III has nearly always risen. To summarize: during the last century, factory output was dominated, though to a diminishing extent, by the Group I industries. During this century there were two rather distinct changes in the structure of output: the great relative gains of Group II (textiles) especially around the time of World War I, and the even greater relative gains of Group III (chemicals, metals, and machines) as Japan prepared for war in the 1930's, and during post–World War II growth.

The corresponding employment structure can also be examined in Tables 4.5 and 4.6.

In this century the total number of factory workers rose ten times. Currently, about 20 percent of the labor force works in factories; in 1909, the figure was barely above 3 percent. These increases, however, were not equally distributed among the three industrial groupings. Group II reached a level of about one million workers in 1919 and since then has had almost a zero rate of growth of labor force. By far the sharpest rates of increase took place in the newer industries represented by Group III. In 1909, they employed about 100,000 workers; by 1919, this had risen to over 400,000; by 1940, to over 2.5 million. Sometime during the 1930's these most progressive industries became the principal source of factory employment. Group I industries absorbed workers at the smoothest rate. Starting with 200,000 employees in 1909, Group I accounted for

---

[10] Group I consists of food and kindred fields; lumber and wood products; ceramic, stone, and clay products; printing, publishing, and allied industries; miscellaneous industries. Group II consists of textile mill products; apparel and other finished products made from fabrics or similar materials; leather and leather products. Group III consists of chemicals, petroleum, and coal products; rubber and rubber products; iron and steel; nonferrous metal products; transportation equipment; machinery; electrical equipment, and measuring and survey equipment.

TABLE 4.5
Shares of Output and Employment for Industrial Groups
(Percent)

Year	Group I Employ-ment (1)	Group I Output (2)	Group I Differ-ence (2)−(1)	Group II Employ-ment (1)	Group II Output (2)	Group II Differ-ence (2)−(1)	Group III Employ-ment (1)	Group III Output (2)	Group III Differ-ence (2)−(1)
1909	24.8%	29.6%	4.8%	62.8%	50.7%	−12.1%	12.4%	19.7%	7.3%
1914	24.9	26.5	1.6	59.4	48.1	−11.3	15.7	25.4	9.7
1919	20.9	20.0	−0.9	54.8	51.0	−3.8	24.3	29.0	4.7
1927	21.4	26.7	5.3	52.7	43.7	−9.0	25.9	29.6	3.7
1931	21.8	27.1	5.3	54.3	38.8	−15.5	23.9	34.1	10.2
1940	18.8	19.0	0.2	24.4	18.4	−6.0	56.8	62.6	5.8
1948	25.7	26.5	0.8	20.4	14.6	−5.8	53.9	58.9	5.0
1953	30.5	27.4	−3.1	23.1	20.1	−2.9	46.4	52.5	6.0
1958	32.0	28.0	−4.0	20.0	14.9	−5.1	48.0	57.1	9.1
1961	33.0	27.9	−5.1	17.2	11.7	−5.5	49.8	60.4	10.6

Source: KTH.
   Note: Employment is in terms of number of workers. Output is gross of intermediate goods in current prices.

TABLE 4.6
Factory Employment

Year	Factory employment (000 workers) (1)	Manufacturing employment (000 workers) (2)	Factory manufacturing *(percent)* (1)÷(2) (3)	Factory/ total employment *(percent)* (4)
1909	821	3,024	27.2%	3.2%
1914	1,010	3,069	32.9	3.9
1919	1,808	4,171	43.4	6.7
1925	1,996	4,903	40.7	7.1
1931	1,842	5,394	34.3	6.2
1937	3,253	6,429	50.6	10.3
1940	4,486	7,160	62.7	13.8
1953	4,658	7,190	64.8	11.8
1958	6,110	8,990	68.0	14.1
1961	8,187	10,160	80.6	18.1
1965	9,650	11,580	83.3	20.3

Source: (1) Japan, Ministry of International Trade and Industry, *Kōgyōtōkei 50-nen shi* (History of the Census of Manufactures for 1909–58; 1961). Entry for 1965 from KTH, *Kigyō-hen* (Report by Enterprises; 1968), p. 228. (2) BST.15; mining is excluded. (3) Total employment from BST.15.

400,000 people by 1931, and by the opening of World War II, it employed virtually as many workers as the textile group.

Changes in the employment structure reflect the general economic history of the period. By 1909, the textile industry already employed about half a million workers and cotton goods production was the most developed modern industry. (The bulk of employment, however, was and continued to be provided by the silk industry.) At the time of World War I, textiles experienced a great surge of employment, directly connected with the war and newly created export opportunities. This was followed, especially during the 1920's and 1930's, by a rather distinct shift in technology toward more capital intensive methods. Under these circumstances, textiles, and especially cottons, could continue to increase their rates of growth of output while slowing down their intake of workers. Labor requirements of Group III have been of a different type. These industries began with much higher levels of capital intensity, and there was no need for the type of "rationalization" experienced by cotton textiles in the 1920's. The uninterrupted and sometimes extremely rapid increase of the labor force in metals, machines, and chemicals resulted from continued rapid expansion with a changing and progressively more capital intensive technology, but one that does not have the "kink" exhibited by textiles sometime during the 1920's. Perhaps the continued increases in employment within Group I may seem unusual—food, lumber and wood products, ceramic, stone, and clay products, etc.—a set of industries with a continually heavy traditional content. Yet certain features of the Japanese economy make this understandable. Three factors must be involved: the highly elastic supply of labor, the labor-using technology in this set of industries, and the persistent and frequently growing demand for traditional products. (All of these features will be discussed in later chapters.)

Changes in the shares of output and employment imply related changes in the levels of partial labor productivity. These are outlined in Table 4.5, where a "zero" entry for the difference between the output and employment proportions would indicate that gross output per worker was equal to the industrial average; positive entries mean above average and negative entries below average output per worker. Obviously, relative labor productivity levels were highest in Group III throughout the entire period of analysis. Group I is rather close to average levels, at least until very recent years. What is much harder to understand is the uniformly below-average position of textiles.[11]

The answer lies in the dual structure of Group II industries. When it is decomposed into its major component parts—silk, cotton, and other—the minuses grow much larger for silk and disappear entirely for the other categories. For example, in 1931, the differences were as follows: −20.6 for silk, 10.4 for cotton, and 10.2 for other. We may safely con-

---

[11] These primitive measures of relative labor productivity cannot be used for analysis in depth. We would need the ratios of gross to net output, relative output prices, sectoral capital stock—all unavailable. The figures cited in the text are meant to indicate only broad trends of change in the industrial structure.

clude that relative labor productivities were highest in all of Group III and cotton textiles, both of which expanded rapidly in the twentieth century.

Changes in Scale Structure

Finally, a few observations concerning the changing scale structure of Japanese industry. Table 4.7 demonstrates that there are distinct differences in the scale distribution of employment among the three industrial groups. Group I is heavily concentrated in small units, with approximately two thirds of its workers engaged in establishments with fewer than 50 workers. This is hardly surprising since the food processing industry has retained to this day many of its handicraft elements, in terms of both technique and organization. We may assume that economies of scale were not large in this line of output. Both Groups II and III show a progressively higher degree of concentration in medium and large-scale employment, although the results are not entirely unambiguous and are most readily interpreted in terms of the periodic expansions and contractions typical of Japanese growth.

During the growth spurt coinciding with World War I, all industrial groups moved in the direction of proportionately larger scale employment, and this movement was most pronounced in Group III, somewhat less strong in Group II, and weakest in Group I. Until the panic of 1927 there was no reversal in the greater weight of larger units, and by 1927, 11.8 percent of workers in Group I, 41.3 percent of workers in Group II, and 44.7 percent of workers in Group III were working in establishments with over 500 workers. Clearly the large unit had come into its own at least in textiles and heavier industries. And then in the 1930's the large establishments in Group III continued to absorb a greater share of workers, while this trend became insignificant for Group I and was actually reversed for Group II, textiles. One must, however, be careful in any generalization concerning the textile industry. As just pointed out, this industrial classification encompasses two very diverse industries, silk and cotton. Silk manufacturing in practically all its stages preserved traditional characteristics. By contrast, the cotton industry can serve as an "ideal type" for early modern growth, and the differences between these two lines of economic activity are clearly reflected in the dynamics of their respective scale structures. More or less half the labor force in silk production was always concentrated in medium-sized units. Beginning in the 1930's, smaller units made significant gains, rising from 18 percent of employment in 1931 to 50 percent in 1958. By contrast, cotton production was always much more large-scale in character. A peak was reached in 1927 when over 65 percent of all operatives were

TABLE 4.7
Industrial Scale Structure by Employment
(Percent)

Year	Small (fewer than 50 workers)	Medium (50–499 workers)	Large (500 & over workers)
	Group I (food and others)		
1909	67.6%	29.5%	2.9%
1914	67.0	27.4	5.6
1919	59.9	33.6	6.5
1927	60.0	28.2	11.8
1931	69.8	25.1	5.1
1940	70.3	23.9	5.8
1948	69.7	24.7	5.6
1953	66.5	26.0	7.5
1958	61.9	30.9	7.2
1961	54.2	35.2	10.6
	Group II (textiles)		
1909	37.4	34.2	28.4
1914	30.4	38.3	31.3
1919	26.7	35.7	37.6
1927	22.7	36.0	41.3
1931	25.5	41.2	33.3
1940	38.2	33.2	28.6
1948	35.7	37.3	27.0
1953	41.7	35.8	22.5
1958	45.4	36.9	17.7
1961	44.9	36.8	18.3
	Group III (heavy and chemical)		
1909	42.9	38.4	18.7
1914	33.6	33.6	32.8
1919	27.8	32.4	39.8
1927	26.4	28.9	44.7
1931	36.1	35.3	28.6
1940	24.5	25.7	49.8
1948	29.5	31.8	38.7
1953	29.1	31.5	39.4
1958	29.0	33.4	37.6
1961	24.1	34.7	41.2

Source: KTH.
Note: Figures show the proportion of workers by scale of establishment to total factory workers in specified industry.

employed in establishments with over 500 workers. Even after that date, *at least* one-third of the workers in this industry were regularly employed in large establishments.

A particular question arises concerning the extraordinary proportional increases in large-scale employment during the 1930's. For all industries, it rose from 25.7 percent in 1931 to 36.2 percent in 1940. By 1948 the proportion had declined to 28 percent. These trends were essentially

TABLE 4.8

Production Structure by Establishment Scale in Manufacturing, 1957

Size (number of workers)	K/L (000 yen per worker)	Index	Y/L (000 yen per worker)	Index	w (average wages per year, 000 yen)	Index	Lw/Y labor share (percent)	K/Y
1. 1-9	69	23.8	186	36.0	114	58.8	34.6	.37
2. 10-29	78	27.0	289	56.0	136	70.1	44.5	.27
3. 30-49	91	31.5	348	67.4	145	74.7	42.1	.26
4. 50-99	120	41.5	420	81.3	157	80.9	38.1	.29
5. 100-199	165	57.1	492	95.3	172	88.7	35.7	.34
6. 200-299	209	72.3	564	109.3	187	96.4	33.6	.37
7. 300-499	309	106.9	696	134.8	205	105.7	29.9	.44
8. 500-999	408	141.2	780	151.1	230	118.6	29.6	.52
9. 1,000-1,999	589	203.8	922	178.6	259	133.5	28.7	.64
10. 2,000-4,999	687	237.7	1,078	208.9	301	155.2	28.3	.64
11. 5,000-9,999	558	193.0	866	167.8	287	147.9	37.8	.64
12. 10,000 & over	651	225.2	897	173.8	329	169.5	37.1	.73
Average	289	100.0	516	100.0	194	100.0	34.4	.44

Source: Japan, Economic Planning Agency, Economic Research Institute, Shihon kōzō to kigyōkan kakusa (Capital Structure and Enterprise Differentials; 1960), Study Series no. 6, Appendix Table 2, p. 142.

Note: Average index of all size classes equals 100.0.

Notation: Y, added value gross of depreciation, including some expenditures for intermediate goods in national income accounts (this helps to explain the low level of Lw/Y); K, fixed capital stock; L, number of workers employed; w, wages.

confined to large-scale heavy-chemical employment, whose share of the work force went from 28.6 percent in 1931 to 49.8 percent in 1940. Of equal interest is the subsequent decline to 38.7 percent in 1948. These changes have to be related to a series of unusual world events. In the late 1930's, with Japan preparing for war, the labor markets became tightly controlled. Workers were mobilized and assigned in increasing numbers to those industries directly connected with the war effort. That can certainly explain the off-trend value for 1940. After the war, as pointed out in Chapter 2, the labor supply situation underwent a one-time structural change as a result of the large repatriation of Japanese living in various parts of the Empire. The greatly eased labor supply may well have improved the relative viability of medium and small enterprises and their share of the work force. Another possible reason for the temporary diminution in the share of large units could have been the deconcentration policies sponsored by the U.S. occupation. That, however, is no more than a guess.

Last, let us make use of the interesting cross-section results for manufacturing (including "nonfactory" production) obtained by the Economic Planning Agency and presented in Table 4.8. These detailed findings for 1957 concerning the structure of production related to size of establishment—the only ones of their kind—should be comparable to

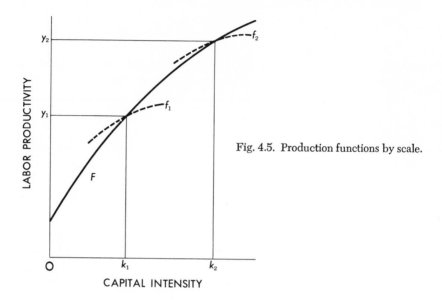

Fig. 4.5. Production functions by scale.

the entries for 1958 in previous tables. With the exception of classes 11 and 12, K/L, Y/L, and w rise together with scale of establishment.[12] However, K/L rises much more rapidly than Y/L, so that generally the level of K/Y is higher for larger establishments, the only exception being class 1. Despite the plausible assumptions of higher-quality labor in larger establishments, the relative share of labor (L_w/Y) declines as the size of the productive unit increases, again with the exception of class 1.

These findings may suggest a production function of the type $Y/L = F(K/L)$ with differential wage rates and a given technology. We do not intend to accept this formulation. Instead, we think that technologies do differ by scale of establishment, and therefore we believe it to be more reasonable, in interpreting Table 4.8, to assume separate production functions for different scales of manufacturing, as for example $Y/L = f_1(K/L)$ and $Y/L = f_2(K/L)$, etc. Relations between $f_1, f_2, \ldots$ and F are illustrated in Figure 4.5.[13]

Points E_1 and E_2 are assumed to represent the conjunction of actual Y/L and K/L levels in two different size classes of Table 4.8. Line F indicates the cross-section path of technological and organizational dif-

---

[12] The exceptions in classes 11 and 12 are probably due to the fact that Table 4.8 is classified by number of workers rather than amounts of capital.

[13] For an analysis in greater detail, see K. Ohkawa, *Differential Structure and Agriculture* (Tokyo, 1972), Part I.

ferences connecting a variety of production functions corresponding to scale levels. These differences imply shifts over time from f_1 to f_2, f_2 to f_3, etc. These shifts would accord with the historical evidence already examined (if the time series and cross section are consistent), i.e. increasingly larger units of factory production and types of activities in which technological advances have been especially prominent.

TECHNOLOGICAL PROGRESS AND THE RESIDUAL

Let us now resume the main thread of the argument. In the wake of this lengthy discussion, it is no longer possible to make simple links between the residual and technological progress. Demand has been shown to influence the residuals of construction and services. Economies of scale have affected principally manufacturing and facilitating industries. Yet technology must also be seen as an element in the latter two sectors, as demonstrated in the ever higher residual growth of manufacturing, the growing dominance of the weighted residual by this industry, and the leading residual growth rates of the facilitating branches during the first spurt. Furthermore, the postwar phenomenon of overall rather than sectoral residual expansion should also be connected to advances in techniques and organization.

The subject of Japanese technological progress in historical perspective deserves detailed and separate study; it cannot be attempted here. We would like only to make a few comments concerning two issues related to this matter. The first pertains to borrowed technology, and the second deals with the unusual opportunities of the years following World War II.

Borrowed Technology

Japan is a classic example of industrialization based on borrowed technology—borrowed of course by the modern sectors. From the very beginning of its modern economic growth until now, manufacturing depended heavily on technological advances from abroad. This was an economical process and is one of the reasons why Japan could develop so quickly. Reliance and dependence on technology developed by the West and for the West does raise a very interesting question. Considering the factor proportions required by borrowed technology (a comparatively high level of capital intensity), how could it be efficiently adapted in an economy with very flexible (cheap) supplies of labor? In large part, the Japanese had very little choice. Remaining competitive meant keeping up to date, and the modern sectors had to take part in world technological progress. The standards were set by the advanced countries of the West, and reflected their own and not Japanese factor proportions. In modern industry, and especially in those areas where foreign competition had to be faced, a rising rate of capital intensity was an imperative and a simple consequence of reliance on borrowed technology. No evidence has been derived for capital shallowing or capital widening. On the contrary, capital deepening has been going on continuously since the measures become available, and it has been most rapid of all in recent years.

This is only part of the story, and it stresses unduly the rigidity of factor proportions. There were possibilities of mitigating the incongruity between required factor proportions and domestic factor prices, and the Japanese explored these paths with great creativity. This subject deserves fuller treatment than we can give it here, but a few suggestions may be helpful. One method of mitigation was the selection of those modern industrial activities relatively most suitable to domestic factor proportions (especially by the private sector). In the postwar period this is best illustrated by the tremendous expansion of the light machinery industry. It grew more rapidly than any other, and also absorbed a great deal of labor. Textiles, which regularly accounted for over 40 percent of manufacturing production between 1891 and 1929, played a similar role before World War II. Another well-known method of mitigation is the fuller utilization of capital through the more intensive use of labor. A multishift system is the classic example, and it is valid for any period of modern economic growth in Japan. After World War II, however, a particularly prevalent form has been the use of secondhand machinery by small-scale enterprises. Last, there is also the possibility of partially substituting capital by labor even in some technologically advanced industries. Subcontracting performed this role both before and after the recent war. As a result of these adaptations, the absorptive capacity for labor by manufacturing was increased.

Borrowed Western technology also concerns the differential structure. Increasingly, capital-intensive methods of production borrowed from more advanced countries resulted in rising labor productivity in modern sectors. Traditional sectors have also had periods of technological progress since 1900 (the situation before that time is not comparable); and especially after World War II, as explained in the next section of this chapter, there has been another acceleration in the growth of agricultural productivity. We have shown that this progress has been largely induced by the modern sectors, in the form of specific machinery and techniques still applicable within a traditional form of economic organization—in this instance the small peasant farm. However, this induced form of progress has been late in coming and its effect is relatively limited. The productivity gap has grown historically, and its evolution is highly correlated with the sharply differing sectoral levels of capital intensity that first become apparent around World War I.

Another aspect of the technology structure problem pertains to the sectoral allocation of labor. Despite the moderating effects of mitigating devices to offset labor-saving techniques, increased employment opportunities in modern sectors were not sufficient to lower the absolute numbers in traditional employment. Probably the best proxy for the traditionally employed is the total number of workers in the unincorporated sectors. As a trend it has risen until very recently, and is only now showing some slight decline. Insofar as international competition required a certain positive rate of capital-deepening in the modern economy, and given the rate of population growth, the high levels of traditional employment were unavoidable. Equally unavoidable were the low levels of productivity in the traditional sectors owing to the impact of surplus labor. Further aspects of this problem will be studied in Chapter 5.

Technological Progress and the Postwar Spurt

In previous chapters as well as in preceding sections of this chapter, much evidence has been presented concerning the unusually large opportunities and achievements of technological progress in postwar Japan. Most of this evidence has, however, been of a rather "formal" and indirect character. Attention has been drawn to high rates of return on capital, declining capital-output ratios, and especially large growth rates of residuals during the 1950's and 1960's. Why were the opportunities and achievements of technological progress so great after World War II? One aspect may be the changed conditions pertaining to the backlog and inflow of foreign technology.

By backlog we mean the difference between the average state of technology within an industry or in the aggregate of all industries and international best practice. Thus the existence of a backlog within a country represents an opportunity for a particular industry or for all industries to bring the level of technology closer to international best practice. The bigger the backlog, the greater and more obvious the opportunity. For most industries and countries, and clearly for Japan, the main way to exploit this opportunity lies in the importation of more advanced techniques from the few leaders of world technology. This process is called inflow. However, the presence of a backlog describes only the possibility of progress, and inflow can only be an *ex post* measure. What needs to be explained is why inflow varies in magnitude from time to time, and this will eventually be considered in Chapter 8, in terms of social capability, i.e. the capacity of various sectors of the society to absorb technical advances.

In drawing a contrast between the periods in Japan before and after World War II with respect to possibilities and actualities of technological inflow, three factors stand out. First of all, the postwar economy possessed the considerable benefit of "spillover" from Japan's own military inventiveness. In a sense Japan was compelled to rely more on its own potential during part of the 1930's and 1940's and this opened up a "swords into plowshares" path of progress. Second, the gap between international best practice and the average technological level within Japan was very much increased by the disruption of normal international relations beginning in the 1930's and ending in the early 1950's with the restoration of Japanese sovereignty. During this long period Japan's relative technological level declined because, on the one hand, progress in this sphere was more rapid among the few countries pushing back the frontiers of technology, and on the other hand, inflow was virtually blocked. Third, the aftermath of World War II presented Japan with the great opportunity of a *simultaneous* technological infusion. The very size of the gap produced by some 15 years of isolation meant that Japan had slipped backward in a number of older and established industries, and also that it was behind in an entire range of new economic activities that originated beyond its frontiers during this period. For a variety of reasons, among which trained manpower may have been the most important asset, Japan was able simultaneously to improve the way of doing familiar things while doing entirely new things. Together, these three factors created an unprecedentedly favorable climate for technological progress and resulted in a rapid closing of the gap.

The long-range effects of spillover are often neglected by the literature on postwar growth, perhaps because the impact of this phenomenon is considered to be only of short-term importance. But this is not necessarily true, as can be seen in the case of the machinery industry. In 1930 the Japanese machinery industry was very small; it constituted only 19.7 percent of total value added in manufacturing. From 1930 to 1940 the value added by the machinery industry rose to an astonishing 48 percent, and the reasons are clear. At that time, the mass production of machinery was strongly pushed by the government since it was related to the production of munitions and armaments. In many senses this was artificial growth and at the expense of more peaceful activities. After the war, the value added by machinery dropped sharply to a level of 20.8 percent in the year 1955; even in 1961 the level was only 32.3 percent.

That is only one aspect of the story. Even though the machinery industry concentrated heavily on the production of arms and similar items, it did receive the opportunity to engage in mass production, to develop know-how and to raise manpower skills. That this effort was directed toward war may have been especially significant in stimulating native inventiveness and skills. International cooperation became increasingly harder to obtain, and from the late 1930's on the Japanese had to stand entirely on their own feet. From the technical point of view, they managed quite well. Japanese ordnance, warships, and planes were generally of acceptable and "competitive" quality.

Much of what was learned and invented before and during the war could be transferred to useful activities. A few of the outstanding examples should be cited. Some aircraft producers (Mitsubishi and Nakajima) switched to the production of motor scooters. Eventually most of the aircraft producers also entered the automobile business (Tachikawa Hikōki, Nakajima, Mitsubishi, Fuji Jūkō). A number of munitions manufacturers started to make sewing machines (Fuji Seimitsu, Aichi Kōgyō, Tōkyō Jūki). Most famous of all is the case of the optics industry. Many of the leading companies in this key postwar export industry were direct descendants of makers of optical war equipment (Fuji Seimitsu, Uryū Seiki, Tōkyō Kōkūkeiki) and relied extensively on what they had learned during the war in making gunsights, bombsights, and so forth. These are only some of the most obvious and direct cases; they barely scratch the surface. Scattered throughout Japanese growth industries there are now men at the helm who first held positions of responsibility in the armed forces. For example, former President Ibuka and current President Morita of the Sony Corporation gained many of their skills while working for the Imperial Navy.

To the best of our knowledge, a systematic study of spillover has not yet been made, and this makes it impossible to compare its influence with the benefits of postwar inflow from abroad. We believe that spillover was important, but also that on balance it was less of a contribution than the importation of foreign know-how. That judgment, however, must remain an *obiter dictum*.[14]

It is generally agreed that the technological gap between Japan and the West was very large at the end of World War II, and has since then been very much reduced. Since a gap of this type is not easily defined, it is also subject to difficulties of measurement. Royalty payments may be one of the most relevant items of information. They rose very rapidly from 1950 to 1961. After 1961, the rate of growth declined substantially. In terms of our periodization, the average annual rates of growth were 31.5 percent for 1951–55, 34.0 percent for 1955–61, and 7.5 percent for

[14] For a more extended discussion and further examples of spillover, see Y. Hoshino, *Nihon no gijitsu kakushin* (Technological Innovations in Japan; Tokyo, 1966), Part 1, chap. 2.

1961–66. This fits well with the pattern of growth discussed in earlier portions of this book. The acquisition rate was very high during the re-habilitation phase, when the base was very low; it surged forward during the investment spurt; and as the gap closed, the rates started to taper off after 1961.[15]

There is another way of looking at the gap, by comparing royalty pay-ments and private fixed investments. Until 1958, royalty payments rose much more rapidly than private investments, and this can be taken as an indicator of the gap's becoming smaller. After 1958 the rates of growth of investment and royalties have been nearly identical. This does not mean that the gap between best practice and average Japanese levels has been eliminated. It does, however, imply that the magnitude of the gap has been stabilized through the early 1960's.[16]

And last is the matter of simultaneous infusion. From the vantage point of postwar Japan, technological backwardness in the late 1940's and early 1950's was made up of two parts. Japan found itself behind leading world levels in a range of older and well-established techniques. These were the activities in which a prewar base had existed, such as branches of engineering, iron and steel, and chemicals, but owing to isolation and war the quality of the base had deteriorated. Japan was lagging even further behind in the "new" activities that were born in the leading countries between the late 1930's and early 1950's. Television, many synthetics, and most other science-originated technologies lacked a prewar base altogether. It is an important indication of Japan's eco-nomic strength that it was able to attack both kinds of backwardness simultaneously.

It is difficult to quantify assertions of this type, although there are some Japanese attempts to do so. These focus on a comparison of 1956 and 1966. In 1956, according to calculations of the government's Science and Technology Agency, simultaneous infusion was in full swing.[17]

[15] See Japan, Kagaku Gijitsu-chō, *Kagaku gijitsu nempō* (Annual Report of the Science and Technology Agency; 1967). The use of royalty figures creates some problems. We have used them in *current* prices. Since royalties represent mainly dollar payments, they should be deflated by an appropriate dollar price index. But dollar prices relative to these rates of growth did not change very much, so that the use of current prices should not make much difference.

[16] Royalty payments are a less than ideal index of technological inflow. Specific industries would have to be studied for a complete picture. Also, the supply side must be considered. A larger postwar inflow may be due in part to a greater desire by foreigners, especially Americans, to sell. These desires appear to have changed in the last few years, when Americans began to insist on joint ventures. For further discussion, see Chapter 9.

[17] See "Japanese Businesses Show Proficiency in Using Foreign Technology," *The Japan Economic Journal*, October 10, 1967.

About half of the imported technology was bought to improve prewar-originated activities; the other half was purchased to engage in entirely new lines of production. By 1966 the situation had been fundamentally altered. Prewar-based activities had caught up, and imports concentrated overwhelmingly on continuing to bring in what was new.

AGRICULTURE

Setting of the Problem

Beginning with Chapter 3, this study has been concerned entirely with nonagriculture as the best available representative of modern sector growth. As our preview has already indicated, this is only a partial story, since account must also be taken of the traditional sector where agriculture is the largest and most typical activity. In this section we will give an account of agricultural growth, stressing the twentieth century, and we shall also attempt to develop an "external inducement" thesis to explain why the rural sector has again grown rapidly after World War II. For comparative purposes, residual growth in agriculture will also be analyzed.

The role of agriculture in Japanese economic development has undergone enormous changes during this century. When Japan first attempted to conquer its absolute and relative economic backwardness in the early years of Meiji, the possibility of agricultural progress was one of its major assets. Throughout the nineteenth century the possibilities of starting modern economic growth hinged in large measure on raising agricultural output through improvements in traditional agriculture. However, with the beginning of this century the importance of agriculture to Japan progressively declined. Industrialization succeeded, other sources of revenue became available, and exports were diversified. Even in later years agriculture remained important especially as a source of employment and as a supplier of labor, but the structure of Japanese output had shifted more and more toward the nonagricultural and particularly the industrial sector.

Nevertheless, the role of agriculture can never be treated as an afterthought in an analysis of Japanese growth, even if the focus is to be on more recent years. The fortunes of the primary sector remained intertwined with those of the rest of the economy, and a balanced picture requires consideration of what was happening in this area.

The dimensions of agricultural growth, from 1885 to the present, are presented in Table 4.9. Agricultural output expanded with increasing rapidity throughout the Meiji era and until World War I. From then on the decline in the growth rate was precipitous during the 1920's, and

TABLE 4.9
Agricultural Growth: Output and Inputs in Terms
of Average Annual Rates of Growth
(Percent)

Period	Output[a] (1)	Arable land[b] (2)	Labor[c] (3)	Land/labor (2)−(3)	Partial productivity Land (1)−(2)	Partial productivity Labor (1)−(3)
1885–97	1.41%	0.46%	−0.16%	0.62%	0.95%	1.57%
1897–1901	2.38	0.55	−0.05	0.60	1.83	2.43
1901–17	1.91	0.75	−0.10	0.86	1.16	2.01
1917–31	0.44	0.15	−0.03	0.18	0.29	0.47
1931–37	0.53	0.31	−0.27	0.58	0.22	0.80
1937–56	−0.60	−0.10	0.45	−0.55	−0.50	−1.05
1956–62	4.06	0.18	−2.80	2.98	3.88	6.86
1962–64	1.18	−0.33	−2.37	2.04	1.51	3.55
1885–1917	1.81	0.62	−0.12	0.74	1.19	1.93
1917–56	−0.05	0.06	0.16	−0.10	−0.01	−0.21

Period	Current inputs[d] Total (4)	Current inputs[d] External (5)	Current inputs[d] Internal (6)	Capital stock[e] (7)	Capital intensity (7)−(3)	Capital output ratio[f]
1885–97	0.76%	1.60%	0.32%	1.09%	1.25%	2.02
1897–1901	1.65	3.65	0.53	0.89	0.94	1.94
1901–17	2.52	4.85	0.29	1.50	1.60	1.83
1917–31	2.11	3.57	−0.48	1.00	1.03	1.71
1931–37	2.16	1.37	0.36	0.69	0.96	1.85
1937–56				0.80	0.35	1.87
1956–62	8.52	10.20	0.77	3.83	6.63	3.02
1962–64	8.62	10.40	0.37	5.05	7.42	3.12
1885–1917	1.74	3.47	−0.33	1.27	1.39	
1917–56	2.10	2.90	0.33	0.65	0.49	

Source: All data from LTES, vol. 9, with the following exceptions. Capital stock for 1885–1937 from WS, part K; for 1956–62 and 1962–64 from SRA, vol. 3, p. 167. Arable land for 1964 from Japan, Ministry of Agriculture, *Nōrinshō tōkeihyō* (Statistical Yearbook of the Ministry of Agriculture; 1966), p. 48. Labor force for 1964 from *ibid.* (1968), p. 13. For detailed methods of estimation and concepts of all these series, see the volumes cited as sources.

Note: All series in seven-year moving averages and 1934–36 prices, with the following exceptions. Five-year averages for 1956 and three-year averages for 1962 and 1964. Output and capital for 1962–64 in 1960 prices.

[a] Added values gross of capital depreciation, prices at the farm level, obtained by using linked deflators.

[b] A sum of paddy and upland fields, excluding pastures, which are unimportant in Japanese agriculture. No adjustment is made for changes in the rate of utilization, as for example the trend of increase in double-cropping.

[c] Number of gainfully occupied persons including all family workers. No adjustment is made for quality and labor days or hours.

[d] Corresponds to intermediate goods, fertilizers, insecticides, etc. "Internal" means of internal origin, that is, the product of Japanese agriculture, such as manures; "external" means of external origin, that is, products from outside Japanese agriculture, like chemical fertilizers and imported feedstuffs.

[e] Capital stock in gross terms.

[f] Figures are for the first year of the period.

there was no recovery when other sectors of the economy boomed in the 1930's. In fact, the trend of decline was reversed only in the second half of the 1950's, when the output of agriculture started to increase after a retardation lasting at least 35 years. Even so, the pace has slowed down somewhat in the 1960's.

The impressive upturn of post–World War II agricultural growth is also evident in the unprecedented rise of the partial productivity of labor at about 7 percent per year. Since labor input is measured only in crude numbers of gainfully employed (hours of work being unavailable), the gains in labor productivity are undoubtedly somewhat overestimated. Furthermore, we note that after the recent war the labor force in agriculture declined more rapidly than ever before, while output grew. This suggests that technological progress must have taken place in the agricultural sector. Indeed, Table 4.9 contains other circumstantial evidence of productivity increases—especially the rates of growth of current inputs, capital, and capital intensity, all of which lend credence to the recorded rates of labor productivity growth after World War II.

Why was it possible for Japanese agriculture to grow again after the very long interruption of the interwar period? This question is taken up in the next section, where the emphasis will be on the change in nature of technological progress. Institutional changes will not anywhere be of primary concern, but in order fully to appreciate the real meaning of the question just posed, a historical setting is needed.

Noteworthy events in Meiji Japan from the economic point of view can generally be placed under the heading of traditional technological progress. In order to make output grow more rapidly, Japanese peasants had to raise the productivity of their land and labor, i.e. they had to improve their methods of production. A number of factors were crucial in this process, but three were of greatest significance: improved seeds, more fertilizer, and a transfer of superior farming methods from more to less developed sections of the country.[18] These steps can be called an overall improvement in traditional technology because during the nineteenth century they relied hardly at all on imported Western scientific knowledge; rather they represented improvements in old ways of doing things and the spread of these superior ways from advanced western to backward eastern Japan. The kind of technology perfected in Japan at that time, frequently referred to as Meiji technology, used land and labor intensively, and was very sparing in its use of scarce capital.

[18] During the Meiji period great improvements also occurred in the quality of Japan's infrastructure, such as the expansion of transport and communication. These advances undoubtedly contributed toward enlarging the market for domestic agricultural products, and must have been an important supporting factor in raising the level of traditional technology.

At the beginning of the twentieth century opportunities for traditional technological progress still existed, but areas of possible improvements were becoming more confined. Most farmers were already using greater quantities of fertilizer; the diffusion of better technologies had already occurred in many areas; and seeds had also reached much higher levels of quality especially in western Japan. Certainly by the beginning of the 1920's, further progress based on traditional technology was unlikely. Diffusion was practically completed, and traditional inputs had reached their most refined level. From then on, agriculture became the sick man of the Japanese economy. Output grew unsatisfactorily, and once again better ways of doing things were needed. However, these would have required a very different type of technology. Traditional methods had reached peak performance and their frontier was incapable of further practical expansion. Instead, the time had come for a more capital-intensive system of cultivation involving more machinery and greater investments. Many factors stood in the way: small units of production, an unfavorable man-land ratio, the large numbers still remaining on the land and excluded from the possibilities of industrial employment, competition of cheap colonial production—all these combined to create over three decades of agricultural depression. And the history of this period— essentially the 1920's and the 1930's, is replete with tenant unrest, cries of parasitic landlordism, and agrarian immiseration. What had worked so well in the nineteenth century had turned to ashes in the twentieth century, and at least through the end of the 1930's no solution was in sight.

The impressive postwar recovery was not accidental. It was the result of a basic change in the circumstances of the farmer. We visualize agricultural growth as influenced by two rather distinct factors: an internal growth potential and external or nonagricultural inducements. These are not always easy to separate for any concrete historical time period; nevertheless, it is useful to keep them conceptually separate. By internal growth potential we mean the sum total of factors *within* agriculture that can lead to a higher rate of growth of output. Some of these would be internal types of technical progress such as traditional seed improvement or the use of more effective *domestic* fertilizers. By external inducements we mean the sum total of factors *outside* agriculture that can lead to a higher rate of growth of output. External inducement generally originates in modern industry and can be measured, though only *ex post*, using indicators such as the growth rate of current external inputs, or the flow of newly designed farm machinery from industry to agriculture in the last ten years or so. Even though internal and external factors are hard to distinguish in practice, at least in theory they need not be confused, since—other things being equal—a favorable change in one, with the other remaining the same, would result in an increased output growth rate. One might also consider a third factor and call it the "social capability" of agriculture to utilize effectively internal and external technological progress.

In the light of this distinction, we propose the following generalizations. First, that postwar agricultural growth is due to renewed internal and external inducements. This is why output grew especially rapidly in recent years. Second, from 1901 to 1917 the internal growth potential was present mainly in the form of the spread of improved seeds all over the country. Until about 1920 the areas planted with *rōnō* varieties increased. These were seeds developed by farmers rather than by agronomists.[19] Outside inducement was present for the first time (note the high growth rate of external input), though rather weak compared with that of recent years. Third, 1917–31 and 1931–37 saw the collapse of both internal potential and outside inducements. Some of the internal reasons have already been cited. On the external side, the depression of the 1920's and the military emphasis of the 1930's were key negative considerations. In addition, the rising impact of cheap colonial rice imports from Korea and Taiwan was another negative factor for the Japanese farmer.[20] Symptomatic evidence is contained in the decline of the current input and capital-intensity growth rate. And fourth, especially from the perspective of outside inducement, there are significant differences between 1901–17 and postwar years. No doubt the most noteworthy of these is the recent decline in the agricultural labor force; at the time of World War I this had been a rather unimportant factor. As a result of alternative employment opportunities, the land-labor ratio rose rapidly in the 1950's even though the amount of arable land had increased more before World War II. This change is reflected in the current movement toward a more capital intensive technology.

Patterns of Technological Progress in Agriculture

From the perspective of agriculture, the years following World War II contained the beginnings of an important technological transformation. Before the war, two types of farm technology had been dominant, one

---

[19] See Y. Hayami and S. Yamada, "Technological Progress in Agriculture," in L. Klein and K. Ohkawa, eds., *Economic Growth: The Japanese Experience Since the Meiji Era* (Homewood, Ill., 1968), particularly pp. 151–52.

[20] See K. Ohkawa and H. Rosovsky, "The Role of Agriculture in Modern Japanese Economic Development," *Economic Development and Cultural Change*, vol. 9 (Oct. 1960), Part II, especially pp. 56–68. Also see Y. Hayami and V. W. Ruttan, *Agricultural Development: An International Perspective* (Baltimore, 1971), pp. 218–28.

biological and the other chemical; progress was concentrated in the areas of plant development (biological) and the application of fertilizers (chemical). Of course, progress is a relative matter; as explained previously, in the 1920's and 1930's both of these methods encountered sharply diminishing returns. After the war, a third type of technology gradually assumed increasing significance. This took the form of advances in the mechanical or engineering categories, especially the new tools and machines that made their appearance in ever greater numbers in recent years.

These types of technology differ in many respects. Speaking in average terms, biological technology, at least in Japan, was more internalized than the other types. Quite a few of the advances in plant technology, notably improved varieties, were developed by farmers themselves or by individuals and organizations that can be included in a broad agricultural classification. Advances related to the use of chemicals and machinery were much less internalized and depended to a critical extent on what has been called external inducement. Chemicals mostly consisted of fertilizers, and especially in this century these were largely produced outside of agriculture. Obviously the same was true of machinery. Furthermore, developments in biological and chemical technology were closely related to one another—for example, improved varieties absorb greater quantities of fertilizer—and neither one of these types of technology has been closely dependent on progress in engineering industries.

There is, however, another difference between these technologies of greater ultimate significance. Both biological and chemical improvements are highly divisible. They can be used with virtually equal efficiency regardless of the size of the cultivating unit. This is not true of mechanical or engineering technology, which is relatively indivisible or "lumpy," and therefore cannot be used equally efficiently by all units. And here there exists the sharpest contrast between the prewar and postwar agricultural economies. Before World War II the dominant technologies offered no particular advantages to the larger unit of production; now this is in the process of changing.

External Inducements

Internal growth potential was especially significant for Japan's agricultural progress during the Meiji era. A combination of circumstances made this true. Modern sectors were still in their infancy and consequently were not equipped to provide economic inducements to progress. More important, perhaps, was the fact that the potential of traditional agricultural technology had not yet been fully exploited. Not only was it possible for traditional methods to be improved, but it was also possible to diffuse these methods on a national level, and for institutional reasons this could not have been accomplished as well under the restrictionist Tokugawa regime. Indeed, if the question had ever been considered in these terms by economic policy makers of the time (to some extent it was), the preferred path of progress must have been rather obvious. Western agricultural machinery was unsuited for paddy rice cultivation in particular and for peasant cultivation in general. The products of chemical technology were largely unavailable and expensive. Biological technology also had to be suited to the conditions of the country, and here again during the nineteenth century Japan had to rely primarily on its own accumulated knowledge rather than on the expertise of Western science. What was true from the perspective of technology was also true from the perspective of economics. Throughout the Meiji era, the ways of doing things indicated by internalized advances were cheaper. They economized capital and were labor intensive, and this fitted Japan's factor proportions.

Although internal growth potential continued to hold out some promise through World War I, during the twentieth century external inducements necessarily assumed a leading potential role as traditional methods reached their ceilings. In this century one must therefore concentrate on the channels of external inducement. Two of these appear crucial: the decline of relative external current input prices to agriculture, and the changing relation between industry and agriculture from the point of view of engineering or mechanical improvements.

Let us start with current input prices. These are peculiarly strategic to agriculture because a close complementarity exists between improved varieties (biological) and the input of fertilizers (chemical). Higher yields require improved varieties capable of absorbing larger quantities of fertilizer, and this makes the linkage between biological and chemical technology very close. Similar linkages can be found in other types of production, but the unusual aspect of agriculture is that improvements and diffusion of biological technology depend more on the conditions under which current inputs are supplied than on fixed investment. For all of these reasons, relative current input prices can be an especially significant inducement for certain types of technological progress in agriculture.

As an index of changes in these relative prices, we can compare the prices received by farmers with the prices of inputs of external origin: fertilizers, insecticides, etc. The facts appear in Table 4.10 and they are

TABLE 4.10
Relative Price Ratios of Inputs in Agriculture
(1934–36 = 100)

Year	Input prices of external origin ÷ prices received by farmers	Prices of capital goods ÷ prices of manufactured goods
1905	205.3	81.1
1919	136.2	86.6
1931	109.8	101.4
1938	100.1	101.8
1954	88.9	89.4
1961	67.2	114.6

Source: LTES, vol. 8, pp. 164–65, 192–93, 258.
Note: Prewar prices in seven-year averages; postwar prices in five-year averages. Postwar prices linked with 1934–36 prices.

very revealing. A clear trend is evident: relative prices of inputs of external origin have fallen sharply during the period. Between 1905 and 1938 the average annual rate of decrease was 2.15 percent; for 1954–61 it was 3.87 percent.

In Table 4.10 the ratio of capital goods to manufactured goods prices has been added to show that the situation outside of agriculture was very different. For nonagriculture, capital goods played the role that intermediate goods fulfilled in pre–World War II agriculture, and the trend of relative prices seems to run in opposite directions. In Japan, because arable land was scarce, its relative price was high even 100 years ago, and it has continued to rise ever since. Labor prices were generally low because this factor was in surplus. Agricultural capital goods prices, combining those of external and internal origin, rose far more than wages (except for 1961—this will be examined below) and less than land. These factor price relations can be expressed quantitatively by taking the price index for current inputs of external origin as 100 (single years), obtaining these results:[21]

Year	Daily male wages	Paddy field prices	Agricultural capital goods prices
1902	100	100	100
1917	112	150	131
1956	199	260	232
1961	365	389	298

One observes a drastic decrease in the prices of current inputs of external origin relative to internal factor prices. In other words, the comparison of Table 4.10 has been strengthened and broadened.

[21] Figures are from LTES, vol. 9, pp. 181–91, 213, 220–21. For a more thorough analysis of these relations, see Hayami and Ruttan, *Agricultural Development.*

The declining trend indicates that external inputs were available to farmers under increasingly favorable price conditions, and the speed at which prices became more favorable was most rapid in the 1950's and 1960's. This must have been a great help in furthering biological improvements. But the fact is that agriculture did not do well, especially between 1919 and 1938, and some of the reasons are also brought out by the figures of Table 4.10. First of all, it should be noted that the trend did not fall with equal rapidity during the indicated intervals. Relative prices fell most rapidly from 1905 to 1919 when agricultural output still grew at a satisfactory pace. After 1919 the rate of decline fell to nearly half its former value, and during the 1930's the trend declined at barely above 1 percent per year. In other words, external inducements weakened considerably after World War I, as did the performance of agriculture in general. Many reasons lie behind this situation, and perhaps the most important of these was that the prices received by farmers remained depressed, particularly in the 1930's, owing to cheap colonial food imports. It was not that modern industry raised the price of inputs to the peasants; it was simply that the peasant did less well with his product in the market. This situation changed only after World War II, when technological progress in modern industry enabled the peasant to purchase inputs at favorable prices while his own output prices were maintained by a more benevolent government. Of course this is not the whole story. As measured here, external inducements only slowed down in the interwar period; they never became an adverse factor. By contrast, the internal growth potential deteriorated much more sharply. Once traditional technology had reached its peak and once it had been diffused nationally and given the continued unfavorable man-land ratio, there was little room for progress. The combination of feeble external inducements and internal weakness resulted in the long stagnation.

Advantages of Larger-Scale Production

Let us begin by establishing an important fact: before World War II net product per worker in agriculture was not strongly associated with the size of the unit of production; after World War II this association became very marked. We shall attempt to show that this development was due to a change in the "state of the art," i.e. the new possibilities of mechanical and engineering improvements.

A sample of the state of affairs in a recent post-war year (1964) is shown in Table 4.11, and it suggests the greater current efficiency of larger-scale production. Net product per worker, either per hour or per year, rises together with the scale of cultivation, and the same applies to

TABLE 4.11
Productivity by Size of Farm, 1964

Scale (chō)	Net product (yen)[a] Per land	Net product (yen)[a] Per labor-hour	Net product (yen)[a] Per worker	K/L (yen)	K per 0.1 chō (yen)	L per 0.1 chō (hours)
1. Under 0.5	¥50,951	¥75	¥120,192	¥234,871	¥41,957	679
2. 0.5–1.0	47,857	96	168,356	301,955	85,352	495
3. 1.0–1.5	42,097	110	201,544	336,100	70,202	381
4. 1.5–2.0	37,827	124	230,607	360,210	59,086	306
5. 2.0–2.5	34,370	143	254,478	340,909	46,044	241
6. 2.5–3.0	34,296	158	284,517	347,912	41,938	217
7. Over 3.0	34,517	200	352,050	372,608	34,516	163
8. Average	40,206	115	208,101	326,113	63,929	350

Source: Japan, Ministry of Agriculture and Forestry, *Ruikeibetsu nōka keizai tōkei* (Farm Economy Survey by Type of Farm; 1966), vol. 8.
Note: This survey provides several classifications of farm households. The ones used here are *sengyō*–farm households *excluding* part-time farmers.
Notation: 1 chō = 2.45 acres = .992 hectares. K, capital stock; L, number of workers or working hours.
[a] Net product is comparable to the net national product concept.

the level of capital intensity. By contrast, net product per unit of land, or partial average land productivity, decreases from class (1) to class (5) and then remains almost unchanged. However, the rise in labor productivity as scale increases and the corresponding decline in land productivity is not at all symmetrical: the gain in output per worker outweighs the loss in output per unit of land. For example, with class (1) as one hundred, in class (5) Y/L rises to 212 while net land product declines to 67.[22] We must also note that, per unit of land, capital and labor are used much more intensively as the unit of production becomes smaller; combined with lower labor productivity this strongly suggests that the amount of arable land and efficient use of factors are closely related.[23] As a whole, this evidence suggests the existence of scale economies in postwar agriculture and this has been confirmed by some recent and more formal econometric studies.[24]

[22] In some ways, this is a regional matter. Declines are especially noticeable in the Kantō and Nansei regions. They are much less evident in Tōhoku and Kansai.

[23] All of the above is based on a 1964 survey. A similar survey for 1960 indicates that the situation was the same. It can be assumed that, for this purpose, 1964 was a representative postwar year.

[24] Two of these are especially relevant. Y. Yuize applied a production function of the Cobb-Douglas type and computed the scale factors (a) when labor input is measured by the size of the labor force, 1.01 for 1952, 1.263 for 1958, 1.075 for 1960, and 1.170 for 1962, and (b) when labor is measured in labor hours, 1.150 for 1952, 1.200 for 1958, 1.197 for 1960, and 1.206 for 1962. In general, the sum of the elasticities of labor, capital, and land exceed unity by 0.15 to 0.20. See Yuize, "Nōgyō ni okeru kyoshiteki seisankansū no keisoku" (Measurement of the Aggregate

That the pre–World War II situation was different can be seen in Tables 4.12 and 4.13. Obviously the direction of postwar trends was already established: product per worker increased while product per unit of land decreased as the farms grew larger. But this is not nearly as important as the extent to which these changes took place. Compared to postwar agriculture, product per worker in prewar Japan was much less closely related to scale, while net product per unit of land dropped at least as sharply. These findings imply weak or absent economies of scale, and once more this is supported by some more formal econometric studies.[25]

Postwar Mechanization

The rising advantage of larger units must be connected with the postwar spread of the third type of agricultural technology, farm mechanization. In an indirect manner, this is already obvious if one looks again at Table 4.9. In prewar Japan the rate of growth of agricultural capital stock was low and declining because peasant production was almost entirely a matter of primitive tools, generous applications of chemical fertilizer, and many strong and able hands. And then, in the 1950's, the figures indicate an enormous increase in the growth of capital stock combined with quite rapid decreases of the agricultural labor force. At the very least this suggests that capital was being substituted for labor, and this is a process normally associated with mechanization.

More direct evidence is the pattern of adoption of power tillers, certainly the most important single item of mechanized farm equipment developed for rice cultivation after· the war. Already during the 1950's power tillers were in use both in small and large farms, but in relative terms their use was much greater among the larger units. This trend continued in the 1960's, with farms of all sizes making greater use of power tillers, and the biggest absolute gains were registered by larger units. Use of power tillers also increased while hours of labor input

---

Production Function in Agriculture), *Nōgyō sōgō kenkyū* (October 1964), no. 18, p. 308.

H. Kaneda's recent results are very similar. Covering the period 1952–61, he combined time series and cross-section observations in ten agricultural districts excluding Hokkaidō. His measured output elasticities are 0.314 (0.025) for land, 0.523 (0.042) for labor, and 0.407 (0.053) for capital. See "The Sources and Rates of Productivity Gains in Japanese Agriculture as Compared with the U.S. Experience," *Journal of Farm Economics*, vol. 49, no. 5 (Dec. 1967), pp. 1443–51.

[25] Using a Cobb-Douglas production function based on cross-section data, Ohkawa measured scale factors for rice (1937–39), 0.979, and for wheat and barley (1940–41), 1.023. See *Shokuryō-keizai no riron to keisoku* (Theory and Management of Food Economy; Tokyo, 1945), chaps. 8 and 9.

TABLE 4.12
Net Farm Product per Input by Scale of Farm Operation, 1922–40

Period	0.5–1.0 chō (1)	1.0–1.5 chō (2)	1.5–2.0 chō (3)	Over 2.0 chō (4)
	Net Product *(Yen)* per 100 Hours of Labor Input			
1922–26	10.6 (100)	11.7 (110)	13.0 (123)	13.1 (123)
1927–30	11.0 (100)	13.5 (123)	13.7 (125)	13.0 (119)
1932–36	11.6 (100)	13.9 (119)	13.0 (112)	14.6 (126)
1937–40	13.8 (100)	16.3 (118)	16.5 (119)	19.5 (141)
Average	(100)	(117)	(119)	(127)
	Net Product *(Yen)* per Unit Area of Cultivated Land			
1922–26	76.4 (100)	68.5 (89)	55.5 (73)	49.4 (64)
1927–30	72.5 (100)	71.6 (99)	58.1 (80)	46.5 (64)
1932–36	74.8 (100)	68.5 (92)	60.5 (81)	54.0 (72)
1937–40	83.1 (100)	79.4 (95)	73.4 (88)	66.3 (79)
Average	(100)	(94)	(81)	(70)

Source: K. Kamiya, ed., *Keizaihatten to nōgyō mondai* (Economic Development and Problems of Agriculture; Tokyo, 1959), Table 6, p. 346.

TABLE 4.13
*Prewar and Postwar Relative Land and Labor Productivities
with Respect to Farm Scale*
(0.5–1.0 chō = 100)

Scale (chō)	Net product per worker			Net product per unit of land		
	Prewar ave.	1960	1964	Prewar ave.	1960	1964
1. Under 0.5	–	78	75	–	105	106
2. 0.5–1.0	100	100	100	100	100	100
3. 1.0–1.5	117	118	114	94	93	88
4. 1.5–2.0	119 ⎤		129	87 ⎤		79
5. 2.0–2.5 ⎤	127 ⎦ ⊢ 152		149 ⎤	70 ⎦ ⊢ 88		72
6. 2.5–3.0 ⎦			164 ⊢			72
7. Over 3.0			208 ⎦			72

Source: For 1960 and 1964, see Table 4.11. For prewar data, see Table 4.12.

declined. This process of substitution, applied to all size classes, and the absolute hours of labor-saving were positively correlated with size of establishment.

The most meaningful measure of mechanization is the labor-machine ratio (a reciprocal of capital intensity in terms of input hours) contained in Panel C of Table 4.14. In the 1950's, according to this measure, the ratio ranged from 8.90 for the smallest farms to 2.51 for the largest farms.

TABLE 4.14
Rates of Utilization of Power Tillers and Differences
of Labor Input by Farm Scale in Rice Farming
(Tōhoku district only)

Class of farms by scale (chō)	0.3-0.5 (1)	0.5-1.0 (2)	1.0-1.5 (3)	1.5-2.0 (4)	2.0 & over (5)
A. Hours of machine use per year					
1957–59 average	19	46	107	160	306
1963–64 average	44	87	174	257	376
Increase	25	41	67	97	70
B. Hours of labor input per year					
1957–59 average	179	336	498	602	773
1962–64 average	126	251	387	473	589
Decrease	53	85	111	129	184
C. B/A, ratio of man-hour to machine-hour					
1957–59 average	8.90	8.19	3.91	3.76	2.51
1962–64 average	2.86	2.88	2.22	1.84	1.57

Source: Keizō Tsuchiya, "Economics of Mechanization in Small-Scale Agriculture," a paper presented to the International Conference on Agriculture and Economic Development, Tokyo, July 3–7, 1967.

During the ensuing half-decade, this differential became much smaller, although it still remained on the order of two to one for 1962–64.

Two general points are suggested by these results. Mechanization is associated with the substitution of machines for labor in such a manner as to favor larger units. At the same time, the pattern of power tiller adoption shows that small farms were also able to mechanize, and have been doing so especially rapidly in the 1960's. Does this contradict the distinction made between the various types of agricultural technology and the particular connection between mechanical and engineering innovations and economies of scale?

In many ways, farm machinery, "lumpy" investments, and scale economies are only just beginning to affect Japanese agriculture; their full impact will be felt only in the future (and only if Japan continues to produce a major share of its own basic food requirements). Until recently, the share of machinery in the capital stock of agriculture was still very small: it was 7 percent in 1954 and 23 percent in 1962.[26] In practice, the partial and incomplete nature of farm mechanization has meant that economies to be gained from larger-scale operations are still rather weak, though certainly stronger than they were before World

[26] LTES, vol. 9, Table 28, p. 211.

TABLE 4.15
Changes in Distribution of Farms by Scale
(Excluding part-time farmers)

Farm class	1955		1960		Change in percentage
	No. (000)	Percent	No. (000)	Percent	
1. Under 0.5 chō	358	17.6%	339	17.3%	−0.3%
2. 0.5–1.0	732	36.2	657	33.7	−2.5
3. 1.0–1.5	545	26.9	536	27.5	0.6
4. Over 1.5	390	19.3	420	21.5	2.2
Total	2,025	100.0%	1,952	100.0%	0.0%

Source: S. Kawano, ed., *Nōgyō mondai* (Agricultural problems; Tokyo, 1963), chap. 2.

War II, and many operations, particularly replanting and harvesting, are still largely carried out by traditional labor-intensive methods. This need not remain true indefinitely, and further improvements in the man-land ratio make it highly probable that incentives for larger-scale operation will continue to rise.

The current situation of initial mechanization—with so many operations as yet traditional—also means that small units are still in a position to take advantage of new methods. This is especially true for power tillers, whose indivisibility can be mitigated through contract (*ukeoi*) and cooperative arrangements. In this way the small farmer need not bear the impossible costs of individual ownership while he can get mechanized help especially at periods of peak labor demand when rural wages are particularly high.

By now, however, there can be little doubt about the higher labor productivity prevailing on larger farms, and if market forces are operating, one should expect a change in scale distribution in this direction. The fact that this has happened is shown in Table 4.15 for the years 1955–60. Units under 1 chō became relatively less numerous, and units with over 1.5 chō increased most rapidly. On the whole, however, the change in size structure has been rather slow—somehow slower than one would have expected it to be on the basis of purely economic reasoning.

In fact, a number of noneconomic factors have been responsible for acting as a brake on the pace of agricultural mechanization and modernization. All of these share the quality of being inimical toward increasing the scale of production. No doubt one of the most important was the statutory limitation on farm size—under 3 hectares, with the exception of 12 hectares on Hokkaidō—introduced by the American-sponsored postwar land reform.[27] Another adverse factor has been the growing asset preference of farmers who are expecting future increases in land prices. Likewise, the fact that farming has become for many a part-time and supplementary occupation has allowed many small-time cultivators to keep their heads above water. Finally, government policy has also prevented a better allocation of resources and a rise in economic efficiency, especially through domestic price supports of rice and protection against agricultural imports.

We have no wish to stress unduly these institutional barriers. Mechanization has just started and is proceeding slowly, primarily because absorbing a surplus labor force is a very slow process. When labor becomes a scarcer factor in agriculture, institutions will without question adapt themselves to the new situation. For this to take place, some time must pass, but it is part of Japan's intermediate-range future. Thus, the recent high rates of growth of output must still be seen as a combination of biological and chemical advances available under especially favorable conditions, together with the beginnings of mechanization. It is our expectation that in the next few decades mechanization will play a much larger role.

The Agricultural Residual

In order to complete the picture of agriculture, and to make it fully comparable to other sectors, we conclude with a brief look at this sectoral residual, as shown in Table 4.16. These measures are necessarily rather rough,[28] but the pattern of crude residual growth is in accord with the findings presented up to now. The weakening of traditional technological progress emerges plainly, as does the era of new opportunities in

[27] Did the land reform favorably affect productivity growth in Japanese agriculture? It is not easy to give a precise answer, since no one has yet succeeded in disentangling the effects of land reform from other factors affecting postwar agriculture. We believe that the influence was favorable under conditions of traditional scale and organization. But the reform has certainly restricted the development of scale economies by placing the traditional tiny holdings on a firmer basis. For a more detailed discussion of this problem, see the relevant chapters in K. Ohkawa, B. F. Johnston, and H. Kaneda, eds., *Agriculture and Economic Growth: Japan's Experience* (Princeton, N.J., and Tokyo, 1970).

[28] Rates of increase are simple "bridge" computations between trough and peak years, based on smoothed series in constant prices. The use of constant elasticities, especially for the long prewar period, could lead to certain doubts, but lack of an adequate data base makes this an unavoidable procedure. There is one computation, restricted to rice farming, for 1888–1901. It indicates elasticities very similar to Ohkawa's results: 0.215 for labor, 0.154 for fertilizer, and 0.631 for land. See M. Shintani, "Meiji chūki suitō seisan ni kansuru sūryō bunseki" (Quantitative Analysis of Rice Production in the Middle Meiji Era), *Nōgyō keizai kenkyū*, vol. 42, no. 3 (Dec. 1970).

TABLE 4.16
Average Annual Growth Rates of the Agricultural Residual
(Percent)

Period	βG_L	αG_K	γG_B	G_I	G_Y	G_R
1901–17	–0.03%	0.43%	0.33%	0.73%	1.91%	1.18%
1917–31	0.00	0.29	0.06	0.35	0.44	0.09
1931–37	–0.08	0.20	0.13	0.25	0.53	0.28
1956–62	–1.20	1.26	0.04	0.10	4.06	3.96
1962–64	–0.78	1.66	–0.08	1.30	1.18	–0.12

Source: Table 4.9. Elasticities (α, β, γ) from Ohkawa, *Shokuryokeizai,* for the prewar period, and from Kaneda, "Sources and Rates of Productivity Gains," for the postwar period.
  Notation:
    L = number of workers.
    K = capital stock.
    B = arable land (unweighted).
    Y = output gross of capital depreciation.
    $G_I = \alpha G_K + \beta G_L + \gamma G_B$.
    α = output elasticity of capital = 0.286 prewar and 0.328 postwar.
    β = output elasticity of labor = 0.280 prewar and 0.430 postwar.
    γ = output elasticity of land = 0.430 prewar and 0.242 postwar.

the 1950's. At this point one must be extremely cautious concerning the negative values of G_R for 1962–64. The period is too short to be used as a basis of interpretation; but it could be an early sign of declining efficiency in Japanese farming, unless a basic transformation occurs soon.

If these residuals are to be adjusted—a task not to be attempted here—it is obvious that accounting for the progress of biological and chemical technology will have a considerable effect. Recent studies suggest that reducing the size of the residual by measuring the contribution of nonconventional inputs can be done with greater success in agriculture than in nonagriculture.[29]

THE EFFECTS OF REALLOCATION

In considering aggregate and sectoral residuals, especially in the context of a two-sector model, there is a problem that we have not yet dealt with—the effects of reallocation.

We have already studied the "attached" qualities of input factors in detail. There exists also an "unattached" effect, namely the reallocation or shift of factors of production within the economy, and its effects will be measured now. Two forms of reallocation will be considered: movements of workers from smaller to larger enterprises within manufacturing, and movements from agriculture to nonagriculture. In theory,

[29] For example, see M. Akino and Y. Hayami, "Sources of Agricultural Growth in Japan, 1880–1965," a paper presented to the Conference on Economic Growth sponsored by the Japan Economic Research Center, Tokyo, June 26–July 1, 1972.

it is clear that both labor and capital can participate in the type of shifts described above. The case of capital, however, is in practice very complicated, and no operational measurements appear possible at this point. Capital is much less mobile than labor, and reallocation of capital may involve big losses that have to be taken into account. We do know that in Japan a significant amount of reallocation of capital does take place, as in the use of secondhand machinery by small-scale industry, but how to measure the effects of all this is beyond our ability at this time.

In order to measure reallocation effects, it will in general be necessary to assume that a proportionality exists between the marginal product and the wages of labor. Insofar as we shall be dealing with postwar nonagriculture, we believe (as shown in the Appendix Note) that the discrepancy between wages and marginal product is not unduly large. We are less confident about prewar years. The case is very different for agriculture, where another method will have to be adopted.

In the case of labor, three types of reallocation should probably be considered: from one industry to another, from smaller to larger establishments, and from unincorporated to corporate enterprise. In principle, all of these could encompass movement from occupations of lower to higher productivity. Actually we will present results only for the establishment and organizational breakdown. There are two reasons for this decision. First, the data are very limited even for postwar years. Second, a considerable overlap must exist between movement from one type of industry to another and movement from smaller to larger enterprise. Either one of these computations should catch the main effect of this shift, and it is more convenient to work with the data pertaining to scale of establishments.

Labor Movement to Larger Enterprises Within Manufacturing

To begin with postwar years, information concerning movements of workers to establishments of different size is confined to manufacturing and is based on *Kōgyō tōkei-hyō* (Census of Manufactures). The initial measurements are confined to 1955–61 and are presented in Table 4.17, which shows the distribution of workers and their wage levels for various sizes of establishments. An inspection of the table readily reveals the nature of manufacturing reallocation during the investment spurt. Throughout these years, and indeed until today, the proportion of Japanese manufacturing workers in small and medium establishments (let us say with fewer than 100 workers) remains very large.[30] Yet it declined

[30] See "The Growth of Factory Production" above, p. 80.

TABLE 4.17
Distribution of Workers and Wage Earnings by Establishment
Size in Manufacturing, 1955 and 1961

No. of workers	Wage earnings (¥000/mo.)				Number of workers (000)				Average annual rate of increase of workers (percent)
	1955		1961		1955		1961		
	Amount	Percent	Amount	Percent	1955	Percent	1961	Percent	
4-9	87.3	54.5%	143.9	55.7%	549	11.09%	626	7.60%	2.21%
10-29	110.3	68.9	188.5	72.9	1,187	23.93	1,678	20.64	7.49
30-99	133.3	83.3	223.3	86.5	1,027	20.72	1,692	20.77	8.68
100-499	175.0	109.4	260.6	101.0	1,017	20.51	1,909	23.48	10.60
500-999	217.1	135.7	310.1	120.2	374	7.54	665	8.16	10.10
Over 999	269.9	168.8	391.5	151.7	805	16.23	1,568	19.27	11.73
Average	159.7	100.0%	258.1	100.0%	4,958	100.0%	8,139	100.0%	8.61%

Source: Annual issues of KTH.

TABLE 4.18
Distribution of Workers and Wage Earnings by Establishment
Size in Manufacturing, 1909–38
(In relatives)

Class	Wage earnings			Number of workers			
	1909	1919	1931	1909	1919	1931	1938
Small (4–49)	100	70.0	46.6	45.7	34.0	37.6	36.4
Medium (50–499)	100	90.0	76.7	33.6	34.5	37.7	27.4
Large (500 and over)	100	140.0	183.0	20.7	31.5	25.7	36.2
Total or average	100	100	100	100	100	100	100

Source: Wages for 1909 and 1919 from KTH; for 1931 from M. Umemura, Chingin, koyō nōgyō (Wages, Employment, and Agriculture; Tokyo, 1961), pp. 209–10. Number of workers from KTH.

during the spurt: from about 56 percent to 50 percent. Furthermore, the establishments adding labor at the most rapid rate were the larger units, and especially those employing over 1,000 workers.[31] At the same time, wage differentials by size of establishment persisted throughout the period, although they did become somewhat smaller. If the assumption of proportionality between marginal productivity and wages is anywhere near the mark, it is clear that as a result of the reallocation of labor, productivity and hence "the residual" will be raised.

The method of measurement is identical to the one employed previously in determining the rate of growth of labor quality. We simply compute an index (base 1955) comparing the structure of employment in manufacturing weighted by the wage distribution in 1961 and 1955. For example, if 1955 wages are used, the index is 105.16 in 1961 and grows at 0.85 percent per year. If 1961 wages are used, the index is 104.19. When the average of base and given year wages is used, the rate of growth of the index is 0.77 percent per year.

We will assume that these increases are ascribable only to the reallocation of labor as a result of movement from smaller to larger units. This is a simplification because we know that wage scales also reflect differences in age, sex, and educational levels. One has to assume that these factors are pretty much the same for all scales of enterprise, or at least that distortions created by these differences are not too large.

Materials for assessing prewar reallocation are very limited. The basic source of information for prewar years remains the Census of Manufactures available since 1909, which shows the distribution of workers within establishments of differing sizes. In order to treat the materials consistently, since classifications have changed from time to time, it is possible to examine the movement of workers only for very broadly grouped establishments. Wage differentials by size of establishment are even harder to obtain. The census provides such information only for 1909 and 1914. In addition, M. Umemura has made estimates for manufacturing and commerce in 1932.[32] His method determined size by the amount of invested capital, rather than in terms of numbers of workers, and we shall have to assume that this does not affect the results to any significant degree. On a more general level, we also know that the differential structure in Japan became noticeable at the time of World

[31] Tables 4.17 and 4.18 indicate the rising share of large-scale employment in the 1930's, and its subsequent decline after World War II. For an explanation, see pp. 86–87 above.

[32] *Chingin, koyō, nōgyō* (Wages, Employment, and Agriculture; Tokyo, 1961), pp. 209–10. These calculations were based on an official survey of the period that was confined to big cities.

War I and its effects were especially accentuated during the 1920's. As shown in Chapter 5, wage differentials were gradually increasing during the 1920's and the early 1930's.

Table 4.18 contains our attempts to reconstruct the prewar wage and employment structure. Necessarily, it is a mixture of fact and assumption. Let us first look at the wage differentials by scale in 1909. In fact, the statistics begin only in 1909 and at that time the differentials were negligible. The 1919 figures are an adjusted version of the 1914 results. The latter indicate a spread from small to large scale, going from 89 to 110. We have widened the spread to account for growing wage differentials during World War I. For 1931 we simply applied the Umemura results obtained for 1932. As mentioned previously, no usable wage differentials are available for 1938. Here we simply assumed that the differentials remained the same as in 1931.

With these data one obtains the following average annual growth rate of crude reallocation indexes (average of base and given year weights for each period): 0.34 percent for 1905–19, −0.39 percent for 1919–31, and 1.17 percent for 1931–38. A few words of amplification may be of some help. First of all, it should be noted that the growth of the reallocation indexes is, prewar and postwar, positively correlated with long swings in investment and output. Certainly the high value for 1931–38 and the negative value for 1919–31 stand out. Both are plausible results. During the 1920's, large and modern industry took on only few additional workers, and this forced new entrants into relatively lower-productivity occupations. In effect this was a reallocation in reverse. During the 1930's, when wage differentials were already large, the somewhat "unnatural" expansion of heavy industry raised the index far above its usual level. It was a higher level than obtained for postwar years.

We can now assess the relative contribution of labor reallocation in manufacturing by comparing the crude shift effect, G_S, with the crude residuals obtained previously, G_R for manufacturing, as shown in Table 4.19. Although there are small differences in the periodization of G_S and G_R, and shifts have not been estimated after 1961, the findings stand out clearly. For every period, and relative to the crude residual, the consequences of labor reallocation have been distinctly minor, despite the fact that our shift measures are maximal since they take no account of age, sex, and educational differences among small and large establishments. We conclude that the reallocation of workers *within modern industry* (as exemplified by manufacturing) had but little influence on either aggregate G_R or G_Y. Indeed, this is not a surprising result. As

TABLE 4.19
*Labor Reallocation in Manufacturing: Average Annual
Rates of Growth*
(Percent)

Category	1908–17	1917–31	1931–38	1955–61
G_S	0.34%	–0.39%	1.17%	0.77%
βG_S	0.17	–0.23	0.68	0.50
$G_{R(M)}$	2.30	2.21	5.65	7.89

Note: G_S is an index of average weights; βG_S figures are from Table 4.2.

pointed out in Chapter 5, the Japanese wage-employment system discourages this type of transfer. We shall see immediately that the major shifts occurred by laborers leaving agriculture.

Labor Movement from Agriculture to Nonagriculture

This situation requires separate and different treatment because, as demonstrated later, it is not possible to assume proportionality between wages and the marginal product of labor. In the literature the common practice has been to compute aggregate residuals (including agriculture), then to estimate the shift from agriculture to nonagriculture, and finally to use these results for purposes of adjustment. We have serious doubts about the appropriateness of these procedures in a differential structure setting. Adjustments for the inequality of wages and marginal product are extremely complex and greatly affect the residuals. That is one reason we have preferred throughout to deal with agriculture as a distinct sector. None of this implies that shifts originating in the net outflow of agricultural workers can be neglected. On the contrary, they are of great importance and can be evaluated by our methods without diminishing the quality of previous measurements.

The reallocation of agricultural workers has been estimated with the following formula:

$$G_{SA} = \overline{W}_1 \beta_1 (G_{L1} - G_L) + \overline{W}_2 \beta_2 (G_{L2} - G_L)$$

G_{SA} is the shift effect of labor between the two sectors, $\overline{W}$ is the weight or sectoral share of output, L is labor employed, G_L is labor's average annual rate of change, and β is the output elasticity of labor. Suffix 1 denotes nonagriculture, suffix 2 denotes agriculture, and no suffix is the aggregate.[33] Agriculture's output elasticity for labor (η) is used for β_2

[33] For a derivation of this equation, see K. Ohkawa, "Makuro seisansei jyōshō eno seisan yōso haibun hendo no koka" (Reallocation Effects of Production Factors), *Keizai kenkyū*, vol. 18, no. 4 (Oct. 1967). The logic of the formulation can

TABLE 4.20
*Effect of the Reallocation of Labor from Agriculture
to Nonagriculture: Average Annual Growth Rate*
(Percent)

Period	$\overline{W}_1\beta_1(G_{L1}-G_L)$ (1)	$+ \; \overline{W}_2\beta_2(G_{L2}-G_L)$ (2)	$= \; G_{SA}$ (3)
1905–19	0.72%	−0.09%	0.63%
1919–31	0.35	−0.10	0.25
1931–38	0.71	−0.10	0.61
1952–55	1.26	−0.50	0.76
1955–61	1.88	−0.42	1.46
1961–65	1.26	−0.19	1.07

instead of the income share, avoiding the use of agricultural wages as a substitute for marginal product. Adopted values of η are 0.28 for the entire prewar period, 0.43 for 1955–61, and 0.355 (an average of prewar and postwar estimates) for 1952–55.[34]

Results of measurement appear in Table 4.20. The first term (1) estimates the positive contribution to total productivity stemming from labor moving from a lower to a higher productivity sector. The second term (2) measures the associated negative effect in agriculture when a decrease of workers lowered output. And the net effect for the economy is shown in column (3). Negative effects, caused by people leaving agriculture, have never been a major problem. That they have increased in the postwar period is understandable, because even in Japan the agricultural population is getting smaller. Positive effects are much more significant throughout the century and especially since the 1950's. The net effect has certainly been large since the war, both absolutely[35] and

be briefly summarized as follows. (1) Previously, βG_L was used as a measure of labor's contribution, and this is again done here. (2) Taking G_L as a standard, we assume that if no shift takes place $G_{L1} = G_{L2} = G_L$ so that $G_{SA} = 0$. The degree of shift from agriculture to nonagriculture is given by $G_{L1} - G_{L2} = S$. As S increases, the positive values of $G_{L1} - G_L$ will grow bigger, and the negative values of $G_{L2} - G_L$ will also be bigger. (3) Thus, a positive contribution of $\beta_1 (G_{L1} - G_L)$ and a negative contribution of $\beta_2 (G_{L2} - G_L)$ are computed to balance both effects, with weights of output shares.

[34] Basic estimates from Kaneda and Yuize for postwar years and from Ohkawa, *Shokuryōkeizai*, for the prewar period. The values of η accord with our historical assessment that there were no significant changes in the lengthy prewar period, that η started climbing around 1955, and that it probably occupied an intermediate position during the rehabilitation years. Direct evidence on this last point is not available.

[35] The rate of growth of GDP in the United Kingdom has not been much higher in the past decade or so.

relative to the magnitude of aggregate nonagricultural residuals. Obviously the possibility of effecting these shifts was one of Japan's economic advantages in recent years.[36]

---

[36] No measurements will be presented for shifts from unincorporated to incorporated enterprises. These entail practical and conceptual difficulties. Statistics are confined to the postwar period—that is one great disadvantage. More to the point, if the estimates are made by assuming that wages and marginal product are proportional in unincorporated units, an underestimation of reallocation is almost certain. Most probably, the effects of these shifts will resemble the agriculture/nonagriculture movement. Both are facets of the same thing: the transfer from traditional to increasingly modern employment.

CHAPTER FIVE

Demand and Supply for Labor in a Dualistic Economy

Many foreign observers, and most of all foreign businessmen, look at postwar Japan as a kind of "paradise." Perhaps no factor is more responsible for this assessment than the labor situation. At a time when most of the economically advanced world faced severe labor difficulties—short supplies, conflict, cost push, etc.—there seemed to be nothing comparable in Japan. To be sure, there were occasional strikes of very short duration, and the rhetoric of conflict was frequently in evidence. There was even talk of impending "labor shortages." Nevertheless, two generalizations hold. First, from the viewpoint of modern enterprise, the postwar labor supply has been extremely favorable — certainly until 1965. Industry had little difficulty in securing the needed quantities of disciplined, loyal, and skillful workers at reasonable wages. Second, in a broad sense this generalization can apply also to the years between 1900 and World War II. It would have to be qualified, and any student of labor history could undoubtedly cite exceptional counterexamples. The fundamental point, however, remains unchanged: during the twentieth century the supply of qualified labor never was a constraint in the development of modern industry. As a preliminary item of evidence, the reader may examine Figure 5.1, where the historical relations between the growth of real wages (deflated by output prices) and labor productivity are traced between 1908 and 1965 for the private nonagricultural sector. During all the upswings, productivity rose much more rapidly than wages, and, other things being equal, most entrepreneurs would feel that this is one of the desirable components of their heaven on earth.[1]

[1] The growth of labor productivity at a higher rate than real wages—both deflated by an index of output prices—has been observed in Japan and in Western countries during business cycle upturns. Our discussion instead focuses on the long swing (Figure 5.1), where we believe the wage lag to be peculiar to Japan. For a comparison with the United States, see Ryūzo Sato, *Keizai seichō no riron* (The Theory of Economic Growth; Tokyo, 1968), Table II.1, p. 302.

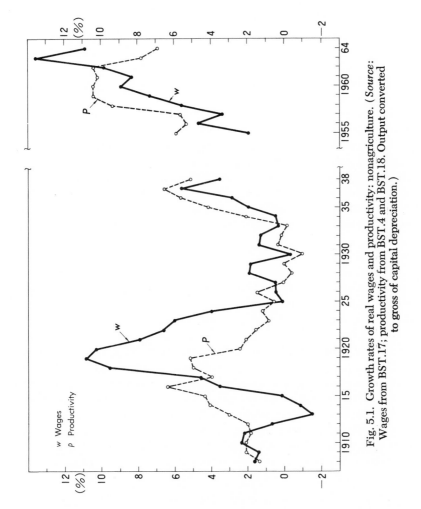

Fig. 5.1. Growth rates of real wages and productivity: nonagriculture. (*Source:*
Wages from BST.4 and BST.18. Output converted
to gross of capital depreciation.)

The demand and supply for labor are by their very nature a broad problem; they can be dealt with from many points of view. An entrepreneur's paradise may be a worker's hell. Sociological and psychological considerations loom large, especially in Japan, where the system of labor relations has retained many idiosyncratic cultural features. Problems of labor are also intensely political, and sometimes there is little resemblance between socialist and capitalist versions of the same problems. In Japan, as in other countries, when it comes to aspects of labor welfare, i.e. labor's gains from industrialization, one can find optimistic and pessimistic schools.

We have chosen a narrower perspective to deal with this range of issues, one that avoids many of the difficult value judgments and follows the preview of Chapter 2. In that chapter we hypothesized that private investment was the most dynamic element in modern economic growth, and that it was a function of the expected rate of return on capital. In turn, we assumed that a wage lag had a favorable effect on the rate of return. Now we shall take up the relations of capital and labor in greater detail.[2] Before getting into specifics of the analysis, it is desirable to provide a general description of the main historical trends as contained in Tables 5.1 and 5.2.

The population of Japan started to grow again in the late Tokugawa era, and throughout the late nineteenth and early twentieth centuries the natural rate rose slightly. A peak was attained at the beginning of the 1930's, when population expanded at about 1.5 percent per year, and with the exception of the immediate aftermath of World War II, the rate of population growth has been declining.[3] Today, Japan's natural rate of increase is among the lowest in the world. Furthermore, neither emigration nor immigration was a significant consideration, so that the demographic patterns have to be explained almost entirely in domestic terms.

As expected, working age population trends reflected growth of the total population. The proportion of working age people rose slowly throughout most of the century, and then much more rapidly after the war as a consequence of a higher rate of natural increase in the 1930's

[2] In the final chapter, wider implications of the labor supply situation, particularly after 1965, will be discussed.

[3] See Tables 2.1, 2.2, and 2.6. The postwar bulge was due to the loss of colonies and repatriation of overseas citizens. Until 1955, 6.3 million Japanese—roughly split evenly between civilians and military personnel—were repatriated from overseas. The most active repatriation years were 1945–48, when a total of 6.1 million people returned. (Japanese nationals repatriated from the United States, Canada, and South America are excluded.) See Japan, *Nihon tōkei nenkan* (Japan Statistical Yearbook), 1955/56, p. 33.

TABLE 5.1

Working Age Population and Participation Ratio

(Percent)

Year	Working age pop./ total pop.[a] (1)	Participation ratio[b] (2)	Labor force ratio (1) x (2)
1905	75.0	71.3	53.5
1920	74.5	65.5	48.8
1925	75.7	63.1	47.7
1930	74.0	62.1	45.9
1935	74.2	60.7	45.1
1940	75.0	60.2	45.2
1948	75.6	59.3	44.8
1950	75.1	57.9	44.8
1955	77.3	59.6	46.1
1960	81.8	58.4	47.7
1965	84.6	57.7	48.8

Source: Working age population from LTES, vol. 2; total population and labor force from BST.15.

Note: Series smoothed by seven-year moving average prewar and five-year moving average postwar.

[a] Before World War II, the working age population was defined as anyone over 10 years of age. The postwar definition includes people between the ages of 15 and 65.

[b] Labor force/working age population.

TABLE 5.2

Rates of Change in the Labor Force
by Industry

(Percent)

Period	Manufacturing	Facilitating industries	Construction	Services	Non-agriculture	Agriculture
			Unweighted			
1908–17	3.12%	1.91%	1.88%	2.23%	2.37%	−0.05%
1912–18	3.89	3.56	1.25	2.20	2.79	−0.84
1918–31	2.29	1.06	1.42	2.01	1.97	−0.26
1932–38	3.70	0.52	1.32	1.43	2.68	−0.25
1955–61	5.29	5.82	7.46	3.81	4.81	−2.34
1962–64	4.00	6.07	5.17	4.11	4.29	−3.72
		Weighted (nonagriculture only)[a]				
1908–17	1.23	0.12	0.13	1.04		
1912–18	1.55	0.22	0.09	1.03		
1918–31	0.96	0.06	0.10	0.91		
1932–38	1.65	0.02	0.08	0.64		
1955–61	2.08	0.34	0.41	1.74		
1962–64	1.58	0.38	0.51	1.82		

Source: BST.15 (excluding the public sector).

Note: Rates of change are simple averages of annual rates of growth.

[a] Weights are the number of workers in each industry.

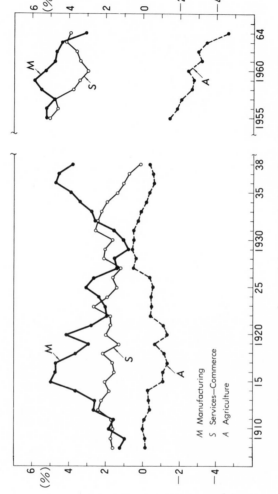

Fig. 5.2. Average annual rates of change in the labor force. (*Source*: BST.15. Public sector excluded.)

and repatriation. The participation ratio (labor force/working age population) has also followed an entirely normal path. It declined, as economic development proceeded, owing to a wider spread and longer duration of education. In combination, these factors created unprecedented growth of the labor force in the postwar years.[4]

Discussion of the industrial or sectoral distribution of Japan's labor force has usually focused on the transfer of workers from traditional to modern sectors. In its simplistic form, one merely observes that the absolute numbers engaged in agriculture remained virtually stable for the entire prewar period. Therefore, net increases of population and labor force "produced" in agriculture were entirely absorbed by the nonagricultural sectors. Some believe that the absorptive powers of nonagriculture were weak, otherwise the absolute numbers in agriculture would have declined. Others can take the view that the absorptive powers were in fact strong since in most other developed countries the agricultural labor force rose absolutely until the 1920's. "Weak" and "strong" are relative concepts, and difficult to make precise. They do, however, point to the essence of the problem. The shift of labor from traditional sectors is the combined result of many different forces, which we will attempt to identify in subsequent sections. But before turning to the mechanism of transfer, a few historical details are needed.

Manufacturing, agriculture, and commerce-services took in labor at different rates though in an interrelated pattern. (See Table 5.2 and Figure 5.2.) The labor force in manufacturing evolved in the familiar long-swing manner, with the expected upswings and downswings. Prewar agriculture did the opposite of manufacturing: in the upswing phase, the growth rate of the labor force declined and was sometimes negative, and in the downswing, relatively more workers entered primary occupations. Services occupied an intermediate position, and the

---

[4] The use of a "labor force" concept creates certain problems for historical analysis. Before World War II, the economic breakdown of the work force was given as "gainfully occupied population" (*yūgyō jinkō*). This does not exactly correspond to employment. Rather it refers to the "usual status" of the individual in question. There is no precise definition about how much work a person had to do in order to be counted as gainfully occupied. Persons were queried about their usual occupations and were listed accordingly. In addition, there are almost no unemployment statistics before the 1950's. For postwar years, unemployed workers are excluded and labor force statistics conform to international standards.

These problems are more apparent than real. Unemployment, usually included in standard labor force definitions, has always been low in Japan—in the postwar years it has been between 0.7 and 1.0 percent—partly because of the persistence of underemployment. The unadjusted use of these series is quite safe.

TABLE 5.3
Net Outflow of the Primary Sector Labor Force

Period	Number of workers[a] (000)	Average annual rates of change (percent)	Ratio to total increase in nonagricultural sector (percent)
1901–5	154	1.04%	68.6%
1906–10	140	0.95	62.8
1911–15	137	0.94	62.8
1916–20	178	1.21	51.6
1921–25	131	0.89	52.8
1926–30	125	0.85	50.2
1931–35	183	1.25	27.2
1936–40	152	1.40	30.5
1951–55	760	4.58	77.0
1956–60	752	5.10	67.0
1961–64	492	3.78	48.5

Source: R. Minami, "The Supply of Farm Labor and the Turning Point in the Japanese Economy," in K. Ohkawa, B. F. Johnston, and H. Kaneda, eds., *Agriculture and Economic Growth: Japan's Experience* (Princeton, N.J., and Tokyo, 1970), p. 85. The last column has been added.
[a] Annual averages for quinquennial years.

rate of change of its labor force was without a clear upward or downward trend.

An interpretation of these movements is not difficult. Manufacturing always relied on workers from agriculture, but the demand was very uneven, related, as it was, to long-term expansions and contractions. Labor supply was governed by the smoother demographic effects, and this led to the opposite reaction of agriculture. It swallowed more or less of the work force depending on opportunities elsewhere. Services were in a more dualistic position. Some parts were modern and contributed to the allocation or reallocation of workers to higher-productivity occupations. Others were traditional and performed the same function as agriculture: holding, and to varying degrees occupying, those people who could not find work in modern economic activities.[5]

More direct measures for the process of transfer from traditional to modern occupations are scarce.[6] Minami's estimates of the net labor

[5] As Table 5.2 shows, the remaining sectors—facilitating industries and construction—are insignificant in the weighted rates. It is the interplay between agriculture, services, and manufacturing that is crucial.

[6] See Henry Rosovsky and Kazushi Ohkawa, "The Indigenous Components in the Modern Japanese Economy," *Economic Development and Cultural Change*, vol. 9, no. 3 (April 1961), especially Table 4. Most attempts to quantify the traditional

force outflow from agriculture to nonagriculture (reproduced in Table 5.3) are the best available source. His figures are also, necessarily, based on certain assumptions, but the trends emerge without ambiguity. Since the proportion of the agricultural to the nonagricultural labor force declines with economic development, one expects the net outflows from agriculture to become increasingly less important to total labor force formation. At the end of the initial phase of growth nearly 70 percent of the new workers were migrants from primary occupations, and by the 1930's this had decreased to 30 percent. Much more unexpected and unprecedented are the postwar figures. With considerable suddenness, the agricultural ratio rose again to early twentieth-century levels of approximately 70 percent, owing entirely to the exceptional circumstances immediately after World War II. In 1942, 13.1 million persons were working in the primary sector. By 1951, this number had risen to 17.0 million, which was *above* the level of 16.2 million in 1902. Two related factors were responsible: large repatriations from the lost empire, and abnormally poor opportunities outside of agriculture while the economy was undergoing rehabilitation. Even in 1951–55, the increases continued and an average of 17.4 million found themselves employed (and underemployed) in primary production. Since then, of course, there has been a very rapid turnaround, and by 1961—at the end of the great postwar investment spurt—the numbers in agriculture were back down to 1935–36 levels. These recent abnormalities must have had a great impact on the nature of the postwar labor supply.

WAGE DIFFERENTIALS

When a labor surplus situation prevails in a dual economy, the marginal worker who cannot enter higher-wage modern industries normally finds employment (or partial employment) in the lower-wage traditional sectors. Under these circumstances, total unemployment is rather uncommon. The requirements for labor, however, do not remain unchanging in the modern sector, and we shall assume that wage differentials between modern and traditional sectors are a good indicator of changing demand-supply conditions in the labor market.

Before examining what happened to wages, a few words of caution are needed. Wages for "traditional" and "modern" sectors do not exist as statistical categories; wages of manufacturing and agriculture have

labor force, usually in terms of unincorporated enterprisers and family workers, have concluded that its absolute numbers have remained almost steady between 1920 and 1960.

TABLE 5.4
Wage Differentials for Selected Years

Year	Daily wages			Ratios *(percent)*		
	w_a	w_n	w_m	w_a/w_n	w_a/w_m	w_n/w_m
1905	31	41	46	75.6%	67.4%	89.1%
1910	41	53	60	77.4	68.3	88.3
1915	46	55	64	83.6	71.9	85.9
1919	120	143	144	83.9	83.3	99.3
1925	165	213	207	77.5	79.7	102.9
1931	90	140	184	64.3	48.9	76.1
1935	91	133	190	68.4	47.9	70.0
1939	171	197	240	86.8	71.3	82.1
1954	275	359	752	76.6	36.5	47.9
1960	423	49,1	1,036	86.1	40.4	47.8
1965	855	816	1,672	104.7	51.1	48.8

Source: LTES, vol. 8, pp. 243–45, and vol. 9, pp. 220–21. For 1965, Japan, Ministry of Labor, *Rōdō tōkei nempō* (Annual Report of Labor Statistics).

Note: Wage differentials are based on series smoothed with a five-year moving average except for 1965, with a three-year average. Daily wages prewar are in sen (1/100 yen) and postwar in yen.

Notation:

w_a, wages of male daily-contract workers in agriculture.

w_n, wages of male daily-contract workers in nonagriculture (construction, manufacturing, wholesale and retail trade.

w_m, average wages of regular male workers in manufacturing.

been used as proxies in the past,[7] and this creates problems. The average wage in manufacturing covers very different lines of activity associated with various levels of compensation, depending on the type and quality of the worker. As a result, the changing composition of employment will affect comparisons over time. Furthermore, the very concept of wages in something as traditional as Japanese farming may appear questionable. Japanese agriculture has only very few independent hired workers, and their wages are subject to large seasonal fluctuations. Nonwage payments in the form of food and lodging are also relatively important. All this means that these indicators had to be presented with caution. Nevertheless, we used wage differentials because they give the best available historical picture of the changing factor price position of the two sectors.

So as to avoid some of these difficulties, the comparisons have now been refined to two new classes: agricultural wages of male daily workers (w_a) and wages of daily workers in nonagriculture (w_n). This ratio (w_a/w_n), based on a more rigorous definition, is used as a proxy for

[7] K. Ohkawa and H. Rosovsky, "Postwar Japanese Economic Growth In Historical Perspective: A Second Look," in L. Klein and K. Ohkawa, eds., *Economic Growth: The Japanese Experience Since the Meiji Era* (Homewood, Ill., 1968), pp. 17–19.

general unskilled wage differentials in modern and traditional sectors. They are listed in Table 5.4, together with average wages of male workers in manufacturing (w_m).

We find that w_a/w_n moves in perfect conformity with output swings (with the exception of 1965, a problem to be considered later). It rises during expansions and falls during contractions (especially toward the end of expansions and contractions). This seems to suggest certain demand-supply relations in the labor market: wage differentials narrow when the demand for labor in the modern sector is more active, and they widen in the obverse case. This has been true also during the post–World War II expansion.[8] Furthermore, the differentials between w_a and w_n are quite narrow (except in 1935 and 1939) considering the implicit differences in costs of living. This suggests that movements out of agriculture were affected by factors other than real income differentials.

The ratio w_a/w_m presents the clearest contrast between the modern and traditional sectors. It sustains two distinct levels: a higher level through 1919 and a lower level from 1931 onward. This means that somewhere between 1919 and 1931 the relative wage of agriculture (or of the traditional sectors) fell sharply and remained in this position more or less until the early 1960's. (Indeed, this pattern closely resembles that of w_n/w_m, especially so after World War II, indicating that for a time the differential structure was strengthened owing to an enlarged labor supply.)

Relations between labor supply and demand have up to now been mentioned in three forms. First, it was observed that wages lagged behind increases in productivity.[9] Second, it was noted that wage differentials narrowed toward the end of each upswing. Last, we observed that

[8] Koji Taira, *Economic Development and the Labor Market in Japan* (New York, 1970), Part I.

[9] The wage-productivity lag—almost equivalent to a rise in the share of capital (α)—permits several interpretations. Two of these require particular attention: biased technological progress in favor of capital, and noncompetitive elements in labor markets. In Chapter 3 Hicksian neutrality was assumed for the private nonagricultural sector. If there was actually bias, the residual measurements would have to be modified.

The possibility of biased technological progress cannot be excluded, but there are two reasons why we continue to use the original assumption. First, accurate empirical evidence about the value of the elasticity of substitution is lacking. This effectively prevents a measure of bias. Second, during downswings we have noticed a decline of α, and an alternating bias in favor of capital and labor during long swings seems highly unlikely.

The second possibility, noncompetitive elements, is much more likely to have been present in the Japanese economy. These cannot be conceived in any singular

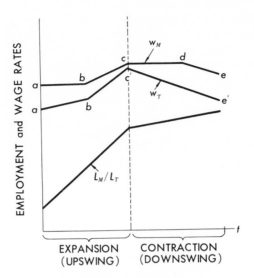

Fig. 5.3. Wage rates and employment in
modern and traditional sectors.

during investment spurts, labor continued to be available at prices favorable to entrepreneurs, and this must be closely related to the wage lag. Now we intend to explore the mechanism of wage differentials in relation to employment in somewhat greater detail.

Figure 5.3 shows what happens to wage rates in modern and traditional sectors during a typical long swing. L_M/L_T is the changing ratio of modern to traditional employment. As far as L_M/L_T is concerned, we assume that during an expansion the ratio of modern to traditional employment increases comparatively sharply. During the contraction, the proportion of modern employment continues to rise, but at a reduced rate. Let us now look at the changing path of absolute and relative wage rates in order to infer certain characteristics about the supply of labor during a long swing.

Wage rates in the modern sector during a typical upswing can be assumed to follow the path traced by line w_M. Here we drew a curve divided into two segments: a–b applies to a period when labor supply is

---

way; flexible supplies of labor, the differential structure, employment institutions all affect the wage lag.

    This finding also creates a systematic distortion in the residuals of Chapter 3, but they are not large enough to require a modification of our broad conclusions.

"unlimited"; within a certain range of expansion the wage rate remains unchanged. However, the requirements of the upswing usually go beyond this range, and segment *b–c* becomes operative, resulting in rising wage rates. Nevertheless, the labor supply remains relatively "flexible," so that wages rise less sharply than productivity increases. Historically, no upswing went beyond the point of flexibility when wage rates increased more rapidly than, or as rapidly as, productivity. This suggests that cost inflation due to wage increases could not have been a factor in ending a long-swing expansion; other reasons must have been involved.

Traditional wages can be assumed to follow the path *a′–b′–c′* during an upswing. During the entire expansion the number of surplus workers becomes smaller since L_M/L_T is sharply rising. Until point *b′* is reached, the impact on wage rates is slight, because the number of surplus laborers remains sizable. When point *b′* is reached, and especially beyond it, the expansion will have continued for some time, and the number of surplus workers will have been reduced by the opportunities of employment. Now, when additional labor is needed in traditional production, and this regularly arises during certain seasons of the year, the relative (short-term) shortage of labor will lead to sharply rising wages in agriculture. As we noted before, w_a/w_m rises during the upswing, and particularly toward the end of the upswing.

Up to this point our analysis has been almost exclusively concerned with periods of expansion. There are two justifications for this. An understanding of postwar growth in historical perspective should concentrate on expansive phases of growth, and furthermore, since 1900 the Japanese economy has displayed only one genuine contraction, the years from 1917 to 1931. Generalizations concerning contractions must therefore be based on a very limited historical record. We do, however, want to say a word or two about the downswing experience partially in order to achieve a more balanced presentation but more important because the downswing of the 1920's was so crucial to the formation of the differential structure.

Let us follow the path of wages. It has already been shown that during a typical upswing money wages will rise, and if inflation is moderate, real wages should also rise. Of course, wages continue to lag behind productivity gains in expansion, but this is a pattern that changes in the downswing, when the ratio of wages to labor productivity rises. At the beginning of contraction, the modern entrepreneur will find that a new high has been reached in the level of money wages, and he will also find that these display downward rigidity. Based on the experience of the

1920's, we know that w_M changed only little through 1931, that w_T declined after a short interval, while the general price level declined. For the downswing, wage rates of the modern sector are illustrated by line *c–d–e*, and for the traditional sector by line *c'–e'*. Wages in the traditional sector are depicted as relatively elastic in the sense that they tend to fall sharply during downswings when surplus labor becomes more plentiful, and as a result w_T/w_M declines. By contrast, in the modern sector we have drawn segment *c–d* to account for the period of rigidity, followed by *d–e* when money wages fall quite gently. The downward rigidity of money wages is an internationally recognized phenomenon, but why does it occur when the supply of labor is flexible? This is a most difficult question. As already mentioned, the available experience with downswings is much too limited for adequate generalizations. But on the whole we tend to believe that modern wages were rigid in a downward direction for some time, and we will discuss this problem in some detail below.[10]

FLEXIBLE SUPPLIES OF LABOR

The previous section dealt with the interaction of demand and supply. From here on we will try insofar as possible to separate these forces so as to clarify some of their distinct behavioral and institutional aspects. Supply will be taken up first, and it involves primarily the more traditional aspects of the Japanese economy. Demand is the next and last topic of this chapter, and there the focus is on the developing modern sectors.

A flexible supply of labor means that a small increase in the wages of the modern sector leads to a relatively large increase in the labor supply, originating largely in the traditional sector. "Unlimited supplies" of labor, in the famous formulation of W. Arthur Lewis, is the limiting case. Using the standard formula $\eta = \Delta Ls/Ls \div \Delta w/w$ (*Ls* is the supply of labor, *w* the wage rate, and η the elasticity), the expectation is a relatively large value for the elasticity of labor supply with respect to wage rates. The real question is the appropriateness of this formulation for Japan.

---

[10] It should be made clear that the mechanism outlined in Figure 5.3 and the text is fully verified by the evidence. Relative wage rates have been covered in Table 5.4. The employment pattern also behaves as indicated. Taking traditional employment as the sum of agriculture and services, and modern employment as the sum of manufacturing, mining, transportation, communication, public utilities, and construction, we find $G_{LM} > G_{LT}$ in the upswing and $G_{LM} < G_{LT}$ in the downswing. See BST.18.

Measuring the degree of flexibility is always difficult because of problems of specifications. (Whose wages and which segment of the labor force need to be included?) Leaving these aside for the moment, let us concentrate on the upswing. The standard elasticity calculation assumes a systematic association between the labor supply and the wage rate, and for Japan this has been confirmed during expansions by empirical evidence: workers moving from the traditional to the modern sector while wage differentials lessen. Yet an association is not the same thing as cause and effect, and we hesitate to adopt a simple interpretation that says that labor moved simply as a result of increases in relative wages offered to traditional workers. We are much more inclined to believe that labor abandoned traditional employment as a consequence of improved job opportunities in the modern sector during upswings. Wage differentials were not nearly as crucial as the availability of jobs. The "push" out of traditional occupations was always steady and strong; it is the "pull" of the modern enterprises that varied.

The downswing of the 1920's can be explained in a similar manner. Wages in and out of agriculture were almost steady (for unskilled labor), and the worker outflow to nonagriculture declined. But a negative elasticity of labor supply with respect to the wage rate does, at first glance, appear illogical. How can one make economic sense out of a situation in which wages outside of agriculture are constant and the numbers flowing out are falling? Does it not imply that the standard elasticity assumptions (or flexibility assumptions) did not apply in the 1920's?

During the long prewar downswing the wage rate was even more irrelevant to the labor supply. This was a time when agricultural underemployment must have risen: population continued to grow, demand in the nonagricultural sector lessened, and the *push* was stronger to get people into any available work. For this period the "job opportunity" thesis also applies: flexible labor supplies because workers were eager for almost any gainful employment. Outflow was again limited by demand.

A direct examination of the agricultural wage-productivity situation will confirm the conditions that have contributed to the historical existence of flexible labor supplies. As can be seen in Table 5.5, the data in 1964 show that Y/L rises for farms as the scale of operations increases; wages remain almost level; consequently, the wage-productivity ratio declines evenly, in line with scale. Using the output elasticities for agricultural labor cited in Chapter 4, we can approximate labor's marginal

TABLE 5.5
Wage-Productivity Relations in Agriculture by
Farm Scale, 1964
(Yen)

Operation scale (chō)	Y/L (1)	Wages (2)	Wages/ productivity *(percent)*
1. Under 0.5	¥638	¥743	116.2%
2. 0.5–1.0	827	787	96.9
3. 1.0–1.5	954	777	81.4
4. 1.5–2.0	1,067	778	72.9
5. 2.0–2.5	1,229	755	61.4
6. 2.5–3.0	1,367	744	54.4
7. Over 3.0	1,760	749	42.5
Average	989	762	77.5

Source: Table 4.11.
  Note: Y/L, net product per worker per day. Wages are daily wages *(hiyatoi)*. 1 chō = 2.45 acres = .992 hectares.

product, and find that it is more or less equal to the wage for those farmers operating in class (4) with 1.5–2.0 chō. For those above that class, the marginal product exceeds the wage. For farmers with less than 1.5 chō, marginal product of labor lies below the wage. See Figure 5.4.[11]

The economic implications of this situation have great significance for Japan's labor supply. Those individuals whose marginal product lies below their wages—and wages are used here in their broadest sense—are underemployed or perhaps more accurately described as "overoccupied." Both descriptions are different sides of the same coin. Workers are overoccupied when, under conditions of decreasing returns, excess

[11] A few words should be added about the data and the derivation of marginal product. The data were produced by the Ministry of Agriculture, and their collection used modern sampling techniques. These surveys are widely acknowledged to be accurate. Wages are averages for male and female day workers, and salary income is excluded. Wage earnings from nonfarm jobs are included.

At point E, wages (w) = marginal product of labor (MP). The marginal product of labor was derived as follows: the output elasticity of labor is multiplied by the average labor productivities of Table 5.5. A variety of output elasticity estimates exist, and these require a number of judgmental modifications. We assumed an elasticity range of 0.43–0.54, based on the results of Kaneda and Yuize (see Chapter 4, note 24, pp. 104–5). Their estimates (0.523 and 0.673) have been adjusted by reducing the scale factor to unity and assuming that the elasticity increases for larger units, in accordance with average measurements.

Wages to be compared with marginal product must also be modified, because the entries of Table 5.5 do not take account of seasonal fluctuations and would therefore overstate the income level. Studies indicate that daily wages are nearly 25 percent above long-term contract wages. (See LTES, vol. 9, pp. 220–21.)

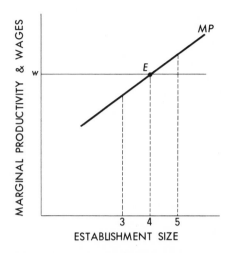

Fig. 5.4. Marginal product of labor in agriculture.

labor is applied. This overly intensive use of labor drives down the marginal product below the wage rate, resulting in underemployment. In 1964, about 78 percent of Japan's two million farm households whose income from farming was larger than from nonfarm sources found themselves in this position.[12] These were the bulk of the population whose terms of employment were still traditional in the sense that work was more a matter of family right than rational economic calculation. Explaining why a situation of this kind could maintain itself would take us far beyond the bounds of our study. One would have to delve deeply into Japan's family system, and similar sociological matters. It should also be stressed that the issue is being discussed from the productivity and not from the income-assets perspective. Farmers can stick it out not only because their families are willing to go along with them, but also because of outside earnings and government price supports. But this does not alter the economics of the matter: the majority are overoccupied at present.

If well over 70 percent of Japan's full-time farm households harbored different degrees of underemployment after World War II, it stands to reason that more farmers were in this condition in the 1930's and earlier, since the gap between marginal product and wages must have been even larger. We do know (see Table 4.12) that output elasticity levels

[12] The total number of farm households is approximately five million.

at that time were much lower. Those numerous people then and now affected by the wage-productivity gap, largely located on the smallest farms, are the ones most anxious to leave agriculture and to find employment in industry. They are the sources of flexibility.

We now come to the so-called "structural changes" in the wage labor situation following 1961, and the end of the first postwar investment spurt. Beginning in about 1961, agricultural wages started to rise absolutely, and what is more significant, they rose sharply, from the same date, relative to nonagricultural wages. Gains were made vis-à-vis incorporated and unincorporated sectors, and wage differentials continued to narrow at a time when, in prewar years, one might have expected a widening in view of the post-spurt setting. This tendency was especially pronounced from 1961 to 1965; since then the tempo of diminishing differentials has somewhat slackened.[13]

A confident interpretation of these new conditions cannot yet be made, but the principal outlines of the future are becoming easier to identify all the time. The downswing pattern of Figure 5.3 no longer applies: all its conditions are now inappropriate. As soon as the elasticity of the labor supply has fallen, the differentials have quickly responded by narrowing, indicating the close historical relationship between flexible labor supplies, the wage gap, and ultimately the differential structure. The nonagricultural demand for workers has not undergone any basic change since the year 1961, and we can therefore assume that a structural change has taken place on the side of supply. The long-run condition of flexibility may have begun to diminish secularly at about that time, and the implications of this new setting will be discussed in Chapter 9.

THE DEMAND FOR LABOR BY THE MODERN SECTOR

Two factors are important in determining the modern sector's demand for labor. One is the relative rigidity imposed by factor proportions (K/L) dictated by a largely borrowed technology. The other is the peculiar Japanese wage-employment system. These are not independent phenomena. In fact, they are closely interrelated, and form a joint force

---

[13] For example, if the ratio of male and female agricultural wages to wages paid in nonagricultural unincorporated enterprises is taken as 100 in 1953, it reaches 177 in 1963. A similar comparison for incorporated enterprises moves in the same years from 100 to 211. See LTES, vol. 9, pp. 220–21. We may note that unincorporated wages rose relative to those paid by corporate enterprise. As explained in the Appendix Note, unincorporated enterprises have very much improved their wage-productivity levels. Agriculture is now the principal remaining lagging sector.

that can explain most aspects of labor demand by the entrepreneurs engaged in modern industry.

Factor Proportions

Let us begin with the matter of flexibility in factor proportions. In Chapter 4 we already observed that Japan was a classic example of industrialization based on increasingly capital-intensive borrowed technology—borrowed, of course, by the modern sectors. We also noted that this posed problems for an economy in which labor was relatively plentiful and capital relatively scarce. However, in modern industry, and especially in those areas where foreign competition had to be faced, a rising rate of capital intensity was an imperative and a simple consequence of reliance on borrowed technology. While it is difficult to verify these propositions rigorously, some evidence already presented is supportive. Employment in modern industries is closely associated with private nonagricultural investment swings, suggesting that the demand for labor is in considerable part determined by capital accumulation in that sector, subject, of course, to factor proportions determined by technological requirements.

To give direct evidence for rigid factor proportions is difficult. Two points can be made. In the nonagricultural sector there has been continual capital deepening since 1885, when the measures start. There is no evidence of either "capital shallowing" or "capital widening." Furthermore, as shown in Table 4.8, in manufacturing a higher K/L is associated with larger enterprises and higher wages. As was also suggested, these associations are seen as concomitants of different levels of technological and organizational progress; i.e. more sophisticated techniques used by larger firms on average require a bigger K/L and better-quality workers.

We must also reemphasize the importance of mitigation techniques discussed in Chapter 4. The selection of modern industries that used relatively more labor (such as textiles), multishift working hours, the use of secondhand machinery, and subcontracting—all these devices raised the absorptive capacity for labor by the manufacturing sector.

The Wage-Employment System

The Japanese wage-employment system in large, modern enterprises has its widely known peculiarities, symbolized by the terms "seniority wage scale" and "lifetime commitment." At this stage, it is not our intention to evaluate the positive or negative aspects of this system, that will come later. We must, however, consider some of its features here, because we believe that the social setting in which wages and employment are determined is closely related to the modern sector's demand function for labor.

The current system is an institutional device gradually developed by modern firms at the beginning of this century. Its purpose always has been to assure an adequate flow of qualified workers, and by now its standard features can be described without difficulty: the level and composition of wages are determined by individual enterprises rather than by an impersonal labor market; wages are closely linked to personal factors such as level of education and specific schools, age, and length of service in an enterprise; on-the-job training is widespread; the particular job and the individual's efficiency matter less to the wage than cost of living and status; there is a strong and reciprocal sense of commitment between the worker and his firm, especially pronounced in large enterprises; the rate of labor turnover is very low for these firms, and there is little movement to or from smaller units. These are the average features, and in recent years—since the middle 1960's—changes in a more "Western" direction are noticeable. However, for our period of analysis the description remains accurate.

Nearly all of these features point in the same direction: a significant proportion of the labor force in nonagriculture—especially in manufacturing and facilitating industries—is, in the eyes of both management and labor, employed with varying degrees of permanence.[14] From the point of view of enterprises, demand for labor must be affected by these conditions: hiring workers becomes a long-run obligation that extends beyond the fluctuations of typical business cycles. Under these circumstances, the entrepreneur may be most cautious in raising wages and employment in a boom, fearing the burden of a large and relatively high-priced work force when the recession arrives.

If the hiring of labor has an important long-run dimension, owing in this case to permanent employment, one must be able to relate it also to investment, since that is where the crucial decisions about the future have to be made. The level and growth of investment determine the changing productive capacity of an enterprise. And each level of long-run productive capacity has to be associated with a certain technologi-

---

[14] There is no way to quantify the proportion exactly. Japanese statistics do list so-called regular and temporary workers, but definitions vary widely, and large categories—e.g. white-collar workers—are excluded. It is not possible to go much beyond the statement in the text.

cally determined "stock" of permanent or "attached" labor. (In other words, both labor and capital become fixed costs.) That is why we shall assume that the secular demand for labor is expressed by $Lw = f(K)$; the total wage bill or the aggregate cost of labor is a function of the capital stock.[15] This is not really a strange way of looking at the matter when it is considered in internationally comparative terms. The future of enterprises in all economies hinges on long-term decisions determining capital accumulation. But in general the corresponding demand for labor represents much less of a contractual arrangement, and therefore no especially steady relation between K and Lw need be expected. In Japan, however, we have *a priori* reasons to assume its presence.

A simple historical test for this proposition, combining the effects of rigid factor proportions and Japanese institutions, is to note the relationships of Lw and K. A close correspondence between G_{Lw} and G_K would support our contentions, and that is how we interpret the facts during the twentieth century (see Figure 5.5). In general, the growth of the wage bill lies close to the growth of capital stock.

Not only are our expectations confirmed, but there exist, in addition, some revealing swing implications. During the two prewar investment spurts, the pace of capital accumulation (G_K) was generally greater than the growth of the wage bill (G_{Lw}) (an exception to this being the last few years of the 1930's; see p. 198), but this relation was reversed in the downswing of the 1920's. By implication, wages lagged behind the growth of capital intensity when the economy went through prewar investment spurts, and fell less sharply in the ensuing downswing. The reason for this, in part at least, can be tied to permanent employment and the enterpriser's time horizon. In the upswing, output growth climbed rapidly, and wage increases were restricted to much lower rates. This is not puzzling: it is part of the wage-productivity lag caused by flexible labor supplies combined with the employer's fear of incurring long-lasting obligations. There was, in effect, no need for him to raise wages. But as the economy approached the boom conditions of long-swing peaks, we see that output, capital stock, and the wage bill were all growing at similar rates. These were the overheated years of expansion, when the situation of temporary labor shortages made higher wages necessary.

What happened in the downswing of 1917–31 is, at first glance, harder to understand. The rate of growth of output declined, followed by that

---

[15] Since this is a long-term relationship, wages are assumed to be in constant prices corresponding to constant capital stock and output prices.

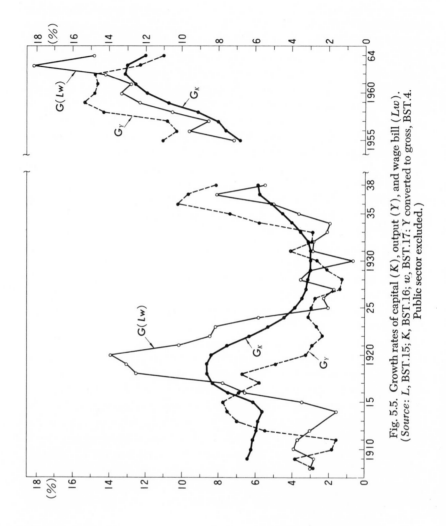

Fig. 5.5. Growth rates of capital (K), output (Y), and wage bill (Lw). (*Source*: L, BST.15; K, BST.16; w, BST.17: Y converted to gross, BST.4. Public sector excluded.)

of capital stock. That would be entirely expected. The same cannot be said of wage costs. These declined only very slowly from their great World War I peak and did not reach a lower-level "equilibrium" until the middle of the 1920's. In an earlier section, we already commented on the difficulty of accounting simultaneously for the downward rigidity of wages and flexible supplies. Perhaps now, by taking the employer's attitude toward the labor force into account, we can come closer to an answer.

The degree of permanence in the labor force is a key issue. With the wage bill resembling fixed costs, Japanese enterprises have always been most interested in maintaining a long-run normal wage level. They are particularly anxious to avoid fluctuations in either direction. Upward movements are successfully dampened—although certainly not avoided. In the downturn of the 1920's, one can only speculate about their motives. Discharging workers would have been a violation of a mutual understanding concerning permanent job rights and, in addition, would have ruined any firm's name. Furthermore, no one could have predicted the long duration of depressed conditions, and Japanese businessmen had particular incentives to hang on to their work forces. Severe wage cuts might have been dangerous. They had invested heavily in their workers, and feared the impossibility of, or costs involved in, replacing them through the labor market. All these factors must have combined to create downward rigidity despite the large pool of underemployed in the traditional economy.

Already in Figure 5.5, but much more clearly in Figure 5.6, a scatter diagram, we can discern a slow drift in the secular trend describing the relations between the growth of aggregate wages and capital stock. Before World War I, all points are located below line E, on which $G_K = G_{Lw}$. Interwar years are fairly well concentrated along line E, and the postwar years are nearly all above the line. These are evidence of important historical changes (quite apart from the previously discussed swing movements). Japan has exhibited a secular movement from an early state in which $G_K > G_{Lw}$ to an intermediate state of $G_K = G_{Lw}$, and to a postwar state in which $G_K < G_{Lw}$.[16] In historical terms, it can be said that the World War I spurt had the advantage of "cheap labor" with

---

[16] In the nineteenth century, G_K also grew more rapidly than G_{Lw}. Data are limited, but preliminary estimates indicate that capital stock rose at 2.2 percent per year in the nonprimary sector for 1885–98, and at 2.0 percent for 1898–1905. Wage data are confined to manufacturing, and they show real rates of increase of 1.2 percent and 0.9 percent for the same periods.

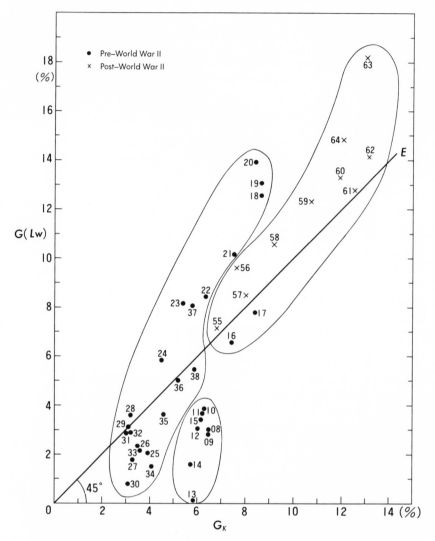

Fig. 5.6. Long-term relation between capital stock and wage bill.

respect to rising capital intensity. Very gradually this advantage has lessened, but even at present wage costs are rising only slightly more rapidly than capital accumulation. Until now, at least in a trend sense, the Japanese economy has not as yet experienced a situation in which aggregate wage costs rise much more rapidly than accumulation; other things being equal, this would be most unpleasant for entrepreneurs.[17]

[17] Some of the structural implications of a rise in postwar Lw/K are discussed in the Appendix Note with reference to corporate and unincorporated enterprises.

CHAPTER SIX

Aggregate Demand and Resource Allocation

Until now we have dealt primarily with the supply-production side of Japanese economic growth. Now we shall focus on the role of demand and resource allocation, and this entails a wide range of topics. All components of aggregate demand are described—although exports are studied in greater detail in Chapter 7—with particular emphasis on investment. The description includes a historical analysis of the investment ratio (I/Y), the changing composition of capital formation, and the distinction between autonomous and induced investment. The analysis concludes with a brief study of the role of savings components in Japanese growth.

THE CHANGING COMPONENTS OF AGGREGATE DEMAND

The compositional trends of aggregate demand are shown in Table 6.1. They are readily identified: a long-term and steady relative decline of personal consumption from 71 percent to 47 percent; the rather steady position of government consumption before World War II and its decline thereafter; the steady but moderate rise of government investments; the steady and very steep rise of private investments especially after the war; and finally, the rise of exports through the 1930's, followed by decline and partial recovery in recent years.

Three questions suggest themselves in connection with these trends. First, what part of aggregate demand was contributed by the growth of private investment? We have put great stress on this activity, and should therefore expect it to play an important role. Second, what part of aggregate demand expansion was contributed by the rate of growth of exports? Some students of Japanese development have used the description "export-led growth," and this conception should find some confirmation in the composition of demand. And finally, we can ask a simi-

TABLE 6.1
The Composition of Aggregate Demand for Selected Years
(Smoothed series, constant prices; *percent*)

Year	C_p	C_g	I_g	I_p	X	I_p*
1907	70.9%	12.3%	4.0%	7.3%	5.5%	3.4%
(1912)	70.9	8.0	4.8	8.6	7.7	4.3
1917	66.8	7.4	3.6	11.4	10.8	7.7
1931	63.5	9.9	6.4	7.2	13.0	4.4
1937	53.6	10.1	8.5	10.8	17.0	9.1
1955	55.4	10.2	6.4	18.6	9.4	12.1
1962	48.2	7.2	8.1	25.9	10.6	19.3
1965	46.9	6.6	8.1	25.4	12.6	18.2

Source: C_p, C_g, and X from BST.6. I_g, I_p, and I_p* from BST.8.
Notation:
C_p, personal consumption.
C_g, government consumption including military expenditures.
I_g, government fixed investment.
I_p, private investment excluding inventory changes.
X, exports.
I_p*, private fixed investment excluding primary investment and residential construction.

lar question about the role of government, especially its autonomous expenditures, with the prime example being public investment.

An answer to these questions is contained in Table 6.2, Incremental Contribution of Aggregate Demand Components, and in Figures 6.1 and 6.2.[1] The table shows the proportion contributed by each part of aggregate demand to the increase of the total; for example, in the case of personal consumption, $\Delta C_p/\Delta V = \Delta C_p/C_p \times C_p/V \times V/\Delta V$. Charts trace the trends and fluctuations of sectoral contributions for the past 60-odd years.

Let us begin with total investment (Figure 6.1). A feature that stands out is the very close resemblance between fluctuations of investment contributions and the growth pattern of aggregate demand. Both move up and down in almost perfect harmony, and we can say with some confidence that investment is a most important element in the movements of aggregate demand. Furthermore, this is also true for private investment (Figure 6.2), and its significance has greatly increased in time: from around 15 percent at the time of World War I to over 33 percent during the postwar investment spurt.

Our second question pertained to exports (Figure 6.1), and the results may be slightly unexpected. The association between the contri-

[1] Table 6.2 contains *period averages* while the figures show smoothed time series. This must be remembered in any comparison of these items.

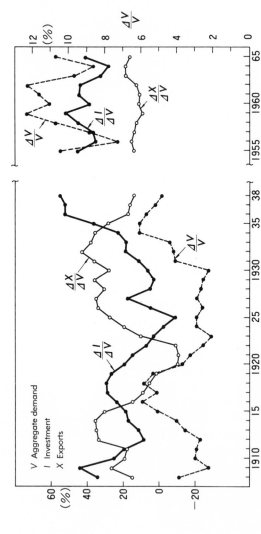

Fig. 6.1. Incremental contribution of aggregate demand components: investment and exports. (*Source*: Table 6.2.)

TABLE 6.2
Incremental Contribution of Aggregate Demand Components
(Period averages; *percent*)

Period	$\dfrac{\Delta C_p}{\Delta V}$	$\dfrac{\Delta C_g}{\Delta V}$	$\dfrac{\Delta I_g}{\Delta V}$	$\dfrac{\Delta I_p}{\Delta V}$	$\dfrac{\Delta X}{\Delta V}$	$\dfrac{\Delta I}{\Delta V}$	$\dfrac{\Delta G}{\Delta V}$	$\dfrac{\Delta I_p{}^*}{\Delta V}$
1908-17	61.5%	-8.5%	4.0%	19.2%	23.7%	23.1%	-4.5%	13.0%
1912-18	52.0	4.8	1.2	18.6	23.4	19.6	6.0	10.2
1918-31	59.5	14.3	11.6	-2.0	16.4	9.6	25.9	-3.2
1932-38	22.5	10.9	15.2	21.0	27.3	36.2	26.1	23.6
1955-61	42.3	3.4	8.5	33.5	12.4	42.0	11.9	26.6
1962-64	43.1	5.2	10.8	25.9	15.0	36.7	16.0	19.9

Source: See Table 6.1.
　Notation: V is aggregate demand.

bution of exports and aggregate demand growth is much less clear than for private investment. At the time of World War I the relation was positive, but in the 1920's export contributions rose markedly while aggregate demand growth continued at low levels. And after World War II, the contribution of exports was distinctly lower, $\Delta X/\Delta V$ having fallen, and it could do much less to affect the performance of demand. This should at least mean that a simple "export-led growth" hypothesis for Japan is not valid. It would be wrong, however, on the basis of this evidence to undervalue the role of exports in demand. They were particularly weighty in the early part of the century, and showed a high value in the early 1930's. Less well known, perhaps, is the complementary relationship between exports and investment (see Figure 6.1): when the contribution of one rose, that of the other fell, and vice versa. This complementarity has persisted for a long time—it is true even now—and is one manifestation of what are frequently called "export drives." As the internal sources of growth weaken, a push is made in the direction of external markets. This certainly happened during the 1920's, when the contribution of exports helped to maintain aggregate demand (it could not, however, lift it). To some extent, this has again happened after 1961.[2]

What about government? (See Figure 6.2.) Beginning with the Russo-

---

[2] It should be noted that exports have an effect upon demand in ways other than through the volume of goods disposed of abroad. They also affect demand through their relation to the balance of payments and the growth in the money supply. To gauge this effect, of course, one needs to consider the growth of exports in current prices rather than in constant prices. Needless to say, the balance-of-payments effect is important during periods when a country operates either on a gold standard or on some other fixed-exchange-rate standard. For Japan, this may have been especially consequential in the period between 1900 and the end of World War I.

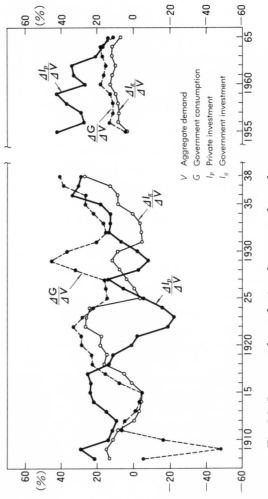

Fig. 6.2. Incremental contribution of aggregate demand components: government consumption, government investment, private investment. (*Source:* Table 6.2.)

Japanese War, the contribution of total government expenditures rose continually, and by the very end of the 1930's, when war preparations were in full swing, it exceeded 50 percent. The drop after the war was abrupt; the public contribution was as low as 10 to 15 percent, and at least until 1965 there has been no sign of change in this situation. In postwar Japan, government was not a major element in demand creation; but it cannot be ignored in the period before the war.

In considering historical alterations in the importance of demand components, the influence of specific historical events should not be left out, and simple causalities must be modified in the light of a variety of factors that are not part of our analysis. For example, the role of exports was important in raising the rate of growth of aggregate demand in both prewar spurts. Partly, this must have been related to the improved competitive position achieved by Japan as a result of increased fixed investments. But external events, economic and noneconomic, were also involved. At the time of World War I the weight of European and American competition was very much reduced in world markets and particularly in Asian markets. In the 1930's the yen was undervalued, and low quality and cheap products—that is to say, Japanese specialties—found receptive markets in a depressed world and in Japan's own colonial territories. Perhaps the clearest instance of an ad hoc effect occurred in the 1930's, when government consumption suddenly accounted for almost 40 percent of the increase in aggregate demand. This was a direct result of military ambition: "Between 1930 and 1935, of the nine hundred and forty-six million Yen increase in central government expenditures, sixty-two per cent was for military uses, fourteen per cent for social welfare, seven per cent for transportation, agriculture, and other economic services, and seventeen per cent for interest on the expanding national debt."[3]

INVESTMENT

The Investment Proportion

The rising share of investment in aggregate demand ($\Delta I / \Delta V$), as well as its role in determining fluctuations in demand, is already clear. These findings provide support for the contention, expressed in the preview, that in Japan investment was the driving force of growth. As we shall show, saving is viewed as a more passive activity. At this point, however, we intend to analyze investment in more detail, especially emphasizing

[3] Hugh T. Patrick, "The Economic Muddle of the 1920's," in James W. Morley, ed., *Dilemmas of Growth in Prewar Japan* (Princeton, N.J., 1971).

TABLE 6.3

The Investment Ratio (I/Y) and Related Terms

(Percent)

Year	I/Y private nonagri.	I/Y total	ΔK/K private nonagri.	K/Y private nonagri.
1907	5.68%	12.75%	6.44%	1.29%
1917	11.78	16.46	8.36	1.39
1931	6.47	15.13	3.04	1.83
1937	12.00	20.53	5.87	1.74
1956	17.38	29.74	7.63	1.88
1962	23.66	36.42	13.12	1.59
1964	21.98	35.68	12.06	1.61

Source: For investment, BST.6 and BST.8. *Y* from BST.4 (converted to gross terms). $\Delta K/K$ from BST.16.

Note: Smoothed series. Figures for 1907, 1956, and 1962 are five-year moving averages; figures for 1917, 1931, and 1937 are seven-year averages; and figures for 1964 are three-year averages.

Notation: I, gross domestic fixed investment; *Y,* gross domestic product; *K,* gross fixed capital stock.

its place in the demand structure of the Japanese economy. For this purpose, the investment ratio (I/Y) is the most appropriate indicator, and its historical evolution is contained in Table 6.3. We already know that capital formation grew more rapidly than output, and therefore during the years under review the trend of I/Y rose substantially. The rise of the total investment proportion was closely associated with investment spurts: when the rate of growth of capital formation spurted, the investment proportion went up sharply; when capital formation grew at more deliberate speeds, I/Y remained relatively stable. Both the level and the rates of increase are particularly remarkable after World War II.

The stability of I/Y during downswings, when a sharp decline might have been expected, is related to a persistent "leader-follower" relation between public and private investment. When the rate of expansion lies above the long-run trend line, private investment grows more rapidly than public investment. The reverse is the case when output growth is below trend values. This relation will be studied in greater detail somewhat later.

The investment ratio is an aggregate measure of resource allocation devoted to capital formation. $I/Y = \Delta K/K \times K/Y$,[4] a simple identity, says that the investment proportion is composed of the rate of capital accumulation (G_K) and the capital-output ratio (K/Y). In terms of Japan's historical experience, both terms have to be evaluated as deter-

[4] For simplicity's sake we will ignore capital retirements, and assume that $I = \Delta K$. Our formulation does not substantially differ from the more usual identity $\Delta K/K = I/Y \times Y/K$, where $\Delta K/K$ is defined as the *desired* rate of capital accumulation. In both formulations, the performance of $\Delta K/K$ is the basic magnitude to be explained.

minants of I/Y; in fact, one cannot disentangle them in any rigorous fashion. They have been influenced by long swings and by trends, and changes in these terms can be related, we believe, to the influence of autonomous incentives arising from expected gains to be derived from altering techniques and unrelated to increases in final demand, as might be expected on the basis of the capital ouput ratio.

To assess the influence of the motives concerning the decision to invest—leaving aside for the moment the problem of their interrelatedness—would require *ex ante* evidence. Of course, all that is available are *ex post* data. They do show, quite unmistakably, that during the twentieth century movements of capital accumulation were more influential than capital-output ratio changes in determining the trend and swing of the investment ratio. For example, during the last two upswings (see Table 6.3) K/Y decreased slightly while I/Y increased very much. The real power lay behind the sharp accelerations of $\Delta K/K$. At the beginning of the century, 1909–17, the rate of capital accumulation jumped by nearly 30 percent while the capital-output ratio rose by about 8 percent. Again, the lift of I/Y from 6.6 to 10.8 percent was more influenced by capital accumulation. We wish to make no exaggerated claims for these empirical observations. But they do serve to underline the implied role not only of induced investment but also of autonomous investment.

The Investment Motive

Viewed from the side of demand for capital, a large amount of investment can be considered as dependent on conditions that produce a high rate of return on existing capital and that permit the economy to absorb a large amount of additional capital without unduly depressing the rate of return. This dependence, which we consider a basic investment motive for private nonagricultural enterprise, can be expressed in the formula $r = Y/K - L_w/K$, saying that the expected rate of return on capital is equal to output per unit of capital minus labor costs per unit of capital.[5]

The expected rate of return can also be expressed as $r = \alpha Y/K$, and long-swing movements of K/Y (Table 6.3) and α, the share of capital (Appendix Note), suggest certain systematic variations in the expected rate of return. During investment upswings the rate of return on capital

---

[5] Assuming marginal equilibrium conditions, this formula can also be stated in incremental terms. See Martin Bronfenbrenner, "Japanese Growth Path: Equilibrium or Disequilibrium?," *Keizai kenkyū*, vol. 21, no. 2 (May 1970). For an econometric estimate of the type of investment function suggested in our text, see K. Odaka and S. Ishiwata, "Effective Demand and Cyclical Growth of the Japanese Economy: 1906–1938," a paper presented to the Second Conference on Economic Growth: A Case Study of Japanese Experience, Tokyo, June 26–July 1, 1972.

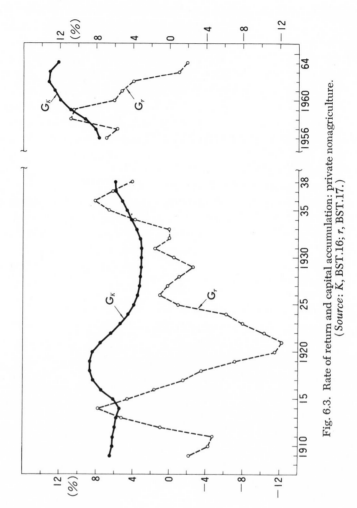

Fig. 6.3. Rate of return and capital accumulation: private nonagriculture.
(*Source: K*, BST.16; *r*, BST.17.)

TABLE 6.4
*Decomposition of the Rate of Capital Return
in Terms of Growth Rates*
(Percent)

Period	Rate of return G_r	Capital-output ratio effect $\frac{1}{\alpha}(G_Y - G_K)$	Labor cost effect $\frac{\beta}{\alpha}G_B$
1908–12	−1.8%	−6.0%	−4.2%
*1913–17	2.6	0.3	−2.3
1918–24	−6.5	−4.8	1.7
1925–32	−1.5	−3.8	−2.3
*1933–38	3.5	3.8	0.3
*1955–61	6.6	10.3	3.7
1962–64	−1.5	−0.5	2.0

Source: Y from BST.4 (converted to gross terms); K from BST.16; r, α, β, from BST. 17.
Note: Investment spurts are marked with an asterisk.
Notation:
$G_L + G_w = G_K + G_B$ is assumed by definition; G_B is a balance defined as $(G_L + G_w) - G_K$.
$G_w = G_\beta + G_Y - G_L$; $G_B = G_Y - G_K + G_\beta$.
$G_r = G_\alpha + G_Y - G_K$ and $\alpha G_\alpha + \beta G_\beta = 0$, since we assumed that $\alpha + \beta = 1$. From these relatives we have
$$G_r = \frac{1}{\alpha}\left\{(G_Y - G_K) - \beta G_B\right\}.$$

must tend to rise, since K/Y rises less rapidly or declines while the income share of capital increases. During investment downswings a reverse tendency must have existed. For trend values, we may assume that r was relatively steady. That these expectations are substantially correct is shown in Figure 6.3, containing the growth rate of the rate of return (G_r) and the growth rate of capital stock (G_K) from 1909 to 1964. Rates of return do rise during investment upswings, reaching peaks with a slight lead, and the expected reverse tendency is equally plain. Furthermore, G_r does not indicate any long-term trend movement. One difference between prewar and postwar Japan should be noticed. Before World War II, G_r was frequently in the negative range, as in 1908–11, 1917–24, 1928–30, and 1932. These were years in which the rate of return on capital was falling absolutely. Since World War II, this has been true only in one (early) year, 1954.

The rate of return on capital can be decomposed into a number of frequently used concepts: Y/K, α, and β. Accordingly, $r = \alpha Y/K = Y/K - L_w/K$. Thus the rate of return is the product of what might be called a "capital-output ratio effect" (Y/K) and a labor-cost effect (L_w/K), and in Table 6.4 we can follow their historical paths and relative level of significance. Investment spurts are marked with an asterisk, and at these times G_r was positive; at other times entries are negative. More to the point are the secular changes in the capital-output ratio

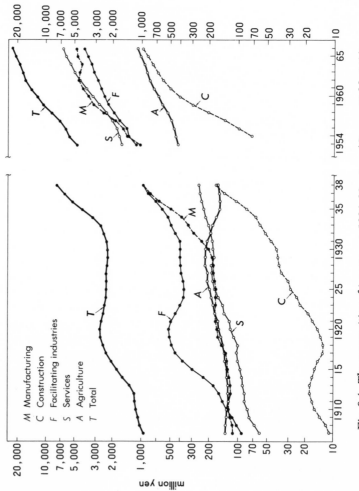

Fig. 6.4. The composition of investment, 1934–36 prices. (*Source:* Table 6.5.)

and labor-cost effects. As already indicated, the capital-output ratio tended to decline during upswings, and therefore its influence has always been beneficial to the growth of the rate of return; indeed it has been increasingly beneficial. Labor costs have had a quite different effect. In the long run they have risen from large minus values in the early part of the century to sizable positive values between 1955 and 1961. The relationship between these two terms is most revealing. During the first spurt, a rising rate of return depended largely on favorable labor-cost conditions; the capital-output ratio effect was weak. A contrast with the postwar spurt is sharp, when rather unfavorable labor-cost conditions are overwhelmed by the increase of Y/K. And finally, the middle spurt occupies an intermediate position: both effects contribute almost equally to the growth of G_r.

The Changing Composition of Investment

Having observed the secular increase in Japan's investment proportion and having speculated about the investment motives of enterprises, we turn next to the issue of allocation. Although investment spurts have recurred regularly in Japanese economic growth, their composition has changed, reflecting the increasing maturity of the industrial structure. Visual evidence is provided in Figure 6.4 where private capital formation has been divided into major industrial components: agriculture, manufacturing (including mining), construction, facilitating industries, and services.

The first investment spurt of this century was due most of all to the rapid increase of investments in private facilitating industries, which include transportation, communications, and public utilities. At the beginning of the twentieth century, total nonagricultural private capital formation in constant prices averaged approximately ¥200 million per year (see Table 6.5). By the end of World War I this had risen to an average of over ¥600 million per year. The level of investment flow rose by some ¥400 million, out of which about ¥350 million were accounted for by facilitating industries.

During the second investment spurt, the lead was taken over by manufacturing industries, with facilitating industries a close second. In the early 1930's private capital formation averaged ¥600 million per year; toward the end of the decade yearly totals were in the neighborhood of ¥1,800 million, i.e. they had tripled. The average annual flow had risen by ¥1,200 million, of which some ¥600 million originated in manufacturing and ¥400 million in facilitating industries.

The postwar investment spurt (1956–62) produced sharp increases in capital formation levels for all industries: tripling for the total, manufac-

TABLE 6.5
Average Private Nonagricultural Investment by Industries: Selected Years
(Million yen; 1934–36 prices)

Year	Manufacturing	Construction	Facilitating industries	Services[a]	Total
1907[b]	¥111	¥11	¥57	¥22	¥201
1917	135	13	402	69	619
1931	232	46	228	113	619
1937	820	143	682	161	1,806
1956	1,504	70	889	709	3,172
1962	4,830	336	1,680	2,065	8,911
1966	5,812	478	2,376	3,382	12,048

Source: Prewar, SRA, vol. 3; postwar, NIS.
   Note: Seven-year averages before World War II; five-year averages after World War II.
   [a] Excludes residential construction.
   [b] Investment by industrial sectors cannot be carried back further.

turing, and services, quintupling for construction, and doubling for facilitating industries—all accomplished in six years. However, when the weight of industrial sectors is considered, it becomes apparent that manufacturing played an even stronger leading role than in the 1930's; it accounted for close to 60 percent of the increases. Furthermore, for the first time, capital formation in the service industries became a significant factor; its contribution (25 percent) was larger than that of facilitating industries (14 percent).[6]

Although these data classify investment by industrial origin, they can equally well confirm the growing significance of durable equipment as compared to construction. All industries engage in construction activities, but the proportion of this kind of investment is greatest for facilitating activities; it represents a much smaller part of manufacturing expenditures.

Finally, a brief look at the changing composition of investment during the two downswings. Clearly the periods in question were very different. In the former, 1917–31, the average flow of private capital

[6] Having identified the sectors whose growth was most responsible for twentieth-century investment spurts, it would now be logical to discuss the experiences of individual industries. Unfortunately the data for this type of analysis are unavailable. The only exception applies to the period 1955–61, for which the EPA has calculated a breakdown of capital formation in manufacturing as part of its effort to improve medium-range planning. For the period, EPA results indicate an average annual real rate of growth of capital formation in manufacturing of 34.4 percent. The individual rates are as follows: metal products 50.4 percent; transport machinery 44.4 percent; other machinery 49.4 percent; petroleum and coal products 38.3 percent; chemical products 23.7 percent; ceramics 25.7 percent; food and tobacco 20.1 percent; textiles 13.7 percent; other industries (timber, pulp and paper, printing, hides, rubber) 20.1 percent.

formation remained unchanged for well over a decade. In the latter, 1962–66, private capital formation continued to rise, though at much lower rates. Nevertheless, there are important similarities. With the exception of the decline in private facilitating investments for 1917–31, all industries continued to raise their levels of investment. But a strong growth leader is missing. Compared with the preceding spurts, the growth rates are not only lower but also more nearly at similar levels for the components.

The changing composition of capital formation can be used to shed some light on another question of historical importance: the distinction between autonomous and induced investment. We have already assumed that both types of investment demand are present, and in the next section an attempt will be made to estimate the significance of the acceleration effect. Now, however, one can use the industrial allocation of investment as a tentative indicator of the autonomous investment proportion.

Autonomous investment is associated with technical progress and innovations. Thus, one can reasonably suppose that the greater the proportion of autonomous within the total investment, the greater the rate of growth of output. The economic forces determining this proportion at any point in time are complex; no simple model can be used. Some of its determinants are nevertheless obvious. For instance, production-oriented investments are more likely to be the result of autonomous influences than are welfare-oriented investments; the same is true of producers' durables as compared with buildings and structures. The major historical point is that Japan's experience indicates not only a rise in the trend of I/Y but also a rising proportion of autonomous investment, and this has been an important element in producing trend acceleration.

A statistical verification of this assertion is necessarily indirect. Within the usual industrial classification, we believe that most innovational investments occur in private manufacturing, mining, and facilitating industries—collectively labeled m'. If this is correct, the ratios $I_{m'}/Y_{m'}$ and $I_{m'}/I$ should support the historical generalization. In fact, both ratios perform as expected: they follow the swing periodization and indicate rising trends. For example, $I_{m'}/I$ was at about 23 percent in 1906; in 1937 the $I_{m'}$ share was 34 percent; and in 1961 it attained about 53 percent. Much the same was true of $I_{m'}/Y_{m'}$: the investment share of sectors containing the bulk of innovational investment rose from 17 percent in 1906 to 42 percent in 1961.

Undoubtedly these ratios overestimate the growing weight of autonomous investment, because not all capital formation within the chosen sectors is innovational and not all outside the sectors is induced.[7] Yet even these crude indicators have their uses. They serve to underline two facts. First, the time series of I/Y that indicates such a clear long swing and rising trend is in considerable part the effect of the innovational sector m' whose time series have an even wider swing and more sharply rising trend. Second, these indicators tell us that the pattern of investment in this century has exhibited a growing bias in favor of productive investment—hence more rapid output growth—and against social overhead expenditures. The Japanese have ignored this bias for a long time, but it has become a key question for the future, and it will be more fully analyzed in Chapter 9.

One last aspect of the long-term pattern that is closely related to the above-mentioned bias needs to be clarified: it is the relation between public and private capital formation. As noted previously, these two originators of investment expenditures have, in the past, adhered to a "leader-follower" relationship. Private investment has been the leader, and when it falters or slows down, government investment has stepped in. As a result, I/Y has, in periods of slower growth, succeeded in maintaining a plateau. All this can be confirmed by referring back to Table 2.4 (p. 34), and especially to Figure 2.4 (p. 32). Here we see that the gap between these types of investment changes in accordance with the historical periodization: it narrows during upswings and widens during downswings. In other words, whenever the Japanese economy experienced its most rapid secular expansions, private investment expanded more rapidly than public investment and vice versa.[8]

THE RELATIONS BETWEEN CONSUMPTION, PRODUCTION,
AND INVESTMENT

Until now we have been concerned primarily with investment demand originating in the promise of adopting improved equipment and/or organization. This is one side of the story. The other has to take account

[7] For example, one could argue that the bulk of innovational investment was confined to a part of manufacturing, namely chemicals, metals, and machinery. In 1960 these absorbed slightly over 25 percent of industrial investment. Making all allowances for error, one might hazard a guess of 30 percent as the proportion of postwar innovational investment.

[8] The growing bias in favor of production as opposed to social overhead investment is simply another way of expressing the public-private relation. Owing to the particularly rigorous investment boom following World War II, the imbalance in public-private or production-welfare allocation is especially severe at the present time. One excellent example of this phenomenon is the secular decline in the proportion of residential buildings in total investment (excluding military investment):

of rising levels of consumption and its changing nature. We shall begin by examining the postwar demand for consumer durables, since this has frequently been considered a notable feature of Japan's recent economic performance. After this brief digression we shall turn to the main issue: the effect of consumption on the pattern of investment.

A Postwar Revolution of Consumer Durables?

The growth of advanced countries after World War II has gone hand in hand with some rapid changes in household consumption patterns. Products once purchased only by the wealthy became items of mass consumption, and new products appeared in a steady stream; in no area was this more evident than in the purchase of consumer durables. European workers started the process by acquiring motorcycles and scooters, and eventually graduated to automobiles. Simultaneously the ownership of a second car became common in the United States. And all over the advanced world, the possession of refrigerators, washing machines, television sets, etc., spread at a rapid pace.

What the impact of this phenomenon meant for the economic growth of America and Europe—frequently it has been called a consumer revolution—is a problem of no direct concern to us. But what this same phenomenon has meant for postwar Japan must be assessed, because statements like "[the Japanese] have broken right through into the revolution of consumer durables" are not at all uncommon.[9]

The meaning of this so-called revolution has never been well defined, and the eye of an observer and even individual consumption statistics can be misleading. By 1964, for example, 80 percent of Japanese wage earners' households had sewing machines, 55 percent owned cameras, 91 percent had television sets, 59 percent had refrigerators, and 72 percent possessed electric washing machines. Prewar consumption levels of all of these items were negligible, and postwar standards placed Japan's urban population for these "small durables" immediately below United States levels. Visual observation especially in the large department stores of Tokyo must reinforce the revolutionary picture; the mass of attractive and modern consumer durables available at low prices is staggering. And when it comes to electronic gadgetry, such as pocket fans and tele-

---

it fell from 23.5 percent in 1905 to 12.2 percent in 1961. By 1970 the ratio had risen to 17.5 percent. See K. Ohkawa, "Problems of Plan Implementation: Japan's Experience in the Resource Allocation Between Public and Private Sectors," in *Economic Planning and Macroeconomic Policy* (Tokyo, April 1971).

[9] "Economist" Correspondents, *Consider Japan* (London, 1963), p. 28.

vision sets with screens the size of postage stamps, the Japanese obviously lead the entire world.

That is only one side of the picture. Consumer durables can be divided into two major classes, big items and little items. During the postwar years, these little items did reach a large majority of Japanese consumers. However, this was not true of big items: automobiles, housing, and expensive leisure goods, such as boats, campers, and vacation homes. In 1964 only 8.8 percent of city households owned passenger automobiles, and to this day a very large proportion of Japanese automobiles, passenger and otherwise, perform as producers' durables. Equally telling is the fact that in 1966 the Japanese automobile industry produced 1.4 million trucks and buses, and only 800,000 passenger cars. The housing situation cannot be summed up in a single measure, but it is well recognized that residential dwellings deteriorated after World War II and that they are still very inadequate today. For all "big items" the situation of the Japanese consumer has improved in the 1960's, but it does not approach the Western European level, not to mention the level obtaining in the United States.

The varied and slightly contradictory aspects of Japan's postwar consumption pattern for consumer durables can be clearly illustrated by comparing the aggregate consumption and production statistics. The production statistics prepared by Miyohei Shinohara (see note 24, p. 171) indicate a most rapid growth for consumer durables between 1955 and 1961. During this interval the production of all manufactured goods rose two and one-half times. That of many individual products grew much more quickly, but the lead belongs to refrigerators, which registered a fiftyfold increase and television sets whose production rose by a factor of 34. These findings should be compared with the changing composition of household consumption by type of goods and services. The proportion of expenditure on durables has doubled between 1958 and 1961, from 3 to 6 percent of the total, but even in 1967 it was only 7.1 percent, a small element in overall household consumption. As a proportion of gross national expenditure, consumer durables registered equally unimpressively (1.9 percent in 1958, 2.7 percent in 1961, and 3.2 percent in 1964). One must conclude that production figures rose so rapidly because the base was so small.

From the perspective of history, one is tempted to argue the opposite of consumer revolution: personal consumption has been one of the surprisingly stable aspects of Japanese society, and certainly until very recently the consumer expenditure pattern in Japan has retained many traditional characteristics. There are numerous impressionistic accounts of this, and Uyeda's, written in 1938 and still quite true today, can be considered typical.[10]

The crowds of men and women, mostly dressed in Western costume, coming out of Tokyo Station every morning and going to work at their offices in the huge ferro-concrete buildings of the Marunouchi district, give the appearance of a thoroughly modernized society. But, when they go home in the evening, they live in small wooden houses, each with a small garden, in a manner not much changed since the beginning of Meiji. They want to wear Japanese clothes, and to eat and drink what their parents had been accustomed to consume.

Less well known is the fact that as recently as 1955 approximately one-half of total consumer expenditures was made for traditional commodities. Income level, and hence urban and rural status, affect the proportion of traditional commodities within the consumer's budget. Lower-income groups consume a larger share of traditional products, if only because their Engel co-efficient—food expenditure as a percentage of income—is higher.[11]

One method for examining the structure of demand is made possible by the national wealth survey for 1955. It includes a survey of the asset holdings of 7,300 families selected as a representative sample for the nation. The survey covered 83 separate items, and since information is also supplied about when assets were acquired, some historical judgments become possible.[12] We classified the assets into the categories traditional, intermediate (containing either hybrid or unclassifiable goods), and modern, and then computed present value by taking into account year of acquisition and price changes. Table 6.6 shows the results.

Two sets of conclusions emerge. In 1955 the value of household asset stock was divided approximately evenly into traditional and modern commodities. If we chose to count residential construction as an indigenous asset—and this would be perfectly legitimate—traditional

[10] Teijirō Uyeda, *The Small Industries of Japan* (Shanghai, 1938), p. 11. See also K. Ohkawa and H. Rosovsky, "The Indigenous Components in the Modern Japanese Economy," *Economic Development and Cultural Change*, vol. 9, no. 3 (April 1961). What we then termed "indigenous" is now called "traditional." See also Keiichirō Nakagawa and Henry Rosovsky, "The Case of the Dying Kimono," *Business History Review*, vol. 37, nos. 1–2 (Spring/Summer 1963).

[11] For example, in 1955 (urban areas only), food expenditures were 54.6 percent for those families with monthly expenditures of 26.8 thousand yen, and 37.4 percent for those units spending 46.8 thousand yen. See Japan, Bureau of Statistics, Office of the Prime Minister, *Kakei chōsa nempō* (Annual Report on the Family Income and Expenditure Survey; 1958), Table 2, pp. 158ff.

[12] See Japan, Economic Planning Agency, *Shōwa 30-nen kokufū chōsa: kakei shisan chōsa hōkoku* (National Wealth Survey for 1955: Survey of Household Assets), vol. 5 (March 1958).

TABLE 6.6
Household Asset Distribution
(Percent)

| Household assets | Years of acquisition | | | Current stock 1955 |
	Before 1941	1941–45	1946–55	
Modern goods	13%	19%	52%	50%
Intermediate goods	5	5	1	2
Traditional goods	81	76	46	48[a]

Source: Computed from *Kakei shisan chōsa hōkoku.*
Note: In order to compute present value, goods acquired before 1941 were deflated by the price index for 1930; goods acquired between 1941 and 1945 with the index for 1943; goods acquired between 1946 and 1950 with the index for 1948; after 1950 yearly deflators were used. For source of price indexes, see Japan, Economic Planning Agency, *Shōwa 30-nen kokufū chōsa: chōsa no hōhō ni tsuite* (National Wealth Survey of 1955: Concerning the Methods of Computation), vol. 6 (March 1958).
[a] Or 73, if residences are considered traditional assets.

goods would constitute 73 percent of all household asset holdings in 1955.[13] Turning to the historical data and the flow pattern in which these assets were acquired, we note a sharp decline in the rate of acquisition of traditional assets. Of the assets purchased before 1941, over 80 percent are classifiable as traditional and only about 13 percent as modern. The pattern of acquisition after World War II indicates that modern goods are now in the majority. If this trend continues, one may expect that traditional durable goods, with the possible exception of housing, will eventually fade into insignificance.

These observations concerning the supposed consumer revolution and the long-run personal consumption pattern support the analysis of savings to be presented at the end of this chapter. There we will note a certain conservatism displayed by the Japanese public in discussion of their savings habits, and it has been quantitatively illustrated here. This is not to say, of course, that increases in consumption played an insignificant part in postwar or historical growth; but we must approach a different dimension of the problem.

Consumption and Production

The role of consumption or demand increases in postwar Japan cannot be confined to any one type of commodity or industry. Prewar per capita increases in private consumption were rather small and declined in relative importance as a trend. In recent years the contrast is very marked.

[13] See H. Rosovsky, *Capital Formation in Japan, 1868–1940* (New York, 1961), chap. 9. On the average, Japanese residences have changed very little since the beginnings of the Meiji era. Until the last five or ten years major construction materials and methods have been very little influenced by the West.

Now, overall increases in consumption for almost all (including traditional) types of goods and services have been at unprecedented levels. To satisfy these increases in demand required substantial amounts of capital and labor; the consequence was induced investment and employment especially in industries providing consumer goods and services. It is this link between consumption and the structure of production that will be examined in this section.

The case we will make for postwar Japan can be summarized as follows. First, postwar increases in overall private consumption, ultimately due to the income-raising effects of autonomous investment, have created a situation in which derived demand or the acceleration principle has been much more important than in the past.

Second, the pattern of postwar private consumption is still directed toward commodities and services that in Japan have remained rather traditional both in their techniques and in their organization. This is especially true of household consumption, most of which involves agriculture, commerce, and services.

Next, this pattern of private consumption has given a particular character to derived demand. Satisfaction of consumption demand, as opposed to investment demand, requires *relatively* large amounts of labor and capital. To put it differently, consumption goods industries use factors less efficiently than investment goods industries.

And finally, these differences in the levels of efficiency have contributed toward raising the value of the accelerator. A given increase in consumption meant additional expenditures for goods and services produced by industries with relatively high marginal capital output ratios. Thus, derived demand redirected investment from more productive types (autonomous) to less productive types (induced).[14] At the same time, this process induced a great deal of capital formation (and employment) in the postwar years.

A number of steps are needed to verify these propositions. First, one

---

[14] The terms "autonomous" and "induced investment" present problems, and sharp distinctions are rarely possible. But the definitions proposed many years ago by A. H. Hansen still seem valid: "Autonomous investment springs notably from changes in technique. Autonomous or independent investment (more or less independent of *current* sales) is opened up by inventions, new discoveries, new products and new processes. Induced investment, on the other hand, is the result of an increase in final demand or sales volume." See *Business Cycles and National Income* (New York, 1951), p. 190. One may ask why induced investment in a follower country should contain less technological progress than autonomous investment. No general answer can be suggested. In Japan, however, we have shown that, until quite recently, consumption has retained a close tie to traditional demand where the possibilities of borrowing are extremely limited.

TABLE 6.7
Distribution of Total Consumption by Industries

Industry	Values (billion current yen)			Percentages to total[a]					
				1955		1960		1965	
	1955	1960	1965	Total	House-hold	Total	House-hold	Total	House-hold
Agriculture	¥493	¥586	¥1,149	6.6%	7.1%	5.0%	6.1%	4.6%	5.3%
Manufacturing "A"	2,620	3,889	6,823	35.1	37.0	33.3	38.1	27.3	30.2
Manufacturing "B"	261	649	1,703	3.5	3.1	5.6	5.6	6.8	7.2
Chemicals	(143)	(268)	(648)	(1.9)	(1.7)	(2.3)	(2.2)	(2.6)	(2.6)
Metals	(24)	(20)	(163)	(0.3)	(0.3)	(0.2)	(0.2)	(0.7)	(0.7)
Machines	(94)	(361)	(892)	(1.3)	(1.1)	(3.1)	(3.2)	(3.5)	(3.9)
Construction[b]	266	670	1,810	3.6	3.5	5.7	6.7	7.2	8.3
Facilitating industries	527	736	1,475	7.1	5.9	6.3	7.4	5.9	6.8
Public utilities	(104)	(189)	(404)	(1.4)	(1.5)	(1.6)	(2.0)	(1.6)	(2.0)
Trans. communications	(423)	(547)	(1,071)	(5.7)	(4.4)	(4.7)	(5.4)	(4.3)	(4.8)
Commerce-services	3,281	5,133	12,048	44.1	43.4	44.0	36.1	48.2	42.2
Commerce	(1,638)	(2,155)	(5,759)	(22.0)	(22.4)	(18.5)	(22.1)	(23.0)	(27.1)
Services	(1,643)	(2,978)	(6,289)	(22.1)	(21.0)	(25.5)	(14.0)	(25.2)	(15.1)
Total	7,448	11,663	25,008	100.0	100.0	100.0	100.0	100.0	100.0

Source: Japan, Gyōsei Kanrichō, Tōkei Kijun Kyoku (Statistics Standard Bureau), *Shōwa 30-nen sangyō renkanhyō* (Input-Output Table for 1955); *Shōwa 35-nen sangyō renkanhyō* (Input-Output Table for 1960); *Shōwa 40-nen sangyō renkanhyō* (Input-Output Table for 1965).

Note: Manufacturing "A" includes the more traditional categories, including mining; manufacturing "B" includes chemicals, metals, and machinery. All figures in parentheses are subtotals.

[a] The first column for each of the three years is the total, and the second column is a distribution percentage of household consumption.

[b] Private residential construction from national income statistics.

has to visualize the economy as divided into two large sectors. One sector is heavily influenced by autonomous or innovational investment opportunities. This is the modern sector where the technologically most progressive industries are located—those relying most intensely on borrowed technology that can, it is hoped, result in lower levels of K/Y. The other sector is a "follower" in the sense that innovational investment leads to increases in income per capita, creating additional need for a wide variety of more traditional consumer goods and services as well as government services. Here the promise of innovation is much smaller, and essentially K/Y can be considered as given. The modern sector creates demand for both consumption and investment goods, whereas we shall consider acceleration as being confined specifically to the capital requirements of follower or traditional sectors. (Obviously there is a degree of overlap between the two concepts.)

To quantify the acceleration process, one can use the standard formula $GY \times \sigma = I/Y$ (where σ is the incremental capital-output ratio). If σ is relatively stable, as was the case except for agriculture, it can be applied as an indicator of capital requirements in follower sectors. (No attempt will be made to quantify the full investment and consumption impact of derived demand. This would require elaborate econometric calculations.)

The distribution of consumption demand in 1960. Japan possesses multisector input-output tables that we shall use to analyze both the structure of consumption and the linkages between consumption and production. Table 6.7 deals with the structure of total (household, government, and business) consumption. It is based on a highly simplified version of the input-output table and can substantiate most previous suppositions.[15] The very moderate percentage of consumption directed toward manufacturing "B," the leading and most innovational sectors of chemicals, metals, and machinery, is particularly striking. In 1955 it received only 3 percent of average household expenditures, and the machinery industry alone received only 1 percent. Of course, these industries were expanding rapidly, but even after ten years of record growth, the whole category was still only 7 percent, and machinery stood at 4 percent. By comparison, manufacturing "A," the more traditional

---

[15] In 1965, government and business consumption were 13.7 and 8.4 percent, respectively, of the total. By international standards, the former is low and the latter is high. The reasons for these levels are generally agreed upon: postwar government social expenditures have been small; postwar business entertainment expenditures have been enormous.

TABLE 6.8

Sectoral Incremental Capital-Output Ratios in the Production of Consumption Goods

Sector	1955			1960			1965		
	σ	ε	σc	σ	ε	σc	σ	ε	σc
Agriculture	1.75	6.6%	0.116%	11.30	5.0%	0.565%	6.61	4.6%	0.305%
Manufacturing "A"	1.54	35.1	0.541	2.16	33.4	0.721	2.16	27.3	0.590
Manufacturing "B"	1.32	3.5	0.046	1.49	5.6	0.083	1.81	6.8	0.123
Construction	0.59	3.6	0.021	1.05	5.7	0.060	1.42	7.2	0.102
Facilitating industries	2.99	7.1	0.212	3.82	6.3	0.241	4.03	5.9	0.238
Commerce-services	1.87	44.1	0.825	1.78	44.0	0.783	2.14	48.2	1.032
Total		100.0	1.761		100.0	2.453		100.0	2.390

Source: Gross domestic fixed capital formation by industries from NIS (1970); gross domestic product by industries at market prices from *ibid.* Investment and output in current prices, smoothed by five-year moving average. These include the public sector.

Note: Manufacturing "A" includes the more traditional categories, including mining; manufacturing "B" includes chemicals, metals, and machinery.

Notation:

σ, incremental capital-output ratio derived as follows: $G_y \sigma = I/Y$.

ε, consumption distribution percentage; see Table 6.7.

$\sigma_c = \sigma \times \epsilon =$ incremental capital-output ratio in production for final consumer demand.

categories, occupied a much larger place in the consumption pattern of households, government, and business.[16]

It should also be stressed that the agricultural percentages of Table 6.7 are unduly low because of the classification system. All processing of primary products has been included under manufacturing "A." If these activities were considered as part of agriculture, in 1960 its entry would have risen from 5.0 to nearly 30 percent.

The character of acceleration. Having described the relationship between postwar consumption expenditures and industrial production, we come next to quantifying and characterizing the impact of the accelerator. Table 6.8 gives the incremental capital-output ratio in the production for final consumer demand (σ_c).[17] This has to be contrasted with the incremental capital-output ratio in the production for capital formation (σ_i), which, similarly calculated, was 1.20 in 1955, 1.56 in 1960, and 1.82 in 1965.[18] Thus σ_c is definitely greater than σ_i, and between 1955 and 1965 the difference became larger.[19]

Let us now try to summarize the conclusions regarding consumption,

[16] Obviously the use of manufacturing "B" to represent autonomous investment and manufacturing "A" to represent induced investment should not be interpreted too rigorously. Intermediate zones are present, and our results yield only approximations.

[17] There is no inconsistency between the rise of σ in Table 6.8 and the findings in previous chapters to the effect that the postwar capital-output ratio (K/Y) declined, especially during the spurt. Earlier we were concerned with *private nonagricultural* investment. In the table now being discussed, agriculture and the public sectors should be included. Both increase capital-output ratios. The values for agriculture fluctuate very much from year to year. It would therefore be wisest to consider the three yearly entries as an average.

A more elaborate calculation should take into account the effects of intermediate goods. This requires a complicated procedure, and given the quality of data, final results are not necessarily improved. In addition, those industries with which we have been especially concerned—agriculture, commerce, and services—use comparatively small proportions of intermediate goods.

[18] The industrial distribution of production for capital formation is much more concentrated than production for consumption. In 1960, 95 percent of investment goods were produced by manufacturing "B" and construction. The distribution percentages were as follows: agriculture 0.5, manufacturing "A" 0.6, manufacturing "B" 65.8, construction 29.2, facilitating industries 0.3, and commerce-services 3.6. This distribution was also used for 1955 and 1965.

[19] The ratio σ_c/σ_i was 1.47 in 1955, 1.57 in 1960, and 1.31 in 1965. In Table 6.8, σ has been estimated in current prices, since the national income statistics do not supply industrial output deflators. This biases the estimates, and σ_c/σ_i can be considered a most conservative estimate. Taking 1960 as 100, the consumption price index was 91.6 in 1955, and 133.2 in 1965; the investment goods index was 83.0 and 111.6 for the same years. Adjusting with these indexes gives 1.86 and 2.79 for σ_c in 1955 and 1965.

production, and investment. In general, the propositions stated at the beginning of this section have been confirmed within the limits of available data. Postwar private sectors, *including* business, and the public sector have continued to purchase goods and services primarily from those production activities with high marginal capital-output ratios, thereby inducing large quantities of investment. (The high values of σ for agriculture, services, and facilitating industries tell the story.) Purchases for capital formation purposes had much lower incremental capital-output ratios.

The mechanisms underlying these findings have to involve complicated interactions. Stated in very simplified terms, we are inclined to underscore the following linkages. The process begins with autonomous or innovational investment in the private sector because of economic opportunities arising from (frequently imported) technological and organizational progress. These activities eventually lead to increases in per capita income, which, in turn, will raise the demand for the goods and services of less progressive or non-innovational sectors. This brings in the sizable acceleration process, because the kinds of products and services desired are far less amenable to technical progress and therefore have high incremental capital-output ratios. Of course, some of the derived demand will also accrue to those sectors, particularly manufacturing "B" and construction, that produce investment goods.

One last point: can one compare the power of prewar and postwar acceleration? In the absence of necessary statistics, it is not worthwhile to spend much time on this matter. Still, it seems obvious that acceleration must have been much weaker before World War II. The growth rate of income certainly was much lower. What happened to comparative levels of the marginal capital-output ratio of various industries is less certain. In agriculture it rose very much after the war; for facilitating industries it declined. On balance it probably did not change too much in either direction, and the critical difference remains the greatly increased growth of income after the war. This is what made acceleration so powerful. And this is why the postwar investment boom was so pervasive. It is true that engineering, steel, and chemicals had the most impressive records of capital formation; but at the same time almost *all* sectors displayed spectacular rates of investment growth.[20]

[20] See our "Postwar Japanese Growth," in L. Klein and K. Ohkawa, eds., *Economic Growth: The Japanese Experience Since the Meiji Era* (Homewood, Ill., 1968), especially Figure 1.3.

TABLE 6.9
The Composition of Domestic Savings
(Percent)

| Year | Gross aggregate ratio[a] (1) | Net ratio[b] (2) | Proportion to domestic savings | | | | |
			Private[c] (3)	Corporate (4)	Government (5)	Capital consumption[d] (6)	Net foreign claims (7)
1908	15.6	7.9	23.7	2.0	20.6	51.6	-4.1
1917	32.6	22.4	57.8	2.2	15.3	48.7	-21.8
1924	15.6	5.3	-14.5	0.6	44.5	57.5	-12.5
1931	15.7	6.7	24.5	3.3	13.2	60.2	-2.0
1937	24.5	16.3	50.4	9.5	23.0	38.8	0.2
1956	27.7	20.4	47.6	12.0	19.4	33.0	0
1962	33.9	25.6	45.9	12.7	21.4	32.7	-1.9
1966	36.0	26.7	48.3	12.3	16.5	35.2	1.5

Source: Savings from BST.10. GNP from BST.5. Foreign claims from BST.11. Corporate savings from Y. Yamada, *Nihon kokumin shotoku suikei shiryō* (A Comprehensive Survey of National Income Data in Japan; Tokyo, 1957).
Note: Smoothed series. Figures for 1908, 1956, 1962, and 1966 are five-year moving averages; figures for 1917, 1924, and 1931 are seven-year averages; and figures for 1937 are three-year averages.
[a] National savings/GNP.
[b] Net savings/NNP.
[c] Corporate savings are included.
[d] Available data do not permit allocation of capital consumption to public and private sectors.

SAVINGS

It is not our intention to provide an overall analysis of the role of sav-ings in Japanese economic development. A complete treatment of this subject is necessarily lengthy and would have to be interdisciplinary in approach. Instead, we intend to confine ourselves to those aspects of savings that directly affect our particular approach to Japan's growth. Investment plays a key role in our framework, and the study of savings will therefore focus on the financing of investment. How did savings sup-port the rapid growth of capital formation? This is the main question we will attempt to answer.

The time path of the long-term aggregate savings ratio has a configu-ration that is already familiar: it closely resembles the long swings of in-vestment and aggregate output (Table 6.9). In either net or gross versions, peaks are attained in 1917 and 1937, and the postwar level is much above any of the prewar entries.

These findings suggest an additional though obvious point of impor-tance. Over time, and especially in this century, the savings ratio has risen sharply, especially during expansion periods. In 1908, for example, net savings were only 8 percent of net national product; by 1917 they had climbed to 22 percent; and in 1966 the ratio nearly reached 27 percent. This deserves stressing, because sometimes the impression is given that Japan's savings ratio has always been in a remarkably high range. No doubt this is the case at present, but it took at least 60 years to reach this position.

Just as the aggregate savings ratio has changed its level since the turn of the century, so has its composition altered. That personal savings have been unusually large in Japan is well known, and fully confirmed by Table 6.9. Personal savings (in the table, private minus corporate savings) were usually the most important component of domestic savings, and attained especially large shares toward the end of long-swing expansions—56 percent in 1917, 41 percent in 1937, and 33 percent in 1962. At the same time, corporate savings are assuming an ever more important role. They remained at a net level of 3 percent or under of aggregate savings until 1931, and in 1956 they reached 12 percent. (In gross terms corporate savings are, of course, much larger.) Keeping in mind the very sizable and rising private investments through this period, it is also evident that the corporate sector has not in the past and does not now generate nearly sufficient savings to finance its own activities. In large measure the deficit must have been supplied by personal savings. Statistical proof for this assertion is available only since 1952, when regularly only some 60 percent of personal savings are absorbed within that sector, mainly for the purchase of housing and producers' durables. The remainder was undoubtedly placed in the hands of businesses (and government) via the banks, post office savings, and other financial intermediaries.

These flows are a peculiar characteristic of the Japanese economy, and it may therefore be informative to trace them in greater detail for an illustrative year, fiscal 1961. At that time, the corporate savings–corporate income ratio was 41.5 percent. The corporate savings–investment ratio was 23.5 percent, obviously a considerable shortfall that had to be secured on the outside.

In 1961 the personal sector saved ¥2,307 billion of which ¥1,198 billion (gross) was spent on its own account, essentially for residential buildings and unincorporated private enterprise investments. This is a very heterogeneous sector, being a mixture of households and small proprietorships, the latter mostly engaged in rather traditional pursuits. But the main point is that 63.2 percent of this sector's savings in 1961 flowed outside, ultimately into the eager hands of corporate enterprise.

Small proprietors or owners of unincorporated enterprises played a particularly important role in the generation of personal savings. In 1961

TABLE 6.10
Allocation of Savings Between the Public and Private Sectors
(Percent)

Year	Govt. consumption/GNP	(Govt. savings^a– govt. investment)/govt. investment	Private savings/disposable income	
			Net	Gross
1908	12.9%	−64.2%	5.8%	17.7%
1917	12.9	−5.8	12.6	24.9
1924	10.9	−7.1	−1.0	12.8
1931	15.0	−95.1	6.1	18.5
1937	25.7	−237.2	18.2	32.9
1956	9.7	−19.2	18.8 (13.7)	28.1
1962	8.5	−12.5	23.9 (17.2)	34.3
1966	8.5	−30.3	24.8 (17.9)	36.2

Source: GNP and government consumption from BST.5. Government and private savings from BST.10. Government investment from BST.7. Disposable income from LTES, vol. 1. (Military investment is treated as government consumption.)

Note: Smoothed series, at current prices. Figures for 1908, 1956, 1962, and 1966 are five-year moving averages; figures for 1917, 1924, and 1931 are seven-year averages; and figures for 1937 are three-year averages. Figures in parentheses are household accounts.

^{a}Government savings equal surplus in the current account of general government.

the personal savings–disposable income ratio averaged 18.4 percent. It was 14.4 percent for wage and salary workers, 13.6 percent for farmers, and 21.8 percent for "others," primarily the proprietors. In terms of shares in personal savings, 28.2 percent came from workers, 12.0 percent from farmers, and a hefty 59.8 percent from "others," mostly the owners of unincorporated enterprises. The year 1961 was not unrepresentative, and therefore is a good postwar illustration of how personal savings made up the corporate deficit.[21]

The next step is to trace the historical development of savings from the viewpoint of aggregate expenditures, which is done in Table 6.10. One should start with the government draft on national resources for other than capital formation purposes, and this is the government consumption–GNP ratio. Clearly the prewar draft was much higher than recent levels, permitting a greater formation of national (public and private) savings following World War II. It is also entirely obvious that the prime difference between these two periods is the magnitude of mili-

[21] The above illustration is based on an attempt to arrive at consistent results for national income and family budget data. This unpublished study covered the years 1951–65 and was carried out at the Economic Planning Agency by T. Noda and Y. Ōtani.

tary expenditures, all of which have been treated as consumption in Table 6.10. Before World War II they ordinarily ranged between 4 and 6 percent of GNP. In times of political crisis or conflict, the share shot up to much more elevated levels: 25.1 percent in 1905 at the time of the Russo-Japanese War and 16 percent in 1938 when the country was preparing for the Pacific war. Since World War II, military expenditures have averaged about 1 percent of GNP. There can be no doubt about the resource-liberating effects of this new expenditure pattern.

Next, we come to government savings that measure the public sector's potential contribution to financing both public and private capital formation. The balance between government revenues and current expenditures (the conventional definition of general government savings) measures the public contribution, positive or negative, to financing total investment. Actually, in the Japanese case, government savings were applied nearly entirely to government investments. This balance can be examined in Table 6.10, in the column "(govt. savings − govt. investment) / govt. investment."[22] For the entire period of analysis, the government balance has been negative; therefore in general the public sector has been an absorber of investment resources that otherwise might have been used by private enterprise. Nevertheless, the prewar and postwar contrast is of far greater significance than the historical generalization. From the early twentieth century through the 1930's, government investment deficits rose very sharply, and they attained extremely large magnitudes in the 1930's. In contrast, they became very small in the 1950's and 1960's, even though bond flotation since 1965 has resulted, once again, in rising deficits. We can conclude that in its consumption *and* investment activities, the government made much smaller claims on resources after World War II.

Last, one should examine the net and gross private savings–disposable income ratios. It is already evident that the private sector determined the swings and trend of national savings since the government has been a dissaver. Therefore, everything that was noted earlier concerning the national savings ratio applies here: low initial levels, and excellent correspondence to the long-swing periodization, and a rising trend. Our analysis of domestic savings composition also indicated that, within the private sector, households were the major savers.

Thus far we have established the central role of personal savings in financing investments and in determining the level and movements of

---

[22] In order to make the results comparable for the prewar and postwar periods, military investments have been excluded from this calculation.

aggregate savings. Why should this have been so? Are there specific Japanese conditions backed by theoretical relations that could plausibly explain this long-lasting situation? The following line of reasoning suggests itself. First, empirical studies have shown a close positive relationship between the fluctuations of the personal savings ratio and real disposable income.[23]

Next, there are reasons for assuming that the rate of growth of income affects the personal savings ratio. Two major factors come to mind. First, the Japanese consumer has exhibited an innate conservatism as shown by slow changes in a traditional consumption pattern. Diet, clothes, furniture, entertainment—and other activities connected with daily life—have altered at rates far below those of income growth. Second, personal savings in Japan are in reality a rather mixed category. Farm households and nonfarm unincorporated enterprises (i.e. many small businesses) find it conceptually difficult to separate savings and profits. Both types of enterprises tend to retain profits intended for future investment, and these will temporarily appear as personal savings.

Next, one can also make the usual assumption that the level of personal savings is related to the level of personal income.[24] And last, if the above is accepted, one can expect Japan's savings function to take the following simple lag form: $S_t = A + bY_t + cY_{t-1}$, in which the savings ratio (S_t/Y_t) depends on a constant term, the level of income, and the rate of growth of income.[25]

The savings behavior of individuals and households is undoubtedly much more complicated than any of the suggested behavioral relations. Three causes of high personal savings are frequently given for Japan: a backward social security system, the difficulty of obtaining personal credit, and the necessity of paying for the education of children. In a word, welfare is largely a personal rather than a public matter, and this is seen as heightening the incentive to save. All of these are plausible reasons, although they do open up a series of motives not easy to verify

[23] See K. Ohkawa, "Chochiku ritsu no chōki hendō" (Long-Term Movement of the Savings Rate), *Keizai kenkyū*, vol. 21, no. 2 (May 1970). Between 1908 and 1938, in terms of smoothed series, the two series present nearly a mirror image. Since World War II the similarity is somewhat less clear.

[24] See Miyohei Shinohara, *Structural Changes in Japan's Economic Development* (Tokyo, 1970), chap. 2.

[25] $S_t/Y_t = b + A/Y_t + cY_{t-1}/Y_t$. In a preliminary way we have attempted to fit this equation to the data, taking Y as disposable income, and the results have been encouraging. These calculations indicate that the income growth term accounts for the following percentages of the real savings ratio: 50 in 1908, 27 in 1912, 16 in 1917, 75 in 1924, 50 in 1931, 23 in 1936, 50 in 1953, 40 in 1959, and 31 in 1966.

in an empirical manner.[26] To some extent, the lag between consumption and income growth may be an expression of these concerns, but without a doubt a complete explanation would have to take many more factors into account.

Sometimes it has been argued that if only Japan's savings performance could be explained, then most other factors pertaining to its economic growth would fall into line. That this is not our view should by now be clear. In the present analysis, savings are considered an essentially dependent process whose key determinants are the rate of growth and the level of income. The point is to explain these two items.

[26] For a valuable attempt, see Tuvia Blumenthal, *Saving in Postwar Japan* (Harvard East Asian Monographs; Cambridge, Mass., 1970).

CHAPTER SEVEN

Foreign Trade

EXTERNAL DEMAND: THE GROWTH OF EXPORTS

The role of foreign trade in Japanese economic development has always been subject to a certain mystique. Few will dispute Kuznets's assertion that contact with the outside world is critical for modern economic growth, and clearly the most important task of economic contact takes the form of visible and invisible exports and imports. But in the case of Japan the feeling concerning international economic relations has somehow been even stronger: it is not difficult to find government and business leaders suggesting that international trade has in some sense been "paramount," that it was a necessary and sufficient condition for bringing about economic modernization. Two facts undoubtedly have lent credence to this view. First, there are the historical circumstances of Japanese development: nearly 250 years of self-imposed isolation, followed by virtually uninterrupted and rapid economic growth. Second, there is the well-known fact about the expansion of Japanese exports. Since the 1890's these have expanded at rates much beyond those of world averages. In rough numbers, Japanese exports grew over twice as quickly as world trade volume from the 1880's to World War I, over ten times more rapidly in the interwar period, and about three times as quickly since World War II. No wonder there has been so much talk about "export-led growth."

We intend to argue a rather different set of propositions. Our position is that Japan's rate of growth of exports has been high and well above world averages because the rate of growth of its economy and especially of its industry has been high and well above world averages, and not vice versa. Given the complex interaction between domestic growth and international trade, it is not easy to demonstrate the validity of this view conclusively, but our thinking runs along these general lines.

First, one has to recognize the changing historical role of international trade. What happened in Meiji Japan will not be considered at all since it is outside the period of analysis. We will continue to focus on the years 1900–1965, a long phase of Japanese growth during which manufacturing industries played the leading role in economic development. Consequently, the relationship between trade and these industries will be taken up in particular detail.

Second, export-led growth can be defined as an acceleration in growth caused by an increase in export demand. There were periods in Japanese economic history when this model applied, as in the frequently-referred-to experience of World War I. It does not, however, work equally well for the long run. Even though manufactured exports frequently grew at rates that exceeded those of manufacturing output, we will attempt to show that this was primarily due to a decline in the relative price of these products as a result of productivity gains in manufacturing. The emphasis is on the side of supply, and it is our contention that, in a long-term sense, the most important fact has been the shift of the domestic supply curve. In the language of the standard export function, this would mean that "price effects" outweighed income effects in the long run.

Third, the fact that Japanese exports grew more rapidly than world trade is important because it suggests in which direction the analysis should turn. More rapid growth of exports simply means that Japanese goods were displacing goods of other countries in world markets. If we assume that world demand was relatively indifferent to the national origin of imported products—or at the very least that Japanese products were not preferred simply because they came from Japan—it is then clear that the reason for highly successful export growth must lie on the supply side. Supply, in this sense, has a broad meaning and includes export prices, quality, product differentiation, and financing. Since ours is a framework utilizing primarily the concept of national income, we will concentrate mainly on the relation between prices and export performance, and it will turn out to be largely a study in cost reduction because of relatively low labor costs and rapid technological and organizational advance. Using essentially the same reasoning, we will also try to explain the changing composition of exports and the contrast between prewar and postwar Japan.[1]

[1] A similar conclusion, based on a formal model, has recently been advanced by Y. Shionoya and I. Yamazawa in their paper "Industrial Growth and Foreign Trade in Prewar Japan," presented to the Second Conference on Economic Growth: A Case Study of Japanese Experience, Tokyo, June 26–July 1, 1972.

TABLE 7.1
Demand Components of Manufacturing
(Percent)

Year	Exports (1)	Consumption[a] (2)	Producers' durables (3)	Construction[b] materials (4)	Fixed investment (3) + (4) (5)	Total (6)
1905	24.4%	61.1%	7.1%	7.4%	14.5%	100.0%
1912	28.1	54.3	9.4	8.2	17.6	100.0
1919	27.3	48.6	16.4	7.7	24.1	100.0
1926	29.3	55.3	7.8	7.6	15.4	100.0
1931	30.5	52.3	10.1	7.1	17.2	100.0
1938	27.1	41.0	25.1	6.8	31.9	100.0
1955	15.8	61.8	11.8	10.6	22.4	100.0
1960	13.5	51.9	17.9	16.7	34.6	100.0
1965	14.2	52.7	16.4	16.7	33.1	100.0

Source: For prewar years, from Y. Shionoya, "Patterns of Industrial Development," in L. Klein and K. Ohkawa, eds., *Economic Growth: The Japanese Experience Since the Meiji Era* (Homewood, Ill., 1968), chap. 3. Postwar, from Input-Output tables (see Table 6.7).

Note: Prewar percentages are seven-year averages, with the exception of 1938, which is a five-year average. Postwar percentages are for single years.

[a] Consumption includes private and public sectors.

[b] Construction materials are listed despite the fact that durables used in construction are not final demand. They are, however, directly purchased from the manufacturing sector, and that is the point at issue in this analysis. Hence column (5) is headed "fixed investment."

The Export of Manufactures

To understand Japan's export performance in the twentieth century, one has to concentrate almost exclusively on the manufacturing industry. Around 1900 the products of this sector were 65 percent of total exports; during the 1930's manufactured exports attained 75–80 percent; and in the postwar years the share topped 90 percent.[2] During this long period, the growth of exports (G_X) and the growth of manufacturing output (G_{Ym}) developed a regular pattern, especially after World War I. As shown in Figure 7.1, during the upswing of the 1930's and again in the 1950's, G_{Ym} was larger than G_X. During most of the 1920's and again in the first half of the 1960's, both investment downswings, G_X was larger than G_{Ym}. This may be considered the "normal" pattern of the last 50 years. Around World War I the situation was very different, since during that investment spurt G_X exceeded G_{Ym} by a considerable margin until 1916, followed by a steep decline of G_X lasting until 1921. Let us leave the World War I situation aside for the moment, and first attempt to make sense of the period since about 1923.

Table 7.1 contains the demand components of manufacturing for

[2] In the same time span, the share of manufactured imports in the total declined from approximately 80 percent to 25 percent.

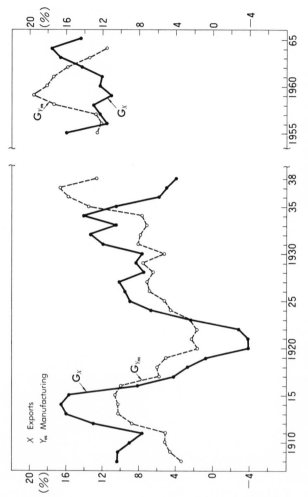

Fig. 7.1. Exports and manufacturing. (*Source*: Exports, BST.12; Y_m, BST.4.)

1905–65. It is there to place the role of exports in perspective. Throughout the period, the proportion of exports in the final demand of manufactured products, excluding intermediate goods, was relatively large, but there is a prewar and a postwar break. After World War II, exports have become much less important—their proportion was nearly halved—and fixed investments have been their replacement in the final demand structure. The trend points in the direction of domestic demand assuming a bigger lead over foreign demand.[3]

Of greater relevance to the so-called normal pattern is the competitiveness of domestic and foreign demand. When the domestic market becomes more active, it is reasonable to expect the export proportion to stagnate or decline, and vice versa. A favorable home market is always more attractive to the entrepreneur: sales are easier and less risky, and the price may be more favorable. When the home market weakens, the entrepreneur's horizon naturally extends to overseas opportunities with greater eagerness, and those are precisely the periods when the Japanese are said by foreign competitors to mount export drives or to engage in dumping. From Japan's point of view, however, foreign sales perform a useful demand-stabilizing task. This is how we interpret the relative movements of G_X and G_{Ym} since the 1920's, and the interpretation is, at least indirectly, supported by the evidence. In Table 7.1 it is particularly instructive to compare columns (1) and (3): after 1919, a rise or fall in the proportion of producers' durables is accompanied by a movement in the opposite direction for exports.[4]

The period centering on World War I does not fit this line of reasoning because, in contrast to the situation since the 1920's, "export-led growth" has a distinct plausibility. Export demand, at that time, held to extraordinary levels for about six years, directly as a consequence of World War I, when, as stated previously, the temporary disappearance of European producers created shortages and opportunities for the Japanese. The unusual aspects of this episode are confirmed by the prevailing relative price structure. As we shall see below, Japanese export prices (P_X) declined secularly compared with either import (P_M) or general prices (P). Taking 1934–36 as 100, P_X/P fell, almost in a

---

[3] These statements are somewhat abstract, and special historical circumstances no doubt contributed toward these movements. After World War II, the geographical orientation of Japan's trade was drastically rearranged away from Asia and toward North America, and its prewar share of world trade has not yet been recovered. Similarly, the steep decline of export growth toward the end of the 1930's was also influenced by a deteriorating political situation.

[4] This relation was already noted in our discussion of exports, investment, and aggregate demand. See Chapter 6 above.

straight line, from 209 in 1905 to 74 in 1937. There was only one exception, when these relative prices rose from 170 in 1913 to 187 in 1918. In this sense, the World War I position of Japan was abnormal—relatively increasing export prices, due to external factors outweighing internal economic conditions—a situation that has not been repeated since then.[5]

Price Effects

Our hypothesis is that the "price effect" has been the most important explanatory factor for the pattern of export growth, and this immediately raises a paradoxical issue.[6]

The empirical record indicates that the long-run development of the Japanese economy was accompanied by a moderate but sustained inflation. There were . . . some exceptions: the Matsukata deflation brought a price decline lasting from 1881 to 1886; World War I caused hyperinflation, and was followed by declining prices throughout most of the 1920's. However, in terms of the long run these exceptions were not frequent.

This passage was intended to describe only the years before World War II, but subsequent events have made it fully valid also for recent years. How was this rise in general prices compatible with declining relative, and not infrequently declining absolute, export prices?

The answer is contained within the structure of the Japanese economy, and specifically it is related to its dual or differential aspects. At least during this century, and perhaps earlier as well, the dispersion of domestic relative prices was wide but it also had a tendency toward bimodality, which reflected opposite pressure stemming from modern and traditional sectors. In broad trend movements, prices of goods produced by the modern economy tended toward relative decline, whereas goods emanating from traditional sectors showed signs of relative increase. General expenditure prices throughout the period were still heavily weighted by traditional production and consumption; therefore these indexes gave evidence of the sustained inflation. Export goods, in

---

[5] In terms of the usual methods of measuring export functions, the "normal" pattern means that the price elasticity must always exceed the income elasticity. When this pattern does not apply, for example from 1908 to 1916, income elasticities could have been larger. For the period 1924–37, M. Baba and M. Tatemoto fitted an export function with a price elasticity of −1.029 (0.103) and an income elasticity of 0.690 (0.255). Other measurements, which include the years of World War I, could give rather different results. See "Foreign Trade and Economic Growth in Japan: 1858–1937," in L. Klein and K. Ohkawa, eds., *Economic Growth: The Japanese Experience Since the Meiji Era* (Homewood, Ill., 1968), chap. 6.

[6] Kazushi Ohkawa and Henry Rosovsky, "Economic Fluctuations in Prewar Japan," *Hitotsubashi Journal of Economics*, vol. 3, no. 1 (October 1962), p. 14.

TABLE 7.2
Representative Indexes of Relative Prices

Year	Exports	Imports	Agriculture	Manufac-turing	Textiles	Machinery	General expenditure prices
1906	100.0	100.0	100.0	100.0	100.0	100.0	100.0
1912	69.5	89.1	104.1	85.6	80.4	74.3	120.5
1917	74.7	106.3	92.2	102.7	94.5	112.5	165.4
1924	70.6	90.4	100.5	79.2	80.4	60.0	250.0
1931	41.7	56.6	68.1	59.4	44.8	53.2	191.6
1938	43.5	77.9	95.3	74.2	50.0	67.7	249.8
1953	100.0	100.0	100.0	100.0	100.0	100.0	100.0
1955	86.3	93.6	101.7	91.2	82.2	89.9	105.1
1960	79.9	74.6	95.7	82.6	64.1	83.2	118.5
1965	57.9	61.0	110.7	65.2	51.1	62.7	149.1

Source: BST.14, except for textiles and machinery from LTES, vol. 8 (prewar), and from Japan, Economic Planning Agency, Economic Research Institute, *Keizai bunseki,* no. 27 (March 1969) (postwar).

Note: The original price indexes are three-year averages for the prewar period and single years for the postwar period. Individual indexes have been expressed as ratios of the general price index, and then converted to 1906 or 1953 comparison bases.

contrast, were increasingly modern and therefore illustrate the modern price pattern.

Evidence for these claims is given in Table 7.2. The suggested pattern is easily identified. For example, while general expenditure prices more than doubled between 1906 and 1938, relative export prices declined nearly 60 percent, and the relative prices of textiles fell by about 80 percent. These are the extreme cases, but the dual price structure is also observable in other forms. Relative prices of manufactures declined, while those of agriculture fluctuated, reaching 95 in 1938. The backwardness of the commerce-service sector is also spectacularly apparent; a similar calculation (not included in the table) shows the relative price of this sector to be 110 at the end of the 1930's. These price movements continued after World War II in intensified form. Between 1953 and 1965, general expenditure prices rose by 50 percent, but relative export prices declined to 58 and manufactures to 65. And the relative prices of agriculture, partially supported by the government, increased to 111.

One further question requires consideration. Why did the relative prices of the traditional economy rise? Basically we see this as a result of growing demand pressure combined with the inability to raise sufficiently the rate of growth of productivity. The resulting pressure on prices was damped by a flexible labor supply and by food imports from the colonies, but it was not sufficient to prevent a sustained and moderate inflation.

The situation of the modern economy was very different. Its output could yield lower relative prices because labor was "cheap" and the opportunities for productivity growth through technological progress were enormous. This permitted the modern economy to make inroads in both domestic and foreign markets, even though the rate of progress at which these inroads were made was faster abroad largely because foreign consumers on the whole had higher incomes per capita. It should be stressed that the decline of relative export prices was not peculiar; rather it was part of a much broader phenomenon, namely the relative decline of nearly all modern prices due in large measure to technological progress. There is a need to emphasize this point, because the rapid growth of Japan's exports has so often been interpreted very differently and, we believe, incorrectly. Too often the role of low wages is over-stressed whereas technological progress is forgotten. And sometimes, especially when dealing with the 1920's and 1930's, there is much talk of "social dumping." This term is hard to define, and however it be defined, some such thing may have taken place from time to time in certain industries. But it is equally likely that some of these charges simply reflect the growing power of Japan's modern industries to stand on two sturdy legs: relatively cheap labor and a great inflow of technology.[7] Neither one of these is necessarily antisocial.

A decline in the prices of any particular industry is bound to reflect a multitude of factors especially when international transactions are involved. Some of these factors, especially those related to cost reduction, are quantitatively presented in Table 7.3, where wages, prices, and productivity changes are compared for seven manufacturing industries between 1925 and 1938.[8] Of these the textile industry was espe-

---

[7] It has been suggested to us that exports may have had a particularly beneficial effect in furthering the exploitation of scale economies. This is plausible because manufacturing has relatively large economies of scale (Chapter 4), and this finding included export demand. However, the role of exports in this regard should not be overestimated. The export proportion to the total output of manufacturing (including intermediate goods) maintained a level of around 20 percent prewar, and it was without a distinct trend. During the postwar years the proportion declined.

These are the aggregate dimensions of the question. No doubt the conclusion has to be modified for specific industries. For example, it would seem as if export demand played a major role in allowing the Japanese automobile industry to attain scale economies in the 1950's and 1960's.

[8] The interval and especially the initial year are determined by data availability. This introduces a cautionary point. In the preceding paragraph we spoke of the growing trend divergence between modern and traditional prices, and this appears to be contradicted in Table 7.3. But the interval presented here does not illustrate a trend change; instead it largely covers a period of manufacturing expansion including an investment spurt during which modern prices (and especially investment-related prices) were under considerable pressure. This explains the rather rapid price increases in metals and machinery.

TABLE 7.3

*Average Annual Rates of Change in Productivity, Wages, and
Output Prices in Manufacturing Industries, 1925–38*

Industry	Labor productivity[a] (1)	Prices (2)	Wages (3)	Value productivity (1) + (2) (4)	Managerial gains (4) − (3) (5)	Productivity-wage gap (3) − (1) (6)
Textiles	4.48	−2.87	−1.64	1.61	3.25	−6.12
Wood products	3.80	−0.18	−0.42	3.62	4.04	−4.22
Food	2.83	−0.75	−0.60	2.08	2.68	−3.43
Metals	4.44	4.47	0.13	8.91	8.78	−4.31
Machinery	4.83	1.64	−0.07	6.47	6.54	−4.90
Chemicals	3.64	0.22	0.32	3.86	3.54	−3.32
Ceramics	3.65	−2.25	−0.42	1.40	1.82	−4.07
Others	4.92	1.11	−1.00	6.03	7.03	−5.92
Total manufacturing	3.83	−0.48	0.89	3.35	2.46	−2.94

Source: Output from Y. Shionoya, "Patterns of Industrial Development," in Klein and Ohkawa, eds., *Economic Growth*, chap. 3. Labor force from LTES, vol. 2. Wages and Prices from LTES, vol. 8, pp. 247–49, 192–93.

Note: Rates of change calculated between the two terminal years, and based on three-year averages centered on 1925 and 1938.

[a] Y/L in constant prices.

cially export-dependent,[9] and the table can reveal some of the reasons underlying its international competitiveness.

Within this array of manufacturing industries, the partial productivity of labor (Y/L) grew especially rapidly in textiles, metals, machinery, and others. However, only textiles were able to combine above-average productivity growth with sharply declining prices. In no other sector did prices decline with equal speed; indeed prices rose in the remaining industries where productivity gains were impressive. For textiles, a combination of these circumstances meant a very low rate of increase of value productivity (column 4, productivity in current prices); only ceramics made slower gains. But the growth of value productivity is not necessarily the determining element in an industry's competitive position. Textile enterprises were favored by wages that fell more rapidly than in any other sector (column 3),[10] and consequently the productivity-wage gap in this industry led all of manufacturing. Thus, despite declining output prices, what we have called "managerial gains" in textiles (column 5)—wage costs in relation to value productivity—continued to increase at above-average rates between 1925 and 1938.

[9] During the period under consideration, the export-output ratio—percentage of exports to domestic output—was 70 to 75 percent for raw silk and 50 to 60 percent for cotton fabrics.

[10] See Chapter 5. Real wages declined for unskilled workers, and particularly young girls.

Do these computations shed light on the export capability of Japan's textile industry? We think so, especially if Japan's exports were price-elastic, because the ability to withstand or promote low prices was the combined effect of productivity gains due to technological progress and lagging money wages. Neither factor taken alone can be considered the decisive advantage.

Postwar Export Shifts

Up to this point, the discussion of export growth has dealt largely with the prewar period. In many ways the situation changed considerably after World War II, but our basic postulate remains valid. Before the war, Japanese exports were dominated by the products of "light industry," among which textiles occupied a preeminent place. Most of the industries engaged in international trade were heavily dependent on exports, i.e. they specialized in this type of business. To a limited extent this type of export composition began to change in the 1930's. Textiles became less important and the proportion of machinery rose. Basically, however, the overall character remained unaltered. In the first half of the 1950's, approximately 30 percent of exports still consisted of fibers and textiles, and another 20 percent was classified as sundries. Only 14 percent was in the category of machinery. By the first half of the 1960's, after the great investment spurt, major changes in composition had taken place. Fibers and textiles were down to 8 percent and sundries to 14 percent, and machinery with 39 percent had assumed its position of leading component, followed by metals and metal products (26 percent).[11] The nature of the industries participating in export activities also underwent a transformation. Those with lesser foreign market dependence expanded their exports more rapidly, and of course their contribution to total export growth became progressively more significant. What this meant in terms of actual commodities sent abroad was a shift away from toys, sewing machines, clothing, etc., in the direction of plastics, business machines, and automobiles.

The problem now becomes explanatory. Why the shift in composition and why the rapid growth of new and different export industries? One may, of course, stress the importance of relative wage costs. In fact, the rates of increase of cash wages per worker differed widely among types of industries, but close examination has shown that increases in wages were inversely proportional to the growth of exports, but only until about 1955.[12] No doubt relative wage levels are of some importance in

---

[11] See H. Kanamori, "Economic Growth and Exports," in Klein and Ohkawa, *Economic Growth*, chap. 10, p. 311.
[12] *Ibid.*, pp. 316–17.

TABLE 7.4
Productivity and Wages in Manufacturing Industries:
Average Annual Rates of Growth, 1952–61

Sector	Residuals (percent)	Money wages per year (000 yen) 1952	Money wages per year (000 yen) 1961	Money wages, rate of increase (percent)
Chemicals	18.83%	¥158.4	¥322.9	8.26%
Paper, pulp	12.73	173.9	263.8	4.84
Transportation machinery	11.79	175.4	325.1	6.97
Wood and wood products	9.39	85.5	180.6	8.66
Petroleum, coal products	8.83	168.7	388.8	9.70
General and electrical machinery	8.74	150.8	282.6	7.25
Rubber products	7.46	146.4	243.5	5.81
Metals and metal products	5.07	170.1	323.5	7.41
Textiles	4.40	85.2	167.6	7.80
Leather and hide products	3.71	117.0	222.3	7.39
Ceramics, clay, stone products	2.70	127.5	241.2	7.30
Printing	2.02	142.3	311.0	8.25
Food and tobacco	1.41	98.6	182.3	7.07

Source: Residuals are from T. Watanabe and N. Igaizu, "Gijitsu shimpō to keizai seichō" (Technological Progress and Economic Growth) in M. Kaji, ed., *Keizai seichō to shigen haibun* (Economic Growth and Resource Allocation; Tokyo, 1967), p. 127. Wage data are from a special unpublished survey of the Economic Planning Agency.

determining the possibilities of foreign sales, and they may have been especially important in the old customary types of exports, such as textiles and toys. In the last four or five years there has been more and more talk in Japan about competition from Taiwan, Hong Kong, and Korea, and this must be rooted in competitive power largely based on lower labor costs. As a general explanation of export growth and composition, however, we believe that changes in wage costs have been of minor significance; certainly they have been of less significance than before World War II. What really mattered was the speed and the possibility of technological progress—to be sure, combined with a flexible labor supply.

Support for this point of view is contained in the relative residuals of Table 7.4. These were computed for 13 different industries from 1952 to 1961 in the manner described in Chapter 4, together with rates of increase in money wages. On the whole, differences in wage growth are rather minor, while the growth of residuals differs enormously over the whole range of industries. We do not know enough about the exact export performance of each industry, but it is perfectly obvious that the postwar shift has been in the direction of those kinds of production exhibiting the fastest expansion of residuals. To see this, one only needs to compare the experience of textiles and ceramics (old-line exports) with that of transportation and electric machinery (new exports). In other words, the crucial variation from the point of view of export competitiveness has been the rate of technological progress and not the rate of wage changes.

The Balance of Payments

Our survey of Japanese economic development in the twentieth century has been largely concerned with domestic factors. With the exception of a discussion of exports and frequent stress on borrowed technology, there has been only occasional mention of other international matters. In this brief section we intend to deal with this hitherto neglected topic.

In 1970 the Japanese government adopted a tight money policy to curb an "overheated" economy. This was a thoroughly familiar step that had occurred previously, at regular four- or five-year intervals. Whereas the policy measure of 1970 was the same as in former years, the reasons for its adoption were fundamentally different. Formerly, tight money was employed to achieve external equilibrium; now the intention became the restoration of internal equilibrium. This was a change of epochal significance. Until the end of the 1960's, Japan had always—after some years of rapid growth—encountered the external restraint of foreign payments deficits. At present, Japan is accumulating foreign reserves, and this constraint seems to have disappeared. To understand how this new situation came about requires some historical background.

We begin by summarizing Japan's experience with respect to the external constraint between 1900 and 1965.

1. Japan repeatedly faced crises connected with payment deficits. These were a ceiling, periodically blocking further rapid growth.

2. The foreign reserve position was largely determined by the trade balance, so that expansions of exports and imports were paramount in determining when the ceiling came into existence.

3. Because of an extremely poor natural resource endowment, the import of raw materials and fuels was Japan's severest "supply restraint."

4. This restraint remained operative despite successful import substitution activities for goods other than raw materials and fuels.

5. But import substitution could not possibly go far enough, and an adverse balance of payments repeatedly compelled Japan to devalue the yen during the 1920's and 1930's.

6. Occasionally, the external situation was unusually favorable. This was the case at the time of World War I, and also during the Korean war. Out of the 70 years now being considered, not too many can be placed in the "unusually favorable" category.

These generalizations apply to the entire period. Next, let us examine the historical background more closely, beginning with the prewar current account. In million yen, the balance of trade looked like this in cumulated amounts for each period (BST. 11), with the deficits (or surpluses) in terms of their ratio to the import of commodities and services (including income payments):

Period	Million yen	Percent	Period	Million yen	Percent
1904–13	−1,032	−15.2%	1932–36	−288	−1.7%
1914–19	2,813	30.6	1937–40	599	2.4
1920–31	−3,406	−9.9			

During 1904–13, deficits were big and closely related to expenditures of the Russo-Japanese War. (The deficit for 1904–5 alone was 425 million yen.) World War I altered the situation radically, and for a brief period Japan accumulated foreign exchange at a record pace. Soon, however, the exchange position became more normal and dreary. In the 1920's, deficits were an almost annual event, and the World War I surplus was quickly dissipated. With the advent of the 1930's and its investment spurt, deficits became somewhat smaller owing to yen devaluation.

Capital account statistics are not available for Japan proper, and to include these effects one has to rely on tentative estimates for the Japanese Empire, including its overseas territories. Given their limitations, these show (Table 7.5) that capital inflows to a very considerable extent mitigated the current account deficits just before the first world war. Later, the war surplus was large enough to permit both sizable capital outflows and an overall surplus. During the 1920's, despite the large quantities of "red ink" on current account, capital inflows were smaller.

TABLE 7.5

Balance of Payments, 1900–1940

(Million current yen)

Payments	1900-1907	1908-13	1914-19	1920-31	1932-36	1937-40
Current	−492	−366	3,037	−2,863	187	890
Capital[a]	818	176	−1,282	1,335	−324	n.a.
Long-term	899	525	−1,410	−353	−946	n.a.
Short-term	−81	−349	128	1,688	622	n.a.
Gold	56	36	−659	272	78	n.a.

Source: Current payments, for Japan proper, are from BST.11. Capital and gold payments, for the Japanese Empire, are from Y. Yamamoto, "Kokusai shūshi tōkei no chōki sōgōka ni tsuite" (Long-Term Estimates of the Balance of Foreign Payments), *Jimbun Gakuhō*, no. 38 (March 1969).

Note: There is a discrepancy between current and capital accounts because the former applies to Japan proper and the latter to the entire Empire. Capital accounts for Japan proper are not available.

[a] Based on government capital accounts. Short-term capital is a residual estimate and includes errors and omissions.

And finally, in the 1930's, the deficit was related to the outflow of capital.

These deficits, surpluses, and capital movements are, of course, closely tied to the economic history of the period. Japan adopted the gold standard in 1897 and stuck with it until 1917. Despite this, deficits were large for 1904–13 and were covered only by substantial long-term foreign loans. In this sense, just before the outbreak of World War I, Japan faced a severe external disequilibrium: growth for nearly a decade had been backed by net inflows of foreign resources. The war itself brought this situation to an abrupt reversal, but within Japan the economic boom also created a very rapid inflation, and by 1917 domestic prices had climbed more than in most other countries. During the 1920's, the time had come to pay for the previous excesses. They were most difficult years, when the government pursued its dual aims of deflation and returning to the gold standard at the prewar par. Little success was achieved in either direction. The deflation did not manage to bring Japan's prices into line,[13] and the return to gold lasted only from January 1930 to December 1931. When gold was abandoned a second time, the exchange rate of the yen fell rapidly from $49.38 (1931) to $28.12 (1932) per ¥100. Eventually the yen was pegged to sterling at 43 percent of the old gold par rate. This enormous devaluation, together with government deficit spending, in time helped both domestic business and exports. Toward the middle of the 1930's, the current account was nearly balanced, and capital exports were largely yen destined for satellite development in Manchukuo.[14]

Now we can see the entire period up to World War II in perspective. As a whole, growth was inflationary; the value of the yen depreciated domestically between 1900 and 1919, and did not significantly appreciate in the 1920's. By the 1930's further depreciation vis-à-vis foreign currencies was an absolute necessity.

Before saying a few words about the postwar situation, let us consider a question that may have arisen in the minds of some readers. In this chapter we have stressed the divergence between domestic and export prices; as a trend, the former rose and the latter declined. Furthermore, supply conditions were considered nearly always favorable for exports. Why, then, the need for downward yen revaluation and a Jap-

[13] With 1913 = 100, Japan's wholesale price index was 149.8 in 1934, compared with a United States figure of 108.4 and a United Kingdom value of 105.6.

[14] For a detailed account of this period, see Hugh T. Patrick, "The Economic Muddle of the 1920's," in James W. Morley, ed., *Dilemmas of Growth in Prewar Japan* (Princeton, N.J., 1971).

anese price level internationally out of line by 1920? There is no contradiction. Export prices did decline relative to domestic prices. Import requirements were also large and rising, and this pressure was intensified by the domestic inflation. Deficits in the balance of payments came about because even the rapid expansion of competitively priced exports was insufficient to cover desired imports. It was hoped that depreciation would ameliorate both aspects of the problem by providing a further push for exports and less attraction for imports.

Japan's post–World War II exchange rate was fixed at ¥360 to the dollar in 1949 (at 1/160 of the yen value in 1934–36), and at least until the late 1960's this rate worked well. Compared with prewar times, no long-run international disequilibrium was evident; instead of thoughts of devaluation, after 1969 there was increasing talk of the need for upward revaluation, which finally came in 1971. Short-term payments crises did occur several times after World War II, but each time the government imposed tight money conditions, expansion was briefly slowed down, and within less than two years rapid growth resumed.

A full explanation of Japan's very different international position after the war ultimately involves all the subjects covered in this book. Most directly, however, one can point to price stability. Postwar deficits were not accompanied by rising wholesale prices (with the possible exception of 1953). During the investment spurt, domestic prices remained remarkably stable. After that, since 1961 the price level did rise but wholesale and export prices continued to be steady. Basically this was due to the high rate of growth of productivity, which permitted rapid shifts of supply curves. Compared with the prewar period, Japan was now able to meet its import requirements without difficulties. Cost reduction in modern sectors was one aspect of increased export capability. Another element was the favorable external situation, including a most advantageous exchange rate and low import prices.

Japan has come a long way in this century. With respect to external restraints, this can be appreciated most clearly by comparing upswings and downswings since 1900. Before World War II, Japan's exchange position was always precarious, and both upswings entailed specific accommodations to this fact: taking advantage of opportunities created by World War I and depreciation in the 1930's. No successful accommodation was achieved in the 1920's. Then, for a period of approximately 20 years, from 1950 to 1970, Japan's international position remained in equilibrium, and external restraint became merely a matter of short-run adjustment. And now we have come full circle to a new disequilibrium: large and perhaps chronic surpluses in 1970 and 1971, and upward readjustments of the yen, one of the strongest currencies in the world. It is, of course, impossible to analyze this situation only from the Japanese perspective. Prewar and postwar conditions were closely tied to world economic conditions, and to a large variety of political decisions.[15] And yet, the transformation of Japan from a country of chronic deficit to that of chronic surplus is one measure of its economic achievements during the twentieth century.

One further matter relating to external constraints must be mentioned. After World War II, Japan's foreign trade proportions declined markedly, especially compared to the period 1910–40. Although the reasons for this are hard to pinpoint, there is no doubt that this decline must have contributed to an easier situation with respect to any external constraint.

Import Requirements

The long-run performance of Japan, described in Chapter 2, consisted of two trends moving in opposite directions: a relative decline in imported semifinished and final manufactured goods and a relative rise in the purchase of raw materials of foreign origin. To be specific, in 1905 manufactured goods accounted for 53.2 percent of total imports, and materials and fuels, excluding food products, for 46.8 percent. In 1965 manufactured imports had fallen to 28.2 percent while fuels and raw materials had climbed to 71.8 percent.[16] Japan's growing need for raw materials is the "real" side of external restraints, as opposed to the monetary side just discussed, and these requirements should be looked at not in relation to GNP but to manufacturing output; that is where most of the raw materials and fuels were used.[17] Two countervailing forces are present: import substitution of semimanufactured goods, and a rising inflow of materials and fuels, needed to accommodate the rapid expansion of manufacturing, for which import substitution was nearly impossible in a resource-poor country.

While the trend of import substitution in prewar Japan presents no conceptual difficulties, and while it has much in common with the ex-

[15] What if the United States had insisted on a less favorable exchange rate in 1949? What if Britain had remained neutral in World War I and had not opened Asian markets to Japan? What if the Great Depression had not ruined Japanese silk exports? Obviously there is no end to questions of this kind.

[16] BST.13. Food imports maintained a steady proportion of 10 to 15 percent of imports, except for the early 1950's when they briefly rose to 30 percent.

[17] For the import proportion to GNP, see BST.6 and BST.12. In constant prices, the ratio rose from 13 to 15 percent in 1900–1919 to 21 to 23 percent in the 1930's. After the war, the ratio fell to 9 to 12 percent. A decrease in the price of primary goods was an important factor in generating the decline.

perience of other industrialized countries, the time dimension of import substitution does deserve observation. All of the preceding chapters have discussed the major output and investment spurts of Japanese economic history, and in Chapter 4 a special effort was made to link investment spurts with periods of rapid technological progress. Now we can show that spurts (and rapid technological progress) are also positively correlated with accelerated import substitution. It is a logical connection. First of all, the possibility of import substitution must be related to acquiring new know-how, and this is precisely what occurred during spurt periods. Second, the very duration of spurts—longer than business cycles and usually lasting seven years—depended to some extent on successful import substitution. Otherwise, the pressures of increased investment and more rapid manufacturing growth would quickly have brought about unsupportable foreign payments deficits owing to excessive import expansion.

There are many possible ways to document the association between spurts and accelerated import substitution. One of these is Figure 7.2, in which the ratios of imported producers' durables and unfinished goods to each sector's domestic output are shown from 1895 to 1939 in current prices. This period includes the investment spurts of 1913–19 and 1931–38. Despite the irregularities inherent in annual series, the graph indicates unmistakably that the import ratio fell especially when the economy experienced one of the two prewar investment spurts. Import substitution must have speeded up at these times, unless the relative prices of domestic products rose during investment spurts, thereby distorting the picture. This was not the case.[18]

One more point needs to be mentioned. During both World War I and the 1930's the accelerated import of manufactures would have been hampered even if desired by some segments of the economy. Between 1914 and 1919 European and later American suppliers were diverted from normal international trade. Toward the end of the 1930's the Japanese government encouraged a policy of self-sufficiency, and some of the supplier countries were less and less anxious to ship manufactures to a potential enemy. For these reasons one could perhaps argue that both phases of rapid import substitution were the result of largely ad hoc circumstances. We cannot deny that these international disturbances may have been contributory causes both to import substitution

---

[18] For example, with 1905 as 100, by 1919 the prices of imported materials had risen to 213, imported semimanufactures to 292, and imported finished goods to 364. During the same interval, domestic manufacture prices rose to 202. In later years these relative prices remained more or less the same. See BST.14.

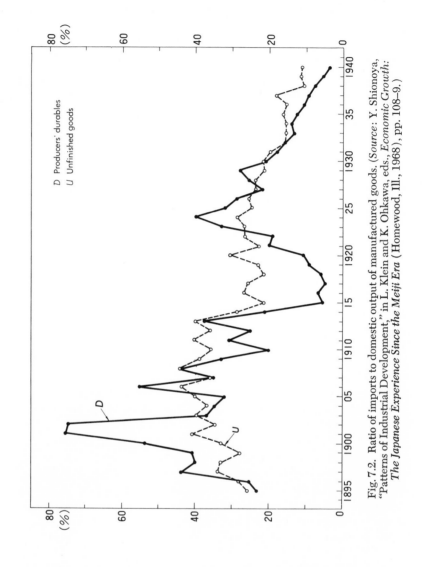

Fig. 7.2. Ratio of imports to domestic output of manufactured goods. (*Source:* Y. Shionoya, "Patterns of Industrial Development," in L. Klein and K. Ohkawa, eds., *Economic Growth: The Japanese Experience Since the Meiji Era* (Homewood, Ill, 1968), pp. 108–9.)

TABLE 7.6
Regional Distribution of Japan's Foreign Trade:
Exports and Imports, Selected Years
(Percent)

Region	1903	1914	1919	1930	1940	1951	1965
Asia:							
Exports	44%	45%	41%	46%	62%	52%	33%
Imports	54	49	45	36	43	29	33
North America:							
Exports	30	36	44	39	21	16	35
Imports	15	18	38	34	39	46	37
Europe:							
Exports	24	16	10	9	7	11	15
Imports	30	28	8	20	6	8	12
Others:[a]							
Exports	2	3	5	6	10	21	17
Imports	1	5	9	10	12	17	18

Source: Prewar, H. Ōuchi, ed., *Nihon keizai tōkeishū* (Collected Statistics of the Japanese Economy; Tokyo, 1958); postwar, M. Shinohara and S. Fujino, eds., *Nihon no keizai seichō* (The Growth of the Japanese Economy; Tokyo, 1967), chap. 11.
[a] South America, Africa, and Oceania.

and to investment spurts. But the point is that the investment spurts are historical facts—no doubt the combined results of endogenous and exogenous causes—and import substitution was one necessary aspect of a prolonged period of rapid growth.

The end of World War II created many complicated changes in Japan's international economic relationships. Of immediate import was the loss of its large empire, an occupation by victorious foreign powers, and considerable alterations in diplomatic and political relationships. Abrupt and short-term changes were combined equally with long-term changes and it is not a simple matter to disentangle these forces.

Both elements are illustrated in Table 7.6 where the regional distribution of Japan's foreign trade (export and import) is given from 1903 to 1965. Before World War II, Japan's trade as a whole was largely confined to Asia and the West; South America, Africa, and Oceania (classified as "others") were relatively less important. Until the 1930's, when the play of economic forces still took precedence over politics, these regional ties experienced considerable rearrangement. Europe became less of an import and export market, the import share from Asia declined somewhat, and most noticeably the relative position of North America—essentially the United States—was strengthened in the trade pattern.[19] A much greater concentration toward Asia is seen in the figures for 1940, and it suggests the strengthening of imperial economic ties during this troubled decade. In actuality, of course, colonial trade had been increasing in importance for some time, and it was now reaching its peak. When the Russo-Japanese War ended in 1905, the ratio of colonial to all foreign trade was still small: 3 percent for imports and 4 percent for exports. By the end of World War I, it had risen to 20 per cent of all imports and 18 percent of all exports. In 1930 the economic significance of the colonies—all located in Asia—was still rising, and they accounted for 24 percent of imports and 26 percent of exports. Peak dependence was undoubtedly reached in 1942, when overseas possessions accounted for 41 per cent of Japan's imports and 60 percent of its exports. This was the "co-prosperity sphere" at its greatest just before the disaster.[20]

The regional distribution of postwar trade in 1951 still reflects unhealed wounds caused by the catastrophe of the 1940's. Very low exports to, and very high imports from North America both are evidence of war damage and occupation, and a rather high proportion of exports to Asia—no longer to China and Korea but more to Southeast Asia—simply gives evidence once more of the fact that Japan in 1951 could sell mainly the products of light industry in international markets. More relevant are the changes between 1951 and 1965. In these we recognize some continuation of prewar trends and some novel features. The preeminence of the North American relationship—both for exports and for imports—is not new, because from a long-run standpoint no special significance need be attached to the events of the 1930's, since they were the direct consequences of the collapse of the silk market combined with increasing political conflicts. The relative decline of Asian markets is new, and it is counterbalanced by the reestablished importance of Europe and more active ties with other parts of the world (South America, Africa, and Oceania). In our opinion, the loss of colonies is not a primary cause in explaining these shifts. As far as exports are concerned, we already saw that these changed drastically toward sophisticated and highly fabricated products in the 1960's, and these naturally found their market in the more advanced areas of the world. Furthermore, the Asian countries were increasingly capable of producing most of Japan's traditional exports themselves.

[19] The decline of Europe is especially impressive if Meiji figures are added. In 1896, for example, Europe accounted for 30 percent of Japan's exports and 52 percent of its imports. H. Ōuchi, ed., *Nihon keizai tōkeishū* (Collected Statistics of the Japanese Economy; Tokyo, 1958).

[20] Colonial trade figures from Ōuchi.

What about postwar imports? To some extent import substitution has continued. At the same time, it must be recognized that import substitution has become rather less significant for postwar investment spurts and for continued growth in the 1960's. In 1940, about 7 percent of all manufactured goods available in Japan were imported; and this ratio was considerably higher in earlier years. Since 1951 the ratio has averaged slightly above 2 percent, and imported manufactured goods have become insignificant in total supply. It seems that import substitution, which must be confined to manufacturing, has been virtually completed, and in contrast to prewar years, during the spurt there was no decline in the imported proportion of either producers' durables or unfinished goods.[21] Undoubtedly this is a key difference in the prewar and postwar comparison.

The other category of major imports, raw materials and fuels, is of a noncompetitive nature, meaning that Japan has only little power in mitigating this external restraint through substitution. In saying this, we do not intend to minimize favorable effects accruing from special types of technological progress that were material-saving or permitted material substitution. Japan's efforts in "improvement engineering" have, in fact, frequently taken the form of reducing so-called "standard unit requirements" of fuels and materials. Furthermore, the Japanese have made enormous efforts to acquire direct control of certain raw materials in other countries, such as oil in the Middle East and timber in Canada. Despite these successes, import requirements in this category have continued to increase almost in parallel with the output of manufacturing. In addition, the growth of these imports has been found to be almost unrelated to their relative price changes, and this clearly underlies their imperative nature.[22] With import substitution virtually completed, one is inevitably led to an important conclusion concerning future import requirements: they will continue to expand at a rate approximately equal to that of manufacturing, and, given Japan's rapid expansion, this could raise serious problems for the world economy.

[21] The proportion of imported producers' durables maintained a steady level of about 5 percent during the 1955–61 investment spurt; the proportion of unfinished goods rose from 22 to 30 percent. See Y. Shionoya, "Kōgyō hatten no keitai" (The Pattern of the Industrial Structure), in M. Shinohara and S. Fujino, eds., *Nihon no keizai seichō* (Economic Growth of Japan; Tokyo, 1967), p. 174.

[22] According to Y. Shionoya and I. Yamazawa, "Industrial Growth and Foreign Trade in Prewar Japan," a log-linear import function for this category gives significant results with two variables: (1) prices of raw materials and fuels related to prices of domestic manufactures and (2) output (gross of intermediate goods) of manufacturing. The elasticity with respect to variable (2) is close to unity for both prewar (1905–34) and postwar (1953–65) periods, whereas the coefficient of variable (1) is statistically insignificant. The constant is small in both cases.

One can easily appreciate the magnitude of this problem by looking more closely at recent history. Japan's rapid growth during the decade of the 1960's and the shift toward "heavier" industries has led to high rates of increase in the consumption of natural and particularly mineral resources. Major mineral requirements have been increasing more rapidly than GNP—indeed, in many instances more rapidly even than the index of industrial production. According to a recent Ministry of International Trade and Industry (MITI) survey, the following average annual growth rates for resource consumption prevailed for 1965–70: petroleum 18.8 percent; coal 16.2 percent; iron ore 19.1 percent; nickel 26.3 percent; and aluminum 19.1 percent. Generally speaking, these rates were above those for 1960–65.[23] Of course, a country's resource consumption pattern is a complicated matter, and in Japan, as elsewhere, technological progress meant that certain savings in materials and fuels were achieved during this period. Nevertheless, the figures do strongly imply that the possibilities of mitigating resource requirements have been limited.

Against the background of these great and growing needs, we must consider Japan's well-known position of resource poverty. Its consequences are obvious: natural resources are an exceptionally high share of imports. For example, in 1968, materials and fuels constituted 58.1 percent of imports; comparative figures for some other countries were: Italy 35.1 percent; United Kingdom 26.8 percent; West Germany 25.8 percent; and the United States 18.1 percent.[24] Furthermore, during the long postwar economic expansion, Japan's import dependency has risen sharply. Between 1960 and 1970, the import dependency of coal went from 35.8 to 78.5 percent; iron ore rose from 68.0 to 87.9 percent; and copper went from 50.6 to 75.6 percent. (And during the entire decade, petroleum, nickel, and aluminum maintained levels of about 100 percent.) For the overall category of "major mineral resources," import dependency rose from a level of 55 percent in 1960 to 90 percent in 1970.

These trends have important and potentially disturbing implications for the economic and political future of Japan. In effect, they mean that if rapid growth is to continue—and in the absence of an entirely unanticipated technological revolution—Japan will need an ever larger

[23] See Japan, Ministry of International Trade and Industry, *Shigen mondai no tembō* (Perspective on Resource Problems; 1971), p. 2.

[24] For mineral resources and fuels the comparative figures were: Japan 35.1%; Italy 21.6%; United Kingdom 15.7%; France 16.4%; West Germany 15.7%; United States 11.4%. *Ibid.*, p. 12.

share of world resources. Already today these shares are not at all inconsiderable,[25] and to expand them very much may become difficult. Certainly the Japanese fully appreciate the gravity of this situation, and the government is now promoting a policy called *kaihatsu yunyū* (development imports), which attempts to assure an adequate supply of importable raw materials through the direct investment of Japanese capital in supplier countries. However, it is difficult to see how this can entirely solve the problem. This is so because the fundamental problem is political and not economic. No doubt Japanese entrepreneurs could find, exploit, and/or purchase natural resources all over the world—if allowed to do so. But all sorts of nationalistic sentiments and fears of domination may check these efforts at any time. One must conclude that Japan's gargantuan appetite for oil, coal, nickel, and the like may yet prove to be a constraining factor in maintaining the levels of growth achieved in the 1960's.

[25] In 1969, Japan consumed the following proportion of "free world" mineral production: petroleum 9.1%; iron ore 15.8%; copper 14.3%; lead 7.4%; zinc 15.8%; aluminum 11.0%; nickel 19.0%. *Ibid.*, p. 5.

CHAPTER EIGHT

The Economics of Trend Acceleration

TWENTIETH-CENTURY GROWTH PATTERN

The main purpose of this book is to explain the rapid growth of Japan's postwar economy in historical perspective. By "historical perspective" we mean the twentieth century, because it is our belief that from about 1900 through the 1960's a single historical model can explain the observed features of Japan's remarkable economic performance. In this chapter we will outline what we think needs to be explained and how we plan to explain it. Various assumptions and behavioral relations will be elaborated and tested insofar as possible by available historical data.

The years 1901 to 1966 constitute an identifiable historical unit—or to use a term previously employed, a growth phase[1]—because during this long period certain important characteristics of Japanese economic growth have persisted. In other words, this period established a specific growth pattern whose principal features we may briefly review.

1. During the 60-odd years with which this study is concerned, the trend rate of growth of aggregate product has been very rapid. Among the 15 to 20 countries that have established a long-term record of modern economic growth, only the United States and Canada (and perhaps Sweden and the Soviet Union) have turned in achievements of similar magnitudes. Thus, in overall distribution of historical national growth rates, a conservative estimate of Japan's performance would place it in the top quartile.

2. Japan's trend rate of growth of aggregate product has been accelerating during the period of analysis. Average growth rates, according

[1] See Kazushi Ohkawa and Henry Rosovsky, "A Century of Japanese Economic Growth," in W. W. Lockwood, ed., *The State and Economic Enterprise in Japan* (Princeton, N.J., 1965); and their "Postwar Japanese Growth," in L. Klein and K. Ohkawa, eds., *Economic Growth: The Japanese Experience Since the Meiji Era* (Homewood, Ill., 1968).

to our periodization of the time series, alternate between periods of comparatively faster and slower growth, but the trend rate is rising: the economy developed more rapidly in the 1930's than in the early part of the century, and the sharpest acceleration occurred after World War II.[2]

3. The more than 60 years between 1901 and 1966 have been subdivided into segments of unequal length, and each one of these represents an upswing or a downswing of a long swing. Long swings have been an enduring feature of Japanese growth during this century, and they have been especially prominent in the rate of growth of private and total capital formation.

4. Long swings in the rate of growth of capital formation and aggregate product between 1901 and 1966 have had certain systematic associations with some other standard measures of economic performance.

a) In this century, capital formation grew more rapidly than output, and therefore the trend of I/Y rose substantially. And rise of the investment proportion was closely associated with investment spurts: when the rate of growth of capital formation spurted, the investment proportion went up sharply; when capital formation grew at more deliberate speeds, I/Y remained relatively stable. This stability during downswings, when a decline might have been expected, has been related to a "leader-follower" relation between public and private investment. When the economy is in a period of growth above the trend line, private investment grows more rapidly than public investment. The reverse is the case when output growth is below trend values.

b) The proportion of total domestic savings to total product (S/Y) presents essentially the same pattern as the development of I/Y. As a trend, the domestic savings proportion rose steeply during this century, and the path of increase closely resembled that of the investment proportion.

c) Movements of the private nonagricultural capital-output ratio (K/Y) present a somewhat more complicated picture because they combine divergent influences of trends and swings. During an upswing or investment spurt, the values of K/Y generally declined. In a trend sense, however, K/Y gradually increased from the beginning of this century until the first half of the 1930's. From then until the beginning of the 1960's, the values of K/Y generally declined.

d) Capital and labor relative income shares (α and β) show a regular

[2] Many of the industrialized countries grew much more rapidly after World War II, but this should not be confused with trend acceleration. The latter implies a gradual gathering of speed going back before the 1940's.

pattern in the long-swing framework. During upswings α rises and β declines, and the opposite happens in downswings. The secular performance of relative shares is much more difficult to define because of severe prewar data limitations. However, as indicated below, we will assume that α and K/Y move in a similar manner.

e) Another growth characteristic of this period is the steady and uninterrupted rise in capital per worker (K/L) in the nonprimary private sector. The failure of a strong upturn from 1931 to 1937 was undoubtedly due to the abnormally heavy weight of military investments. If these were to be included, we can safely assume that the growth of capital per worker would have indicated a steadily rising trend.[3]

5. The movements of K/Y and α imply systematic changes in the rate of return on capital, r. During investment upswings the rate of return on capital must rise, since K/Y rises less rapidly or declines while the income share of capital increases. During investment downswings a reverse tendency must have existed. For trend values, we may assume that the rate of return was relatively steady, because $r = Y/K - Lw/K$, and the secular performance of K/Y and Lw/K went in opposite directions and therefore canceled each other.

6. Elsewhere we have characterized the Japanese economy of this period as affected by a special type of dualism called "differential structure." A dual economy implies the presence of two sectors, one traditional and the other modern, operating with different organization, techniques, and incentives. The trends are pretty clear. During the period in question the gap in output per worker in modern (manufacturing) and traditional (agriculture) sectors grew larger. The wage gap also grew larger for most of the period, although it appears to have turned a corner in the 1960's. The swing pattern of the productivity-wage relation is equally distinct. For private nonagriculture, wages increase less rapidly than labor productivity in the upswing, and productivity grows less rapidly than wages in the early years of a downswing. This phenomenon has been tied to what we have called a "flexible" labor supply and previously described peculiarities in Japan's wage-employment system.

7. Two characteristics of Japan's export growth pattern should be noted.

a) During all the designated time intervals the average annual rate of growth of exports (in constant prices) exceeded that of GNP.

[3] See S. Ishiwata, "Military Capital in Japan Before World War II" (Project Report No. 7), in K. Boulding and N. Sun, "The Effects of Military Expenditures upon the Economic Growth of Japan" (mimeo.; International Christian University, Tokyo, 1967).

b) Relative to domestic prices, the prices of exports declined during the entire period because the goods sold abroad increasingly consisted of manufactured goods, a sector in which productivity gains were large.

8. Finally, two observations can be made about the pattern of Japanese imports. On the one hand, the proportion of imported manufactured goods declined during almost the entire period, showing both the rapidity and the extent of the import substitution process. On the other hand, imports of materials and fuels climbed to very high levels, underlining the dependence on a range of imports for which, owing to Japan's poor resource base, no substitution was feasible. Until the end of the 1960's, Japan continued to have repeated balance-of-payments deficits. These were taken care of either by exogenous factors (World War I) or by recurring currency devaluations (in the 1930's and the new exchange rate after World War II).

The list of historical continuities or regularities is now complete. Two side issues should be briefly considered. Are there other regularities? Does our list apply as well to the period before 1900 or to the future? The answers to these questions are not difficult. There may be other regularities, but as we will attempt to show, our list suffices to explain the main empirical observations. As for the second question, two points should be made. What is usually referred to as Meiji economic growth is outside of our main emphasis, because the mechanism of Meiji growth was, as we have seen, quite different. Meiji growth was closely related to the traditional sectors both in terms of domestic output and in the structure of exports; modern sectors were until the Russo-Japanese War quite insignificant when viewed against the background of economic aggregates. Private capital formation spurts, a rising investment proportion, a differential structure—all these acquire real meaning only in this century. What about the future? No one can predict with certainty, but we do have reason to believe that at least some of the regularities of 1901–66 will change in the 1970's and 1980's. Most of these will be discussed in Chapter 9, but one possible change may be mentioned now. The ratio I/Y and the domestic savings ratio have risen secularly and have reached levels of over 30 percent. Here are a pair of world records for market economies, and it is difficult to believe that these ratios have not reached something very near an upper limit. Whatever happens, our present concern is the explanation of the historical past and not the prediction of future events.

Given the list of regularities and/or continuities, we come now to the next step in the analysis, which is to ask: What needs to be explained? At the most general level, we would like to give answers to two related questions: Why was post–World War II economic growth in Japan so rapid by world standards and by prewar Japanese standards? How can one account for the long swing and the trend acceleration in Japanese economic growth during this century?

Our suggestion is that one model or mechanism can apply unchanged for the period of analysis. For this purpose we need a model capable of generating swings and trend acceleration and comparatively more rapid postwar growth. The model we propose to use is restricted to the *private modern sector*; in empirical terms this must be taken to mean private nonagricultural production. It is a necessary and undamaging simplification: the excluded traditional and public sectors have not been major *direct* contributors to trend acceleration.

Three behavioral assumptions are made, based on standard economic theory and observed history. These are (1) that private investment was the main agent of economic modernization as the carrier of new and largely imported technology; (2) that the private investment decision is mainly determined by profit expectations, based among other things on the experience of the recent past as affected by the capital-output ratio and labor-cost conditions; and (3) that, as a first approximation, the growth form of a simple aggregate production function of the type $G_Y = G_R + \alpha G_K + \beta G_L$ can describe the main trend of output for the private modern sector. G_R (being the "residual" or total productivity) refers to the rate of growth of technical-organizational progress and to other "unknown effects," and accounts for shifts of the production function through time.

LONG SWINGS

Next, let us attempt to explain the long swings of private investment; these are, of course, one of the observed historical regularities. Our view of the swing phenomenon does not require anything resembling a self-contained cycle theory, and for this reason the term "long cycle" or "Kuznets cycle" has been avoided. From the evidence presented, it is already plain that the duration of upswings and downswings varies greatly, that causes of upswings and downswings also vary, and that ad hoc phenomena such as wars and the international economic setting played key roles. Nevertheless, these observed long swings do have significant common characteristics, and our explanation will initially concentrate on these.

It is most convenient to begin by looking at an investment spurt, which can be outlined first as a simple or theoretical case; then we can turn to a less simple and more true-to-life version. In the simple case we rigorously retain the specifications of the production function in which α is held constant. Even with this restriction, the rate of return on capital *r* could rise, owing to a fall in K/Y attributable to technological and organizational progress and rising demand. A rise in *r*, actual and expected, would mean a greater amount of capital formation as well as a shift toward more capital-intensive production for private modern output.

The simple case has been mentioned only to show that technological progress and demand alone could give rise to an investment spurt. But it is a much too simple and unrealistic formulation. We have shown that α rises in the upswing, and it is our view that this is primarily the effect of a wage lag.[4] Lagging wages are related to the differential structure and should be related to the demand for labor by the modern sector. By a flexible supply of labor we simply mean that additional labor is available without requiring significant wage increases. The labor supply was flexible because underemployment persisted in the traditional sectors, resulting in productivity differentials that characterized the Japanese economy, and flexibility was additionally supported by a growing population and by the comparatively small labor requirements of the modern sector.

The end of the upswing and the ensuing downswing are harder to systematize because there are only two downturns on record, with each one strongly affected by different ad hoc events.[5] Still, the common

---

[4] Three possible reasons can explain the increase of α in the upswing: first, the elasticity of substitution may not be unity; second, technological progress may be biased in favor of capital especially in the upswing (i.e. *not* neutral as assumed by the long-run production function); and last, many noncompetitive elements may be present, particularly a wage lag behind increases in the partial productivity of labor. All these reasons would raise the rate of return on capital and intensify the investment spurt.

Precise measurement of the elasticity of substitution is extremely difficult, and whether technical change in Japan has or has not been biased—and in which direction—is also a most difficult empirical problem. The production function suggested here is meant only as a broad first approximation. For the moment, one can safely continue to think in terms of neutrality. At the same time it is clear that in Japan the wage lag was present, especially in early upswings, and that both commodity demand and technological influences and lagging wages raised the rate of return on capital in the modern sector. They were present at the same time and interacted with one another: this is the essence of the less simple and more empirical case.

[5] Given that the end of the period of analysis is 1965, the postwar downswing is very short, and it may well be inappropriate to consider these years within a longswing framework. Two replies can be made to these doubts. First, the downswing is an adjustment process following a spurt, and it need not take a long time. Second, our view of long swings is rather elastic, and for this reason words like "cycles" have been avoided. Postwar progress in effective demand policies may have made it possible for Japan to avoid severe depressions, which could have extended the downswing beyond 1965.

features stand out. Toward the end of the upswing, the expected rate of return on capital falls, owing to a rise in K/Y caused by a slowdown in demand increase, despite the continued though much slower growth of capital stock and a consequent decline in the rate of actual technological progress that has to be explained by considering specific historical circumstances. At the same time, Lw/K tends to rise—or at least it ceases to decrease, probably due to permanent employment practices and relatively rigid factor proportions. All of these factors combine to pull down the growth of private capital formation, and during the downswing I/Y and G_R maintain lower average levels while to some extent government activity helps to sustain the aggregate investment proportion (I/Y) at a new plateau. After some time, the rate of return on capital will rise again, when, owing to a renewed wave of technological or organizational opportunities, K/Y begins to decline, and another private investment spurt will have started.

What has just been described may be called the internal mechanism of Japanese long swings, and our intention has been to highlight the role of technological progress. This is, however, a very narrow view of the broad economic process represented by these swings, and there is at least one fundamental question that remains unanswered. It may be possible to explain upper and lower turning points in these economic terms if the swing is taken as given. But why does Japanese capital formation record relatively long spurts followed by periods of adjustment that take the form of downswings? After all, is it not reasonable to suppose that technological and organizational progress, especially if borrowed, should proceed smoothly, and that it, in turn, should induce a smooth increase in capital formation?

An explanation for this question cannot be confined to economic reasoning or endogenous economic relations. Instead, we must consider the actual history of Japan, together with the upswings and downswings as sequential units. Each recorded investment spurt was preceded by a period of adjustment. This is true even of the first spurt occurring in the second decade of this century, which followed the adjustment process of the late 1890's and early 1900's associated with balance-of-payments difficulties and the Russo-Japanese War. As we already know, periods antecedent to investment spurts share certain characteristics. The rate of capital formation is low; capacity, in the broadest sense, is underutilized; and technological and organizational progress grows slowly, since these magnitudes are closely tied to the progress of investment.

At the same time, Japan's social capability to absorb borrowed technology has continued to expand independently of upswings or downswings of investment or aggregate output. We shall have more to say about this phenomenon in discussing trend acceleration in the next section and institutional innovation in Chapter 9. The main point is that relatively smoothly expanding social capability is an endogenous aspect of resource underutilization in periods of retrenchment, as well as a growing potential asset for the next investment spurt.

One must ask one more question: What brings about downswings? We have already said that ad hoc events have to be considered, and no single answer is possible. To some extent, the previously noted rise in K/Y and consequent decline in r can be connected with the exhaustion of technological progress, particularly in certain industries in which overheated investment became prominent. But one has to adopt a broader and more varied set of reasons. For example, balance-of-payments difficulties induced by internal and external price changes, coupled with rising import demand, created long-term difficulties after World War I. And of course the results of World War II were a war-induced interruption of productive investment and gave rise to a period of rather prolonged isolation.

A special comment concerning exports may also be helpful in connection with downswings. It might seem that the limits of export expansion would create particular difficulties in sustaining a spurt. Japan's exports are price-elastic, and prices tend to rise toward the end of upswings. Imports are not especially price-sensitive and depend on output and income; therefore they will be rising at the same time. One would logically expect balance-of-payments difficulties to put a premature stop to growth spurts.

In actuality this did not happen, since spurts lasted on the average some seven years. Aside from continuing import substitution, reasons for weakening the export constraint are varied. World War I gave Japan an export boom of considerable length. Yen devaluation was a factor in the 1930's and following World War II. In recent years, until 1968, balance-of-payments crises were distinctly short-term phenomena, indicating that the basic export potential of the economy has been strengthened, i.e. that the price effect continued to be beneficial even after many years of rapid growth.

The lower turning point of the long swing should be thought of in similarly broad dimensions. Renewed technological opportunities play their part, especially from the sectoral point of view, but the expected rate of return will also rise because unexploited social capability has continued to increase, and in addition one can always identify favorable exogenous factors, such as World War I–related export possibilities and defense expenditures in the 1930's. These beneficial shocks, combined with the internal mechanism, produce the investment spurt.

To summarize, the Japanese long swing has to be considered the combined result of a broad range of influences—economic and noneconomic, endogenous and exogenous. The capital-output ratio and the wage lag outline the underlying tendencies, but sociopolitical factors and the outside world may be most crucial in determining amplitude and actual dates.

TREND ACCELERATION

We turn next to an explanation of the trend, or the potential long-term growth path of the Japanese economy, and begin by considering its connection to investment spurts. (Interrelations between the trend and technological-organizational progress will be considered in the next section.) These periods of accelerated capital formation and output growth should approximate the maximum growth capacity of the economy under a particular set of historical circumstances. At these times, productive capacity continues to be fully utilized, and the actual rate of technical progress must be close to potential levels.[6] Figure 8.1 permits a convenient comparison of the three growth spurts that have formed the core of the historical period under consideration. Each successive spurt is made up of higher average annual rates of output growth (GNP), confirming not only trend acceleration but also a rising maximum growth capacity for the Japanese economy.

Unlike long swings that are observed historical phenomena, the trend is always an abstraction. Combining the maximum potential growth of spurt periods and the adjustment years of downswings, we can think of the trend as a synthetic representation of a "normal" long-term growth path, in which expected and steady rates of capital return for enterprises are such as to lead to a "normal" rate of capital formation. As will be shown below, the trend conceived of in this way can also be considered an "equilibrium" growth path.

The heart of the matter remains the relationship between swings and the trend, and a hypothesis concerning trend acceleration. We will proceed in the usual order, from simple abstractions to more realistic historical conditions.

Let us assume the existence of a simple constant r growth path for the private modern sector described by the equation $G_R = (1 - \alpha) [G_K - G_L]$ and by line OE in Figure 8.2. This is simply the previously used

---

[6] These presumptions are close to standard business cycle theory, where peak-year output is often considered to be potential or maximum output.

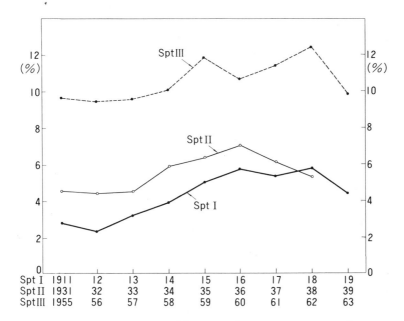

Fig. 8.1. A comparison of three growth spurts: average annual
rates of growth of GNP.

production function when K/Y and α are taken as constants.[7] If these
assumptions are correct, it follows that there is a long-run steady relation between the growth of the residual and the rate of growth of capital
per worker. Movement toward the growth path is achieved by K/Y and
r fluctuating about the path. Below line OE, K/Y is rising while r is falling; above the line the opposite is true, and these shifts represent the
movements of the long swings of private investment. In Figure 8.2, each
swing phase, plotted in terms of its own average values, is a deviation
from the path. Since line OE is intended to approximate Japan's actual
historical development, each point (U_1, D_1, etc.) also represents a certain rate of growth maintained by the modern private sector during an
upswing or a downswing.

The "equilibrium" growth path OE contains most of the necessary in-
gredients of trend acceleration if—as was indeed the case in Japanese
economic history—the trend rate of growth of K/L keeps rising. In terms
of the simple model suggested in Figure 8.2, the growth path is as follows. We have assumed that on line OE, $G_r = 0$, and this represents an
unchanging rate of return on capital at which private enterprises invest

[7] Because $G_Y - G_R = \alpha G_K + (1 - \alpha)$, G_L can be written $G_R = G_Y - G_K + (1 - \alpha)$
$[G_K - G_L]$. If $G_Y = G_K$, the above formulation is derived.

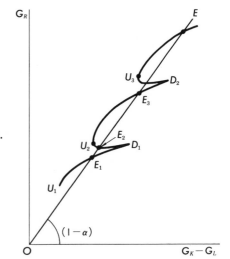

Fig. 8.2. The equilibrium growth path.

at a normal pace. Now, let us suppose that the economy starts at U_1 where $G_Y > G_K$ and r is rising. As capital accumulation proceeds, the economy moves toward the equilibrium point E_1 where $G_Y = G_K$. If capital accumulation goes beyond E_1—as was usually the case—the economy overshoots the equilibrium point and enters the area where $G_K > G_Y$ and r is decreasing. Both will eventually slow down capital accumulation, as indicated by a change in direction of $U_1E_1D_1$ toward E_2. At the new "equilibrium," given the possibility of further technological progress, the economy will again enter the area of $G_Y > G_K$ and favorable conditions for r. And another upswing will have begun, eventually proceeding toward E_3, etc. It must be noted that each point on line OE is at a higher level, corresponding to a greater G_R. Why this should have been true poses the central question: Why is a higher rate of growth of K/L associated with a higher rate of residual growth? Or, to put it slightly differently, why does the modern private sector tend toward a kind of historical "equilibrium" path at ever higher levels of G_R? In a preliminary way we have dealt with it in discussing capital formation spurts and adjustment processes and in suggesting the idea of rising social capability to import technology. This will be explored more fully in the next section.

Any model is a one-sided exaggeration, and ours is no exception. Changes of the rate of return in the real world are far more complicated than thus far suggested. The rate of interest and the rental value of capital stock affect the rate of return, and it must also be recognized that K/Y itself had a clear historical trend. These factors have to be discussed when assumptions are relaxed, historical complications are taken into account, and elements outside the framework are introduced. And yet it will always be useful to keep the main relations of the model in mind. In our view, they contain the key relationships that have created Japan's amazing modern economic growth.

In progressing now toward a more realistic consideration of historical events, we have to deal with the two major simplifications: secular changes of K/Y and related movements of Lw/K (or relative income shares). That the assumption of a constant path for K/Y cannot adequately represent historical reality in Japan has already been established, and therefore the original equation $G_R = (G_Y - G_K) + \beta(G_K - G_L)$ has to be reconsidered.

Previous chapters have already indicated that between 1900 and the present there were three different relations between the growth of capital stock and output: $G_Y < G_K$, $G_Y = G_K$, and $G_Y > G_K$. The first corresponds to the rising capital-output ratio lasting through the 1920's, the second to the flattening out of the ratio in the 1930's, and the third to the postwar decline. Therefore, even if β remains unchanged, it is not possible to identify a unique association between G_R and $(G_K - G_L)$, as was suggested in Figure 8.2. Instead, we have to consider the relative importance of the two terms that have changed in relation to the growth of the residual: $(G_Y - G_K)$ and $\beta(G_K - G_L)$.

Figure 8.3 provides this slightly artificial decomposition for the private nonagricultural sector using G_R^* and G_Y^* (terms adjusted for the rate of utilization as outlined in Chapter 3). With the help of the chart, one can date the altering performance of the capital-output ratio with considerably greater precision. Using $G_Y^* - G_K^*$, we see that between 1909 and 1927 the capital-output ratio was rising; during 1928–38 the capital-output ratio started to decrease; and after World War II, from 1956 to 1965, the decline in the capital-output ratio was very considerable. In historical terms there appears to have existed a negative correlation between the movements of $G_K - G_Y$ and G_R^*.

The causes of this change have been considered at many points in earlier chapters. Before World War II, and particularly before the 1930's, new investment was concentrated in social overheads, and this is here reflected in relatively high levels of $\beta(G_K - G_L)$, declining levels of $G_Y^* - G_K$, and a comparatively low G_R^*. At this time, the increases in capital per worker were as important as in later years, but their role in raising total factor productivity was more potential than actual. As the

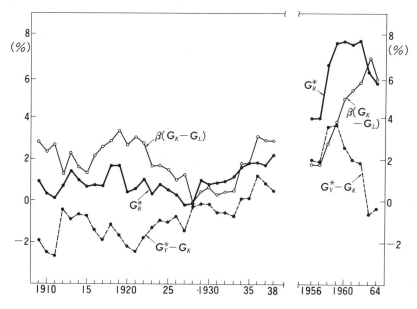

Fig. 8.3. Decomposition of $G_R{}^*$.

composition of capital formation became more directly relevant to output growth, first in the 1930's and much more so in the 1950's and 1960's, the continued increases in capital intensity combine with declining capital-output ratios to achieve record levels of output and residual growth.

Information provided in Chapter 5 indicates that the assumption of constant relative income shares is not valid for the entire period of analysis. Keeping in mind the relation $Lw/K = Y/K \times Lw/Y$, let us consider the secular movements of Lw/K. In fact, they are systematically associated with the historical path of the capital-output ratio. A falling level of Y/K (or a rising capital-output ratio), combined with declining wage costs per unit of capital, corresponds well to the first 20 or so years of this century. From then until World War II, Japan was close to the equilibrium path assumed above: relatively steady levels of Y/K and Lw/K. After the war, the pattern of rising Y/K (declining capital-output ratios) is associated with rising labor costs. Of course, the actual situation does not fit these cases every single year, but there is no doubt about the general direction and timing of these shifts.[8]

[8] These patterns meet the following conditions:

$$G_Y < G_K, \quad G_K + G_L > G_w \quad \text{(early pattern)}$$
$$G_Y = G_K, \quad G_K + G_L = G_w \quad \text{(middle pattern)}$$
$$G_Y > G_K, \quad G_K + G_L < G_w \quad \text{(postwar pattern)}$$

Why these patterns existed and what caused the changes cannot be easily explained. One would need in-depth studies of individual technological and organizational improvements, encompassing the entire period of analysis, and these are not available. A few speculative remarks may therefore not be out of place. The composition of capital formation has already been mentioned as a possible reason for rising capital-output ratios from 1900 to the late 1920's. One can also think of other explanations. When modern economic growth was still in its infancy—through the first investment spurt of this century—to take advantage of the full efficiency of borrowed technology must have presented considerable difficulties, and this could be one of the reasons for a rising capital-output ratio. At that time, favorable labor cost conditions were especially crucial in preventing declines in the rate of return and its concomitant, lack of development. Gradually, this situation became more favorable, industry by industry, as the Japanese acquired more experience. It took a relatively long time, and if these speculations are correct, one can perhaps say that modern industry in the aggregate had achieved advanced-country efficiencies sometime in the 1930's. After World War II, maybe owing to extensive application of "improvement engineering" (see Chapter 9), the Japanese surpassed advanced-country efficiencies in many industries, and gains in output per unit of capital could make up for rising labor costs without creating adverse investment conditions. If our assessments are correct, the role of "cheap labor," taken in the aggregate, can be placed in historical perspective. In one sense it was always a major asset, but its importance has diminished from a time when its absence might have prevented the introduction of Western technology to the postwar era when its presence is merely an additional competitive advantage.

These observations may be sufficient to demonstrate that the previously described long-term growth path, with its simple assumptions, has to be modified so as to bring the explanation closer to historical reality. To do so would require a much more complicated model, and we have no intention of attempting this task. In our opinion it is not a necessary task, because the demonstrated association between G_R and $G_{K/L}$ will remain the basic force underlying trend acceleration. As was pointed out in the section "A Preview of the Explanation" (Chapter 2), the two essential elements of trend acceleration are borrowed technology, with rising levels of K/L used by the modern sector, and an increasing social capability of absorbing this technology. We hope that our model provides a sufficiently realistic framework within which to understand this process.

Our model has been developed within the framework of a specific equation. Readers will remember that the equation involves four assumptions: disembodied technological progress, neutrality, conditions approximating competition, and constant returns to scale. Neutrality and competitiveness have already been discussed at earlier stages of the analysis, and something has to be added now concerning the remaining assumptions.

We are aware of the fact that our method of estimating total factor productivity is faulty in some respects, and therefore the unexplained residual may contain the influences of embodiment and increasing returns to scale.

In Chapter 4 we said that the embodiment hypothesis was too restrictive for our interpretation of Japanese growth, and now we add a brief justification of this view. Our analysis started with the relation between $G_{K/L}$ and G_R. Both capital and labor enter into the basic term used as a first approximation in observing the performance of inputs in relation to the production function. A rigorous embodiment hypothesis would consider only G_K. No doubt capital accumulation alone can affect the growth of the residual—in that sense the embodiment hypothesis is partially justified. But empirical findings, especially the historical movements of K/Y, suggest the presence of technological progress not directly related to capital accumulation. These will be explored more fully in the following section. That increasing returns to scale were a factor is also implied in Chapter 4; this too will be taken into account.

Of course, the unexplained residual may contain other things as well. A conspicuous example is improvements of "human capital." Measures of labor quality, especially those based on the small wage differentials with respect to education (see Chapter 3), cannot adequately account for the growth potential represented by an educated labor force. Fuller utilization of high-quality labor can also raise the residual.

All of the problems just identified are exogenous, i.e. they are not explained within our analytical framework. To take them into consideration necessitates a broadened vision of economic processes that we shall refer to as interaction.

INTERACTIONS

In the previous section we have attempted to establish and elaborate the relation between the growth of capital per worker and the residual. Under plausible though restrictive assumptions, one can demonstrate the basic tendency of the model to generate trend acceleration. Going beyond these restrictive assumptions is extremely difficult, as is usually the case when one tries to combine theory and history. To begin with, an unexplained residual is a magnitude that cannot be defined with sufficient precision. In a sense, it is an "unknown," making it difficult to explain why it has risen over time or why the production function has "shifted." Trend acceleration, on the other hand, is an observed fact. Therefore we will now try to link trend acceleration and an ill-defined residual in terms of Japan's historical experience. At best, this is an assignment that can be performed only in a preliminary and speculative manner. Our own work and that of other researchers have not yet reached levels that could allow definitive conclusions. Nevertheless an understanding of Japanese trend acceleration requires a historical and even a noneconomic approach, and we will try to suggest its main outline.

Rising Per Capita Income, Learning by Doing, and Institutions

The relationship between G_R and $G_{K/L}$, which we have observed statistically, is not meant to be taken as a statement of simple causality. Quite the contrary: to gain a realistic picture of this relationship requires the supposition of complicated and positive interactions. Let us take these up first as they would exist in a closed economy.

1. The repeated investment spurts, which we have labeled the "driving force" behind modern economic growth, have been explained by variations in the level of r (the expected rate of return on private investment). The level of r itself has been related to technological and organizational progress (via K/Y) and to the distributive mechanism (the relative levels of α and β as affected by a differential structure).

2. Periodic private investment spurts of long duration have two effects. (a) One of these is the supply-production effect, in which an investment spurt will result in more rapid capital accumulation, a higher rate of increase in capital per worker, and output growing more rapidly than capital accumulation. It would also be reasonable to suppose that new investment, which served as a carrier for imported technology on which Japan depended, contributed toward raising G_R. This is the most direct or simple explanation. (b) Investment spurts also raise the level and rate of growth of distributed income per capita. This would be especially true in an economy in which underemployment was a persistent characteristic. And the rate of growth of income per capita can also affect G_R; this is the first interaction.

3. Japan's borrowing of technology was not, in general, limited by the availability of suitable items. Japan was and is a "follower country," and there was always room for introducing improvements of foreign origin. However, there were a set of limiting factors that we shall call the

amount or level of "social capability." We use that term to designate those factors constituting a country's ability to import or engage in technological and organizational progress. And it is our belief that a higher rate of growth of income per capita raises social capability, largely in three ways.

a) By improving "human capital"[9] (better schools, improved diet, etc.), thereby making labor more suitable for work with advanced technology. As a result of public and private investment in education, including vocational training, we were able to observe in Chapter 3 that in Japan high-quality labor was available at relatively low prices, and this undoubtedly increased the country's capability of absorbing new methods from abroad. Furthermore, this reservoir of qualified laborers disposed of less capital per worker than its counterparts in the United States and Western Europe. At any one time, therefore, this particular reserve of capability is large, especially in the twentieth century. It is also an unmeasured potential that does not appear in our quantification of increases in labor quality.

b) By widening the market and thereby improving the possibility of exploiting economies of scale. We have been unable to make wholly satisfactory measurements of scale economies, but the discussion in Chapter 4 linking output growth and labor productivity strongly suggests scale influences in certain industries, especially manufacturing. Possibilities of exploiting these economies, as revealed by our analysis, imply an interaction between technological progress (G_R) and widening of the market.

c) By raising the savings ratio, particularly in the household sector. The frequently repeated thesis concerning investment as the driving force of Japanese growth does not imply a minor role for savings. As shown in Chapter 6, Japan's rising savings ratio was an endogenous consequence of secular growth and not a characteristic determined by initial conditions. The close association of household savings ratio movements with long swings and trend acceleration meant an especially stable source of finance for domestic investment.[10]

4. This then is what we mean by "interaction" between G_R and $G_{K/L}$. In the simple case one can move from increases in K to a higher level of

---

[9] See Theodore W. Schultz, *Investment in Human Capital* (New York, 1971).

[10] Before World War II, growth was more inflationary because $I > S$ *ex ante*. A rising savings ratio is sometimes the product of income redistribution in favor of upper-income groups. We do not believe that this was a major factor in Japan, although income distribution data are such as to prevent proof of this assertion.

G_R. But G_R can rise because income has risen, and this can lead to a higher level of $G_{K/L}$.

Opening this model to foreign trade creates no difficulties. The possibility of exporting obviously raises the level of aggregate demand and improves the possibility of exploiting economies of scale. On the supply side, the case of the direct or simple explanation seems especially applicable as seen by the secular relative decline in export prices.

Interaction is not confined to the household sector or to demand. It also appears within the process of production at the level of business enterprise. In Chapter 1, we describe Japan's unusual position as a latecomer, in the form of a sizable gap between a backward economy and a far less backward sociopolitical structure. As a result, Meiji Japan had considerable capability in exploiting modern technology and organization. This initial gap can go a long way toward explaining nineteenth-century growth. But the real challenge is to explain accelerated growth in the twentieth century, while economic backwardness was *decreasing*.

Simon Kuznets has outlined some of the difficulties, and has also hinted at the answer, when he wrote:[11]

Much of the stock of technology accumulated with the passage of time in developed countries may not be relevant to the needs of the backward latecomer. . . . Another part of the stock may not be easily borrowable because it is not suited to the conditions of the backward country. . . . Borrowing in such cases may require the capacity for substantial modifications, and this capacity is not likely to be attained until the backward country has advanced sufficiently in the process of its growth. Thus *relevance* of the existing stock of unexploited technology may change over time in the process of growth itself —increasing because the once backward country acquires greater capacity for modification, or because its scale of priorities shifts toward the more advanced components of technology. . . . The argument calls for a more systematic examination of the concept of relevant stock of technology, and greater attention to the factors involved in the capacity to borrow and to transform.

Japanese economic history suggests that it was possible to *expand* the range of *relevant* borrowable stock in the twentieth century, and this must have been one of the main forces leading to trend acceleration. Some of the ways in which this was accomplished have already been discussed when we considered the rigidity of factor proportions in the modern economy and "mitigation." These types of activities are part of a broader interaction process that stresses the gains in experience achieved through new capital formation in enterprises. What we have in mind is

[11] Simon Kuznets, "Notes on Japan's Economic Growth," in Klein and Ohkawa, *Economic Growth*, pp. 391–92.

very close to Kenneth Arrow's concept of "learning by doing," and this may have been an unusually active force in Japan.[12] Research and development activities were of no real significance until well after World War II. In their stead, domestic technical knowledge progressed by means of education and capital formation. (And on-the-job training was also closely related to capital formation.) Working with new and more advanced machinery and equipment, conceived or manufactured in more advanced countries, raised levels of competence and experience for management and labor, thereby broadening the relevant horizon of technology.

The notion of interaction between capital formation and shifts of the production function has been broadened from the conventional factor of rising income per capita to "learning by doing." More unconventional factors have to be considered even if we want to give only a preliminary picture of historical trend acceleration. In Chapter 9 we discuss illustrations of institutional advances in Japan, all of which raised its capability to import Western technology. These include *zaibatsu*, permanent employment, administrative guidance, and the formation of the Ministry of International Trade and Industry (MITI) after World War II. Some of these institutional innovations are private, others are public; they are treated as illustrations because other examples could have been selected. Whether or not institutional development of this type fits into a narrow interaction pattern—relating G_R and $G_{K/L}$—is hard to determine, but there can be little doubt concerning the positive contribution of these elements to trend acceleration. A more detailed presentation of these institutions can be postponed, but two points should be stressed while we are considering theoretical issues. First, the new institutions are *antecedent* to spurts or increases in capital formation.[13] Second, these types of institutional advance are likely to be *additive*: they combine with each other to improve the environment for enterprise in importing technology.

One brief digression is in order, relating to the traditional sector of the Japanese economy. Why has borrowed technology had such a limited impact on traditional production, or, to put it in more Kuznetsian language, why was the range of relevance of Western technology so nar-

---

[12] Kenneth J. Arrow, "The Economic Implication of Learning by Doing," *Review of Economic Studies*, vol. 29 (1962).

[13] For example, *zaibatsu* were founded in the 1880's and 1890's, but their major impact on the economy was not felt until the first two decades of the twentieth century. Similarly, although MITI was created right after World War II, its role in furthering and guiding the import of technology did not become important until the middle 1950's.

row? To a considerable extent, the answer has already been given in Chapters 4 and 5, but for the sake of a balanced presentation we summarize matters here.

The traditional sector—agriculture and small-scale industry—is the repository of surplus labor. It needs labor-intensive technology because its factor prices are most unfavorable to relative capital-intensive modern progress, and because in many lines of activity borrowable technology cannot yield sufficient gains in productivity. (The classic example would be the low relevance of Western farm machinery to paddy cultivation.) Of course, traditional technology need not be static, and interaction with the modern sector does occur. We have given evidence of both in describing Japanese agriculture. In general, however, the international backlog of technology has been quite irrelevant for the traditional economy.

What has been called the differential structure is one aspect of the failure of borrowed technology to achieve a broader degree of relevance. On the one hand, this failure resulted in the differential level of labor productivity. On the other hand, the comparatively rigid factor proportions of modern technology, in spite of imaginative mitigation, together with population growth contributed toward the continuance of surplus labor.

Recent changes in this situation can also be related to trend acceleration, and especially to the gathering force of this phenomenon since 1900. A differential structure obviously limits the relevant borrowable stock of technology; weakening of this structure enlarges borrowable stock. To some extent this has happened throughout the twentieth century as the weight of the traditional economy declined. However, its disappearance was a very slow process, and it is only in recent years, particularly in the 1960's, that the limiting powers of the traditional economy have been diminished.

Summary

Let us conclude by restating some of the major connections stressed in this section. The connection between the growth of capital per worker and the growth of the residual is not obvious unless one stipulates either an acceleration in externally supplied unexploited technology or an acceleration in human quality. We have tried to indicate that both existed in Japan because of the widened range of relevant technology and the gains of "learning by doing."

Trend acceleration built around the notion of successive investment spurts also entails the requirement that the capacity for more rapid growth precede the observed increases in I/Y and S/Y. If possible, one should be able to pinpoint factors accounting for the acceleration during each spurt, and also for the initial acceleration. Furthermore, since trend acceleration may be unique to Japan, ideally it should be possible to identify responsible factors specific to that economy. The preliminary nature of our discussion has been mentioned often enough, and these difficult assignments have to be relegated to the future. Yet, some of what has been covered in this chapter does indicate possible connections. We have emphasized that social capability grows more smoothly than capital formation, and that downswings are periods of adjustment in which reserves of capability can be built up. We have also pointed to the antecedent and additive nature of institutional innovations; and we have always placed great stress on external and exogenous elements when each spurt is considered as a period of concrete economic history. That leaves entirely unanswered only the initial acceleration of the twentieth century. Without benefit of detailed study, and leaving to one side obvious external factors, we are tempted to assign a considerable role to the gap described in Chapter 1; that is to say, a utilization of potentials accumulated in Meiji Japan.

CHAPTER NINE

Beyond Measurement

Many topics of undoubtedly great importance for Japanese development in the twentieth century have not been analyzed in the preceding eight chapters. The role of government, for example, has frequently been considered a most crucial aspect of Japan's economic modernization, and we have had very little to say about its activities. This is also true for financial and monetary problems, so frequently emphasized by other students of Japanese economic history. One could also add the "human equation" to the list of omitted topics, and this would include such things as labor-management relations, entrepreneurship, motivation, and the capacity for group action. It is also a fact that our approach has taken a macroeconomic form and that we have presented only little material at levels below broad economic sectors. And these omissions relate only to the economy. Obviously noneconomic factors, such as the political, social, and international environment, also had a decisive influence on Japan at all times.

What we have not taken up in detail falls into two overlapping categories. As we said at the very beginning, our purpose has not been to write a "neutral or general" study. Instead, we focused on private investment spurts, technological progress, and trend acceleration in a national income framework. That is why government policy, financial relations, and individual industries can be assigned a secondary place. Some other admittedly very interesting aspects of Japanese growth, for example, political or entrepreneurial action, are necessarily matters of speculation. They are usually beyond measurement, at least as that term is commonly understood by economists.

Having come now to the concluding chapter, we would like to liberate ourselves, and our readers, from the narrower confines of the analytical framework by dealing with some of the omissions in a rather speculative manner. Investment spurts and trend acceleration will still be stressed, but most of the discussion will center on the last 20 years. Two major topics are discussed below: some aspects of public and private institutional development, and the short- and longer-run economic future of Japan.

Before turning to these more general matters, we shall add a few words concerning the years 1966–70. The period 1900 to 1965, which up to now usually defined the entire period of analysis, has been analyzed in a long swing setting. In this final chapter, we intend to discuss the entire postwar period, including 1966–70, as 15 or more years of uniformly and unprecedentedly high growth. This will necessarily blur long-swing distinctions, and a bit of explanation should be helpful.

Compared with the years before World War II, the Japanese economy has grown at an exceedingly rapid pace for all years between 1955 and 1970, and this has been an essential part of trend acceleration. Even during the downswing of 1962–65, aggregate output rose at 8.6 percent in real terms,[1] and the average rate of growth for 1966–70 was 12.3 percent per year.

Could the period 1966–70 fit into a long-swing pattern? No answer can be given to this question so soon after the events. All we can do is to describe what has been taking place. Following the lower rates of growth during most of the first half of the 1960's, private investment picked up again, although the high point achieved in 1967 (27.0 percent) was well below the previous peaks of 1960 and 1961. Perhaps this period can be considered a renewed private investment spurt; perhaps eventually the entire span 1956–71 (?) will have to be taken as a very long upswing, briefly interrupted in 1962–65.[2] It is equally likely that our framework, which makes private investment the critical element, cannot apply as well after 1965 when other factors become more positive. As we have noted in Chapter 7, Japan's balance-of-payments "ceiling" appears to have lifted and a rather different explanatory approach may be called for in the future.

SOME ASPECTS OF INSTITUTION BUILDING

The Social Capability to Import Technology

The notion that imported technology played a critical role in Japanese economic modernization is not exactly revolutionary. It is an interesting

---

[1] We must stress again that upswings and downswings refer primarily to private investment, and the post-1961 downswing was real enough, as the following annual growth rates of $\Delta I_P/I_P$ show: 38.8 percent in 1960; 29.4 percent in 1961; 1.1 percent in 1962; 10 percent in 1963; 16 percent in 1964; and −9.1 percent in 1965.

[2] A rather similar event occurred in 1901–17.

finding *only* if the Japanese overcame greater obstacles and/or did it better than other countries. We are tempted to answer "yes" to both questions.[3]

Students of economic development have long been aware of the fact that technology is created in advanced countries, and that its developmental direction is responsive to the mix of factor proportions and skills existing in these countries. And it is equally well known that this creates an obstacle for less developed countries attempting rapidly to absorb sufficient quantities of imported technology. An especially serious obstacle exists because, if an underdeveloped country wishes to develop an export market, considerations of cost and quality may require the use of up-to-date methods. Given this situation, it may be important to create specific institutions designed to raise a less developed country's capability to import technological and organizational progress. Japanese economic history shows both the significance of the rapid absorption of imported technology via the repeated investment spurts and also the development of specific institutions that facilitated the entire process.

Throughout this century a number of specific institutions come to mind that raised Japan's social capability to absorb technological and organizational progress of foreign origin. They share some common characteristics: a loose antecedent relationship with individual investment spurts, an additive dimension meaning that methods developed in one spurt continue beyond it and may assume even greater importance at a later time, and finally, close ties to the functionings of modern enterprise that set them apart from the earlier reforms of Meiji times.

Let us briefly reconsider each one of the investment spurts in this light. The first one was associated with two institutions of lasting significance: *zaibatsu* and permanent employment. It is true, of course, that the most famous zaibatsu (Mitsui, Mitsubishi, Sumitomo, and Yasuda) originated in the Meiji era, but they reached their greatest power toward the end of the 1920's, and it was largely based on the rapid industrialization that had occurred in the first two decades of this century. Although it is difficult to generalize, perhaps one can say that in the nineteenth century commerce was the major activity of zaibatsu; around World War I it was industry with particular emphasis on coal mining, shipbuilding, engineering, and glass; and in the 1920's it became finance.

The zaibatsu were leaders in the development of technologically more

[3] That the Japanese did it better than other countries is implicit in the rate of growth of national income and the residual.

sophisticated industries. They were major importers of Western technology and innovators. They provided a low-income Japan with the possibility of exploiting scale economies, and their diversification permitted what Lockwood has called "combined investment," i.e. the simultaneous development of complementary industries.[4] Zaibatsu also economized what must have been a scarce factor, i.e. individuals capable of running modern businesses, and through the operation of their affiliated banks they were most adept at mobilizing scarce capital resources. Given that the issue of that day, as now, was growth rather than economic democracy, there developed in Japan a certain kind of bigness that was unacceptable elsewhere but quite suitable in this setting.

Permanent employment is another peculiarly Japanese invention that came into prominence between 1900 and 1920. It was very much out of keeping with the nineteenth-century industrial labor situation, when piracy of workers was common and turnover rates were extremely high. Now a growing number of workers, especially in large enterprises, were hired on a lifetime basis, and more attention was devoted to noncash benefits such as housing, stores, and medical care. Undoubtedly an immediate reason for the creation of this system was the desire of enterprises to undermine the powerful and troublesome regional labor recruiters, and the consequent "Balkanization" of labor markets was most convenient for the big producers.[5] But there must have been a more fundamental and long-run reason, because permanent employment gave the Japanese entrepreneur a labor force without incentives to oppose technological and organizational progress even of the labor-saving type. It was also the type of labor force in which the enterprise had incentives to invest through, *inter alia*, on-the-job training. Of course, we are not speaking of the entire work force; this system was essentially confined to modern large-scale industry, and there were always temporary workers who could be and were laid off when business conditions deteriorated.

The 1930's were far less productive and interesting when it comes to the development or expansion of business institutions. Yet this decade does show the considerable resilience of Japanese enterprise, and some of its creations have had, in our opinion, a lasting influence.

Three factors characterized the growth of industry. First, there was an increasing emphasis on military-related heavy industry, and by 1936

---

[4] See W. W. Lockwood, *The Economic Development of Japan* (Princeton, N.J., 1954), p. 227.
[5] See Koji Taira, "Characteristics of Japanese Labor Markets," *Economic Development and Cultural Change*, vol. 10, no. 2 (January 1962).

one can speak of *junsenji keizai* or quasi-wartime economy. Second, the expansion of colonial economies, particularly in Manchukuo, became more important to Japanese business circles. Third, there arose an intense conflict between the zaibatsu and both the military and the remaining representatives of the traditional economy. The military found the zaibatsu not sufficiently cooperative in their attempts to prepare the economy for war, and the peasants and small industrialists tended to blame the enormous combines for their suffering during the Great Depression. Amidst these events, two items merit particular attention: the rise of the *shinzaibatsu* (new zaibatsu) and the cartelization movement.

Shinzaibatsu were new combines that came into being as a result of rising military requirements. They were especially closely involved in producing military equipment and in exploiting resources of the colonies; Nakajima and Nissan are excellent examples. Shinzaibatsu are mentioned only to underscore the element of flexibility: when the established zaibatsu became somewhat recalcitrant and insisted on directing business in accordance with preferences of private gain, there appeared to be no difficulty in finding other entrepreneurs who were willing to make their plans fit the strategic plans of the military.

The cartelization movement of the 1930's, especially strong between 1930 and 1932, was a direct outgrowth of the depression. At a time when economic conditions were extremely precarious, government and business jointly attempted to govern "excessive and unregulated competition" through schemes to control output and prices and the allocation of markets and sales quotas. Some 45 diverse industries were affected, including alloy iron, anthracite, steel plates, chemicals, coal, oil, and pig iron. Although once again attempts of this type were not unknown before the 1930's, nothing on this scale had ever been attempted previously. The details of this episode are not significant[6] since the majority of cartels never operated as intended; there were always too many firms prepared to violate the agreements. What is most significant is that the cartelization movement established the habit of "administrative guidance" that has become a useful tool of Japan's postwar technology policy. This will be discussed below.

Turning now to postwar Japan and its magnificent economic achievements, one must recognize immediately that fortuitous events and good luck played some role. The war and especially the defeat pushed aside

---

[6] For an excellent account of this period, see G. C. Allen, "The Development of Industrial Combinations," in E. B. Schumpeter et al., *The Industrialization of Japan and Manchukuo, 1930–1940* (New York, 1940), chap. 20.

older leadership groups and opened the way for new men with new energies. In this atmosphere, talent became more important than pedigree. Sustaining the defeat presented two other opportunities. Physical destruction eliminated much antiquated capital equipment and eventually led to Japan's possessing a rather young and up-to-date capital stock. Losing a war to the United States was an opportunity of another kind, bringing with it large amounts of aid and military protection at very low cost. And finally, the Korean war, and to a lesser extent the Vietnamese war, have provided windfall gains to the Japanese economy.

The years since World War II have also given birth to an institution that has, on balance, greatly increased Japan's capability to import foreign technology. And here we are referring to the "notorious MITI," or, officially, the Ministry of International Trade and Industry, which is dedicated to the interests of producers, especially those who operate on a large scale. It is notorious abroad because of its rather unfriendly attitude toward trade liberalization and direct foreign investment. It is equally notorious in Japan because of its power in affecting the destiny of individual firms and industries.

Although MITI is a direct descendant of the prewar Ministry of Commerce and Industry, its postwar activities are quite new in an age when technology has assumed supreme importance. The ministry reviewed the import of technology; it had to grant approval for licensing agreements and joint ventures; it allocated foreign exchange necessary for the importation of equipment or the purchase of know-how. MITI officials continually survey the foreign technology scene, encourage and discourage certain lines of advance, set priorities—in a word they have attempted to reach and implement a national and rational policy of technological change. The popularity of this ministry is not great, even among certain industrialists, but in view of Japan's performance as a technology importer it would be hard to argue that private initiative has been stifled by excessive government interference.[7]

As Japanologists know, MITI operates in mysterious ways, and methods of implementation are not easily described. A few rather sparse examples will have to suffice.

Earlier, mention had been made of "administrative guidance" that came into being as a result of the postwar "advice cartels" run by MITI.

[7] Some may be surprised that the Economic Planning Agency is not taken up as a major new institution. However, compared with MITI it is a midget. The powers of the EPA are largely "indicative" and it has been subject to strong political pressures. See Tsunehiko Watanabe, "National Planning and Economic Development: A Critical Review of the Japanese Experience," *Economics of Planning*, vol. 10, nos. 1–2 (October 1970).

These were (and are) informal and sometimes unsuccessful cartel arrangements jointly set up by the industry and government. They have no statutory standing, but do not lack muscle in matters of output, capacity, or pricing policy. A Japanese minister once explained why he opposed wholly owned direct foreign investment. Something like this was said: "Assume that 'administrative guidance' discussions are taking place in an industry, and that one of the firms is foreign. We decide that for the good of all, production will have to be reduced by 20 percent in the next quarter. And what if the foreigner then asks: Mr. MITI bureaucrat, show me the law that authorizes you to give this order. And once the question is asked, 'administrative guidance' is dead." Presumably no Japanese would dare ask such a question! What is the connection to improving the inflow of technology? Merely that through the industry-wide "harmonization of new investment" (a MITI phrase) that takes place at sessions of this type, and in other ways, the flow can be shaped, controlled, and made more effective.

Japan must be the only capitalist country in the world in which the government decides how many firms there should be in a given industry, and then sets about to arrange the desired number. Thus it is well known today that in the opinion of the government there are too many automobile and computer firms, and we can expect the requisite reductions to take place soon—a process that has already occurred in the paper, petrochemical, synthetic fiber, cement, and steel industries. Spurred by the inevitability of trade liberalization, MITI in the 1960's has been especially concerned with arranging these mergers. Their purpose is clear: to control effectively the expansion of capacity and to form strong (large) and technologically up-to-date firms that can compete with the best foreign producers.

A final example can be taken from the computer industry. Within the past year MITI decided that Japanese producers of computers *must* in the future provide for software compatability, i.e. all software will have to be usable on any domestic machine. This is a major technological decision that imposes certain constraints on hardware architecture, but its economic advantages could be enormous in local and world markets. American experts remain skeptical concerning the possibility of achieving an "impossible dream"; but too often we have underrated Japan's capacity in these matters.[8]

[8] Some will, no doubt, wonder why in this recital nothing has been said concerning improved education as a means of raising Japan's social capability to import technology. Two reasons are involved. First, education is a matter of national policy, and therefore less specifically related to business. Second, and more important, as

John Diebold summarized the matter very well in a recent address:[9]

Again and again we encounter this phenomenon — innovations with great promise for important segments of our future, applied with enthusiasm by talented people, turning into business disasters! I have come to believe that this is not a series of chance mishaps, confined to education, or computers or other advanced technologies in isolation; rather it is a basic problem growing more common as, in the tasks we undertake, we encounter the realities of our age: rapid technological change acting as an agent for major social change, which in turn demands widespread *institutional* change for business success.

Diebold was talking about the present situation in advanced countries, but his observation and conclusion apply equally to the process of historical development. For the developing country, a major task is to bring in new technologies and forms of organization, and this may require specific institutions designed to raise a country's capability to take advantage of the gap between itself and more advanced countries.

This view could easily be subject to misinterpretation. We are not recommending zaibatsu, shinzaibatsu, cartels, and MITI without reservations, and some of the evils associated with all these institutions will be discussed below. However, it would be a mistake to judge Japan by the standards of Western liberalism. In this connection, two issues should be kept in mind. First, Japan's "establishment" has been growth-oriented for nearly a century. It set a target of catching up with the West, and since increased welfare would have interfered with the rate at which the target was attainable, leaders were generally willing to postpone other problems. Japan is just now getting tired of "growth at any cost," and its leaders are showing increasing concern for all aspects of the quality of life. Perhaps Japan has been too growth-oriented—who can really say?—but that is hardly the point. We should judge the institutions not in terms of our own political preferences, but in terms of their efficiency in furthering growth; that is the point.

The second issue is related to the common features of these institutions. In general, they are disliked by liberal economists because they imply trusts rather than antitrusts, state interference, monopoly or oligopoly power, etc. We would not presume to defend these monsters, but we should again retain a proper perspective. Usually there are two

already mentioned, Japan entered the Meiji era with relatively respectable educational levels, and by the beginning of the twentieth century schooling was already widespread. In 1905, the country-wide attendance in primary schools was 95.62 percent. See Japan, National Commission for UNESCO, *The Role of Education in the Social and Economic Development of Japan* (Tokyo, 1966), p. 52.

[9] "New Rules and Opportunities for Business as We Enter the Post-Industrial Era," Keynote Address, Third Tri-Annual International Productivity Congress, Vienna, 1971, p. 13.

types of objections voiced: one on behalf of consumers and the other on behalf of innovation. As for the former, all one can say is that the Japanese consumer may have suffered, but it could have been short-run suffering for long-run gain, and in any event consumer sacrifice was a price willingly paid by those in charge. The matter of innovation is also not simple. Much of the literature tells us that monopolies and oligopolies have little incentive to innovate since they can exist comfortably on monopoly profits.[10] This may be a plausible position when a firm or an economy finds itself at the technological frontier. Then, in the absence of competition, there may be little urge to explore new ways of doing things. For a "follower country," however, we should look at the situation differently. Now the issue is not to exercise inventiveness and to push into the unknown, but rather to adopt what is known and proved elsewhere. To be sure, there are risks and costs, but basically the opportunities for increased profits are much clearer. Furthermore, we must always remember the international dimension (and perhaps also that the attitude of the United States toward monopolies and cartels developed in a setting in which international markets were relatively unimportant). Most of Japan's modern industries, by definition already using imported technology, were intent eventually on exporting their products. And this meant competing with the best foreign firms, frequently under difficult circumstances. Therefore, the Japanese had great incentives to reduce costs by using the latest and best methods, and this is exactly what happened, most prominently in textiles before the war and in nearly everything else after the war.

No doubt we are protesting too much, since surely no one will claim that Japan's Combines or state intervention has led to technological conservatism. Our main point is simply that Japanese economic history demonstrates the need for specific institutions to improve technological import capabilities, and that some of the fears associated with certain forms of organization have been, from this point of view, exaggerated.

In considering the sweep of Japanese economic history, we are struck by the notion that government-business relations were, from the local point of view, well arranged. Japan retained some advantages of capitalism, i.e. efficient producers, while reaping certain benefits of socialism, i.e. considerable public control of the economic effort and direction. Harmony of this variety was undoubtedly not the result of explicit policy. One can, however, identify two basic and useful strands of long-run policy. In general, the government, at least since the 1880's, stayed

---

[10] As is well known, J. A. Schumpeter did not share this view. See his *Capitalism, Socialism, and Democracy* (New York, 1942), chap. 8.

out of areas in which the private sector had comparative advantage. The government engaged in very little production and did so only when national defense was involved or where bottlenecks prevented private entry. For example, silk and cotton textiles were left pretty much alone, but in the early 1900's the government did establish the Yahata steel works. Furthermore, public investment programs were concentrated by and large in the non-spurt periods, and therefore did not compete too much with private investment.

Another aspect of Japan's rising social capability might be called, somewhat awkwardly, the conscious development of factor proportion mitigation, and it has been dealt with elsewhere (see Chapter 4). We are referring to the previously mentioned incongruity between advanced technology and the factor proportions of historical latecomers. The Japanese handled this problem in a number of imaginative ways, all of which are still relevant today. Modern industry encompasses a wide spectrum of techniques, and it is possible to concentrate on its more labor-intensive components. This is why Japan selected textiles in the early part of the century and also why the light machinery industry has been so important in postwar Japan. (One is particularly tempted to stress this in view of Asia's rather high-quality labor resources compared with those, say, in nineteenth-century Russia.) Japan also demonstrates the possibility of fuller utilization of scarce capital by the more intensive use of labor through the wide use of multishift production. It is also possible, even in modern enterprises, to substitute labor for capital through subcontracting. This has been a very economical way of tying small-scale industry into the modern production process.

All of the above is widely known. There is, however, another sphere in which Japan has managed to squeeze more out of scarce capital, and this is in developing the art (should one say science?) of "improvement engineering." A review of Japanese economic modernization would quickly reveal that it has been a history virtually devoid of core inventions. The basic techniques have come from the United States and Europe, but not infrequently these have been systematically improved by the importers. By now this sort of activity has become a deeply engrained tradition among certain Japanese enterpreneurs, and many historical and current examples can be cited. In the Meiji era, when the Japanese first began to build textile machinery, they discovered that it was possible to substitute wood for iron in the beams of the machines, so long as the joints were made of iron. A significant cost reduction was achieved. In the 1930's they pioneered in scientific cotton blending, i.e. turning out a desired quality of cloth based on using the cheapest possible varieties of raw cotton. (One has the feeling that the British, at least at that time, considered the method *infra dig!*)

A most interesting set of examples comes from recent years. Japanese small and medium-sized computers are available abroad with a four- to five-year warranty, while competitive U.S. and European firms until recently offered nothing similar. The reasons for Japan's advantage are closely related to improvement engineering. All computers destined for export are subject to rigorous inspection, the costs of which are fully tax-deductible. (This has been a common practice for many Japanese products beginning with raw silk in the 1880's.) At the same time, two key production improvements are also involved. Both apply to the memory core—a weak link from the point of view of reliability and durability. In the core many wires cross and some touch, and these have a tendency to corrode at points of contact. Some time ago, Japanese manufacturers began to gold-plate cross points. Furthermore, when a core is made, quantities of dirt enter into wiring, causing eventual failures. Japanese manufacturers now wash cores before they are installed.

No major innovations were involved in any of these improvements, but their economic impact has in all instances been considerable. Improvement engineering reduces the real cost of imported technology by making it more productive. At the margin it will permit the adoption of some techniques that otherwise would not have been profitable. If, by means of these efforts a technique is made more economical, it could also result in a greater domestic and foreign market, leading to otherwise unexploitable economies of scale. The very act of improvement engineering can also raise the quality of certain categories of workers. It is largely an activity of "carefully taking apart and putting together a little better"; it is concrete and directly related to production, especially when compared to basic research. In contrast to the pursuit of core innovations, this type of activity is less risky and much cheaper: in effect, one is working in already proved directions.

Finally, a word about the human element in Japan's recent success story. Thus far we have concentrated on relatively "pure" economic factors. Somehow account has to be taken of the tremendous burst of entrepreneurial energy in postwar Japan. The Japanese have a long history of entrepreneurial achievements; throughout this century they have been strong, imaginative, and sometimes ruthless competitors. Still, as with so many other indicators, there is an extraordinary quality attached to the 1950's and 1960's; one need think only of the long list of triumphs in electronics, steel, shipbuilding, automobiles, and many other industries. Behind each one of these stands a group of innovating business leaders. Is there any reason for believing that recent years were in some way particularly hospitable to the flowering of entrepreneurial talent? We are convinced that there was something special about the postwar era—and so are some very knowledgeable Japanese. World War II destroyed Japan's "proper order of things," and this may be the exceptional ingredient that favored entrepreneurship. One hundred years ago, the Meiji Restoration destroyed the Tokugawa system and liberated the long pent-up energies of all classes. What happened after that is history: Japan became the only non-Western nation to achieve modern economic growth. With time, however, the new order developed rigidities especially from the point of view of new enterprise. New ventures and ideas came to be judged not only in terms of their intrinsic merit but also in terms of who made the suggestion, what his connections were, where he had been to school, etc. These rigidities were wiped away when the World War II establishment was displaced. For a time, talent and ability counted more than age, university degrees from the right schools, and family or banking connections. A new and vital entrepreneurial class emerged, and it has served Japan brilliantly ever since.

The Darker Side

In any attempt to squeeze relevance out of a nation's historical experience, the temptation to "accentuate the positive" is strong. One cannot, however, review certain aspects of Japan's long-term record without commenting also on its darker side. The obligation is particularly strong because our account has stressed the economic achievements of modern Japan. That is not the whole story.

Twentieth-century Japan enjoyed rapid economic growth, but by the 1930's this came to be combined with an aggressive, totalitarian military government, which eventually plunged the country into a disastrous war. It would be extremely simple-minded to draw a direct connection between economic growth on the one hand and military aggression on the other. Nevertheless, the question remains: Was there something in Japan's economic structure as it developed in this century that encouraged, fostered, and supported the political forces leading the country to war and eventually to inevitable defeat at the hands of the United States and its allies?

A fundamental aspect of the problem must have been the unequal development of the Japanese economy from around 1900 until at least the middle of the 1960's. Frequently this has been referred to as an aspect of "dual economy," while we have preferred the term "differential structure." Whatever one chooses as label, there cannot be any doubt about what was happening. Throughout these years—cyclical fluctuations apart—the modern economy was progressing at a satisfactory pace. Using continually improved techniques it could, by and large, provide better standards for capitalists and workers. By contrast, the traditional sectors—essentially agriculturalists, craftsmen, and small entrepreneurs—were not able to participate in this progress. The particular set of factor proportions under which they were forced to operate —little land, many workers, and expensive capital—effectively prevented the adoption of superior Western techniques. And gradually, a growing wedge came between the modern and traditional economies. In the modern sectors, productivity and wages rose rapidly; in the traditional sectors productivity and wages either stagnated or rose much more slowly. By 1931, for example, the ratio of output per worker in agriculture relative to manufacturing stood at 26 percent; his wage was approximately 50 percent of what industrial workers earned. (In the middle of the 1880's these figures were respectively 50 percent and 70 percent.) The impact of these differences is easy to imagine. With the coming of the 1920's and 1930's there is much discussion of an "agricultural problem," and a "small-scale industry problem," and the meaning of "problem" was clear. It simply meant that these sectors were depressed, that their incomes were low and frequently inadequate, and that they were a source of social discontent. E. O. Reischauer labeled the situation "something new and as yet unique in the world— an industrialized nation supported by the toil of people living not far above the subsistence level."[11] While this statement is exaggerated, and certainly not unique to Japan—what would one say about prewar Italy or the Soviet Union?—there can be no doubt about the identity of the toilers. They were not the large businessmen or landlords; they were not the male workers in the large zaibatsu plants; they were not the bureaucrats. Instead, one found them among the small owner-cultivators and tenants in the countryside, in small-scale industry, and in many traditional and some modern services. And let us remember that these groups represented *well over 50 percent* of the gainfully employed population.

As usual, the evolution of this situation—or to put it another way, the symptoms—appears most openly in agriculture. One has only to look at the frequently cited statistics on the number of tenancy disputes: 85 in 1917, over 2,000 by 1927, and nearly 7,000 in 1936. The economic factors underlying these disputes were numerous: resentment against

[11] *The United States and Japan* (Cambridge, Mass., 1954), p. 62.

landlord absenteeism, demand for rent reduction during poor harvests, the decline in farm prices especially since 1925, and foreign competition. (If the price of rice is taken as 100 in 1926, it stood at 50.0 in 1931; similarly, the price of silk was 27.3 and the price of all commodities was 72.8. Cash income of "average farm families" during the period fell by about 60 percent.) At the bottom of it all there was a set of most intractable given conditions: too many people, too little land, and the task of feeding a growing population. In the 1920's the "tenant problem" was at the forefront. By the 1930's it had become the "problem of the villages" and the "problem of agriculture," focusing "on the bigger conflict of interests between the peasants as a whole on the one hand, and 'the towns,' 'the capitalists,' and 'the government' on the other."[12] This is seeing the issues in broader and better perspective. One could, of course, put it in even broader terms by calling it the "problem of the differential structure," and it was equally intractable.

What does all this have to do with Japanese militarism and aggression? What are the possible links between the distress of the traditional sector, including agrarian distress as the main component element, and "the rise of totalitarianism at home accompanied by expansion abroad?" Many links are plausible.[13] A powerful motive for expansion may have been to secure opportunities for emigration to relieve domestic underemployment. Severe domestic dissatisfaction, especially on the part of those in less productive occupations, created dangers for the rulers of Japan, and members of these groups—army leaders, politicians, bureaucrats, industrialists—may have seen expansion as a means of diverting attention from distress at home and as a way of healing rifts in the social structure by fostering a sense of national unity in the face of common danger. There was also a close relation between young officer rebels of the 1930's and the peasantry from which some of them came, whose supposed "traditional values" they widely admired.[14] They saw an increasing cleavage in Japanese society between the "Westernized," "individualistic," and "mechanized" towns and the depressed countryside, which still preserved "truly Japanese" techniques, values, and

[12] R. P. Dore, *Land Reform in Japan* (London, 1959), p. 89. Prices from LTES, vol. 9, p. 157 (rice), vol. 8, p. 201 (silk), p. 134 (general expenditure prices).

[13] For an excellent analysis, see Dore, pp. 116–25.

[14] One of the leaders of the abortive 1932 rebellion said at his trial: "No person of feeling could be indifferent to the plight of the villages. . . . While the *zaibatsu* capitalists amass ever greater wealth and indulge every appetite, without giving a thought to the farmers, the tender school children in the starving villages of the north-east go to school without their breakfasts; their families nibble at rotten potatoes." Cited by *ibid.*, p. 94.

personal relations. Of course, to call the towns "Westernized," "mechanized," and "individualistic" does not give a valid picture except in a symbolic sense. The economic and social problems were the same for large segments of the urban population, but it is undoubtedly also true that the army was more directly concerned with and sympathetic to the peasantry. Peasants were, for the usual reasons, preferred as soldiers, and the general anticapitalistic bias of the military also implied an admiration for the virtues of rural life. It was no accident that the doctrines of *nōhonshugi*—a Shinto-based ideology emphasizing agriculture as the foundation of the polity, which by the late 1920's turned right wing and antiurban—appealed to some of the military extremists, and that there was no corresponding ideology extolling the traditional occupations in the cities.

No simple connections between the structure of the economy as it developed in the 1920's and 1930's and Japanese aggression can be made here. Probably none exists. But the economic structure certainly did not help the deteriorating political atmosphere and must be seen as a major contributory factor in the demise of Japan's brief democracy at the end of the 1920's.

And what is there to learn from this sad episode? We know well enough that the differential structure phenomenon is extremely common; it exists today throughout Latin America and much of Asia. We also know that it is an unavoidable aspect of modern economic growth, because sectors applying Western technology inevitably surpass traditional methods in the growth of productivity and wages. After all, that is one meaning of "industrial revolution." Finally, we can also assert that a differential structure is social dynamite, having contributed to explosions in Japan, Pakistan, much of Latin America, and parts of the Middle East. The danger lies not so much in the absolute deterioration of conditions in traditional sectors, although this is common enough, as in their increasing relative deprivation.

These thoughts focus attention on the distributional and welfare aspects of growth. We have not had much to say about this topic because Japan contributed little that was either new or imaginative in these areas. In this sense the magnificent economic achievement of Japan remained flawed until recent times, and when, sitting in the comfortable armchair named hindsight, one considers the last hundred years, it is tempting to say that a few percentage points of the growth rate might well have been sacrificed for greater social welfare. This may sound unduly facile, and as a serious statement it would require extensive amplification.

Nevertheless, when Japan is held up as an admired example, the blemishes of the 1920's and 1930's as well as the immense suffering of the 1940's should not be forgotten.

JAPAN'S ECONOMIC FUTURE

During the late 1940's and early 1950's, before "futurology" had been elevated to its present status of a pseudoscience, most predictions concerning the economic future of Japan were pessimistic. Both Japanese and foreign observers tended to be obsessed by the defeat and destruction of World War II and even more by what seemed to be Japan's obvious disadvantages: a large population living in a destroyed country with sparse natural resources.[15] Today, the errors of 20 years ago may seem unimportant, but we do not believe this. The old forecasts were wrong because the great majority of analysts formed their picture of the future merely by extrapolating current trends. Therefore, they grossly underestimated the gains made possible by the rapid absorption of technological progress—these gains made Japan's resource endowment temporarily insignificant and turned its large and educated labor force into a clear competitive advantage.

When one contemplates what is being said at present concerning Japan's economic future, we seem in danger of once again falling into the trap of seeing tomorrow exclusively in the framework of today.[16]

[15] A rather typical example is the University of Chicago's Round Table of the Air discussion on NBC, December 16, 1951. The following are excerpts from the printed version (no. 716).

Theodore W. Schultz: May I ask what do you see in prospect for the Japanese economy, taking both the short view, the next two or three years, and the next five or ten years? I judge that you see rather serious difficulties?

Norton Ginsburg: Yes, I think there will be very serious difficulties. The Japanese economy, insofar as it has been an export economy in the past, lies dependent, in large part, upon foreign markets and upon imported raw materials in large quantities. And the bulk of those markets and raw materials, with some exceptions, have been in the past in the Far East . . . there are many complications, chiefly Japan's lack of basic raw materials . . .

Earl Pritchard: I certainly agree with the general point which Ginsburg has expressed that Japan is going to have a very serious difficulty of making a go of it economically. She has the problem of finding markets, of getting raw materials . . . Before the war she exported a lot to China. That is closed today; the Southeast Asian countries are not buying too much. Just where do you expect her to find a market?

For the record, it should be added that Professor Schultz took a much more optimistic and realistic view.

[16] This used to be the traditional predictive error concerning Japan. In the Meiji era many foreign observers could not bring themselves to believe that modern economic growth was possible. They understood too well the difficulties of the 1870's and 1880's; they did not foresee that the economic and social regimen would undergo basic change in the 1890's and thereafter.

Those who use the crystal ball most frequently appear to see the future with considerable clarity: the twenty-first century will be Japan's; by the year 2000 Japan will have the largest GNP in the world; even the United States will be surpassed in terms of industrial productivity and standard of living.[17] All of this is possible, but the realization of these predictions depends on a few crucial assumptions. For the past 20 years the Japanese economy has been expanding at the unprecedented rate of slightly over 10 percent per year (in real terms). Most of the rest of the world has been growing much more slowly, on average at more or less one-half the Japanese pace. The gap between Japan and other advanced countries is still large—in 1970 GNP per capita was $1,910 in Japan, $3,020 in West Germany, and $4,850 in the United States—and if it is to overtake the competition by A.D. 2000, two reasonable conditions must hold. First of all, Japan will have to continue running the race at more or less current speed. And second, the other runners must not significantly increase their speed.

Whether or not some advanced countries will be able to challenge Japan's rates of growth cannot be discussed here, although we fail to see how one can be very certain about such a matter in the long run. We shall now examine the first condition: Will the Japanese economy maintain present rates of growth in the future? The year 2000 is far away, and as historical economists we are naturally more comfortable in displaying the easier wisdom of hindsight. To make the question more tractable, let us first ask: Is it likely that Japanese GNP will grow less rapidly toward the end of the 1970's?[18] And then, let us consider the year 2000 in a later section.

We will attempt to show that the possibility of a slowdown cannot be dismissed. For the past 20 years Japan has been a veritable businessman's paradise in which many factors worked toward maximizing the rate of growth of aggregate output. This situation may change during the decade of the 1970's, partly for reasons beyond Japan's internal control. Equally critical may be a conscious change of direction induced by a new set of national priorities. The highest possible rate of growth of GNP does not necessarily lead to optimal national satisfaction. Perhaps the Japanese, who have led the world in growthmanship, will also be first to redirect their energies toward socially more beneficial activi-

---

[17] For example, see Herman Kahn, *The Emerging Japanese Superstate: Challenge and Response* (New York, 1970).

[18] If GNP continues to grow at present rates of over 10 percent per year, by 1980 Japan will reach a level of about $400 billion and a per capita output of about $3,500—all in 1960 prices. United States GNP in 1980 has been forecast at $1,280 billion in 1958 prices.

ties. None of these developments are certainties, but they deserve to be kept in mind when we contemplate the alleged dawning of the Japanese Century.

The Years 1950–1970

Perhaps the best way to understand the implications of the future is to consider once again the reasons for Japan's spectacular economic performance from the middle 1950's to the present. Within this time span Japan not only developed much more rapidly than at any other time in its history; it also did better than any other comparable economy. Why? No one "secret" exists, and the real factors are intertwined in necessarily complicated relationships. Nevertheless, the basic elements in Japan's so-called economic miracle can be identified.

Economists frequently use the concept of the aggregate production function, which says that the growth rate of output is related to the growth rates of the conventional inputs—labor and capital. In specific cases, the relationship between input and output varies both in time and internationally. Two countries—or one country at different historical periods—may have identical rates of growth of input and very different rates of growth of aggregate output. This difference is usually called "the residual," and its existence has generally been ascribed to technological progress, to possibilities of exploiting economies of scale, and to qualitative improvements in input, etc. The point is that in postwar Japan since the 1950's the residual has been growing at an unprecedented rate; to put it somewhat differently, the Japanese have succeeded in squeezing more output out of every unit of input than at any other time in their modern development; the rest of the world has not been able to match these results. Why? Surely a key element must be the massive inflow of foreign technology, which in the 18 years between 1950 and 1968 represented about 10,000 contracts and payments in excess of $1,400 million. These inflows permitted the modernization of old and the creation of new industries under extremely favorable conditions. Foreign technology was, in almost all instances, superior to domestic types, and until recently it was cheap. Foreigners were content to sell know-how for reasonable royalties and license fees; this suited Japanese business and government, both of which were anxious to keep foreign enterprise out of their home market. It was also cheap because the purchase and use of foreign processes avoided expensive and hazardous research and development efforts, since the costs of pioneering were borne by others. Furthermore, Japanese enterprise raised the adaptation of foreign methods to a fine art through the development of what has been called "improvement engineering."

The advantages inherent in acquiring advanced technology are not a Japanese monopoly, and one has to ask why they were so successful. In part, it can be argued that the opportunities were obvious and plentiful in a semideveloped economy recently devastated by war and out of contact with more advanced countries for over ten years. But this was nearly equally true for most Western European economies.

A more distinctive Japanese feature is the level and growth of investment. In this area Japan has topped all competitors. During the 1950's and 1960's, fixed capital formation has averaged well over 30 percent of GNP, with most of this going into private productive investment incorporating recent technological improvements. (Residential housing accounted for only a very small share of this total.) Other countries produced far less impressive figures: for comparable periods, U.S. investment shares were 17 percent, in France they were 19 percent, and in West Germany 24 percent.

What made it possible for such a large share of GNP to be invested in an essentially free market economy? One factor was the high return obtainable from private investment. Capital-output ratios, especially in those industries that imported technology, tended to decline, leading to more output per unit of capital input. Giving the labor force more and better equipment also raised output per worker, but luckily for entrepreneurs this did not lead to a comparable rise in wages. During the 1950's labor productivity rose more than wages; for most of the 1960's productivity has kept pace with wage increases. In European countries as well as in the United States, wage increases outstripped labor productivity gains in this period.

The labor situation remained unusually favorable in Japan until the late 1960's. Real strikes, i.e. lengthy work stoppages, were almost unknown, and the national unions continued to dissipate their energies on problems of foreign policy. On the shop floor, where it counted, the employer dealt with docile and cooperative enterprise unions. Labor supply remained elastic owing to the large reservoir of able, educated workers still available in agriculture and in assorted pockets of traditional underemployment. All this kept cost pressures under control while labor productivity continued to rise at about 9 percent per year in the aggregate—another record.

Undoubtedly, the government deserves considerable credit for Japan's high growth. It taxed moderately—20 percent of GNP, as opposed to 27 percent in the United States and 35 percent in the United Kingdom—supported growth industries by controlling foreign exchange allocations and guiding the inflow of technology, and ultimately guaranteed the availability of industrial bank credit through the Bank of Japan. Busi-

ness and government worked hand in hand toward the common ob-
jective of rapid economic growth; sometimes it was hard to know where
one entity began and the other left off. Of course the fact that defense
expenditures were less than 1 percent of GNP helped both government
and business. It is perhaps worth recalling that Japanese defense was
so inexpensive because of American guarantees.

The public also supported the all-out growth effort primarily by sup-
plying the savings needed to finance the enormous investments. In the
1960's personal savings were about 20 percent of disposable income, as
compared with 12 percent in West Germany and 7 percent in the United
States. Why and how the Japanese manage to be so frugal is a frequently debated issue among social scientists. Some of the most crucial
factors may be repeated here. The individual Japanese is largely responsible for his own welfare—clearly this is related to the low level
of government expenditures—and he must provide for education, retirement, and "rainy day" emergencies. Welfare is private and not yet public, and this heightens the incentive to save in order to make up for the
inadequacies of Japan's social security system. It is also true that personal income has been rising rapidly during the past 20 years while consumption expenditures have risen, but with a time lag of between one
and two years. In other words, the Japanese have been rather conservative consumers, and the lag alone will assure a large and growing pool
of savings. The reason for the extent of the lag—even its existence—may
be puzzling in view of the manifest prosperity of the people. However,
this prosperity has its misleading aspects. In the consumption of necessi-
ties and small consumer durables—food, clothing, radios, TV, refrigerators, etc.—the Japanese can compare themselves favorably with nearly
all other countries. This is not so when it comes to housing or automobiles—only 7 percent of Japanese owned private cars in 1969, as opposed
to 39 percent in the United States and 18 percent in West Germany.
These large items are difficult to acquire largely because consumer
credit is still an underdeveloped commodity. When and if it does become
available, the consumption lag may disappear.

Japan's postwar growth has also been greatly supported by an expansion of exports running at about 15 percent per year, which is more
than twice the rate of expansion of world trade. Again, we believe that
the absorption of new technology is relevant in explaining this phenomenon. Foreign customers purchased a rising proportion of Japanese
goods because these represented good buys in terms of price and quality.
And indeed, while domestic consumer prices rose over 50 percent in the
decade of the 1960's, export prices for many commodities declined and

in the aggregate remained almost stable. The incongruity between domestic and export prices is complicated, but one reason undoubtedly is the fact that Japanese exports have increasingly concentrated on those commodities in which cost-reducing technological progress has made its largest contributions. In the last few years the most rapidly rising exports have been transportation equipment, machinery, and iron and steel. All of these industries have had especially rapidly declining capital-output ratios indicating the massive absorption of technical and organizational progress, in good measure of foreign origin. Obviously the government has also had a lot to do with building up these strong and increasingly competitive export industries through its explicit methods of preferential credit rationing, tax exemptions, extraordinary depreciation allowances, readier permission to import know-how and—at times—tight protection against foreign imports.

We should also keep in mind that the past 20 years created an especially congenial climate for trade expansion. Japan's largest customer, the United States, espoused free trade, and there was little difficulty in penetrating markets in South and Southeast Asia, and Latin America.

Implications for the 1970's

Next, we should consider the meaning of what took place during the last 20 years. What are its implications for the future, especially for this decade? Were these years a specific growth phase and the consequence of transitory economic opportunities, or do they represent a style of growth that will maintain itself for the next 30 years? There are two separate aspects to this problem. First, we have to speculate about the quality in the 1970's of those economic factors so vital in creating rapid growth in the past. Second, we speculate about the possibility of new factors affecting the direction of economic development in Japan.

Let us begin with the inflow and absorption of foreign technology. There seems to be general agreement on the following points: in the 1950's and 1960's Japan lagged behind the technological leaders (primarily the United States and to a lesser extent West Germany); since the middle 1960's this technological gap has been rapidly growing smaller; and Japanese business is now making great efforts through increased research and development expenditures and similar devices to develop its own advanced technology. The facts have recently been thoroughly analyzed by James Abegglen.[19] He notes that since 1958 approximately 10 percent of total manufacturing in Japan was carried out using foreign technology. However, if only the modern sectors are

[19] See James Abegglen, ed., *Business Strategies for Japan* (Tokyo, 1970), chap. 7.

considered, the dependency on foreign technology would rise to 25–30 percent. Although the number of technical agreements has continued to increase all the time, "the proportion of agreements representing technology new to Japan and previously unlicensed is dropping steadily, from 70 percent in 1961 to only one-third in 1966." This is one sign that the gap is closing, "both because Japan is achieving technical parity with the nations of the West and because of an increasing reluctance of Western business to make technology available on license."[20] As Abegglen points out, the private sector has responded to this pressure by a considerable research and development effort. In 1964 about 115,000 employees were classified as research workers; France and West Germany reported slightly over 30,000 each. Obviously these efforts have yielded some favorable results: "In 1960 Japan paid about $95 million for foreign technology, and received payments of only $2 million for sales of Japanese technology; . . . in 1967 while Japan paid out about $239 million, receipts totalled about $26 million."[21]

It seems to us that the long-run implications of the present situation are frequently misunderstood. There are many reasons for believing that in the coming decades Japan will create numerous significant and profitable technological advances. No doubt Japan will also continue to avail itself of progress made elsewhere. There is, however, a fundamental difference between closing a gap (or eliminating a lag) and depending on the extension of a domestic or foreign technological frontier. In the former case, if other conditions are right, one can proceed at great speed. Gains can accrue in a relatively short time. In the latter case, one may face lengthy bottlenecks. The technological frontier is inevitably surrounded by uncertainties, hesitations, and false starts—soon an element of easy success in Japanese development may disappear. It would be fruitless to attempt to quantify the effect of Japan's reaching technological parity sometime in the 1970's. On balance, however, it seems clear that reaching this point will make continued high-speed growth more difficult. Probably the rate of growth of residuals will decline, and it may not be possible for labor productivity to maintain a rate of expansion two or more times larger than that of competing countries. Of course, the residual can be said to contain technological *and organizational* progress, and reaching parity may have less impact on the latter

[20] *Ibid.*, p. 117. Of course, overall parity is still a good distance away. At this time, technological renovation is moving from production and processing sectors to packing, marketing, and leisure industries. Technical advances are also moving from large to small establishments. See Japan, Economic Planning Agency, *Economic Survey of Japan, 1968–69*, p. 110.

[21] Abegglen, p. 131.

item. But we remain skeptical. The recent waves of mergers and con-
solidations generally encouraged by the government may lead to a rise
in efficiency. They may also once again bring about prewar-style rigidities, together with all the adverse features that this term implies.

Let us turn our attention now from technology and capital to labor,
wages, and employment. Japan's current position has frequently been
described as "second and fourteenth": the second largest GNP in the
capitalist world and number fourteen from the top in income per capita.
Low income per capita in the aggregate is a direct consequence of low
productivity in certain backward sectors, primarily agriculture, forestry,
and fisheries, the service industries, and small and medium-sized enterprises. However, a growing body of evidence indicates that certain
changes are now discernible within the long-established differential
structure; these began in the first half of the 1960's. Tendencies toward
both narrowed wage differentials and smaller labor supply elasticities
have been described in Chapter 5. In 1967, for the first time since World
War II, the ratio of labor demand to supply (active openings/active
application job seekers) exceeded 1.00 (in 1959 the ratio was 0.44). And
the Japanese government estimates that from 1976 to 1980 the working-
age population will rise by only 1 percent per year. Since 1967, wage
differentials have continued to narrow, though at a somewhat slower
pace.

Productivity differentials, however, present a very different picture:
the gap between advanced and backward sectors is still there, and it
is still widening. This sharp contrast in wage and productivity gaps is
a new phenomenon of the late 1960's, and its consequences must be
taken into account in evaluating Japan's economic future. Two problems, in particular, require attention: wage-income-price relations, and
patterns of labor shift.

The wage-income-price relations of Japan up to the present differ fundamentally from those of other advanced countries. In Western Europe
and the United States, cost push or inflationary wage increases have
generally been recognized as one of the primary causes of rising prices.
This has not been true in Japan, where the causes of inflation are structural. In the past, until the early 1960's, the differential structure meant
that low-productivity sectors also paid low wages, and the prices of their
goods and services remained relatively low, though as a trend they were
slowly rising. Now the situation has changed. Labor shortages are reducing wage differentials without affecting productivity levels. Given
the persistent strong demand for the output of the more backward sectors—they supply much of the food and many other daily needs—their

prices have been rising. This is the mechanism of Japan's inflation in the 1960's and today: it is a new version of the differential structure.[22]

The performance of Japanese prices clearly illustrates what has been happening. During the 1960's, these relative movements were observable: rising retail prices vs. stable wholesale prices;[23] rising consumer goods prices vs. stable investment goods prices; and rising domestic vs. stable export prices. All these contrasts reveal the key role of backward sectors in raising the price level as against the stabilizing influence of modern industry.[24]

The transfer of workers from less to more productive occupations has as yet been unaffected by the new differential structure. Higher wages are required to get the needed numbers, but the ever rising productivity attainable in modern industry has kept demand strong. Net outflows continue unabated, despite rising prices, wages, and incomes in agriculture and other traditional sectors.

So much for the current situation. What of the future? This is the crucial question. No easy answer is possible, but we can say what appears to us a distinct possibility. On the one hand, modern industry will continue to require a large number of workers. On the other hand, labor supply will be less plentiful and pressure for rising wages emanating in backward sectors should be powerful. If this is combined with more limited technological opportunities in the coming decade, the appearance of cost push sometime during the 1970's is not only conceivable— rather it is highly likely.

The reaction of organized labor to this possible situation should also

---

[22] For a rigorous proof of these contentions, see Ryoshin Minami and Akira Ono, "Price Changes in a Dual Economy," in R. F. Kosobud and R. Minami, eds., *Econometric Studies of the Contemporary Economy of Japan* (Chicago, forthcoming).

[23] A division into wholesale prices originating in modern and traditional sectors would show divergent movements: stability and sometimes decline in the former and increases in the latter. In the aggregate, however, traditional wholesale prices are not very significant, since the important service sector does not enter into consideration.

[24] For a few years before 1970, some increases occurred in wholesale prices, and it was widely believed that signs of cost push were appearing in modern sectors. But this turned out to be a premature conclusion. When the government adopted a tight money policy to curb an excessive rate of growth, wholesale prices stabilized. We may therefore conclude that the pressure came from the demand side.

Some might also argue that recently labor costs in relation to productivity, or labor's relative share, have started to increase in modern industry, and this is offered as an explanation of the recent inflation. As a long-term trend we identified a similar phenomenon when discussing labor costs per unit of capital in Chapter 5. But to link this observation with rising prices is too simple. At the same time, one has to consider output per unit of capital, and this gives no support to cost push up to the present.

be considered. Until now the Japanese worker has done well. His real wages have increased despite inflation, and individually and collectively he has had a somewhat superficial sweetheart agreement with his bosses at the plant level. Yet one may have doubts about the future. Management has shown little resistance to sizable wage increases, largely because these were more than matched by gains in productivity. But will management not be tempted to resist if it becomes more difficult to raise productivity levels? If this happens, if prices continue to go up, if labor shortages still exist, we can safely assume more severe and open worker-management conflict in the 1970's. When will the Japanese economy experience a wave of Western-style strikes, defined as rather lengthy work stoppages against individual enterprises in order to achieve a set of economic demands? Many of the largest employers are peculiarly vulnerable to this tactic: they export a relatively large share of output, and interruptions of shipments would lose foreign clients; they are heavily indebted to banks and therefore carry unusually heavy overhead burdens. Perhaps the Japanese labor unions will adopt these tactics in the 1970's. If so, it could lead to some significant changes.

Foreign trade is another area in which changes cannot be excluded, although these are always difficult to predict. The business cycle boom that began in 1965 has relied far more on the contribution of exports than previous postwar booms.[25] Also, as a trend, Japan's share in world trade has more than doubled in the last 15 years, and plans for the future remain ambitious. The Japan Economic Research Center estimates a 10 percent share of world exports by 1975, with an 18 percent share of the U.S. market and 35 percent of the Asian market.[26]

We are not especially concerned with the targets for 1975. Our query is: Can this great expansion continue beyond the 1970's? Let us briefly dwell on some of the straws in the wind. Japan's export capability depends on its own prices as well as on world prices. Should cost push develop in the 1970's, it stands to reason that export prices will not escape this pressure, and no one can argue that this is a competitive advantage in world markets.

This is all the more dangerous because a rise in protectionist sentiment is in evidence in many parts of the world. Talk of Japanese dumping is more frequent, and various industries are seeking relief from foreign

[25] For 1965–69 exports contributed nearly 12 percent to total increases in gross national expenditure. During the preceding boom (1958–61), the comparable contribution stood at 7 percent.

[26] See Saburō Ōkita, *Essays in Japan and Asia* (Tokyo, 1970), p. 19.

competition. If the United States adopts quotas, tariffs, and other restrictions, this will undoubtedly hurt Japan's trade account. In Asia also there is a rising nervousness about Japanese economic and political intentions, usually expressed as a fear of "domination." Perhaps the Japanese will reach 18 percent of the American market and 35 percent of the Asian market, but it is also likely that the attempt will generate strong resistance.[27]

We have tried to suggest that some of the very favorable factors in Japanese growth may be transitory. At least some of the possible changes are beyond simple policy control; they can perhaps be called part of the economic maturation process. Now we would like briefly to consider the likelihood and consequences of new socioeconomic priorities.

A recent article in the influential *Japan Economic Journal* said:[28]

The Japanese economy has passed the time when it should be satisfied only with the expansion of gross national product. It, instead, has entered the state in which it should pay closer attention to the level and distribution of stocks.

Environmental improvement based on social investments is the principal theme in this stage.

By now this has become a familiar refrain, and anyone concerned with Japan will be familiar with criticisms of "growth at any cost," *kōgai* (public nuisances), and assorted horror stories concerning pollution. No longer can these topics be called a partisan matter. Both the ruling Liberal Democratic Party and the opposition parties agree that the "agonies of a growing economy" must somehow be rectified. The question is: Are we confronting merely another fad of Western origin or do they mean it?

Given 20 years of great prosperity, the Japanese have, according to their own sources, accumulated an impressive list of agonies. The best known of these is the lag in social overhead capital. Despite a growth rate of government investment, measured against per capita national income, that exceeds those of more advanced nations, Japan continues to fall behind in filling its needs. Measured in terms of number of rooms per person, diffusion of water supply and sewage, ratio of paved roads, or area of city parks, Japan lags sadly behind countries with which it

[27] In this discussion no attempt has been made to assess the impact of rising military expenditures, because we do not believe that Japan in the next ten years will engage in large-scale rearmament. We could easily be wrong, but everyone will agree that the low level of military expenditures up to the present has been a distinct advantage in maintaining rapid growth, and that large-scale rearmament would contribute very little toward future economic development.

[28] "China Trade Causing Headache," *The Japan Economic Journal*, May 19, 1970.

likes to compare itself. (Medical facilities are the only exception.) The ratio of social capital stock to national income fell steeply from the early 1950's until the early 1960's, and since then it has not risen significantly. The ratio of living-related social capital stock—houses, environmental sanitation, health and welfare, education—to national income, which the government would like to see at 0.5 or 0.6, actually stands at about 0.35.[29]

Many reasons can explain the present impasse. Funds are always a problem especially when taxes are low. Public investments have been more affected than the private sector by price increases because of their larger labor content. A great inflation in land prices has been another stumbling block. However, the fundamental reasons lie elsewhere. As first priority the government consistently maintained a policy of maximizing the rate of growth of aggregate output; other needs remained in a subordinate position. This implied encouraging private capital formation, a balanced budget, and a chronic shortage of resources available for the enlargement of social consumption.

Modern economic growth has also led to an ever more unpleasant and dangerous set of public hazards or nuisances. To understand the problem, one only needs to know that Japan has the largest per-area gross national product in the world. More economic activity takes place in less space than in any other country, and the consequences in terms of noise and water and air pollution are not hard to imagine.[30]

Japan also suffers from a deficiency in social security. The percentage ratio of social security payments to national income was 6.2 in 1966, and it has hardly risen since then. Comparative ratios were 7.6 percent in the United States, 13.8 percent in Great Britain, 19.9 percent in West Germany, 19.2 percent in France, and 15.0 percent in Italy. Japanese (and United States) levels are inadequate, and are made more so by the rapid change in the age structure of the population. A declining birth rate and lengthened life expectancy have raised the proportion of people 65 or over from 5.3 percent in 1955 to a projected 9.9 percent

[29] It may be helpful to provide some international perspective at this point. Taking Britain, France, and West Germany as 100, the Japanese situation in the middle of the 1960's was as follows (*Economic Survey of Japan, 1967–68*, p. 142): per capita annual consumption of vegetables, 121.6; per capita annual consumption of meat, eggs, and fish, 46.7; per capita daily intake of calories, 77.3; number of rooms per household member, 68.4; ratio of diffusion of sewage, 73.1; ratio of population using public water supply, 21.9; extension of paved roads per motor car, 20.4; ratio of paved roads, 13.4; number of teachers per 1,000 elementary school pupils, 107.9; ratio of diffusion of electric washing machines, 153.2; ratio of diffusion of television sets, 166.7; per capita annual consumption of textiles, 94.8.

[30] Air pollution problems are aggravated by Japan's almost exclusive reliance on Middle Eastern oil with high sulphur content.

in 1985. Family units consisting only of old people are on the rise, and they can rely less and less on traditional practices—support from children, family work, etc.—to provide a comfortable old age. This may well be one of the saddest consequences of modern economic growth in Japan. Not long ago one could still see happy old people living in extended families, an especially impressive phenomenon for Americans, who are unfortunately used to a different situation. In this respect, unless great care is exercised, Japan may soon reach U.S. levels.

The agonies and benefits of growth are related to different aspects of the economy. Benefits are closely correlated with the level of income per capita: other things being equal, the richest countries have the highest standards of living. Agonies or adverse side effects also bear some relation to the level of income. However, they are equally closely tied to the rate of income growth, to the progress of technology, and to a variety of noneconomic factors, such as geography. We have not made a systematic comparison of Japan with the rest of the industrialized world. Nevertheless, it seems that Japanese-style growth has produced a lengthy and worrisome set of adverse side effects at comparatively low levels of income per capita. Partly this can be ascribed to the speed of economic development: no doubt the lag in social overhead capital was in some measure due to the steep rise in demand for these services. Partly it is a consequence of resources and physical configuration: air and water pollution are more severe because of population concentration and enforced reliance on certain types of fuel. When Western Europe and the United States were at Japanese levels of income, one heard rather little concerning these unpleasant side effects. Another historical era was involved, society was organized along different lines, and current social priorities were as yet insignificant. All of this is true. It is also true that the problems were less severe in the United States or Europe at these lower levels: in the United States the vastness of the country allowed more leeway, and in Europe both the slower pace of growth and an earlier start permitted some problems to be postponed. Whatever the reasons, we come back to the same conclusion: Japan faces the so-called agonies of growth at lower levels of income per capita than her predecessors in the development race, and postponement of solutions may be neither possible nor desirable.

Japanese planners are well aware of the trade-off issues posed by these problems. Most of them stem from a peculiar political situation. A higher ratio of public investments, badly needed at this time, has in the past been vigorously and successfully resisted by a powerful private sector. Given the fact that sources for financing capital formation are limited, intensified social investments compete with business expansion plans, and leading enterprises have used their considerable influence within the government to minimize the impact of desirable social policies on their affairs. Thus far, obvious steps like increased interest rates or higher corporate taxation have been successfully avoided despite much lip service by business and government leaders in favor of improving the quality of life. Since the 1950's, Japan has been not only a businessman's economic paradise—it has been an economic *and* political paradise: therein lies the problem. But as we have said before, the Japanese are good at institution building, and what is needed now is some national machinery to reach a new consensus concerning overall investment allocations. Presumably the voices of all citizens, representing labor, capital, farming, small business, etc., would be heard.

There are, of course, problems of a more narrow economic character associated with the trade-off between public and private expenditures. Shifting resources from private to public capital formation may lower the output effect of these expenditures because the capital-output ratio is generally higher for social overhead investments.

Undoubtedly these trade-offs have been stated in naïve form. An improvement of the social overhead capital stock should raise the efficiency of private investment. Other types of social expenditures may favorably affect labor force quality. Offsetting possibilities, however, are not likely to change the net trade-offs: the choice of the future lies in curbing either private investment or private consumption. It is this latter alternative that is especially difficult to imagine as Japanese policy, for it would entail asking the people to make consumption sacrifices while their income per capita was still low. This is just the time when desires for more and better consumption are great—and they are growing greater. Japan is on the threshold of becoming a mass consumption society, not a time when any politician—in or out of office—will advocate a large dose of austerity on behalf of the public good.

A Longer Perspective

In the preceding section, we spent some time on Japan's economic future in the 1970's. What about the longer-run destiny of Japan? This is at the moment a rather popular and timely question, and having looked carefully at the past 60 or 70 years, we would like now to speculate about the coming 20 or 30 years. No formal forecast or quantitative projections can be attempted. Instead, we intend simply to pursue some of the future implications stemming from our analysis of the past. In this type of exercise, unknown factors are numerous, and history may

TABLE 9.1
Projected Rates of Growth, 1970–90
(Percent)

Category	Projected annual rates of growth, 1970–90	Annual rates of growth, 1956–68
Manufacturing output	10.5%	11.69%
Agriculture output	2.0 to 2.5	2.78
Labor demand in manufacturing	3.6	4.06
Labor productivity in manufacturing	6.9	7.63
Labor force in agriculture	−3.0 to −3.5	−3.22
Labor productivity in agriculture	5.0 to 6.0	6.08
Total labor force	0.7 to 1.0	1.53

Note: These growth rates are based on a variety of relations discussed in previous chapters. Between the growth rate of aggregate demand (G_Y) and manufacturing output (G_{Ym}) the following long-run relationship (1908–64) exists:

$$G_{Ym} = 1.55 + 1.366 G_Y \qquad (\bar{R}^2 = .707)$$
$$(0.885) \quad (0.138)$$

No similarly steady relationship was found for agriculture, and only a postwar regression has been used, assuming that the constant equals zero. Labor-output relations for manufacturing, in growth rate terms, were calculated from the equations supplied in Chapter 4.

be a poor guide to the hereafter. Nevertheless, the temptation to conjecture is irresistible, and there is probably no sounder method than to consider how the "normal" historical path might change. In doing so, external factors beyond Japan's control have to be largely excluded; there exists no systematic way of discussing them, although we will come back to this matter later.

Toward the end of the 1970's, for reasons already described, we have predicted a slowdown in the rate of growth of Japan's national product. To pursue this prediction beyond the 1970's, it is most practical to concentrate on the demand and supply for labor. For this particular market, the future can be predicted with a fair degree of certainty; it is, after all, widely accepted that sometime soon labor will take the place of capital as a limiting or scarce factor.

By the end of this decade, it is likely that Japan's rate of growth of aggregate output will have fallen from its postwar rate of 10 percent to somewhere in the neighborhood of 6.5 percent. Let us now assume, for discussion's sake, that this rate represents a new long-term average for the next 20 years. Then, as Table 9.1 shows, the other average annual rates of growth are implied.

Just a few additional comments concerning these figures. With these assumptions, labor productivity in manufacturing continues to expand more rapidly than in agriculture; the productivity gap is still being widened. Since the total labor force can only expand slowly for demographic reasons, the high labor requirements of manufacturing can be met only by a continuing reallocation of workers from agriculture to industry.[31] And this is a crucial matter because we believe that the possibilities of substituting capital for labor are technologically limited, although to some degree it will be accomplished so as to combat the trend of rising wages.

If this simple growth path continues until (say) 1990, a picture of the Japanese economy emerges at that time: The proportion of the labor force in manufacturing will be 43 percent if the total labor force rises at 1 percent per year, or 48 percent if the total increases at 0.7 percent per year. Agriculture will contain 8.0 to 9.5 percent of the employed population. The differential of average labor productivity between agriculture and manufacturing will be much larger than it is today; compared to 1970, the relative position of agriculture will fall either 22 percent if the sectoral productivity growth rates differ by 1 percent, or 48 percent if the sectoral difference is 2 percent.

From the present until 1990, therefore, if these assumptions are at all correct, the differential structure will still be a feature of the Japanese economy despite the maintenance of a high net outflow of workers from the backward sectors. Of course, between 1970 and 1990 the weight and significance of those in lower productivity sectors will have declined very much. This is one way of looking at the future, and one certainly should not take these numbers too seriously. It may be interesting, however, to pursue briefly some of the inferences suggested by the numerical example.

At the end of Chapter 1, we said that in the nineteenth century Japan experienced "initial" modern economic growth, and that the period 1900 to 1965 was a much bigger step, which we labeled "the leap toward a semideveloped state." These were the years of private investment spurts and trend acceleration, and in analyzing Japan's short-run future, we have already indicated why we believe this phase to have ended at about the present time. Both the easy availability of technology and labor are less certain assets from now on. National priorities may also be redirected. For these reasons we are inclined to call Japan's next long phase of growth "the movement from semidevelopment to economic maturity." This is likely to be quite a different process. "Economic maturity" is a difficult term to define, but as used here it has a narrow meaning. Let us call it that state in which the incentives of sectoral labor force reallocation have become minimal—in the extreme case impossible. In proceeding from initial growth to semidevelopment, opportunities for labor reallocation increased; that is one way of looking at

[31] For simplicity's sake we will not discuss other possible labor force shifts.

the creation of the differential structure. In moving toward maturity, we can expect that at some point these opportunities will diminish.

When will this situation be attained in Japan and what will be its consequences? A rough indication of "when" is the proportion of the agricultural labor force, and according to the numerical example, in 1990 it will be about 9 percent. This is in excess of current proportions in the United States and the United Kingdom, but for Japan a level slightly below 10 percent may well be a point beyond which labor force shift incentives are minimal. Land resources are unusually poor, and a combination of farm and nonfarm employment is commonplace. We may reasonably assume that when the agricultural labor force declines to about 10 percent, some kind of intersectoral equilibrium will exist in terms of income per head.[32]

No one can name the year when Japan will reach this equilibrium— perhaps in 1990, perhaps earlier or later. It all depends on the long-run rate of growth, and to make a firmer prediction is hazardous. More to the point are the implications of attaining this position—no matter when. From 1900 to the present we spoke of "trend acceleration," and perhaps we can characterize the future as *trend deceleration.* Toward the end of the century the labor bottleneck should loom large, and if the possibilities of substitution are indeed limited, a trend of slower growth is most likely. The previous assumption of 6.5 percent national product growth from now to 1990 was stated as constant average. In reality a decline from, let us say, 8 percent to 4 percent during this interval is even more likely.

These prognostications can in no way be considered pessimistic. Compared with other advanced countries, Japan's growth will still be rapid during the coming 15 or 20 years; only the gap may become somewhat smaller. Rapid growth will continue because labor reallocation has a long way to go, and income levels will continue to rise, creating opportunities for further domestic technological growth combined with continued improvement engineering. In a word, Japan is still a quarter of a century away from facing the difficulties of mature development. To project beyond that stage is quite impossible.

A Japanese economy growing at 6.5 percent per year presents considerable problems for the world, and possible international repercussions must be considered in any estimate of the future. Japan's sustained rapid growth will almost certainly continue to be led by manufacturing.

---

[32] At that point there is no reason whatever for assuming that per capita product in Japan will be the same as that of the United States.

As a result, the growth of exports will have to be large and greater than the growth of world trade. In fact, the pressure to export is likely to become stronger because of what we see as the gradual disappearance of investment spurts.[33] Whether or not the rest of the world can, or desires to, swallow the flood of Japanese manufactures has to be a matter of grave concern. The Japanese may face repeated pressure for upward yen revaluation, and/or a rise of protectionism. To some extent they can attempt to alleviate the situation by larger capital exports, but this raises the specter of Japanese economic domination and has explosive political consequences, especially in Asia. One should not be surprised if, in the coming decade, Japan assumes a most unaccustomed role as champion of free trade, while other advanced countries turn more to defensive tariffs, quotas, and other restraints. Any or all of these eventualities could seriously undermine the projected rates of growth.

On the import side, Japan faces equally serious international repercussions. Import substitution has nearly reached its limit, and now this large and rapidly growing economy displays an ever more voracious appetite for the world's raw materials, of which Japan possesses almost none. It is true that Japan is anxious to exchange its excellent manufactures for the raw materials of less developed countries, and that its large purchases are beneficial to many nations. But few countries see their future as raw material exporters, and Japan's enormous needs now—and more enormous needs in the future—create economic and political apprehensions in diverse parts of the globe. Japan has to face the very real possibility that the world may be unwilling to supply, under any reasonable conditions, the raw materials necessary to sustain for 25 years a growth rate of 6.5 percent. A growth rate of 10 percent, as at present, is almost surely out of the question with this constraint. Even a lower level will demand a kind of economic statesmanship, e.g. repeated upward revaluations, that the Japanese have only rarely displayed in the past.

In discussing Japan's future, our frank purpose has been to act as devil's advocate. This necessarily entails a certain amount of "viewing with alarm," and some will no doubt consider the conclusions excessively pessimistic. Still, we firmly believe that the two major themes that have been stressed are correct: there are certain factors inherent in a higher

[33] Investment spurts in the past came about through a combination of technological opportunities (high Y/K) and favorable wages (low Lw/K). Both factors assured a good rate of return, r. In the future, however, the technological options may be more limited, and labor costs will almost certainly rise. This makes a sustained private investment spurt far less probable.

level of economic maturity that will make it increasingly more difficult to maintain a real annual growth rate of 10 percent, and a government-financed improvement in the quality of life will have the same result. There is no cause for pessimism in these conclusions. If the rate of growth is reduced for the right reasons, Japan may not surpass the West in aggregate income by the year 2000. It may, however, surpass it in aggregate happiness, and this might yet be the real meaning of "Japanese Century" when it arrives.

Will it actually happen? There is some cause for optimism. For a number of reasons we think that the Japanese have a better chance of achieving an intelligent and rational industrial order than many other democratic countries. The level of consensus in the society is still impressive, central government is strong, and the nation has frequently demonstrated a social capability to make basic changes. And yet, the final outcome is not at all obvious. Prime Minister Tanaka appears committed to a policy of maintaining the very high rates of growth while simultaneously raising welfare levels and improving the quality of life.[34] This may prove to be a very difficult task that carries with it the serious danger of a greater and more pervasive inflation. Furthermore, one wonders whether the neglect of the social aspects of growth has not become a habit of the party now in power; in other words, at the margin, will choices inevitably favor more growth? The answers will become clear as the future is transformed into history. As students of Japan's past, we hope for and would welcome a redirection of priorities toward social welfare and quality of life, because these new targets will bring about a more stable Japan capable of more intelligent leadership in Asia.

[34] See Kakuei Tanaka, *Nihon rettō no kaizō-ron* (Restructuring the Japanese Archipelago; Tokyo, 1972).

Appendix Note

Measurement and Decomposition of Relative Income Shares

Three topics are covered in this appendix. First, estimates are made of relative income shares for labor (β) and capital (α); these are needed to derive the residuals already presented in Chapters 3 and 4. Second, the derivation of income shares naturally leads to a discussion of factor compensation: wage rates (w) and the rate of return on capital (r). Third, we will also explore what relative shares reveal about the aggregate and sectoral structure of production by examining in greater detail the major ratios K/Y, K/L, and Lw/K. The analysis is largely confined to the private nonprimary sector after World War II.[1]

RELATIVE SHARES

A proper description of relative shares in Japan means separate treatment for corporations, unincorporated enterprises, and agriculture. The fundamental reason is the particular nature of Japanese dualism, in which modern and traditional methods of production coexist, and in which corporations are largely modern while the remaining units of production are largely traditional. These differences can be observed in Table A.1, where the years are selected to cover the longest possible period based on these data. The table compares corporate and unincorporated output, capital, and employment for 1952 and 1963. We can see that in postwar Japan unincorporated enterprises have retained considerable weight, especially in the employment of labor, where their share is still over 50 percent. Admittedly, the weight of unincor-

[1] Most of the postwar data used in this appendix have been prepared by the authors, based on unpublished materials supplied by the Economic Planning Agency and the official national income statistics. These are the source of all tables. Therefore the concepts and coverage of terms unless otherwise specified are the same as in the official national income statistics (at factor cost). See Japan, Economic Planning Agency, *Shōwa 40-nen kijun: kaitei kokumin shotoku tōkei* (Revised National Income Statistics, 1951–67; 1969), Part 3, pp. 339–415. Output and relative shares are given both gross and net, valued at factor cost. We have generally worked with gross valuations, but net values are also supplied so as to allow international comparisons.

TABLE A.1

Composition of the Private Sector in Terms of Output, Capital, and Labor:
Corporate and Unincorporated, 1952 and 1963

Sector	Output Amount (billion yen)	Output Percent	Capital Amount (billion yen)	Capital Percent	Labor No. of workers (millions)	Labor Percent
		I. Total Private Sector				
1952						
Corporate	2,090	42.6%	9,106	59.4%	9.3	27.3%
Unincorporated	2,813	57.4	6,260	40.6	24.8	62.7
Total	4,903	100.0%	15,366	100.0%	34.1	100.0%
1963						
Corporate	9,600	65.6	26,407	72.3	18.5	44.4
Unincorporated	5,060	34.4	10,120	27.7	23.1	55.6
Total	14,660	100.0%	36,527	100.0%	41.6	100.0%
		II. Private Sector Excluding Agriculture and Financial Sectors[a]				
1952						
Corporate	1,814	59.1	8,896	84.3	8.0	52.3
Unincorporated	1,257	40.9	1,664	15.7	8.0	47.7
Total	3,071	100.0%	10,560	100.0%	16.8	100.0%
1963						
Corporate	8,427	72.8	24,912	87.3	17.4	62.8
Unincorporated	3,270	27.5	3,643	12.7	10.3	37.2
Total	11,697	100.0%	28,555	100.0%	27.7	100.0%

Note: Output in net national product at factor cost, and capital in gross reproducible physical stock at 1960 prices.
[a] Financial sectors include banking, insurance, and real estate.

porated enterprises has decreased during the decade in question, but it remains significant. Sometimes it is suggested that agriculture alone is responsible for the large role played by unincorporated units. Panel II of Table A.1 indicates that this is not entirely true. With agriculture excluded, in 1963 unincorporated enterprises accounted for 27.5 percent of output, 12.7 percent of capital stock, and 37.2 percent of the labor force.

Table A.1 also implies a very different structure of production for the two sectors. For a given quantity of output, unincorporated enterprises use relatively more labor and much less capital, and the differences are very large. Capital-output ratios, taken directly from the table, give evidence of these differences. In 1952, the capital-output ratio was 1.32 for unincorporated and 4.91 for corporate enterprises. This still was a rather abnormal year, but the differences in 1963—1.11 for unincorporated and 2.95 for corporate—are still very large. Without question, these disparities are traceable to the unincorporated sector's heavy use of self-employed labor in the form of proprietors and family workers. Cheap labor of this type permits a maximum use of scarce capital leading to high output per unit of capital input. No doubt, self-em-

TABLE A.2
Labor's Relative Share: Private Corporate Sector,
1952, 1958, and 1964
(Percent)

Sector	1952		1958		1964	
	Gross	Net	Gross	Net	Gross	Net
Manufacturing	66.02%	71.07%	62.61%	72.48%	54.95%	67.18%
Mining	66.67	77.26	71.72	86.56	52.67	69.11
Construction	90.79	94.00	81.09	88.39	73.33	81.58
Commerce	75.60	77.57	72.04	76.73	66.65	71.81
Facilitating industries	69.71	83.95	59.63	77.61	53.37	72.26
Services	73.90	95.18	78.17	93.36	79.89	91.11
Agriculture	77.56	90.34	66.47	84.34	60.08	81.08
Total	67.02	73.41	62.98	72.13	56.83	67.01
Total, excluding agri- culture & finance	69.81	77.04	66.63	77.30	60.37	72.15
(Finance)	41.53	42.42	35.91	37.24	29.77	31.55

Note: Facilitating industries contain transportation, communication, and public utilities. Agriculture includes forestry and fisheries, in which corporate enterprise is relatively prevalent. Total includes finance.

ployment creates considerable conceptual difficulties in distinguishing relative shares, and this will be discussed later. At least, it should be plain that separate treatment of these sectors makes sense.

The Corporate Sector

Table A.2 shows the relative share of labor in gross and net output for 1952, 1958, and 1964. Probably the total, excluding agriculture[2] and finance, gives the most meaningful picture of the overall situation for corporations.

The relative share of labor represents the compensation of labor in total income. It will differ in accordance with definitions and coverage of labor compensation and varying concepts of total income. For our purposes, income shares are generally used as substitutes for the elasticity of labor (and capital) with respect to output. Therefore our coverage includes wages and all other forms of compensation except income transfer items. We also use total income produced, including retained corporate profits. With respect to allowances for capital depreciation, rather than limit ourselves to the conventional net terms, we will present both gross and net versions.

During the period, labor's relative share declined, in gross terms roughly from 70 percent to 60 percent, and in net terms from 77 percent to 72 percent. The decline is very general and, on the whole, rather even.[3] While the ranking of individual broad groups changes somewhat during the selected years, certain industries exhibit persistently high relative shares for labor

[2] Corporate enterprise in agriculture is extremely small.
[3] See also the annual figures in Table A.10.

TABLE A.3
*Decomposition of Relative Shares and Rate of Capital Return:
Private Corporate Sector, 1958*

Sector	K/L	r (pct)	w	Kr/Y (pct)	K/Y	(Y/K)	Lw/K (pct)
Manufacturing	902	15.0%	227.2	37.4%	2.47	(0.40)	25.2%
Mining	809	9.3	253.0	28.3	2.29	(0.43)	31.4
Construction	229	15.6	190.0	18.9	0.97	(1.03)	88.0
Commerce	966	9.6	238.5	28.0	2.92	(0.33)	24.6
Facilitating industries	2,732	7.7	317.4	40.4	5.14	(0.19)	11.6
Services	1,381	5.1	251.2	21.8	4.29	(0.24)	18.1
Total	1,069	8.6	238.0^a	30.2	3.04	(0.33)	24.4

Note: Y and K in 1960 prices, gross of capital depreciation; K/L in thousand yen per worker; w is wage rate in 1960 industrial output prices in units of thousand yen per man-year; Kr/Y is derived from $1 - \beta$, β from Table A.2.
^{a}Average weighted by number of workers in each industry.

(e.g. construction, services, and commerce), and others are persistently low (manufacturing and facilitating industries).

Table A.3, prepared to clarify the structure and levels of relative shares, needs a brief introduction. Most of the symbols and relations used in the table will already be familiar, but a few new concepts require definition: r is the rate of return on capital (K) and is measured by $(Y - Lw)/K$, where Y is output at factor cost and Lw is the total wages of labor;[4] w is the wage rate; Kr is the total return on capital; the relative shares—α, or Kr/Y, and β, or Lw/Y—have already been given in Table A.2. There only β is shown, but of course $\alpha = 1 - \beta$. Table A.3 also contains the component parts of α, β, and r, as indicated by the following relations: (1) $\alpha = Kr/Y = r \times K/Y$; (2) $\beta = Lw/Y = Lw/K \times K/Y$; in other words, from the standpoint of the enterprise, labor's relative share is the product of the ratio of unit labor cost per amount of capital and the output per amount of capital (partial productivity of capital); and (3) if Y, K, and w are given in consistent values at constant prices with the same base year, the formula for β is just another way of deriving the rate of capital return, because $r = Y/K - Lw/K$, which is simply output per amount of capital minus labor costs per amount of capital.

All of these relations can be derived with the information provided by Table A.3. Two further preliminary points need stressing. The results are restricted to 1958, which is more or less the midpoint of the analysis period.

[4] Rates of return can be calculated in many ways, and final results will differ. We have used gross stock, net shares, and constant prices. Others might prefer to use net stock (not available), current prices, and gross shares, and the r's would not be the same. We are making no exclusive claims for the method adopted here, but with the given data it is most convenient. Furthermore, our concern will be primarily the relative levels of capital returns rather than their absolute magnitudes, and these should be less affected by differences in measurement methods.

Whether or not this year is representative can be judged later when the time series are examined.[5] Finally, it will be noticed that some of the measures used here, especially K/Y and K/L, differ rather considerably from the results presented in previous chapters. A number of reasons are involved, among which of prime importance is the fact that the data used in this chapter are confined to corporations, and perhaps for that reason they are more reliable. A subsidiary reason is the difference in valuation: in this chapter at factor cost, and in Chapter 3 at market prices.

Let us now, at last, turn to the tables beginning with A.3. Great differences in the levels of capital intensity are indicated, with facilitating industries at the top and construction at the bottom. However, the relative positions of commerce and services are not low, and this must be due to the elimination of unincorporated production. It indicates that *modern* commerce and services operate at quite high levels of capital intensity.

In general, the range of capital-output ratios is much narrower than differences in capital-labor ratios. For example, the level of construction is one-fifth of facilitating industries for K/Y, instead of one-twelfth as is the case for K/L. Manufacturing is below the all-industry average.

Wage rates have the smallest spread. In the highest-paying facilitating industry, wages are only 1.64 times above the wages in the lowest-paying construction industry. However, it is not entirely correct to use the term "wage rates" for the figures in Table A.3. In reality, these are average wage payments per employee and therefore must reflect differences in the quality and composition of the work force. When mining is excluded—and this industry undoubtedly draws extra pay because of its unusual and unpleasant working conditions—the order of average wage payments is the same as the order of K/L. This association is open to a multitude of interpretations, and one of them is that the greater the amount of capital per worker, the greater the need for more qualified personnel commanding higher levels of compensation. In this connection, we should especially note the relatively low wage level in manufacturing, where young and female workers are numerous.

Table A.3 also contains a decomposition of r, together with the levels of various Lw/K's, or labor cost per amount of capital. Besides revealing the composition of r, the table shows why variations in relative shares have persisted among industries. As mentioned previously, labor's share is a product of the capital-output ratio and labor cost per amount of capital. The capital-output ratio is only one of the determinants. Obviously with a given K/Y, labor's relative share will vary directly with changes in Lw/K: the larger this ratio, the larger the share going to labor.

Here it is best to focus on individual industries, and one can begin with the two extreme cases: construction and facilitating industries. Construction has the highest relative share of output going to labor (see Table A.2), the

[5] The levels of r show considerable variation. Of course, these findings are restricted to a single year and therefore an even level is not necessarily expected. The fact that 1958 was a recession year may also have affected these results.

advantage of the lowest K/Y, the disadvantage of the highest Lw/K, and the highest rate of return on capital (15.3 percent). In other words, construction's high rate of return depends very much on the use of cheap labor. If, for example, average wage payments in this industry had been just 18 percent higher, which would make them equal to manufacturing, the Lw/K of construction would have reached 103.8, and assuming the absence of substitution, the rate of return would have been zero.

The contrast with facilitating industries is vivid. This group of industries has the disadvantage of the highest K/Y, the advantage—despite the highest level of wages—of lowest labor cost per amount of capital, and a rather low rate of return. Obviously these industries are relatively insensitive to changing labor costs.

As we can see in Table A.3, there is a tendency for a low K/Y to be offset by a high wage bill per unit of capital, and for a high K/Y to be offset by a low wage bill. The degree to which this offset occurs determines the level of the rate of return, and the contrast between services and manufacturing is especially interesting. Services have a low Y/K and this is not offset by a small wage bill. For example, its Y/K is about 26 percent above facilitating industries, but its Lw/K is nearly 56 percent higher. The result is a very low rate of return and a large relative share of labor. By contrast, the Y/K of manufacturing is quite high and Lw/K is moderate. Therefore, the rate of return is high, and labor's relative share is rather low. This reasoning cannot be pushed too far. The rate of return must reflect the forces of competition between industries and the possibilities of entry, technological progress, market conditions, etc. All these can also lead to different rates of return for industries, especially in any one year.

Unincorporated Enterprises

For the unincorporated and heavily self-employed economy, the concept of relative shares of labor and capital contains an unavoidable element of artificiality. Individuals in these enterprises frequently received "mixed incomes," partially derived from labor and partially derived from capital, and unambiguous separation is very difficult. Some economists feel that this sector simply operates with a set of different economic principles and that it would be wise to establish a third share called proprietors' or mixed income. This view will not be adopted here because it avoids the fundamental problem of resource allocation. As long as there is some competitive determination of factor prices, the unincorporated or self-employed economy cannot exist in a cocoon, and it should be possible by means of an imputation procedure to arrive at an approximation of relative factor shares. The key problem lies in the method of imputation. Not all methods are equally desirable, and a valid method must take into account the economic realities of unincorporated enterprise in Japan.

There are three conventional systems of imputation, all using information derived from the corporate sector. One method is to assume that relative shares in the corporate economy are the same as in unincorporated sectors. The other two methods assume that either wage rates or rates of return on capital are competitively determined and tend toward equality for corporations and noncorporations. None of these is appropriate or superior for *a priori* reasons; selection must depend on the specific economic situation. Our hypothesis will be that factor prices in the unincorporated sector are subject to market forces and are determined competitively, and we will also argue that, in the light of postwar circumstances, the best results can be obtained by imputing the same rate of return on capital for the enterprise economy and other sectors. The degree to which this hypothesis yields poor results can be considered one measure of market imperfections.

It is not difficult to explain why the frequently used device of assuming identical relative shares for corporations and noncorporations should be rejected for Japan. Using the entries of Table A.1, we can compare Y/K and L/K for corporations and unincorporated enterprises. Unincorporated enterprises are on the average three times more efficient per unit of capital invested; at the same time, their average labor requirements per unit of capital are four times larger. Two implications follow. Since the capital-output ratio is much lower in unincorporated enterprises, if the same relative shares are postulated, it would mean that the rate of return on capital is much higher than for corporations.[6] This does not seem reasonable for postwar Japan. However, if the rate of return on capital is similar for the two sectors, the comparison of Y/K and L/K also indicates how critical a lower average wage must be for noncorporations; of course, this does not necessarily mean different rates for workers of equal quality.

Differences in average capital-output ratios between these two sectors are meaningful, and not the result of a distorted output distribution. An examination of Table A.4 reveals that after agriculture has been excluded, the unincorporated share of output is big for construction, commerce, and services; in each case these units account for over one-third of net output. Unincorporated enterprises are also relatively important in manufacturing, where they account for a steady 19 to 20 percent of output, and because of this steadiness the share of unincorporated manufacturing output has risen relative to the total between 1952 and 1963.

We can now proceed to a description of the system of imputation employed here. The working assumption is that rates of return on capital are equal. To assume a higher rate for unincorporated enterprises seems to us unrealistic, and the supposition of equality may be considered as setting a maximum value. As an example, we outline below an illustrative calculation for aggregate unincorporated relative shares (excluding agriculture and finance) for net output in 1958. All results are stated in 1960 prices.

[6] Because $\alpha = Kr/Y = r \times K/Y$. In the case of other countries where equal relative shares are assumed, the general presumption must be that there are no substantial differences in K/Y.

TABLE A.4
Industrial Distribution of Unincorporated Sector in Terms of Output
(Billion yen, 1960 prices)

Sector	1952			1958			1963		
	Total	Unincor-porated	Unincorporated as pct. of total	Total	Unincor-porated	Unincorporated as pct. of total	Total	Unincor-porated	Unincorporated as pct. of total
Agriculture	1,579	1,551	98.4%	1,750	1,691	96.6%	1,791	1,712	96.6%
Mining	124	26	20.9	163	17	10.4	207	18	8.7
Construction	261	141	54.2	429	193	45.0	846	277	32.7
Manufacturing	1,175	227	19.2	2,330	432	18.9	4,122	814	19.7
Commerce	792	520	65.6	1,649	913	55.4	3,151	1,452	46.1
Financing	262	10	3.8	659	26	3.9	1,173	79	6.8
Facilitating industries	235	22	9.2	510	31	6.1	1,097	67	6.1
Services	486	321	66.0	779	425	54.5	1,274	641	50.2
Total	4,907	2,818	57.4%	8,258	3,729	45.1%	14,661	5,061	34.5%
Total, excluding agri-culture & financing	3,072	1,257	40.9	6,249	2,412	38.6	11,697	3,270	28.0

Note: Output is net of depreciation.

1. Amount of unincorporated capital (K) = ¥2,352 billion.
2. Rate of return on capital for corporations = 6.50 percent.
3. Return on capital in unincorporated sector = (1) × (2) = ¥142 billion.
4. Total product distributed in unincorporated sector = ¥2,017 billion.
5. Amount of product going to non-asset income = (4) − (3) = ¥1,875 billion.
6. Relative share of labor = (1) − (3)/(4) = 92.93 percent.

The next step is to examine the distribution of line (5) or (6). Three kinds of workers lay claim to slices of this particular pie: proprietors, family workers, and hired workers. Proprietors receive compensation for their entrepreneurial activities, and with the system of imputation used here these returns have already been assigned to capital. However, proprietors also receive wages for the work they perform as laborers, and this is a part of the labor share. Here it will appear as a residual. In the case of hired workers, actual data are available about their average wages. We know that hired workers in unincorporated enterprises receive a level of compensation that is, on the average, some 40 percent below that prevailing in corporations.[7] Family workers present the greatest problems. Many may be part-timers and there is no way to consider differences in working hours—one might add that no solid evidence exists to suggest that average working hours per year (say) for family workers are much below those of hired workers. We will use the average wage of hired workers to estimate the compensation of family workers.[8]

Let us proceed with the illustrative calculation.

7. Average annual wage payment per hired worker in the unincorporated sector = ¥151.3 thousand, which is 63.57 percent of the average corporate wage (¥238.0 thousand).
8. The number of hired workers in the unincorporated sector = 2,958 thousand, which is 30 percent of the total labor force in the sector (9,731 thousand).
9. Amount of wage payments going to hired workers = (7) × (8) = ¥448 billion, which is 22.48 percent of the total product distributed in the sector (line 4).
10. The number of family workers is 2,572 thousand.
11. Imputed wage payments to family workers = (7) × (10) = ¥389 billion.
12. Residual to be imputed to proprietors = (5) − (9) − (11) = ¥1,038 billion.
13. Number of proprietors = 4,021 thousand.
14. Average "wage" earnings per proprietor = (12) ÷ (13) = ¥247.1 thousand.

[7] We also know that as a group these workers have much lower qualifications.

[8] Another possibility would have been to treat the earnings of family workers as a residual, to be combined with proprietors' wage earnings, the implication being that these two types of earnings cannot be separated. In view of our stress on the competitive determination of factor prices, this method is not adopted.

TABLE A.5
Imputed Relative Share of Labor and Related Terms by Industry in Unincorporated Sector, 1958

Sector	Share (pct) (1)	Ratio (pct) (2)	Wage(C) (3)	Wage(U) (4)	Wage(U)/ wage(C) (4')	Propri- etors (000) (5)	Family workers (000) (6)	Hired workers (000) (7)	r (pct) (8)
Mining	98.28%	196.0%	253.0	153.3	(60.6)	17	8	47	4.86%
Construction	98.29	157.0	190.9	143.8	(75.4)	414	109	372	10.97
Manufacturing	82.28	76.4	227.2	135.1	(59.5)	799	611	991	9.57
Commerce	94.50	102.9	238.5	159.4	(66.9)	1,990	1,490	848	7.47
Facilitating industries	94.53	106.7	317.4	192.3	(60.6)	48	20	48	3.34
Services	99.76	109.1	251.2	166.4	(66.3)	950	317	652	1.29

Note:

Share, imputed relative share (net) by the method described in the text, using the value of r given in column (8).
Ratio, ratio of imputed proprietors' wage earnings to the average wages in the corporate sector, given in column (3).

Wage(C), corporate wages, EPA data, 1960 prices, thousand yen per man-year.
Wage(U), average wages paid for hired workers in the unincorporated enterprises, 1960 prices, thousand yen per man-year.

How good are these imputations? Many points need to be considered. First of all, let us examine the differentials between the imputed wage earnings of proprietors and corporate employees. In 1958, the year of our example, proprietors' wages averaged 3.74 percent above those of corporate workers. A single year means little, and we have therefore applied this method to other years, with the following results (ratio of proprietors' wage earnings to average corporate wages): 127.8 for 1952; 111.3 for 1955; 116.8 for 1961; and 103.0 for 1963. If 1958 is included, proprietors' wages average about 10 percent above corporate wages during the period, and these seem reasonable differentials in view of the quality differences—sex, age, and education—between these groups. Proprietors are overwhelmingly male, older, and better educated, and one would expect them to receive a somewhat higher wage.

The method of imputation used here can be further evaluated by means of Table A.5, where relative shares are again calculated for 1958, and this time aggregate net output has been subdivided into broad industrial groups. Here one should focus especially on column (2), which again compares proprietors' and corporate wages. Commerce, services, and facilitating industries show differentials that are tolerably close to the aggregates. In the remaining three industries, the situation is very different: proprietors' wages are much higher in mining and construction and much lower in manufacturing. This pattern is realistic and supports our results. Unincorporated proprietors in mining and construction head relatively large enterprises, while in manufacturing they generally run tiny units and depend heavily on a supply of the cheapest possible labor (see column 4).

The imputed relative shares of labor appear in column (1) of Table A.5. Naturally they are very much larger than for corporate enterprise, and the implied structure of production and distribution is shown in Table A.6— again for net output in 1958. Particular note should be made of the ratios that indicate the comparative values—corporate vs. unincorporated—of K/L, Y/K, and Lw/K in different industrial groups. We can observe that the order of Y/K and Lw/K match almost perfectly, and this says that for unincorpo-

TABLE A.6

Decomposition of Relative Shares: Unincorporated Enterprises, 1958

(1960 output prices)

Sector	K/L (000 yen per worker)	K/L U/C (percent)	Y/K (000 yen per worker)	Y/K U/C (percent)	Lw/K (000 yen per worker)	Lw/K U/C (percent)
Construction	34	14.8%	602.2	585%	591.2	661%
Mining	87	10.8	276.0	646	271.1	863
Commerce	155	16.0	135.9	408	128.4	523
Facilitating industries	436	16.0	61.5	317	58.2	501
Manufacturing	333	37.0	54.0	135	44.4	180
Services	412	20.4	53.6	221	52.3	288
Total	242	22.7	85.5	260	79.0	328

TABLE A.7
Labor's Relative Shares and Rate of Capital Return
in Corporate Sector by Industry, 1952–64
(Percent)

Sector	Labor's relative shares			Rates of return on capital		
	1952–55	1956–61	1961–64	1952–55	1956–61	1961–63
Manufacturing	70.73%	65.86%	66.23%	9.59%	13.42%	12.49%
Construction	92.12	88.92	82.00	8.05	11.40	12.83
Mining	83.54	81.78	74.00	10.05	7.23	7.05
Commerce	74.35	68.63	71.50	4.86	11.50	13.83
Services	94.79	91.70	90.95	0.65	1.71	2.38
Facilitating industries	82.02	73.24	70.98	2.41	4.40	5.35

rated enterprises the degree of advantage obtained in output per unit of capital over its corporate competitor is closely associated with the degree of disadvantage in the form of a larger wage bill per unit of capital. Consider two extreme examples. Unincorporated construction squeezes out almost six times as much output per unit of capital, but its labor costs per unit of capital are nearly seven times higher. Unincorporated manufacturing manages to do only 1.35 times better for output per capital, and its labor costs per unit of capital are only 1.8 times higher. In other words, labor costs are such as to allow unincorporated enterprises to remain competitive, but we can seen also how crucial "cheap labor" is to this type of manufacturing. This was not as clear for corporate manufacturing (see Table A.3).

The Industrial Sectors

Sectoral changes in relative shares are given in Table A.7 (corporations only).[9] Undoubtedly the most pervasive common element is the decline in labor's relative share during the active investment spurt years. The situation obviously becomes less uniform after 1961. In some industries—manufacturing and commerce—labor's share rises; other industrial sectors are hard to interpret during this brief period.

Sectoral rates of return also reveal a rather varied picture. Mining is an odd case, because its rate of return declined from 1952–55 to 1956–61, and this continued for 1961–63. Other industries loosely follow the aggregate pattern, by which we mean an increase in rates of return for 1956–61, followed by a plateau at a high level. In most cases—mining and manufacturing apart—capital received a higher return in the early 1960's than in the second half of the 1950's, even though the differences were small.

Some of the factors making for sectoral differences in relative shares can be highlighted by looking at two dissimilar and important industrial sectors. For this purpose manufacturing and commerce have been selected, and we

[9] Analysis in this section is confined to net output. The argument would remain the same for gross output.

can start by looking at Table A.8, where the rate of return is decomposed in the usual manner $(r = Y/K - Lw/K)$. It is immediately apparent that output per unit of capital (Y/K) is consistently higher in commerce than in manufacturing. (The single exception is corporate manufacturing in 1955.) Movements over time are rather similar. With the exception of unincorporated manufacturing, Y/K increased between 1955 and 1961. Y/K continued to rise between 1961 and 1963, and this time the exception is provided by corporate manufacturing. This is, we believe, a more significant exception because it supplies evidence to the effect that the leading sector was losing some of its innovational force while "followers" had the advantage of a declining capital-output ratio. We note also that Y/K is always bigger in unincorporated than in corporate enterprise and that the level is especially outstanding for commerce. This helps to explain why unincorporated enterprise is especially tenacious in this type of activity.

In nearly all instances Y/K and Lw/K move in the same direction, with the exception of corporate manufacturing at the time of the investment spurt. This group of industries succeeded in lowering its capital-output ratio, and at the same time it was able to maintain a high rate of capital accumulation while lowering labor costs per unit of capital. Why this was possible is revealed in Table A.9. Panel I compares corporate manufacturing and commerce, and gives information concerning the growth rates of labor, wages, capital, and output. Between 1955 and 1961, wages rose less in manufacturing than in commerce while employment increases were very similar. For this reason alone, labor costs $(G_L + G_w)$ rose more slowly in manufacturing. Per unit of capital, the differences between manufacturing and commerce were much larger, reflecting a very different pace of capital accumulation. Manufacturing—containing the already identified leading industries—managed to have its capital accumulation move ahead three times more rapidly than commerce without allowing wage rises to get out of hand.

To continue with 1955–61, rates of growth of output were close to one another for corporate manufacturing and commerce. The latter industry had the advantage of a rapidly declining capital-output ratio $(G_K - G_Y)$ accompanied by only moderate investment growth, and this may well have been due to an increasing rate of capital utilization brought about by a surge in effective demand, traceable to the investment spurt. In other words, one of its advantages was the opportunity of following a leader.

Post-spurt developments (1961–63) are rather different. The rate of growth of capital accumulation tripled in corporate commerce, and the level of output continued to grow at the same pace. Following the leader eventually involves a more rapid rate of capital accumulation. In manufacturing the rate of growth of output declined and the rate of investment remained steady. Despite a rise in the capital-output ratio, it has been possible to maintain the rate of return because wage cost increases were, comparatively speaking, moderate.

Table A.9 also covers unincorporated enterprises, and the situation is dif-

TABLE A.8
Decomposition of the Rate of Capital Return: Manufacturing
and Commerce (Net) for Selected Single Years
(Percent)

Year	r	Corporate		Unincorporated	
		Y/K	Lw/K	Y/K	Lw/K
		I. Manufacturing			
1955	9.40%	34.83%	25.43%	46.76%	37.36%
1961	15.73	40.57	24.84	73.89	58.16
1963	12.28	31.22	18.94	77.75	65.47
		II. Commerce			
1955	6.67	23.87	17.20	43.60	36.93
1961	16.29	45.46	29.17	29.81	13.52
1963	14.08	45.76	31.68	33.58	19.40

ferent. Between 1955 and 1961 both groups expanded their labor force and capital at moderate rates by Japanese standards. Big differences, however, are observable in the path of wages: labor costs in unincorporated manufacturing went up much more steeply than in commerce (and incorporated manufacturing). Undoubtedly this explains the rather peculiar pattern where the gap widens between corporate and unincorporated labor shares.[10] The big edge of unincorporated manufacturing was the possibility of decreasing its capital-output ratio; a similar advantage was not achieved by commerce.

Post-spurt developments are again rather different. Rates of employment growth stagnated in contrast to what happened in corporations.[11] Commercial wages rose more rapidly than those in manufacturing, and the gap narrowed. Both groups exhibited enormous increases in rates of capital accumulation, and of course labor costs per unit of capital declined. In other words, since 1961 unincorporated enterprise, as exemplified by manufacturing and commerce, has moved in the direction of capital-deepening. Simultaneously a rise is noticed in both capital-output ratios, especially for manufacturing, and this fact symbolizes some of the problems faced by smaller industry in recent years.

POSTWAR CHANGES IN AGGREGATE RELATIVE SHARES

Aggregate relative shares are a weighted average, with weights being the ratio of sectoral (corporate and unincorporated) to total income. Changes in the aggregate over time are therefore composed of two elements: shifts in

[10] The ratio of average wages in unincorporated to incorporated sectors increased from 56 percent to 68 percent for manufacturing, and from 59 percent to 68 percent in commerce, between 1955 and 1961.

[11] Actually the number of hired workers increased, while self-employed workers diminished in numbers.

TABLE A.9
Average Annual Rates of Growth of Component Terms:
Manufacturing and Commerce
(Percent)

Term	1955-61		1961-63	
	Manufacturing	Commerce	Manufacturing	Commerce
I. Corporate Sector				
G_L	7.44%	7.13%	5.97%	5.84%
G_w	5.15	7.13	8.12	13.49
G_K	14.40	4.94	14.58	15.58
G_Y	17.37	16.83	10.18	15.97
$G_L + G_w$	12.59	14.26	14.09	19.33
$G_L + G_w - G_K$	-1.81	9.32	-0.49	3.75
$G_K - G_L$	6.96	-2.19	8.61	9.74
$G_Y - G_K$	2.97	11.89	-4.40	0.39
II. Unincorporated Sector				
G_L	2.95	1.62	1.09	-0.13
G_w	12.59	4.47	11.65	14.17
G_K	4.88	4.95	25.61	16.53
G_Y	13.22	7.62	9.04	12.87
$G_L + G_w$	15.54	6.09	12.74	14.04
$G_L + G_w - G_K$	10.66	1.14	-12.86	-2.51
$G_K - G_L$	1.93	3.33	24.52	16.66
$G_Y - G_K$	8.34	2.67	-16.57	-3.66

Note: Compound rates of growth between demarcated intervals. Y is net of capital depreciation.

the relative weights of the two sectors and compositional alterations within sectors. In this section we will discuss postwar changes in aggregate relative shares taking the changing weights into account. Specifically, we will try to deal with the three related questions: (1) What role did the changing share of corporate and unincorporated output play in determining the movements of aggregate relative shares? (2) Is there a typical pattern of changes associated with the investment and output periodization? (3) What is the international-comparative position of Japanese relative shares? We are not primarily concerned with comparisons of this type, but a brief look at other countries will prove helpful in interpreting the structure of the Japanese economy.

Aggregate results computed by our methods are summarized in Table A.10 for all available postwar years. The table exhibits considerable short-term fluctuations normally associated with changes in business conditions.[12] These fluctuations are not our major interest, and we will, as usual, focus on the standard postwar intervals: pre-spurt (1952–55), spurt (1956–61), and post-spurt (1962–63).[13]

In Chapter 3 it was observed that labor's relative share declined after

[12] Note, for example, that the frequently used figures for 1958 are on the high side for the relative share of labor. This was due to a recession in that year.
[13] Agriculture and finance continue to be excluded from the discussion.

TABLE A.10
Labor's Relative Shares and Rate of Capital Return, 1952–64
(Percent)

Year	Net output				Gross output			
	A	C	U	r	A	C	U	r
1952	84.51%	77.04%	94.51%	4.57%	78.64%	69.81%	91.26%	4.98%
1953	80.94	74.79	93.01	5.99	75.52	67.11	89.35	6.67
1954	83.43	76.88	93.60	5.51	75.70	67.43	89.40	6.28
1955	83.61	77.29	93.68	5.92	75.22	67.03	89.08	6.82
Average, 1952–55	83.12	76.50	93.70	5.50	76.27	67.85	89.77	6.19
1956	79.51	75.53	91.72	8.03	71.36	65.64	86.80	9.24
1957	78.27	71.29	90.99	8.82	70.30	62.17	86.11	10.11
1958	82.91	77.30	92.93	6.50	73.91	66.63	88.04	7.54
1959	77.50	71.79	89.99	9.07	69.17	62.20	85.43	10.48
1960	73.40	67.78	87.85	11.10	65.67	58.76	83.68	12.80
1961	73.22	67.41	88.15	11.44	64.68	57.58	84.25	13.39
Average, 1956–61	77.47	71.85	90.27	9.16	69.18	62.16	85.72	10.59
1962	76.07	70.84	89.94	9.90	67.04	60.32	86.08	11.62
1963	76.27	71.25	90.30	9.87	67.46	60.98	86.56	11.53
1964		72.15				60.37		
Average, 1962–63	76.17	71.41[a]	90.12	9.88	67.25	60.56[a]	86.32	11.57

Notation: A, aggregate; *C,* corporate; *U*, unincorporated; *r,* rate of capital return in 1960 prices.
[a]Includes 1964.

World War II, and now it can be seen that the decline holds good, net and gross, for all three interval averages.[14] It can also be seen that the corporate sector is much more influential in producing this decline, even though the labor share in unincorporated enterprises follows a similar time path. Finally, it is recognized that differences between pre-spurt and spurt level relative shares are considerable—the average dropped from 83 percent to 77 percent. Two distinct forces are involved. One is a trend effect in the form of a decline in the weight of unincorporated production, and the other is a swing association, to be discussed later. The trend effect is quite powerful. If the weight of unincorporated production had remained the same between 1952 and 1963, the aggregate (net) relative share of labor would have been 79.04 percent, or nearly 3 percentage points above the actual result.[15]

Let us now briefly look at international comparisons. According to Denison,[16] in 1955–59 the labor share was 79.2 percent in the United States and 75.8 percent for the countries of northwestern Europe. In 1960–62 these

[14] Of course, the labor share was unusually elevated in 1952–55 owing to the abnormal situation prevailing during reconstruction and rehabilitation.

[15] A quite strong trend effect necessarily follows from our imputation procedures, which result in much higher relative shares for labor in unincorporated production.

[16] E. F. Denison and J. P. Poullier, *Why Growth Rates Differ* (Washington, D.C., 1967), p. 38.

figures were 79.9 percent and 76.5 percent, respectively, all calculations applying to net output. At first glance, Japanese shares look very similar, since for roughly the same time period they lie between 77.5 and 77.2 percent. Yet this similarity comes about through two very different methods of approximating relative shares. Denison assumed that relative shares of non-financial corporations apply unchanged for unincorporated enterprises, and we rejected the applicability of this view for Japan. Had we used Denison's technique, postwar labor shares in Japan would have been in the neighborhood of 72 percent, which is the actual level for corporations and much below Western quantities.

Denison's methods may be taken as reasonable for the West and we hope that ours are equally reasonable for Japan. It follows that aggregate labor shares *are* very similar, but that corporate labor shares are much lower than in the West, while they are much higher for unincorporated production in Japan. Other things being equal, one could add that Japan's modern sectors have an advantage over Western competitors in their lower labor costs per unit of output.[17] In contrast, traditional sectors have the disadvantage of higher labor costs per unit of output, but as has already been shown, this is offset by an extremely low capital-output ratio.

What happens to the pattern of relative shares when compared to investment or output swings is also evident in Table A.10. Pre-spurt, the labor share is almost steady; then it clearly declines during the spurt; and post-spurt it "rises," although here we are limited to two years and an insignificantly small change. Some light can be shed on this pattern by looking at the rate of return on capital (r) and its components (Y/K and Lw/K). The rate of return follows the movements of capital formation and accumulation very closely. From 1956 to 1961, when investment growth rates continually rose, r presented a mirror image of this movement. At either end of this upswing, rates of return remained at a plateau, but the level was much higher in the early 1960's than in the early 1950's.

Between 1955 and 1961 the rate of return on net output for corporations rose by 5.52 percentage points, from 5.92 to 11.44 percent. If these corporate rates and their changes can be used for noncorporations, it is possible to decompose the rate of return in order to determine what factors contributed to the upswing. This has been done in Table A.11, taking K as 100. During the postwar investment spurt, output per unit of capital increased (i.e. the capital-output ratio declined), and this raised the aggregate rate of return by 6.54 percent. At the same time, capital intensity and wage payments changed, reducing the rate of return by 1.02 percent, yielding a net increase of 5.52 percent. For corporations, both the gains due to a rise in Y/K (8.87 percent) and increases in labor costs (3.35 percent) were above average. Unincorporated enterprises had much more moderate increases of Y/K during the boom (1.58 percent), but their labor costs per unit of capi-

---

[17] "Other things being equal" refers to the possible offset of higher interest rates and higher prices for capital goods.

TABLE A.11
Decomposition of the Rate of Return
(Percent)

Category	1955	1961	Change
Aggregate			
Y/K (output per unit of capital)	35.64%	42.18%	6.54%
Lw/K (labor cost per unit of capital)	29.72	30.74	1.02
Corporate			
Y/K	26.02	34.89	8.87
Lw/K	20.10	23.45	3.35
Unincorporated			
Y/K	86.31	87.89	1.58
Lw/K	80.39	76.45	-3.94

tal *decreased* by 3.94 percent.[18] The main point, however, relates to the aggregate: during the investment spurt, a decline in labor's relative share and a rise in the rate of return on capital was caused by realizing greater output per unit of capital rather than by declining labor costs per unit of capital.

In the all-too-short post-spurt period, the situation is rather different in nearly all respects. In the first place, the rate of return decreased from 11.44 to 9.87 percent, and this 1.57 percent decline is decomposed as shown below, again with K taken as 100.

	Corporations	Unincorporated enterprises	Aggregate
Y/K in 1963	33.84%	89.76%	40.91%
Change since 1961	-1.05	1.87	-1.27
Lw/K in 1963	23.97	79.89	31.04
Change since 1961	.52	3.44	.30

For the aggregate economy (excluding agriculture and finance) the post-spurt decline in Y/K (-1.27 percent) has had much more influence in lowering the rate of return than the minor increase in labor costs (0.30 percent). But corporations and unincorporated enterprises were not at this time operating under the same circumstances. In corporations, output per unit of capital declined by 1.0 percent; in unincorporated production it rose by 1.87 percent. Labor costs per unit of capital rose in both groups, but much more steeply for unincorporated enterprises (3.44 percent) than for modern corporations (0.52 percent). These figures suggest some characteristics of the post-spurt growth mechanism. A rise in the capital-output ratio of corporations must be related to a combination of two factors, one being a decrease in the rate of utilization due to a decline in the rate of growth of

[18] This result is in large measure an effect of our assumptions: we applied the same rate of return to both sectors while imputing only very moderate wage increases to unincorporated enterprises—a 19 percent rise as opposed to a 40 percent rise for corporate enterprise.

aggregate demand, and the other being the fading away of opportunities for technological progress. The considerable increases in labor costs for the unincorporated sector present a clear divide before and after 1961. As shown here, wage differentials between modern and traditional units widened when the rate of capital formation was rising, and became smaller when capital formation began to grow more slowly.

THE ESTIMATION OF PREWAR INCOME SHARES

It is, of course, even more difficult to derive accurate income shares before World War II. Since this information is required for the estimation of residuals, we provide here a very brief review of the procedures that were used.

Prewar estimates since 1919 preserve the distribution between corporate and unincorporated sectors. For the corporate sector, $Y_1 = A_1 + W_1$, where A_1 is asset income (a sum of retained corporate earnings and personal asset income including dividends, rent, and interest, and excluding government interest payments and rent income accruing to owners of agricultural land). W_1 is the compensation of workers, excluding government employees; $\alpha_1 = A_1/Y_1$, and $\beta_1 = W_1/Y_1$.

For the unincorporated sector, $Y_2 = A_2 + W_2$. An imputation procedure has been used to estimate W_2 and A_2. No wage income is attributed to unpaid family workers, on the assumption that all their incomes are to be attributed to proprietors. Compensation for the proprietors' labor as workers is estimated by average corporate wages in the same industries, and the residuals $(Y_2 - W_2)$ are assumed to equal A_2; $\alpha_2 = A_2/Y_2$, and $\beta_2 = W_2/Y_2$. In the nonagricultural sector, aggregate α and β are derived as a weighted average.

Before 1919 data availability does not allow a breakdown into corporate and unincorporated sectors. Therefore, for the years 1905–18, the aggregate values of β have simply been extrapolated backward by means of gainfully occupied population statistics and wage indexes, with α derived as a residual.

A word about the sources. Data for prewar national income distributed can be found in Yūzō Yamada's *Nihon kokumin shotoku suikei shiryō* (A Comprehensive Survey of National Income Data in Japan; enlarged and revised edition, Tokyo, 1957). These are revisions of the Hijikata estimates and were used for 1919–29. For the 1930's we used unofficial Economic Deliberation Council (Keizai Shingi Chō) estimates in *Nihon keizai to kokumin shotoku* (The Japanese Economy and National Income; Tokyo, 1954). In some cases, minor adjustments have been made by Ohkawa for such items as compensation of government employees and rent to owners of agricultural land.

Number of employees and number of unincorporated enterprises are taken from the above-mentioned sources. However, the number of unincorporated enterprises for 1919–29 were separately estimated by Ohkawa.[19]

[19] For a general reference, see K. Ohkawa, "Changes in National Income Distribution by Factor Shares in Japan," in J. Marshal and B. Ducros, eds., *The Distribution of National Income* (New York, 1968).

Basic Statistical Tables

Basic Statistical Tables

The 18 tables that follow contain the primary data upon which the analysis of this book is based. Although the list is fairly comprehensive, and conforms to the scope originally suggested by Professor Moses Abramovitz, all of the tables contain information used in writing the book.

The compilation of long-term economic statistics for Japan is a continuing process, necessarily entailing repeated revisions and refinements. Since the publication of our original studies in the late 1950's and early 1960's,[1] much progress has already been made, and quite a bit of work still awaits completion, especially for pre–World War II series. We have made an effort to employ the latest revisions, some of which are as yet available only in unpublished form. Having used many different sources and the work of many different people in various stages of completion, it is not possible either to describe all estimation procedures in full detail or to discuss at length the original raw data used by the various scholars. The printed sources to which we refer (nearly all in Japanese) generally supply much of the needed background information. In addition, K. Ohkawa intends to prepare a special volume in English, tentatively titled *National Output and Expenditure of Japan Since 1886*, which will comprehensively survey all matters relating to sources and estimation procedures.

The Basic Statistical Tables, in most cases, cover the period 1905–70. No entries are given for earlier years because the reliability of those series is not yet sufficiently established. For the period 1941–51, with the exception of 1945, estimates of the Economic Planning Agency have been used, although conditions in Japan were frequently so chaotic as to make these numbers also rather unreliable.

Despite the great efforts of numerous investigators, prewar data are probably not of sufficient accuracy to be used on a single-year basis. For the

[1] K. Ohkawa and others, *The Growth Rate of the Japanese Economy Since 1878* (Tokyo, 1957), and H. Rosovsky, *Capital Formation in Japan, 1868–1940* (New York, 1961).

record, they are presented this way in the Basic Statistical Tables, but as readers will remember, smoothed series or period averages have been used in the main text. Unless specified, all tables are in calendar years.

GENERAL BACKGROUND ON SOURCES

Unless otherwise specified, postwar series (1941–70) are reproduced from Keizai Kikaku-chō (Economic Planning Agency, Government of Japan), *Kokumin shotoku tōkei nempō* (Annual Report on National Income Statistics). In source citations this report is abbreviated NIS (National Income Statistics).

Four main sources were used for the prewar (1905–40) series:

K. Ohkawa, ed., "Nihon keizai no chōki bunseki: chūkan hōkoku" (A Long-Term Analysis of the Japanese Economy: Interim Report), Tōkei Kenkyū Kai (Statistical Research Association; mimeo.), Tokyo, 1971.

K. Ohkawa, ed., *Chōki keizai tōkei no seibi kaizen ni kan-suru kenkyū* (Studies on Long-Term Economic Statistics), Tōkei Kenkyū Kai (Statistical Research Association), Tokyo, vols. 1 (1967), 2 (1968), 3 (1969).

K. Ohkawa, M. Shinohara, and M. Umemura, eds., *Chōki keizai tōkei* (Estimates of Long-Term Economic Statistics of Japan Since 1868), Tōyō Keizai Shimpō-sha (The Oriental Economist Publishing Co.), Tokyo.

Vol. 1, K. Ohkawa and N. Takamatsu, *Kokumin shotoku* (National Income), forthcoming.

Vol. 2, M. Umemura and K. Akasaka, *Jinkō to rōdōryoku* (Population and Labor Force), forthcoming.

Vol. 3, K. Ohkawa and others, *Shihon Stokku* (Capital Stock), 1965.

Vol. 4, K. Emi, *Shihon keisei* (Capital Formation), 1971.

Vol. 6, M. Shinohara, *Kojin shōhi shishitsu* (Personal Consumption Expenditures), 1967.

Vol. 7, K. Emi and Y. Shionoya, *Zaisei shishitsu* (Public Expenditures), 1966.

Vol. 8, K. Ohkawa and others, *Bukka* (Prices), 1965.

Vol. 9, M. Umemura and others, *Nōringyō* (Agriculture and Forestry), 1966.

Vol. 10, M. Shinohara, *Kōkōgyō* (Mining and Manufacturing), 1972.

Work sheets of K. Ohkawa and N. Takamatsu at the Institute of Economic Research, Hitotsubashi University, Tokyo. Most of the work sheets will appear in the forthcoming vol. 1 of LTES by K. Ohkawa and N. Takamatsu entitled *Kokumin shotoku* (National Income). These materials will also be published in Ohkawa's forthcoming book *National Output and Expenditure of Japan Since 1886*, together with detailed explanations concerning estimating methods.

In indicating the sources of the appendix tables, these four compilations are abbreviated as follows:

IR (Interim Report)
SRA (Statistical Research Association)
LTES (Long-Term Economic Statistics)
WS (Work sheets)

Gross National Product: Current Prices
(Million yen)

Year	Net domestic product at market prices	Net factor income from abroad	Net national product at market prices	Provisions for consumption of fixed capital	Statistical discrepancy	Gross national product at market prices	Statistical discrepancy/ GNE (percent)
1905	2,726	-26	2,700	269	187	3,156	5.9%
1906	3,137	-69	3,068	293	90	3,451	2.6
1907	3,634	-51	3,583	335	-290	3,628	-8.0
1908	3,622	-57	3,565	329	48	3,942	1.2
1909	3,526	-55	3,471	321	169	3,961	4.3
1910	3,574	-61	3,513	336	254	4,103	6.2
1911	4,162	-66	4,096	358	201	4,655	4.3
1912	4,573	-66	4,507	411	50	4,968	1.0
1913	4,691	-67	4,624	433	155	5,212	3.0
1914	4,320	-68	4,252	430	-17	4,665	-0.4
1915	4,790	-64	4,726	473	-280	4,919	-5.7
1916	5,843	-31	5,812	609	-346	6,075	-5.7
1917	7,813	2	7,815	871	-201	8,485	-2.4
1918	10,702	26	10,728	1,170	-229	11,669	-2.0
1919	14,136	38	14,174	1,307	-270	15,211	-1.8
1920	13,453	17	13,470	1,800	360	15,630	2.3
1921	13,830	5	13,835	1,573	-419	14,969	-2.8
1922	14,216	17	14,233	1,623	-193	15,663	-1.2
1923	14,181	19	14,200	1,709	-910	14,999	-6.1
1924	15,067	-8	15,059	1,745	-1,176	15,628	-7.5
1925	15,734	-11	15,723	1,589	-1,002	16,310	-6.1
1926	15,484	-18	15,466	1,538	-952	16,052	-5.9
1927	14,945	-3	14,942	1,558	-157	16,343	-1.0
1928	15,526	-24	15,502	1,605	-538	16,569	-3.2
1929	15,817	-20	15,797	1,631	-1,081	16,347	-6.6
1930	13,257	-25	13,232	1,394	140	14,766	0.9
1931	11,954	-24	11,930	1,214	260	13,404	1.9
1932	12,921	-38	12,883	1,370	-557	13,696	-4.0
1933	14,514	-53	14,461	1,570	-716	15,315	-4.7
1934	15,696	-26	15,670	1,604	-228	17,046	-1.3
1935	16,787	-14	16,773	1,674	-85	18,362	-0.5
1936	18,639	25	18,664	1,805	-1,067	19,402	-5.5
1937	22,046	8	22,054	2,428	-798	23,684	-3.4
1938	25,018	40	25,058	2,748	183	27,989	0.7
1939	31,877	17	31,894	3,140	-3,622	31,412	-11.5
1940	37,026	70	37,096	3,870	-4,383	36,583	-12.0

Gross National Product: Current Prices
(1941-44, million yen; 1946-70, billion yen)

Year	Net domestic product at market prices	Net factor income from abroad	Net national product at market prices	Provisions for consumption of fixed capital	Statistical discrepancy	Gross national product at market prices	Statistical discrepancy/ GNE *(percent)*
1941	38,598	259	38,857	3,157	2,882	44,896	6.4%
1942	45,474	367	45,841	3,666	4,877	54,384	9.0
1943	53,419	348	53,767	4,272	5,785	63,824	9.1
1944	60,941	165	61,106	5,257	8,140	74,503	10.9
1945							
1946	359		359	24	92	475	19.4
1947	1,061	-1	1,060	57	192	1,309	14.7
1948	2,205	-1	2,204	108	353	2,665	13.2
1949	3,017	-1	3,016	158	202	3,376	6.0
1950	3,723	-2	3,721	207	18	3,946	0.5
1951	5,018	-11	5,007	280	155	5,442	2.8
1952	5,520	45	5,565	434	260	6,259	4.2
1953	6,406	43	6,449	553	53	7,055	0.8
1954	7,199	32	7,231	701	-96	7,836	-1.2
1955	7,844	25	7,869	791	-36	8,624	-0.4
1956	8,652	18	8,670	934	122	9,726	1.3
1957	10,120	10	10,130	1,044	-97	11,077	-0.9
1958	10,543	3	10,546	1,129	-152	11,523	-1.3
1959	11,735	-7	11,728	1,300	-103	12,925	-0.8
1960	14,144	-16	14,128	1,590	-219	15,499	-1.4
1961	16,758	-37	16,721	2,037	368	19,126	1.9
1962	19,073	-50	19,023	2,413	-236	21,200	-1.1
1963	21,840	-66	21,780	2,855	-171	24,464	-0.7
1964	24,933	-98	24,835	3,513	491	28,839	1.7
1965	27,780	-99	27,681	4,024	-82	31,787	-0.3
1966	31,940	-99	31,841	4,760	193	36,794	0.5
1967	37,866	-107	37,759	5,506	278	43,543	0.6
1968	44,920	-150	44,770	6,670	267	51,707	0.5
1969	52,030	-168	51,862	8,098	280	60,240	0.5
1970	61,857	-159	61,698	9,571	-287	70,982	-0.4

Sources and remarks: Prewar: IR, pp. 149–50, with a slight recent revision for investment in agriculture. "Statistical discrepancy" includes possible effects of inventory changes that have not been estimated. The large entries for 1939 and 1940 may be due to unrecorded military expenditures. Therefore, in calculating growth rates in the main text, the discrepancy is assumed to be 5.75 percent in 1939 and 6.10 percent in 1940. Postwar: 1941–51, NIS (1962), pp. 120, 143; 1952–65, revised NIS (1969), pp. 60–61; 1966–70, NIS (1972), pp. 36–37. Figures for 1945 are not available; figures for 1946–51 are for fiscal year. Net national product and domestic product at factor cost have been converted to market prices.

Gross National Product: Constant Prices
(1934-36 prices, million yen)

Year	Net domestic product at market prices	Net factor income from abroad	Net national product at market prices	Provisions for consumption of fixed capital	Statistical discrepancy	Gross national product at market prices
1905	5,854	-47	5,807	472	383	6,662
1906	6,223	-122	6,101	492	167	6,760
1907	6,667	-81	6,586	514	-561	6,555
1908	6,727	-96	6,631	537	80	7,248
1909	6,645	-96	6,549	562	306	7,417
1910	6,940	-106	6,834	584	479	7,897
1911	7,159	-107	7,052	615	311	7,978
1912	7,373	-101	7,272	645	76	7,993
1913	7,249	-100	7,149	680	238	8,067
1914	7,599	-110	7,489	706	-62	8,133
1915	8,508	-109	8,399	725	-506	8,618
1916	9,097	-47	9,050	754	-450	9,354
1917	9,637	3	9,640	804	-272	10,172
1918	10,401	24	10,425	867	-244	11,048
1919	10,878	27	10,905	940	-220	11,625
1920	10,290	12	10,302	1,013	250	11,565
1921	11,537	4	11,541	1,071	340	12,272
1922	11,012	13	11,025	1,116	-177	11,964
1923	10,974	14	10,988	1,148	-714	11,422
1924	12,590	-6	12,585	1,187	-964	12,808
1925	12,001	-8	11,993	1,222	-779	12,436
1926	12,063	-14	12,049	1,264	-730	12,583
1927	11,569	-3	11,566	1,312	70	12,948
1928	12,902	-20	12,882	1,358	-464	13,776
1929	13,380	-17	13,363	1,401	-929	13,835
1930	12,440	-24	12,416	1,439	121	13,976
1931	12,370	-30	12,340	1,473	254	14,067
1932	13,762	-40	13,722	1,507	-619	14,610
1933	15,291	-55	15,236	1,556	-766	16,026
1934	16,148	-27	16,121	1,618	-229	17,510
1935	16,848	-14	16,834	1,690	-87	18,437
1936	18,083	24	18,107	1,775	-1,043	18,839
1937	19,588	7	19,595	1,851	-737	20,709
1938	19,514	32	19,546	1,941	15	21,502
1939	22,931	12	22,943	2,064	-2,735	22,272
1940	23,614	47	23,661	2,202	-2,914	22,949

Gross National Product: Constant Prices
(1960 prices, billion yen)

Year	Net domestic product at market prices	Net factor income from abroad	Net national product at market prices	Provisions for consumption of fixed capital	Statistical discrepancy	Gross national product at market prices
1953	7,072	43	7,115	641	638	8,394
1954	7,965	32	7,997	818	-2	8,813
1955	8,577	26	8,603	915	182	9,700
1956	9,114	18	9,132	997	509	10,638
1957	10,131	9	10,140	1,036	487	11,663
1958	10,950	3	10,953	1,183	77	12,213
1959	12,195	-7	12,188	1,336	-133	13,391
1960	14,144	-16	14,128	1,593	-217	15,504
1961	16,018	-36	15,982	1,935	331	18,248
1962	17,581	-50	17,531	2,230	-474	19,287
1963	19,382	-66	19,316	2,593	-746	21,163
1964	21,464	-97	21,367	3,125	-232	24,260
1965	22,968	-97	22,871	3,448	-1,014	25,305

Sources and remarks: Prewar: IR, pp. 64–65, with a slight recent revision for investment in agriculture. These prewar series are estimated on the assumption that statistical discrepancies are the same as in current price series, and that the real output of the service sector can be approximated as a residual of the domestic account, the foreign account being excluded. This was done to avoid the use of unreliable deflators for the service sector. Postwar deflators: NIS (1969), pp. 82–83; no deflators are available after 1965. No price indexes have been used to link prewar and postwar series because of the tentative nature of the series.

Net Domestic Product by Industry at Market Prices: Current Prices
(Million yen)

Year	Agriculture (including forestry & fishing)	Mining & manufacturing	Facilitating industry	Construction	Services	Total (NDP)
1905	856	545	144	86	1,095	2,726
1906	1,101	624	170	114	1,128	3,137
1907	1,303	757	193	176	1,205	3,634
1908	1,301	674	201	158	1,288	3,622
1909	1,160	662	208	156	1,340	3,526
1910	1,104	715	231	157	1,367	3,574
1911	1,473	761	260	171	1,497	4,162
1912	1,681	860	278	188	1,566	4,573
1913	1,712	928	284	194	1,573	4,691
1914	1,317	972	298	186	1,547	4,320
1915	1,258	1,184	345	197	1,806	4,790
1916	1,555	1,662	467	190	1,969	5,843
1917	2,122	2,297	600	244	2,550	7,813
1918	3,237	3,081	773	344	3,267	10,702
1919	4,977	3,780	778	478	4,123	14,136
1920	3,916	3,391	1,086	699	4,361	13,453
1921	3,781	2,911	1,231	673	5,233	13,830
1922	3,412	3,173	1,288	761	5,582	14,216
1923	3,557	2,927	1,300	820	5,577	14,181
1924	3,857	3,101	1,416	823	5,870	15,067
1925	4,172	3,196	1,595	852	5,964	15,734
1926	3,506	3,135	1,646	862	6,335	15,484
1927	3,340	3,102	1,528	820	6,155	14,945
1928	3,162	3,507	1,608	844	6,405	15,526
1929	3,138	3,874	1,653	836	6,316	15,817
1930	2,118	3,069	1,575	727	5,768	13,257
1931	1,783	2,773	1,531	616	5,251	11,954
1932	2,189	3,234	1,442	624	5,432	12,921
1933	2,689	3,680	1,400	890	5,855	14,514
1934	2,452	4,326	1,533	892	6,493	15,696
1935	2,805	4,721	1,615	985	6,661	16,787
1936	3,253	5,224	1,676	1,429	7,057	18,639
1937	3,676	6,927	1,844	1,719	7,880	22,046
1938	3,918	8,890	1,944	1,822	8,444	25,018
1939	5,842	11,787	2,223	2,264	9,761	31,877
1940	5,858	14,582	2,472	2,661	11,453	37,026

Net Domestic Product by Industry at Market Prices: Current Prices
(1941-44, million yen; 1946-70, billion yen)

Year	Agriculture (including forestry & fishing)	Mining & manufacturing	Facilitating industry	Construction	Services	Total (NDP)
1941	7,092	12,736	2,842	1,266	11,639	35,575
1942	8,233	15,241	3,391	1,603	13,309	41,777
1943	8,315	18,088	4,168	1,876	15,653	48,100
1944	10,104	20,740	5,134	2,243	18,551	56,772
1945						
1946	140	70	16	25	110	361
1947	343	229	36	48	312	968
1948	625	521	105	83	629	1,963
1949	751	778	202	102	905	2,738
1950	879	938	250	137	1,179	3,383
1951	1,128	1,293	330	171	1,603	4,525
1952	1,319	1,518	447	236	2,000	5,520
1953	1,217	2,041	550	324	2,274	6,406
1954	1,369	2,181	621	343	2,685	7,199
1955	1,622	2,274	717	358	2,873	7,844
1956	1,498	2,763	788	434	3,169	8,652
1957	1,666	3,308	922	540	3,684	10,120
1958	1,690	3,208	1,006	537	4,102	10,543
1959	1,709	3,786	1,111	664	4,465	11,735
1960	1,837	4,908	1,298	835	5,266	14,144
1961	2,053	5,805	1,562	1,079	6,259	16,758
1962	2,220	6,342	1,783	1,196	7,532	19,073
1963	2,201	7,288	2,038	1,385	8,928	21,840
1964	2,401	8,158	2,266	1,621	10,487	24,933
1965	2,575	8,845	2,461	1,842	12,057	27,780
1966	3,002	10,061	2,875	2,140	13,862	31,940
1967	3,635	12,572	3,105	2,575	15,979	37,866
1968	3,908	15,093	3,459	3,234	19,226	44,920
1969	3,954	18,263	3,954	3,590	22,269	52,030
1970	4,020	21,836	4,639	4,392	26,970	61,857

Sources and remarks: Prewar: IR, slightly changed because of recent revisions of primary and service sectors. GDP series are not available. Postwar: 1941–51, NIS (1962), pp. 140–41; the series at factor cost has been tentatively converted to market prices by using the ratio for each industry in subsequent years; 1952–65, revised NIS (1969), pp. 302–3; 1966–70, NIS (1972), p. 285. Figures for 1945 are not available; figures for 1946–51 are for fiscal year.

Net Domestic Product by Industry at Market Prices: Constant Prices
(1934-36 prices, million yen)

Year	Agriculture (including forestry & fishing)	Mining & manufacturing	Facilitating industry	Construc-tion	Services	Total	Private nonagri-culture
1905	1,551	754	201	178	3,096	5,780	3,643
1906	1,902	831	247	220	3,428	6,628	4,228
1907	2,026	933	287	300	3,592	7,138	4,669
1908	2,082	875	313	298	3,475	7,043	4,483
1909	2,042	890	325	286	3,494	7,037	4,538
1910	1,917	961	362	287	3,639	7,166	4,771
1911	2,176	1,008	405	302	3,610	7,501	4,821
1912	2,172	1,063	424	314	3,683	7,656	4,990
1913	2,206	1,169	465	326	3,465	7,631	4,936
1914	2,232	1,282	412	335	3,666	7,927	5,217
1915	2,258	1,476	466	340	3,593	8,133	6,366
1916	2,521	1,660	556	280	5,041	10,058	7,085
1917	2,482	1,786	518	268	5,619	10,673	7,804
1918	2,479	1,930	571	292	5,799	11,071	8,238
1919	2,784	2,035	653	344	5,822	11,638	8,354
1920	2,545	1,745	876	350	5,322	10,838	7,865
1921	2,519	1,955	1,061	404	6,009	11,948	8,710
1922	2,491	2,118	1,108	458	5,998	12,173	9,055
1923	2,475	1,912	1,063	477	6,073	12,000	8,906
1924	2,539	2,020	1,241	491	6,866	13,157	8,451
1925	2,749	2,189	1,422	573	5,975	12,908	9,388
1926	2,565	2,417	1,514	618	5,979	13,093	9,676
1927	2,742	2,547	1,419	605	5,659	12,972	9,312
1928	2,635	2,856	1,454	646	6,459	14,050	10,492
1929	2,960	3,261	1,561	648	6,233	14,663	10,801
1930	2,664	3,190	1,544	702	5,383	13,483	9,907
1931	2,449	3,497	1,527	650	5,463	13,586	10,248
1932	2,757	3,818	1,429	648	5,878	14,530	10,908
1933	3,101	3,615	1,385	862	6,818	15,781	11,667
1934	2,645	4,339	1,532	920	6,827	16,263	12,596
1935	2,788	4,783	1,720	989	6,456	16,736	12,819
1936	3,052	5,162	1,679	1,382	6,835	18,110	13,707
1937	3,089	5,280	1,703	1,453	7,985	19,510	14,748
1938	2,995	6,327	1,697	1,366	7,366	19,751	15,305
1939	3,400	7,820	1,985	1,450	9,296	23,951	18,991
1940	3,000	8,706	2,189	1,323	9,386	24,604	19,821

Net Domestic Product by Industry at Market Prices: Constant Prices
(1960 prices, billion yen)

Year	Agriculture (including forestry & fishing)	Mining & manufacturing	Facilitating industry	Construction	Services	Total	Private nonagriculture
1953	1,239	1,999	605	401	2,828	7,072	5,294
1954	1,396	2,181	670	411	3,307	7,965	5,837
1955	1,722	2,322	741	436	3,356	8,577	6,239
1956	1,639	2,680	799	487	3,510	9,115	6,953
1957	1,735	3,092	901	533	3,870	10,131	7,834
1958	1,811	3,227	1,003	587	4,322	10,950	8,590
1959	1,949	3,813	1,111	704	4,618	12,195	9,677
1960	1,837	4,908	1,298	835	5,266	14,144	11,860
1961	1,839	5,817	1,482	969	5,911	16,018	11,854
1962	1,849	6,478	1,659	1,022	6,573	17,581	15,512
1963	1,724	7,376	1,922	1,137	7,223	19,382	17,302
1964	1,783	8,257	2,064	1,268	8,092	21,464	19,779
1965	1,766	8,899	2,118	1,391	8,794	22,968	21,482

Sources and remarks: Prewar: IR, pp. 151–52. Postwar: NIS (1967), pp. 76–77. The latter do not give industrial output deflators, which were taken from WS, section P. Until 1965, GDP series are not available. The industrial classifications are as follows: primary (agriculture, forestry, and fisheries); manufacturing (includes mining); facilitating (transportation, communication, and public utilities); services (wholesale and retail trade, banking, insurance and real estate, and services and public administration). This breakdown applies also to the remaining tables. Estimates of private sector output from WS, section Y.

Gross National Expenditure: Current Prices
(Million yen)

Year	Private consumption expenditure	General govt. consumption expenditure	Gross domestic fixed capital formation	Exports of goods & services & factor income received from abroad	Less: Imports of goods & services & factor income paid abroad	Gross national expenditure at market prices
1905	2,351	626	516	401	738	3,156
1906	2,461	485	540	540	575	3,451
1907	2,672	338	634	617	633	3,628
1908	3,060	307	663	506	594	3,942
1909	3,060	320	598	539	556	3,961
1910	3,145	339	689	586	656	4,103
1911	3,488	407	860	618	718	4,655
1912	3,855	370	857	723	837	4,968
1913	4,128	339	860	836	951	5,212
1914	3,531	344	806	790	816	4,665
1915	3,554	366	793	994	788	4,919
1916	4,082	361	1,035	1,637	1,040	6,075
1917	5,318	423	1,816	2,347	1,419	8,485
1918	7,599	582	2,702	3,003	2,217	11,669
1919	11,072	881	2,937	3,230	2,909	15,211
1920	11,075	1,085	3,596	2,968	3,094	15,630
1921	11,286	1,120	2,868	1,998	2,303	14,969
1922	11,719	1,198	2,975	2,309	2,538	15,663
1923	11,921	1,164	2,500	2,095	2,681	14,999
1924	12,274	1,187	2,930	2,561	3,324	15,628
1925	12,863	1,073	2,704	3,167	3,497	16,310
1926	12,496	1,133	2,826	2,880	3,283	16,052
1927	12,283	1,391	2,892	2,857	3,080	16,343
1928	12,370	1,668	2,743	2,900	3,131	16,569
1929	11,942	1,612	2,815	3,160	3,182	16,347
1930	11,001	1,479	2,323	2,358	2,395	14,776
1931	9,926	1,684	1,946	1,895	2,047	13,404
1932	9,945	1,839	2,030	2,294	2,412	13,696
1933	11,000	2,046	2,466	2,845	3,042	15,315
1934	12,257	2,005	2,923	3,424	3,563	17,046
1935	12,825	2,117	3,346	3,985	3,911	18,362
1936	13,505	2,184	3,622	4,382	4,291	19,402
1937	15,298	2,609	5,660	6,006	5,889	23,684
1938	17,101	3,046	7,977	5,684	5,819	27,989
1939	17,630	3,402	9,822	6,601	6,043	31,412
1940	20,005	4,821	11,698	7,253	7,194	36,583

Gross National Expenditure: Current Prices
(1941-44, million yen; 1946-70, billion yen)

Year	Private consumption expenditure	General govt. consumption expenditure	Gross domestic fixed capital formation	Increase in stocks	Exports of goods & services & factor income received from abroad	Less: Imports of goods & services & factor income paid abroad	Gross national expenditure at market prices
1941	20,701	13,495	9,308	2,414	6,117	7,139	44,896
1942	23,734	17,118	10,187	4,416	5,031	6,102	54,384
1943	26,001	22,855	14,158	1,716	4,889	5,795	63,824
1944	26,554	27,672	17,390	3,265	3,950	4,328	74,503
1945							
1946	333	55	78	28	5	24	475
1947	915	102	263	83	28	82	1,309
1948	1,741	282	516	236	81	191	2,665
1949	2,261	394	623	208	217	327	3,376
1950	2,397	437	639	368	469	364	3,946
1951	3,018	552	1,093	570	908	699	5,442
1952	3,861	668	1,277	385	788	720	6,259
1953	4,665	780	1,549	142	789	870	7,055
1954	5,162	864	1,698	140	854	882	7,836
1955	5,529	894	1,705	421	979	904	8,624
1956	6,012	936	2,290	507	1,189	1,208	9,726
1957	6,597	1,009	2,946	740	1,334	1,549	11,077
1958	7,057	1,105	2,941	252	1,318	1,150	11,523
1959	7,722	1,209	3,435	418	1,531	1,390	12,925
1960	8,823	1,382	4,682	551	1,774	1,713	15,499
1961	10,106	1,607	6,370	1,382	1,860	2,199	19,126
1962	11,747	1,864	7,136	459	2,142	2,148	21,200
1963	13,769	2,200	7,875	884	2,349	2,613	24,464
1964	15,945	2,554	9,404	1,083	2,889	3,036	28,839
1965	17,929	2,949	9,767	776	3,563	3,197	31,787
1966	20,586	3,328	11,344	1,037	4,164	3,665	36,794
1967	23,554	3,733	13,965	2,296	4,467	4,472	43,543
1968	27,296	4,277	17,327	2,366	5,528	5,087	51,707
1969	31,320	4,925	20,938	2,228	6,818	5,989	60,240
1970	36,292	5,853	24,921	3,132	8,272	7,488	70,982

Sources and remarks: Prewar: IR, pp. 147–48, slightly changed because of a recent revision of agricultural investment. Personal consumption expenditures based on Shinohara, LTES, vol. 6, with regional price differences adjusted by Ohkawa. Shinohara's calculation goes somewhat beyond "personal" consumption expenditures since business consumption expenditures are included. There is no way to separate this item, and we may assume on the basis of postwar input-output data that its size roughly corresponds to "increases in stocks," for which no reliable prewar estimates exist. Postwar: 1941-51, NIS (1962), pp. 120, 149; 1952-65, revised NIS (1969), pp. 78-79; 1966-70, NIS (1972), pp. 54-55. Figures for 1945 are not available; figures for 1946-51 are for fiscal year.

Gross National Expenditure: Constant Prices
(1934–36 prices, million yen)

Year	Private consumption expenditure	General govt. consumption expenditure	Gross domestic fixed capital formation	Exports of goods & services & factor income received from abroad	Less: Imports of goods & services & factor income paid abroad	Gross national expenditure at market prices
1905	5,272	1,552	688	346	1,196	6,662
1906	5,238	1,136	866	443	923	6,760
1907	5,378	755	926	451	955	6,555
1908	6,015	691	1,035	440	933	7,247
1909	6,132	719	991	492	917	7,417
1910	6,389	734	1,146	579	951	7,897
1911	6,306	815	1,389	601	1,133	7,978
1912	6,487	719	1,271	697	1,181	7,993
1913	6,692	657	1,297	779	1,358	8,067
1914	6,516	722	1,271	764	1,140	8,133
1915	6,896	870	1,176	1,009	1,243	8,618
1916	7,289	762	1,252	1,281	1,230	9,354
1917	7,622	763	1,598	1,525	1,336	10,172
1918	8,055	842	2,038	1,657	1,544	11,048
1919	8,813	1,032	2,283	1,323	1,826	11,625
1920	8,680	1,060	2,471	1,136	1,782	11,565
1921	9,253	1,045	2,649	1,014	1,689	12,272
1922	9,827	1,116	2,381	1,078	2,438	11,964
1923	9,998	1,099	1,883	927	2,485	11,422
1924	10,207	1,116	2,052	1,194	1,761	12,808
1925	10,407	1,005	2,215	1,430	2,621	12,436
1926	10,556	1,084	2,338	1,529	2,924	12,583
1927	10,861	1,304	2,395	1,710	3,322	12,948
1928	11,177	1,595	2,368	1,824	3,188	13,776
1929	11,102	1,531	2,505	2,012	3,315	13,835
1930	11,152	1,475	2,430	2,017	3,098	13,976
1931	11,425	1,841	2,197	2,091	3,487	14,067
1932	11,232	1,981	2,302	2,488	3,393	14,610
1933	11,999	2,173	2,565	2,606	3,317	16,026
1934	12,757	2,061	2,955	3,483	3,746	17,510
1935	12,747	2,108	3,355	4,096	3,869	18,437
1936	13,082	2,135	3,559	4,197	4,134	18,839
1937	13,748	2,454	4,326	4,988	4,807	20,709
1938	13,915	2,544	5,386	4,614	4,957	21,502
1939	13,332	2,641	6,906	4,020	4,627	22,272
1940	13,341	3,524	7,071	4,005	4,992	22,949

Gross National Expenditure: Constant Prices
(1941–52 at 1934–36 prices; 1952a–65 at 1960 prices; 1965a–70 at 1965 prices;
1941–52, million yen; 1952a–70, billion yen)

Year	Private consumption expenditure	General govt. consumption expenditure	Gross domestic fixed capital formation	Increase in stocks	Exports of goods & services & factor income received from abroad	Less: Imports of goods & services & factor income paid abroad	Gross national expenditure at market prices
1941	9,410	6,134	4,607	1,316	4,433	4,992	20,908
1942	8,956	6,460	3,901	2,071	3,246	3,814	20,820
1943	8,469	7,445	4,771	820	2,910	3,330	21,085
1944	7,006	7,301	4,723	1,218	2,310	2,445	20,113
1945							
1946	6,826	1,123	2,545	812	102	534	10,874
1947	7,410	828	2,965	1,273	247	757	11,966
1948	8,391	1,360	2,973	1,734	352	889	13,921
1949	9,297	1,619	2,756	1,230	753	1,186	14,469
1950	10,077	1,838	2,741	1,277	1,614	1,307	16,240
1951	11,040	2,022	2,929	2,009	2,187	1,757	13,430
1952	12,927	2,395	3,581	1,365	2,354	2,262	20,360
1952a	4,635	1,075	1,612	401	782	542	7,963
1953	5,241	1,105	1,857	137	783	729	8,394
1954	5,497	1,110	1,994	141	838	767	8,813
1955	5,945	1,119	2,021	426	958	769	9,700
1956	6,437	1,107	2,494	485	1,123	1,008	10,638
1957	6,850	1,118	2,978	718	1,287	1,288	11,663
1958	7,374	1,206	3,079	259	1,365	1,070	12,213
1959	7,969	1,277	3,537	416	1,531	1,339	13,391
1960	8,823	1,356	4,696	554	1,778	1,703	15,504
1961	9,661	1,433	6,050	1,372	1,915	2,183	18,248
1962	10,611	1,576	6,564	460	2,264	2,188	19,287
1963	11,738	1,637	7,088	861	2,442	2,603	21,163
1964	13,123	1,804	8,270	1,047	2,976	2,960	24,260
1965	13,856	1,867	8,333	737	3,681	3,169	25,305
1965a	18,112	2,943	9,765	705	3,563	3,197	31,891
1966	19,599	3,103	10,919	949	4,114	3,582	35,102
1967	21,598	3,272	12,894	2,090	4,374	4,382	39,846
1968	23,748	3,499	15,750	2,180	5,356	4,946	45,587
1969	25,973	3,721	18,432	2,110	6,429	5,656	51,009
1970	27,942	3,981	20,965	2,841	7,463	6,830	56,362

Sources and remarks: Prewar: IR, pp. 155–56, with same adjustments as in BST.5. Postwar: 1941–52, NIS (1962), pp. 160–61; 1952a–65, current price series from BST.5, deflators from NIS (1967), pp. 82–83; 1965a–70, NIS (1972), pp. 58–59. Figures for 1945 are not available; figures for 1946–51 are for fiscal year.

Gross Domestic Fixed Investment by Sector and Type: Current Prices
(Million yen)

	Private		Government				Total (excl. dwellings & military)	
			Nonmilitary					
Year	PDE	Construc-tion	PDE	Construc-tion	Military	Dwellings	PDE	Construc-tion
1905	181	52	22	53	77	73	203	105
1906	165	85	26	58	64	73	191	143
1907	186	79	34	100	70	90	220	179
1908	184	69	43	131	80	97	227	200
1909	139	73	43	121	65	92	182	194
1910	160	124	46	134	64	95	206	258
1911	213	184	53	167	77	107	266	351
1912	277	103	63	150	80	121	340	253
1913	282	93	64	148	81	132	346	241
1914	244	104	64	136	86	114	308	240
1915	257	94	63	116	75	125	320	210
1916	453	127	69	103	75	146	522	230
1917	970	235	82	141	140	174	1,052	376
1918	1,473	367	119	171	227	237	1,592	538
1919	1,309	502	163	262	290	273	1,472	764
1920	1,383	670	195	464	377	384	1,578	1,134
1921	650	539	209	528	428	373	859	1,067
1922	674	589	191	631	355	410	865	1,220
1923	498	384	211	632	241	390	709	1,016
1924	551	793	246	626	192	394	797	1,419
1925	435	665	253	623	243	350	688	1,288
1926	405	837	294	670	199	338	699	1,507
1927	430	848	299	712	203	276	729	1,560
1928	499	608	282	734	220	283	781	1,342
1929	578	622	294	730	187	294	872	1,352
1930	456	543	270	567	173	221	726	1,110
1931	258	479	247	480	176	233	505	959
1932	288	369	270	514	309	241	558	883
1933	540	434	283	558	357	252	823	992
1934	862	523	278	531	428	250	1,140	1,054
1935	1,005	637	291	596	467	280	1,296	1,233
1936	1,164	652	311	599	517	293	1,475	1,251
1937	1,857	916	334	542	1,607	341	2,191	1,458
1938	2,752	789	380	507	3,157	281	3,132	1,296
1939	3,787	967	434	507	3,617	348	4,221	1,474
1940	4,445	1,202	458	688	4,195	500	4,903	1,890

Gross Domestic Fixed Investment by Sector and Type: Current Prices
(1941-44, million yen; 1946-70, billion yen)

Year	Private (excl. dwellings)	Government (excl. dwellings)	Dwellings	Total (excl. dwellings)
1941	7,086	1,611	611	8,697
1942	7,415	2,082	690	9,497
1943	10,752	2,629	777	13,381
1944	13,116	3,624	650	16,740
1945				
1946	37	30	11	67
1947	95	146	22	241
1948	212	258	47	470
1949	289	299	35	588
1950	389	190	60	579
1951	609	411	71	1,020
1952	712	474	96	1,186
1952a	721	371	180	1,092
1953	862	459	229	1,321
1954	904	515	271	1,419
1955	888	532	285	1,420
1956	1,373	571	346	1,944
1957	1,856	683	407	2,539
1958	1,718	772	451	2,490
1959	2,019	909	507	2,928
1960	2,909	1,107	666	4,016
1961	4,102	1,419	850	5,521
1962	4,238	1,880	1,019	6,118
1963	4,453	2,182	1,240	6,635
1964	5,388	2,407	1,609	7,795
1965	5,086	2,738	1,942	7,824
1966	5,834	3,278	2,232	9,112
1967	7,575	3,592	2,798	11,167
1968	9,689	4,159	3,479	13,848
1969	11,994	4,709	4,235	16,703
1970	14,425	5,408	5,087	19,833

Sources and remarks: Prewar nonagriculture: LTES, vol. 4, pp. 226–29, except for private producers' durable equipment, which is based on new and as yet unpublished estimates of S. Ishiwata. Prewar agricultural investment: WS, section A. Postwar: 1941–52, NIS (1962), pp. 148–49; military expenditures on durables and buildings and structures are considered government current expenditures, as in more recent postwar series; 1952a–62, revised NIS (1969), pp. 78–79; 1963–70, NIS (1972), pp. 54–55. Figures for 1945 are not available; figures for 1946–51 are for fiscal year.

Gross Domestic Fixed Investment by Sector and Type: Constant Prices
(1934–46 prices, million yen)

Year	Private PDE	Private Construction	Government Nonmilitary PDE	Government Nonmilitary Construction	Government Military	Dwellings	Total (excl. dwellings & military) PDE	Total (excl. dwellings & military) Construction
1905	247	102	28	122	112	154	275	224
1906	333	154	32	122	96	143	365	276
1907	230	127	40	173	95	164	270	300
1908	266	114	56	221	123	173	322	335
1909	220	130	60	218	104	173	280	348
1910	235	220	64	245	113	180	299	465
1911	308	309	74	299	125	197	382	608
1912	350	168	80	258	119	218	430	426
1913	380	157	80	249	118	234	460	406
1914	347	187	83	242	128	210	430	429
1915	307	160	72	201	121	228	379	361
1916	433	195	63	157	89	235	496	352
1917	745	243	55	153	93	225	800	396
1918	1,101	300	65	149	105	240	1,166	449
1919	1,142	355	109	185	185	225	1,251	540
1920	1,126	410	130	256	257	226	1,256	666
1921	794	338	167	317	718	238	961	655
1922	608	343	158	383	555	261	766	726
1923	393	245	202	375	343	243	595	620
1924	426	459	210	379	238	262	636	838
1925	393	510	223	421	317	265	616	931
1926	403	584	278	473	256	264	681	1,057
1927	438	615	287	495	255	220	725	1,110
1928	486	483	272	535	271	238	758	1,018
1929	550	529	280	545	254	263	830	1,074
1930	555	535	282	500	241	234	837	1,035
1931	333	492	290	489	270	244	623	981
1932	329	379	313	537	446	253	642	916
1933	515	427	295	560	463	253	810	987
1934	840	518	276	531	474	261	1,116	1,089
1935	1,024	615	292	599	475	277	1,316	1,214
1936	1,163	623	313	596	501	248	1,476	1,219
1937	1,227	778	273	476	1,129	297	1,500	1,254
1938	1,787	614	272	388	2,031	208	2,059	1,002
1939	2,544	1,120	308	335	2,288	215	2,852	1,455
1940	2,944	577	325	382	2,536	228	3,269	959

Gross Domestic Fixed Investment by Sector and Type: Constant Prices
(1941–52 at 1934–36 prices; 1952a–65 at 1960 prices; 1965a–70 at 1965 prices;
1941–52, million yen; 1952a–70, billion yen)

Year	Private (excl. dwellings)	Government (excl. dwellings)	Dwellings	Total (excl. dwellings)
1941	3,634	826	313	4,460
1942	3,090	867	288	3,957
1943	3,813	932	276	4,745
1944	3,813	1,053	189	4,866
1955				
1946	1,283	1,024	366	2,307
1947	1,277	1,974	399	3,251
1948	1,420	1,731	315	3,151
1949	1,429	1,478	176	2,907
1950	1,541	748	236	2,289
1951	1,749	1,180	203	2,929
1952	2,047	1,362	376	3,409
1952a	913	434	259	1,347
1953	1,054	519	284	1,573
1954	1,097	578	320	1,675
1955	1,065	606	351	1,671
1956	1,484	604	407	2,088
1957	1,853	676	445	2,529
1958	1,768	809	502	2,577
1959	2,066	938	534	3,004
1960	2,920	1,106	671	4,026
1961	3,943	1,328	733	5,271
1962	4,060	1,663	842	5,723
1963	4,238	1,864	987	6,102
1964	5,068	1,968	1,228	7,036
1965	4,758	2,149	1,433	6,907
1965a	5,085	2,739	1,941	7,824
1966	5,664	3,148	2,106	8,812
1967	7,191	3,275	2,427	10,466
1968	9,149	3,748	2,851	12,897
1969	11,058	4,108	3,270	15,166
1970	12,845	4,458	3,662	17,303

Sources and remarks: Prewar nonagriculture: LTES, vol. 4, pp. 230–33, except for Ishiwata's series for private producers' durables. Prewar agricultural investment: WS, section A. Postwar: all current series from BST.7. Price deflators, 1941–52, NIS (1962), p. 168 (a single series without breakdown into sectors or types); 1952a–65, NIS (1967), pp. 74–75; 1965a–70, NIS (1970), pp. 62–63. Figures for 1945 are not available; figures for 1946–51 are for fiscal year.

Gross Domestic Fixed Investment by Industry
(1934-36 prices, million yen)

Year	Agriculture (including forestry & fishing)	Mining & manufacturing	Facilitating industry	Construction	Services	Total	Private nonagriculture
1905	160	111	91	8	30	400	197
1906	188	94	86	11	46	425	185
1907	184	119	81	12	63	459	205
1908	169	136	108	11	87	511	241
1909	191	105	97	14	71	478	182
1910	192	116	104	13	88	513	218
1911	181	134	152	17	86	570	289
1912	187	144	176	23	90	620	336
1913	193	133	202	23	75	626	344
1914	189	119	195	20	110	633	358
1915	196	92	185	14	84	571	297
1916	222	122	249	14	92	699	407
1917	197	134	441	12	103	887	622
1918	189	136	674	9	114	1,122	864
1919	202	183	704	12	137	1,238	931
1920	208	178	718	13	92	1,209	856
1921	250	199	485	16	96	1,046	642
1922	228	199	381	25	147	980	602
1923	257	136	293	17	166	869	424
1924	240	177	302	24	127	870	439
1925	244	164	310	28	230	976	519
1926	258	156	386	38	173	1,011	447
1927	270	185	422	32	205	1,114	541
1928	279	183	451	36	184	1,133	592
1929	284	238	459	44	213	1,238	665
1930	300	193	456	50	172	1,171	589
1931	296	161	331	40	153	981	408
1932	272	197	323	35	171	998	418
1933	292	274	409	50	204	1,229	652
1934	273	450	565	67	218	1,573	1,009
1935	264	530	646	82	251	1,773	1,185
1936	270	540	769	95	283	1,957	1,332
1937	224	615	744	93	284	1,960	1,463
1938	249	927	907	151	217	2,451	1,949
1939	281	1,351	1,135	212	246	3,225	2,694
1940	295	1,379	1,313	298	266	3,551	3,011

Gross Domestic Fixed Investment by Industry
(Current prices, billion yen)

Year	Agriculture (including forestry & fishing)	Mining & manufacturing	Facilitating industry	Construction	Services	Total	Balancing item
1951	96	434	254	7	375	970	-197
1952	130	299	333	10	389	1,115	-46
1953	162	375	427	13	512	1,445	-43
1954	199	324	381	17	534	1,391	-64
1955	189	362	420	11	523	1,488	-17
1956	215	664	594	45	658	2,093	-82
1957	234	846	750	47	758	2,596	-39
1958	223	714	751	64	801	2,550	-2
1959	281	1,067	825	96	1,003	3,211	-61
1960	299	1,746	987	156	1,245	4,342	-90
1961	391	2,323	1,252	256	1,666	5,802	-86
1962	385	1,955	1,397	295	1,971	6,227	224
1963	450	2,188	1,552	316	2,313	6,946	127
1964	471	2,458	1,627	329	2,904	7,936	147
1965	543	2,052	1,948	368	2,958	7,894	24
1966	634	2,454	2,232	510	3,527	9,613	255
1967	909	3,751	2,406	713	4,024	11,874	70
1968	1,066	4,734	2,826	784	4,789	14,344	145
1969	1,262	6,042	3,410	931	6,183	17,669	-160
1970	1,380	6,778	3,889	1,150	7,255	20,515	62

Sources and remarks: Prewar: SRA, vol. 3, p. 167. Postwar: 1952–62, revised NIS (1969), pp. 242–43; 1963–70, NIS (1972), pp. 226–27. The balancing item represents the discrepancy between commodity flow estimates of aggregate fixed investment and expenditure estimates by industrial categories. No industrial deflators are available. Estimates for private sector from WS, section K.

BASIC STATISTICAL TABLE 10
National Savings
(Current prices, million yen)

Year	National savings	Provisions for consumption of fixed capital	Saving of private sector	Saving of general government	Saving of general govt. (excl. military)	Net foreign claims
1905	190	269	242	-321	-398	-324
1906	516	293	347	-124	-188	-26
1907	638	335	190	113	43	4
1908	600	329	67	204	124	-62
1909	602	321	83	198	133	4
1910	643	336	95	212	148	-49
1911	782	358	218	206	128	-79
1912	766	411	87	268	188	-92
1913	771	433	19	319	238	-90
1914	799	430	65	304	219	-6
1915	1,019	473	291	255	180	225
1916	1,667	609	707	351	276	633
1917	2,783	871	1,424	488	348	965
1918	3,537	1,170	1,800	567	341	836
1919	3,321	1,307	1,329	685	395	383
1920	3,536	1,800	1,107	629	253	-59
1921	2,626	1,573	273	780	351	-242
1922	2,794	1,623	180	991	656	-181
1923	1,963	1,709	-668	922	681	-537
1924	2,246	1,745	-449	950	758	-684
1925	2,424	1,589	-284	1,119	876	-281
1926	2,499	1,538	-132	1,093	894	-363
1927	2,711	1,558	227	926	723	-180
1928	2,559	1,605	199	755	536	-184
1929	2,841	1,631	411	799	612	27
1930	2,321	1,394	463	464	291	-2
1931	1,823	1,214	533	76	-100	-122
1932	1,998	1,370	687	-59	-368	-32
1933	2,463	1,570	1,033	-140	-495	-3
1934	2,886	1,604	989	293	-135	-37
1935	3,528	1,674	1,576	278	-189	181
1936	3,798	1,805	1,494	499	-18	177
1937	5,853	2,428	2,565	860	746	193
1938	7,922	2,748	5,016	158	-2,999	-55
1939	9,225	3,140	5,294	791	-2,826	-597
1940	11,853	3,870	7,017	966	-3,229	155

National Savings

(Current prices: 1941-44, million yen; 1946-70, billion yen)

Year	National savings	Provisions for consumption of fixed capital	Saving of private corporations	Saving of households & private nonprofit institutions	Saving of general govt.	Statistical discrepancy	Net foreign claims
1941	10,846	3,157	1,781	10,069	-7,043	2,882	-876
1942	13,689	3,666	2,176	11,374	-8,404	4,877	-914
1943	15,297	4,272	2,519	14,124	-11,403	5,785	-577
1944	21,053	5,257	2,986	20,120	-15,450	8,140	398
1945							
1946	100	24	-1	8	-23	92	-5
1947	352	57	-4	-40	148	191	7
1948	773	108	2	-8	317	354	21
1949	905	158	38	-43	552	200	75
1950	1,179	207	192	410	351	19	172
1951	1,821	280	214	717	452	158	159
1952	1,744	434	152	442	452	264	81
1953	1,617	553	214	394	403	53	-74
1954	1,819	701	300	549	370	-101	-18
1955	2,207	791	222	853	377	-36	82
1956	2,785	934	274	952	504	121	-12
1957	3,462	1,044	555	1,219	738	-94	224
1958	3,287	1,129	443	1,248	619	-152	96
1959	3,983	1,300	478	1,547	761	-103	131
1960	5,285	1,590	956	1,864	1,094	-219	52
1961	7,398	2,037	1,050	2,402	1,543	366	-353
1962	7,577	2,413	966	2,691	1,746	-239	-18
1963	8,479	2,855	916	3,022	1,849	-163	-280
1964	10,313	3,513	1,163	3,202	1,946	489	-173
1965	10,878	4,024	955	3,875	1,943	81	335
1966	12,832	4,760	1,448	4,338	2,091	195	449
1967	16,192	5,506	2,289	5,518	2,599	280	-72
1968	20,071	6,670	3,272	6,609	3,250	270	373
1969	23,930	8,098	3,724	7,556	4,271	281	764
1970	28,763	9,571	4,757	9,309	5,410	-284	709

Sources and remarks: Prewar: WS, section S (residual estimates). The exclusion of military investments before World War II reduces national savings by an equal amount. Postwar: 1941-51, NIS (1962), p. 138; domestic savings converted to national savings; figures for 1945 are not available; figures for 1946-51 are for fiscal year; 1952-65, revised NIS (1969), pp. 68-69; 1966-70, NIS (1972), pp. 44-45. The prewar series are rough because inventory changes and statistical discrepancies are not taken into account. For net lending to the rest of the world, see BST.11.

Foreign Accounts
(Current prices, million yen)

Year	Exports of goods and nonfactor services (1)	Merchandise (FOB) (2)	Factor income received from abroad (3)	Total (1) + (3) (4)	Imports of goods and nonfactor services (5)	Merchandise (FOB) (6)
1905	390	335	12	402	700	502
1906	530	441	10	540	497	437
1907	602	452.	15	617	567	512
1908	493	399	14	507	523	461
1909	519	437	20	539	481	431
1910	567	502	19	586	576	521
1911	599	523	19	618	634	581
1912	701	618	22	723	750	684
1913	810	717	26	836	859	795
1914	767	671	24	791	725	671
1915	967	793	27	994	697	636
1916	1,588	1,252	49	1,637	960	884
1917	2,260	1,793	86	2,346	1,335	1,201
1918	2,894	2,177	109	3,003	2,134	1,902
1919	3,103	2,444	127	3,230	2,820	2,501
1920	2,861	2,267	107	2,968	3,005	2,682
1921	1,908	1,503	90	1,998	2,218	1,941
1922	2,225	1,885	84	2,309	2,470	2,216
1923	2,007	1,699	88	2,095	2,612	2,394
1924	2,483	2,191	78	2,561	3,239	2,972
1925	3,068	2,687	99	3,167	3,387	3,109
1926	2,788	2,432	92	2,880	3,174	2,923
1927	2,758	2,399	100	2,857	2,977	2,714
1928	2,816	2,425	84	2,900	3,023	2,747
1929	3,058	2,621	102	3,160	3,060	2,766
1930	2,267	1,888	91	2,358	2,279	2,006
1931	1,818	1,491	76	1,894	1,947	1,686
1932	2,205	1,820	89	2,294	2,285	1,936
1933	2,853	2,367	93	2,846	2,896	2,464
1934	3,319	2,813	105	3,424	3,432	2,970
1935	3,857	3,292	129	3,986	3,769	3,272
1936	4,226	3,605	156	4,382	4,160	3,641
1937	5,840	5,114	166	6,006	5,774	4,903
1938	5,473	4,705	211	5,684	5,573	3,963
1939	6,527	5,979	74	6,601	5,987	4,403
1940	6,931	5,875	322	7,253	6,947	4,910

Foreign Accounts

Factor income paid abroad (7)	Total (5) + (7) (8)	Net exports of goods & services & net factor income from abroad (4) − (8) (9)	Transfers from the rest of the world (10)	Less: Transfers to the rest of the world (11)	Net lending to the rest of the world (9) + (10) − (11) (12)	Year
37	737	−335	13	2	−324	1905
79	576	−36	13	3	−26	1906
66	633	−16	23	3	4	1907
71	594	−87	28	3	−62	1908
75	556	−17	24	3	4	1909
80	656	−70	24	3	−49	1910
84	718	−100	24	3	−79	1911
88	837	−115	26	3	−92	1912
93	952	−116	29	3	−90	1913
91	816	−25	25	6	−6	1914
91	788	−206	22	3	225	1915
80	1,040	597	38	2	633	1916
84	1,419	927	40	2	965	1917
83	2,217	786	52	2	836	1918
89	2,909	321	64	2	383	1919
89	3,094	−126	70	3	−59	1920
84	2,303	−305	67	4	−242	1921
68	2,538	−229	51	3	−181	1922
69	2,681	−586	52	3	−537	1923
86	3,324	−763	83	4	−684	1924
110	3,497	−330	53	4	−281	1925
109	3,283	−403	44	4	−363	1926
103	3,080	−222	45	3	−180	1927
108	3,131	−231	50	3	−184	1928
122	3,182	−22	53	4	27	1929
116	2,395	−37	38	3	−2	1930
100	2,047	−152	32	2	−122	1931
127	2,412	−118	89	3	−32	1932
146	3,042	−97	99	5	−3	1933
131	3,563	−139	105	3	−37	1934
143	3,911	74	111	4	181	1935
131	4,291	91	91	5	177	1936
158	5,889	117	n.a.	n.a.	193	1937
171	5,819	−135	n.a.	n.a.	−55	1938
54	6,043	−558	n.a.	n.a.	−597	1939
252	7,194	59	n.a.	n.a.	155	1940

(continued)

Foreign Accounts
(Current prices: 1941-44, million yen; 1946-70, billion yen)

Year	Exports of goods and nonfactor services (1)	Merchandise (FOB) (2)	Factor income received from abroad (3)	Total (1) + (3) (4)	Import of goods and nonfactor services (5)	Merchandise (FOB) (6)
1941	5,754	4,551	363	6,117	7,035	4,079
1942	4,585	3,612	446	5,031	6,023	2,929
1943	4,431	3,240	458	4,889	5,685	2,944
1944	3,478	1,479	472	3,950	4,021	1,947
1945						
1946	5	5		5	24	22
1947	28	28		28	81	67
1948	81	75		81	190	155
1949	217	193		217	326	262
1950	469	333		469	362	319
1951	908	577	1	909	696	574
1952	732	465	56	788	709	612
1953	724	454	65	789	849	738
1954	794	581	60	854	854	735
1955	921	723	58	979	872	742
1956	1,130	894	59	1,189	1,168	941
1957	1,278	1,028	60	1,338	1,499	1,172
1958	1,270	1,034	48	1,318	1,104	901
1959	1,483	1,229	49	1,532	1,334	1,099
1960	1,715	1,432	59	1,774	1,638	1,336
1961	1,795	1,494	65	1,860	2,096	1,695
1962	2,070	1,750	71	2,141	2,027	1,605
1963	2,270	1,941	80	2,350	2,467	2,000
1964	2,802	2,413	88	2,890	2,851	2,270
1965	3,452	3,000	111	3,563	2,987	2,316
1966	4,033	3,469	131	4,164	3,435	2,651
1967	4,315	3,682	152	4,464	4,213	3,265
1968	5,353	4,589	174	5,527	4,762	3,679
1969	6,751	5,643	247	6,818	5,573	4,312
1970	7,939	6,828	332	8,271	6,996	5,402

Foreign Accounts
(Current prices: 1941-44, million yen; 1946-70, billion yen)

Factor income paid abroad (7)	Total (5) + (7) (8)	Net exports of goods & services & net factor income from abroad (4) – (8) (9)	Transfers from the rest of the world (10)	Less: Transfers to the rest of the world (11)	Not lending to the rest of the world (9) + (10) – (11) (12)	Year
104	7,139	-1,022	146		-876	1941
79	6,102	-1,071	157		-914	1942
110	5,795	-906	329		-577	1943
307	4,328	-378	776		398	1944
						1945
	24	-19	14		-5	1946
1	82	-54	61		7	1947
1	191	-110	131		21	1948
1	327	-110	185		75	1949
2	364	105	67		172	1950
3	699	210	-51		159	1951
10	719	69	18	6	81	1952
22	871	-82	9	1	-74	1953
28	882	-28	12	2	-18	1954
32	904	75	17	10	82	1955
40	1,208	-19	17	10	-12	1956
51	1,550	-212	18	30	224	1957
45	1,149	169	19	92	96	1958
56	1,390	142	19	30	131	1959
75	1,713	61	22	31	52	1960
102	2,198	-338	26	41	-353	1961
121	2,148	-7	24	35	-18	1962
146	2,613	-263	24	41	-280	1963
186	3,037	-147	26	52	-173	1964
210	3,197	366	23	54	335	1965
231	3,666	498	24	73	449	1966
259	4,472	-8	26	90	-72	1967
325	5,087	440	29	92	377	1968
416	5,989	829	31	96	764	1969
491	7,487	784	35	110	709	1970

Sources and remarks: Prewar: 1905-36, Yūzo Yamamoto, "Kaigai shūshi" (Foreign Account) in WS; 1936-40, Japan, Economic Planning Agency, *Nihon keizai to kokumin shotoku* (The Japanese Economy and National Income; 1959), pp. 188-89. Postwar: 1941-51, NIS (1962), pp. 132-35 (income transfers are available only in net terms); figures for 1945 are not available; figures for 1946-51 are for fiscal year; 1952-65, revised NIS (1969), pp. 266-67; 1966-70, NIS (1972), pp. 248-49.

BASIC STATISTICAL TABLE 12
Foreign Trade
(Constant prices: 1905-52 in millions of 1934-36 yen; 1952a-65 in billions of 1960 yen; 1965a-70 in billions of 1965 yen)

Year	Imports	Exports	Year	Imports	Exports	Year	Imports	Exports
1905	1,135	336	1931	3,317	2,007	1951	1,745	2,178
			1932	3,214	1,974	1952	2,209	2,333
1906	797	435	1933	3,159	2,612	1952a	534	727
1907	856	439	1934	3,608	3,377	1953	708	719
1908	822	428	1935	3,728	3,964	1954	639	779
1909	793	474				1955	631	901
1910	835	561	1936	4,008	4,048			
			1937	4,713	4,851	1956	785	1,067
1911	999	583	1938	4,747	4,442	1957	1,246	1,229
1912	1,057	675	1939	4,584	3,975	1958	1,027	1,314
1913	1,227	755	1940	4,821	3,827	1959	1,285	1,483
1914	1,012	741				1960	1,705	1,718
1915	1,099	982	1941	4,906	4,149			
			1942	3,738	2,926	1961	1,782	1,848
1916	1,135	1,242	1943	3,230	2,608	1962	2,108	2,189
1917	1,257	1,469	1944	2,200	1,928	1963	2,457	2,359
1918	1,486	1,597	1945			1964	2,779	2,886
1919	1,770	1,271				1965	2,961	3,566
1920	1,728	1,095	1946	534	102			
			1947	752	247	1965a	2,987	3,452
1921	1,628	969	1948	886	362	1966	3,358	3,986
1922	2,373	1,039	1949	1,184	743	1967	4,127	4,227
1933	2,421	888	1950	1,297	1,586	1968	4,628	5,187
1924	1,715	1,158				1969	5,263	6,193
1925	2,539	1,386				1970	6,384	7,166
1926	2,827	1,481
1927	3,212	1,650
1928	3,078	1,771
1929	3,188	1,947
1930	2,948	1,939

Sources and remarks: Prewar: Total exports and imports of BST.11, deflated by export and import price indexes of BST.14. Postwar: 1941-52, NIS (1962); price deflators from p. 168; figures for 1945 are not available; figures for 1946-51 are for fiscal year; 1952a-70, price deflators for 1952a-65 from NIS (1967), pp. 82-83; for 1963a-70, NIS (1972), pp. 62-63.

Commodity Composition: Exports and Imports
(Current prices, million yen)

Year	Food-stuffs	Raw materials	Mineral fuels	Chemicals	Semi-finished materials	Investment goods	Consumption goods	Total
				Exports				
1905	43	93	14	2	108	3	55	318
1906	51	138	16	2	132	4	76	419
1907	45	151	19	2	129	8	75	429
1908	43	139	18	1	105	7	62	375
1909	49	159	17	2	116	3	65	411
1910	51	172	16	2	140	3	71	455
1911	56	166	19	3	156	4	80	484
1912	63	207	21	3	182	7	89	572
1913	69	248	25	5	221	8	95	671
1914	69	212	25	5	223	7	85	626
1915	81	213	21	12	290	11	116	744
1916	108	353	25	27	418	38	204	1,173
1917	176	466	32	30	624	121	216	1,665
1918	219	485	40	30	838	123	314	2,049
1919	164	732	48	18	888	41	356	2,247
1920	158	486	51	21	883	49	358	2,006
1921	78	465	39	13	472	25	147	1,239
1922	97	735	24	9	535	26	178	1,604
1923	89	619	22	9	484	17	172	1,412
1924	111	765	23	10	652	18	184	1,763
1925	136	984	34	19	809	26	214	2,222
1926	144	819	32	16	742	23	200	1,976
1927	135	824	26	16	685	24	204	1,914
1928	158	806	25	19	644	27	233	1,912
1929	163	860	24	20	740	37	261	2,105
1930	139	471	23	16	548	38	200	1,435
1931	106	391	16	14	407	28	158	1,120
1932	108	425	16	15	530	27	242	1,363
1933	162	452	17	22	725	52	398	1,828
1934	173	398	14	22	1,022	98	398	2,125
1935	199	529	14	28	1,128	104	460	2,462
1936	203	572	16	37	1,177	123	504	2,632
1937	248	632	15	41	1,393	172	620	3,121

(continued)

303

Commodity Composition: Exports and Imports
(Current prices: 1947-65, billion yen; 1905-20, million yen)

Year	Food-stuffs	Raw materials	Mineral fuels	Chemicals	Semi-finished materials	Investment goods	Consumption goods	Total
				Exports (continued)				
1947	1	2	1	0	5	0	1	10
1948	2	11	3	1	23	2	10	52
1949	9	14	3	0	98	16	30	170
1950	20	23	2	2	177	23	49	296
1951	26	30	0	5	325	28	72	486
1952	37	36	3	4	272	35	72	459
1953	48	37	3	3	223	63	80	457
1954	49	42	2	6	319	63	103	584
1955	49	47	2	8	388	77	149	720
1956	65	56	3	9	422	161	180	896
1957	68	63	1	9	465	205	213	1,024
1958	85	65	3	11	433	203	230	1,030
1959	97	77	3	12	477	236	337	1,239
1960	97	69	5	15	611	258	398	1,459
1961	97	86	6	18	590	315	401	1,513
1962	119	109	5	37	670	333	487	1,760
1963	102	119	6	46	752	387	531	1,943
1964	120	114	7	35	942	463	691	2,372
1965	122	169	9	91	1,138	712	785	3,026
				Imports				
1905	96	165	19	9	144	33	18	484
1906	83	140	14	13	131	26	18	425
1907	82	189	16	16	136	36	17	492
1908	70	155	18	16	117	43	14	433
1909	53	169	16	15	99	25	15	392
1910	48	225	18	20	116	21	15	463
1911	64	225	18	24	157	40	18	526
1912	89	294	19	25	150	37	17	631
1913	145	346	18	30	149	44	18	750
1914	105	321	19	29	102	30	14	620
1915	70	354	16	19	86	13	12	570
1916	56	454	13	30	189	28	23	793
1917	70	576	20	41	305	40	33	1,085
1918	265	872	37	47	446	61	44	1,772
1919	511	1,078	52	83	445	90	70	2,329
1920	316	1,232	58	92	512	110	95	2,415

Commodity Composition: Exports and Imports
(Current prices: 1921-37, million yen; 1947-65, billion yen)

Year	Food-stuffs	Raw materials	Mineral fuels	Chemicals	Semi-finished materials	Investment goods	Consumption goods	Total
				Imports (continued)				
1921	219	758	46	32	353	124	62	1,594
1922	296	870	61	49	392	124	84	1,876
1923	249	1,018	71	60	327	125	123	1,973
1924	353	1,179	90	66	475	151	128	2,442
1925	405	1,438	82	76	375	123	67	2,566
1926	360	1,276	88	92	370	116	72	2,374
1927	333	1,131	102	81	357	91	76	2,171
1928	319	1,078	127	87	379	114	88	2,192
1929	290	1,108	136	104	345	129	96	2,208
1930	229	650	124	69	309	91	68	1,540
1931	172	510	114	53	270	56	54	1,229
1932	169	978	146	33	193	63	60	1,642
1933	185	1,304	156	41	288	67	60	2,101
1934	174	1,378	171	55	322	81	71	2,252
1935	195	1,398	202	73	407	104	75	2,454
1936	220	1,663	236	86	352	140	57	2,754
1937	230	1,766	340	96	1,033	223	79	3,767
1947	9	5	3	2	0	0	0	19
1948	27	14	13	3	1	0	2	60
1949	115	103	34	12	14	0	5	283
1950	123	195	19	1	5	2	3	348
1951	202	423	58	3	23	15	13	737
1952	231	345	81	4	25	22	18	726
1953	245	404	102	6	39	38	27	861
1954	260	390	95	7	34	48	19	853
1955	261	417	102	9	41	39	14	·883
1956	233	618	145	15	81	53	14	1,159
1957	241	728	241	21	185	90	17	1,523
1958	223	469	183	20	51	102	16	1,064
1959	213	631	198	29	75	109	17	1,272
1960	234	773	262	31	139	119	24	1,582
1961	281	1,013	330	41	166	164	32	2,027
1962	254	911	370	43	128	215	37	1,958
1963	370	1,057	436	53	151	256	53	2,376
1964	477	1,152	499	71	292	247	76	2,814
1965	497	1,229	574	58	244	230	87	2,919

Sources and remarks: John Brode, "Tables of Japanese Foreign Trade, 1868-1965" (Cambridge, Mass., 1967; unpublished). Exports FOB, imports CIF prices. The original source is Ministry of Finance, *Dai-Nihon Nihon) gaikoku bōeki nempō* (Annual Reports of the Foreign Trade of Japan). Coverage: Japan proper except for 1905-20, when Korea is included. Note on classification: military goods are classified as "consumption"; raw silk and fertilizers are included as "raw material."

Price Indexes (Deflators): Output and Expenditure
(1934-36 = 100)

Year	Consumers' goods & services	Investment goods	Implicit deflator (aggregate)	Agriculture (including forestry & fishing)	Mining & manufacturing
1905	44.6	75.0	47.3	55.2	72.2
1906	47.0	62.3	51.0	57.9	75.1
1907	49.7	68.5	55.2	64.3	81.1
1908	50.9	64.0	54.3	62.5	77.0
1909	49.9	60.3	53.3	56.8	74.4
1910	49.2	60.1	51.9	57.6	74.4
1911	55.3	61.9	58.3	67.7	75.5
1912	59.4	67.4	62.1	77.4	80.9
1913	61.7	66.3	64.6	77.6	79.4
1914	54.2	63.4	57.2	59.0	75.8
1915	51.5	67.5	57.0	55.7	80.2
1916	66.0	82.6	65.5	61.7	100.1
1917	69.8	113.7	83.2	85.5	128.6
1918	94.3	132.6	105.4	130.6	159.6
1919	125.6	128.7	130.7	178.8	185.7
1920	127.6	145.5	135.0	153.9	194.3
1921	122.0	108.3	122.0	150.1	148.9
1922	119.3	124.9	130.6	137.0	149.8
1923	119.2	132.8	131.1	143.7	153.1
1924	120.2	142.7	122.0	151.9	153.5
1925	123.6	122.1	131.0	150.1	146.0
1926	118.4	122.4	127.7	136.7	129.7
1927	113.1	120.8	126.0	121.8	121.8
1928	110.7	115.8	120.2	120.0	122.8
1929	107.6	112.4	118.0	106.0	118.8
1930	98.7	95.6	105.6	79.5	96.2
1931	86.9	88.6	95.2	72.8	79.3
1932	88.5	88.2	93.6	79.4	84.7
1933	91.7	96.2	95.5	86.7	101.8
1934	96.1	99.0	97.3	92.7	99.7
1935	100.6	99.7	99.6	100.6	98.7
1936	103.3	101.8	103.0	106.6	101.2
1937	111.3	130.8	114.2	119.0	131.2
1938	122.9	148.1	130.2	130.8	140.5
1939	132.2	142.2	141.0	171.8	151.9
1940	150.0	165.5	159.4	195.3	167.5

Facilitating industry	Construction	Services	Imports	Exports	Year
71.8	48.2	35.4	61.7	115.9	1905
68.7	51.7	32.9	62.3	122.0	1906
67.3	58.6	33.5	66.3	136.9	1907
64.3	59.1	37.1	63.6	115.1	1908
64.1	55.3	38.3	60.6	109.5	1909
63.8	54.6	37.5	69.0	101.2	1910
64.1	56.2	41.5	63.4	102.8	1911
65.6	59.8	42.5	70.9	103.8	1912
61.1	59.5	45.4	70.0	107.4	1913
72.4	55.4	42.2	71.6	103.5	1914
74.1	57.9	50.3	63.4	98.5	1915
84.0	67.9	39.1	84.6	127.8	1916
115.9	91.0	45.4	106.2	153.9	1917
135.3	118.0	56.3	143.6	181.2	1918
119.1	139.0	70.8	159.3	244.2	1919
123.4	200.0	81.9	173.6	261.3	1920
116.0	166.7	87.1	136.3	197.0	1921
116.2	166.0	93.1	104.1	214.2	1922
122.3	172.0	91.8	107.9	226.0	1923
114.1	167.5	85.5	188.8	214.5	1924
112.2	148.5	99.8	133.4	221.4	1925
108.7	139.4	106.0	112.3	188.3	1926
107.7	135.4	108.8	92.7	167.1	1927
110.6	130.7	99.2	98.2	159.0	1928
105.9	128.9	101.3	96.0	157.1	1929
102.0	103.6	107.1	77.3	116.9	1930
100.3	94.3	96.1	58.7	90.6	1931
100.9	96.3	92.4	71.1	92.2	1932
101.1	103.2	85.9	91.7	109.2	1933
100.1	97.0	95.1	95.1	98.3	1934
93.9	99.6	103.1	101.1	97.3	1935
99.8	103.4	103.3	103.8	104.4	1936
108.3	118.3	98.7	122.5	120.4	1937
114.6	133.4	114.6	117.4	123.2	1938
112.0	156.1	105.0	130.6	164.2	1939
112.9	201.1	122.0	144.1	181.1	1940

(continued)

Price Indexes (Deflators): Output and Expenditure
(For 1941–52, 1934–36 = 1; for 1952a–65, 1960 = 100; for 1965a–70, 1965 = 100)

Year	Consumers' goods & services	Investment goods	Implicit deflator (aggregate)	Agriculture (including forestry & fishing)	Mining & manufacturing
1941	2.20	1.95	2.15		
1942	2.65	2.40	2.61		
1943	3.07	2.82	3.03		
1944	3.79	3.44	3.70		
1945					
1946	48.8	29.0	43.6		
1947	123.5	74.0	109.4		
1948	207.5	149.0	191.4		
1949	243.2	202.0	233.3		
1950	237.9	235.0	243.0		
1951	273.4	353.2	295.4		
1952	284.6	348.1	307.6		
1952a	83.3	82.5	78.6		
1953	89.0	86.2	84.4	98.2	102.1
1954	93.0	85.7	88.7	98.1	100.0
1955	93.0	86.4	88.7	94.2	97.9
1956	93.4	93.7	91.4	91.4	103.1
1957	96.3	100.8	95.4	96.0	107.0
1958	95.7	95.5	94.3	93.3	99.4
1959	96.9	97.3	96.5	94.3	99.3
1960	100.0	99.8	100.0	100.0	100.0
1961	104.6	105.3	105.2	111.6	99.8
1962	110.7	108.2	109.9	120.1	97.9
1963	117.3	110.1	115,6	127.7	98.8
1964	121.5	112.4	118.8	134.7	98.8
1965	129.4	116.7	125.8	145.8	99.4
1965a	100.0	100.7	100.2		
1966	105.0	104.3	104.8		
1967	109.1	108.5	109.3		
1968	114.9	109.8	113.4		
1969	120.6	112.8	118.1		
1970	129.9	117.8	125.9		

BASIC STATISTICAL TABLE 14 *(continued)*
Price Indexes (Deflators): Output and Expenditure
(For 1941-52, 1934-36 = 1; for 1952a-65, 1960 = 100; for 1965a-70, 1965 = 100)

Facilitating industry	Construction	Services	Imports	Exports	Year
			1.43	1.38	1941
			1.60	1.55	1942
			1.74	1.68	1943
			1.77	1.71	1944
					1945
			45.1	47.0	1946
			107.7	112.3	1947
			214.4	223.9	1948
			275.6	287.7	1949
			278.7	290.9	1950
			397.9	415.4	1951
			331.8	352.7	1952
			132.8	100.8	1952a
90.8	80.9	80.4	119.3	100.8	1953
92.7	83.3	81.2	115.0	101.9	1954
96.7	82.1	85.6	117.6	102.2	1955
98.6	89.2	90.3	119.8	105.9	1956
102.3	94.6	95.2	120.3	104.0	1957
100.2	91.4	95.1	107.5	96.6	1958
100.0	94.3	96.7	103.8	100.0	1959
100.0	100.0	100.0	100.6	99.8	1960
105.4	111.4	105.9	100.7	97.1	1961
105.2	111.7	114.6	98.2	94.6	1962
106.0	121.8	123.6	100.4	96.2	1963
109.8	127.8	129.6	102.6	97.1	1964
116.2	132.4	137.1	100.9	96.8	1965
			100.0	100.0	1965a
			102.3	101.2	1966
			102.1	102.1	1967
			102.9	103.2	1968
			105.9	106.1	1969
			109.6	110.8	1970

Sources and remarks: Prewar: columns (1), (2), and (3) are implicit deflators, calculated from corresponding items in BST.5 and BST.6 (WS, section P). Columns (4), (5), (6), and (7) from WS, section P, based on unpublished data of SRA. Column (8) is also an implicit deflator from SRA, vol. 3, pp. 152-53. Columns (9) and (10) from LTES, vol. 8, pp. 152-53. Postwar: 1941-52, NIS (1962), p. 168; aggregate price index derived from BST.5 and BST.6; 1952a-65, NIS (1967), pp. 82-83; 1963a-70, NIS (1972), pp. 62-63. Figures for 1945 are not available; figures for 1946-51 are for fiscal year.

Population: Total and Gainfully Occupied (Labor Force Employed) by Industry
(Thousands)

Year	Total population	Agriculture (including forestry & fishing)	Mining & manufacturing	Facilitating industry	Construction	Services	Total gainfully occupied	Private nonagriculture
1905	46,746	16,205	3,094	625	538	4,542	25,004	7,774
1906	47,132	16,117	3,154	642	557	4,637	25,107	7,841
1907	47,654	16,126	3,180	732	547	4,671	25,256	8,018
1908	48,224	16,069	3,248	713	613	4,721	25,364	8,174
1909	48,850	15,926	3,384	691	613	4,805	25,419	8,369
1910	49,489	15,943	3,353	705	614	4,907	25,522	8,413
1911	50,179	16,051	3,373	687	637	4,923	25,671	8,435
1912	50,925	16,060	3,417	709	669	4,991	25,846	8,596
1913	51,671	16,094	3,534	661	682	5,072	26,043	8,764
1914	52,399	16,068	3,531	706	666	5,226	26,197	8,917
1915	53,110	15,520	3,897	746	701	5,532	26,396	9,560
1916	53,768	15,489	3,837	799	673	5,839	26,637	9,343
1917	54,365	15,539	4,285	785	698	5,561	26,868	9,989
1918	54,711	14,784	4,684	923	698	5,843	26,932	10,554
1919	55,032	14,834	4,764	972	690	5,766	27,026	10,577
1920	55,885	14,663	4,966	1,043	701	5,838	27,211	10,906
1921	55,963	14,731	4,746	1,020	707	6,201	27,405	10,984
1922	56,666	14,772	4,899	1,023	730	6,209	27,633	11,150
1923	57,389	14,110	5,399	1,089	745	6,530	27,873	12,013
1924	58,119	14,452	5,226	1,102	767	6,352	27,899	11,742
1925	58,876	14,394	5,330	1,118	790	6,471	28,103	11,979
1926	59,736	14,349	5,412	1,099	825	6,747	28,432	12,312
1927	60,741	14,276	5,725	1,091	802	6,590	28,484	12,432
1928	61,659	14,363	5,719	1,121	839	6,783	28,825	12,654
1929	62,595	14,573	5,795	1,135	853	6,815	29,171	12,780
1930	64,450	14,689	5,872	1,162	846	7,050	29,619	13,101
1931	65,457	14,865	5,785	1,156	836	7,295	29,937	13,169
1932	66,433	15,014	5,659	1,107	834	7,610	30,224	13,081
1933	67,431	14,891	5,835	1,060	860	7,896	30,542	13,296
1934	68,309	14,752	6,137	1,091	818	8,030	30,828	13,629
1935	69,254	14,571	6,461	1,121	833	8,228	31,214	14,176
1936	70,133	14,609	6,708	1,137	846	8,308	31,608	14,472
1937	70,630	14,538	6,887	1,189	863	8,228	31,705	14,529
1938	71,012	14,466	7,111	1,239	885	8,154	31,855	14,814
1939	71,379	14,395	7,401	1,308	918	8,175	32,197	15,263
1940	71,933	14,323	7,686	1,371	948	8,170	32,498	15,566

Population: Total and Gainfully Occupied (Labor Force Employed) by Industry
(Thousands)

Year	Total population	Agriculture (including forestry & fishing)	Mining & manufacturing	Facilitating industry	Construction	Services	Total gainfully occupied	Private nonagriculture
1941	72,218	13,662	7,900	1,611	1,009	7,200	31,382	
1942	72,880	13,132	8,406	1,706	1,039	6,594	30,877	
1943	73,903	12,602	8,913	1,803	1,070	5,987	30,375	
1944	74,433	12,074	9,421	1,897	1,101	5,384	29,877	
1945	72,147							
1946	75,750	17,446	5,480	1,687	1,242	6,969	32,824	
1947	78,101	17,811	6,107	1,709	1,320	6,382	33,329	
1948	80,002	17,610	6,165	1,743	1,390	7,187	34,095	
1949	81,773	17,409	6,222	1,777	1,461	7,991	34,860	
1950	83,200	17,208	6,280	1,811	1,531	8,796	35,626	
1951	84,541	16,989	6,511	1,858	1,581	9,413	36,352	
1952	85,808	16,769	6,743	1,906	1,631	10,031	37,080	17,305
1953	86,981	16,680	7,790	1,910	1,630	11,360	39,370	18,073
1954	88,240	16,190	8,010	1,860	1,710	12,120	39,890	18,664
1955	89,280	16,530	8,050	1,900	1,800	12,840	41,120	19,454
1956	90,170	16,140	8,480	2,030	1,830	13,475	41,955	20,614
1957	90,930	15,800	9,080	2,130	2,000	14,000	43,010	22,181
1958	91,770	15,210	9,490	2,220	2,069	14,250	43,239	22,972
1959	92,640	14,620	9,590	2,350	2,270	14,880	43,710	24,052
1960	93,420	14,490	10,020	2,450	2,360	15,310	44,630	24,827
1961	94,290	14,090	10,620	2,530	2,550	15,360	45,150	26,374
1962	95,180	13,690	11,200	2,660	2,700	15,470	45,720	27,508
1963	96,160	12,960	11,530	2,760	2,720	16,110	46,080	28,543
1964	97,180	12,500	11,730	2,940	2,890	16,640	46,700	29,775
1965	98,270	12,120	11,940	3,030	3,080	17,280	47,450	31,042
1966	99,030	11,750	12,200	3,300	3,550	18,110	48,930	32,280
1967	100,190	10,720	12,720	3,220	3,810	19,450	49,920	33,424
1968	101,320	10,550	13,180	3,330	3,870	19,950	50,880	
1969	102,520	10,420	13,470	3,390	3,820	20,320	51,420	
1970	103,720	10,060	13,660	3,510	3,990	20,810	52,030	

Sources and remarks: Total population prewar: based on unpublished materials of M. Umemura and K. Akasaka, forthcoming in LTES, vol. 2. Total population postwar: 1941–68, Statistics Bureau of the Prime Minister's Office, *Nihon no suikeijinkō, Jinkōsuikei shiryō* (Population Estimates of Japan, Population Estimate Series; 1965), no. 36, p. 46; 1969–70, *ibid., Jinkōsuikei geppō* (Monthly Report on Current Population Estimates; Jan. 1972), pp. 4–5. Gainfully occupied population prewar: WS, section L, original estimates by M. Umemura (SRA, vol. 3, pp. 132–39), with unpublished revisions by R. Minami. Gainfully occupied population postwar: agriculture, 1941–52, from interpolated census data, except for 1946, which is from Y. Yamada, *Nihon kokumin shotoku suikei shiryō* (A Comprehensive Survey of National Income Data in Japan; Tokyo, 1957), p. 153. Other industries: 1941–44, our estimation based on data provided in Japan, Economic Planning Agency, *Nihon keizai to kokumin shotoku;* 1946–52, interpolated census data; 1953–70, for all industries interpolated census data using the Labor Force Survey as an index. Employment in the private sector from WS, section L. Figures for 1946–51 are for fiscal year. There is a conceptual difference between the prewar concept of "gainfully occupied persons" and the postwar definition of "labor force." For an explanation, see Chapter 5.

Gross Reproducible Capital Stock by Industry
(At 1934–36 prices, million yen)

Year	Agriculture (including forestry & fishing)	Mining & manufacturing	Facilitating industry	Construction	Services
1905	4,266	898	2,376	95	2,222
1906	4,396	964	2,647	108	2,304
1907	4,485	1,065	2,884	115	2,352
1908	4,586	1,176	3,128	125	2,417
1909	4,692	1,227	3,436	146	2,573
1910	4,770	1,349	3,721	153	2,641
1911	4,848	1,459	4,113	171	2,730
1912	4,915	1,554	4,542	188	2,825
1913	4,985	1,626	4,952	216	3,073
1914	5,039	1,691	5,348	214	3,177
1915	5,130	1,776	5,581	216	3,265
1916	5,220	1,920	5,718	219	3,342
1917	5,314	2,092	6,627	234	3,425
1918	5,385	2,252	7,610	248	3,550
1919	5,491	2,455	8,746	267	3,747
1920	5,592	2,591	9,937	286	3,887
1921	5,711	2,835	10,671	297	4,064
1922	5,821	2,912	11,417	318	4,239
1923	5,802	2,947	11,919	319	4,405
1924	6,067	2,986	12,444	348	4,563
1925	6,203	3,122	12,981	366	4,696
1926	6,339	3,018	13,951	393	4,838
1927	6,490	2,992	14,858	425	5,028
1928	6,648	3,087	15,604	443	5,108
1929	6,807	3,266	16,126	461	5,270
1930	6,968	3,282	16,712	494	5,448
1931	7,118	3,225	17,380	506	5,636
1932	7,253	3,251	17,977	520	5,880
1933	7,360	3,496	18,581	558	6,088
1934	7,443	3,942	19,199	615	6,274
1935	7,522	4,375	19,980	694	6,485
1936	7,613	4,801	20,986	790	6,743
1937	7,644	5,407	21,857	868	6,999
1938	7,736	6,061	22,679	1,011	7,189
1939	7,884	7,260	23,580	1,130	7,431
1940	8,016	8,553	24,225	1,470	7,705

Gross Reproducible Capital Stock by Industry
(At 1934-36 prices, million yen)

Private nonagri-culture	Riparian works	General govt. buildings	Dwellings	Total	Year
4,903	982	396	10,972	22,207	1905
5,267	995	418	11,040	22,872	1906
5,543	1,008	455	11,105	23,469	1907
5,824	1,030	513	11,199	24,174	1908
6,234	1,055	568	11,282	24,979	1909
6,561	1,075	617	11,385	24,711	1910
7,178	1,106	665	11,504	26,596	1911
7,454	1,150	707	11,660	27,541	1912
8,025	1,190	744	11,822	28,608	1913
8,418	1,219	774	11,916	29,378	1914
8,690	1,256	805	12,083	30,112	1915
8,938	1,288	833	12,248	30,788	1916
9,981	1,310	862	12,397	32,261	1917
11,132	1,327	892	12,569	33,833	1918
12,518	1,351	941	12,735	35,733	1919
13,846	1,373	1,013	12,849	37,528	1920
14,796	1,402	1,079	12,982	39,041	1921
15,570	1,434	1,152	13,140	40,432	1922
16,058	1,463	1,245	13,266	41,366	1923
16,464	1,492	1,364	13,426	42,690	1924
17,007	1,518	1,488	13,543	43,917	1925
17,679	1,543	1,643	13,680	45,405	1926
18,419	1,576	1,816	13,810	46,995	1927
19,032	1,608	2,035	13,957	48,490	1928
19,553	1,636	2,199	14,117	49,882	1929
20,034	1,666	2,306	14,263	51,139	1930
20,500	1,687	2,379	14,429	52,360	1931
21,022	1,747	2,455	14,583	53,666	1932
21,802	1,827	2,546	14,805	55,261	1933
22,680	1,879	2,661	15,013	57,026	1934
23,809	1,944	2,819	15,213	59,032	1935
25,253	1,994	2,952	15,336	61,215	1936
26,753	2,044	3,089	15,459	63,367	1937
28,253	2,081	3,182	15,643	65.582	1938
30,387	2,124	3,290	15,826	68,525	1939
32,626	2,148	3,374	16,013	71,504	1940

(continued)

Gross Reproducible Capital Stock by Industry
(At 1960 prices, billion yen)

Year	Agriculture (including forestry & fishing)	Mining & manufacturing	Facilitating industry	Construction	Services
1953	5,787	4,266	8,154	150	5,016
1954	6,101	4,631	8,561	168	5,165
1955	6,353	4,922	8,980	177	5,341
1956	6,586	5,337	9,484	211	5,533
1957	6,779	6,029	10,091	242	5,848
1958	6,959	6,764	10,782	280	6,140
1959	7,258	7,508	11,563	335	6,464
1960	7,615	8,820	12,431	410	7,003
1961	7,969	10,345	13,820	569	7,692
1962	8,486	12,106	15,400	721	8,512
1963	8,891	13,722	17,211	860	9,412
1964	9,448	15,821	19,298	1,036	10,573
1965	9,999	17,417	21,816	1,152	11,620

Gross Reproducible Capital Stock by Industry
(At 1960 prices, billion yen)

Private nonagri- culture	Riparian works	General govt. buildings	Dwellings	Total	Year
11,244	891	809	9,798	34,871	1953
11,998	941	1,190	9,985	36,742	1954
12,659	992	1,551	10,166	38,482	1955
13,558	1,033	1,832	10,495	40,511	1956
15,852	1,066	2,162	10,946	43,163	1957
16,231	1,109	2,550	11,430	46,014	1958
17,738	1,164	2,984	11,746	49,022	1959
20,126	1,220	3,507	12,312	53,318	1960
22,978	1,282	4,066	12,875	58,618	1961
26,175	1,347	4,807	13,607	64,986	1962
29,345	1,429	5,597	14,496	71,618	1963
33,444	1,564	6,469	15,590	79,799	1964
36,767	1,714	7,424	16,932	88,074	1965

Sources and remarks: Prewar: LTES, vol. 3, pp. 160–62, and SRA, vol. 3, p. 170. LTES, vol. 3 (Capital Stock) also supplies net series for prewar years. Agricultural capital from WS, section K. Postwar: SRA, vol. 3, p. 167. Capital stock values are given at the end of the calendar year. Private capital stock from WS, section K.

[a] Excluding dwellings for 1953–65.

Major Ratios, Relative Income Shares, Rates of Capital Return and Wages:
Private Nonagriculture
(Smoothed series at 1934-36 prices)

Year	Capital-Output ratio (K/Y)	Output-Labor ratio (Y/L) *(yen per head)*	Capital-Labor ratio (K/L) *(yen per head)*	Factor share *(pct.)* Capital (α)	Labor (β)	Wages *(yen per head a year)*	Rates of capital return (in rates of change, *pct.*)
1908	1.26	560	705	42.4	57.6	315	
1909	1.29	573	740	42.6	57.4	323	-2.08
1910	1.35	574	773	42.6	57.4	324	-4.24
1911	1.41	575	809	42.4	57.6	326	-4.75
1912	1.41	593	837	42.9	57.1	333	1.00
1913	1.40	619	865	44.7	55.3	340	5.26
1914	1.37	650	892	47.0	53.0	343	7.86
1915	1.35	678	916	48.8	51.2	348	4.60
1916	1.36	703	956	49.9	50.1	355	1.66
1917	1.39	722	1,004	50.2	49.8	363	-1.63
1918	1.42	749	1,061	49.3	50.7	385	-3.60
1919	1.47	770	1,129	47.3	52.7	411	-7.18
1920	1.54	773	1,189	44.0	56.0	435	-11.46
1921	1.61	778	1,251	40.3	59.7	458	-12.24
1922	1.67	782	1,306	37.6	62.4	479	-10.36
1923	1.71	786	1,346	35.4	64.6	496	-8.00
1924	1.73	795	1,380	33.7	66.3	511	-6.28
1925	1.75	802	1,403	33.5	66.5	515	-1.03
1926	1.76	807	1,422	34.2	65.8	513	1.04
1927	1.79	808	1,449	34.9	65.1	509	0.25
1928	1.83	804	1,471	35.2	64.8	512	-1.03
1929	1.84	811	1,497	34.7	65.3	520	-2.59
1930	1.85	823	1,526	34.5	65.5	531	-0.53
1931	1.83	841	1,543	34.7	65.3	546	1.60
1932	1.83	847	1,557	34.8	65.2	552	0
1933	1.84	853	1,578	35.0	65.0	560	0
1934	1.81	882	1,603	35.8	64.2	578	3.68
1935	1.85	936	1,637	37.0	63.0	599	6.60
1936	1.79	997	1,674	38.2	61.8	634	8.10
1937	1.76	1,054	1,727	39.2	60.8	667	6.17
1938	1.74	1,106	1,791	40.0	60.0	699	4.15

Major Ratios, Relative Income Shares, Rates of Capital Return and Wages:
Private Nonagriculture
(Smoothed series at 1960 prices)

Year	Capital-Output ratio (K/Y)	Output-Labor ratio (Y/L) *(thousand yen per head)*	Capital-Labor ratio (K/L) *(thousand yen per head)*	Factor share *(pct.)* Capital (α)	Factor share *(pct.)* Labor (β)	Wages *(thousand yen per head a year)*	Rates of capital return (in rates of change, *pct.*)
1954		308		24.7	76.0	234	
1955	1.93	325	627	25.5	74.5	242	
1956	1.88	341	643	26.5	73.5	251	6.82
1957	1.84	360	660	27.4	72.6	261	5.67
1958	1.75	392	687	29.0	71.0	278	10.74
1959	1.68	430	724	30.6	69.4	299	10.30
1960	1.64	473	776	31.6	68.4	324	6.04
1961	1.61	519	836	32.6	67.4	350	5.18
1962	1.59	572	907	33.4	66.6	381	3.94
1963	1.60	614	980	33.4	66.6	409	-0.95
1964	1.61	655	1,056	33.0	67.0	439	-1.91

Sources and remarks: K/Y, K/L, Y/L computed from smoothed series (seven-year averages prewar, and five-year averages postwar), based on annual data of BST.4 (Y), BST.15 (L), and BST.16 (K). Prewar and postwar relative shares from WS, section O. For a description of estimation procedures, see Appendix Note. All terms have been converted into gross shares, wages for the private nonagricultural sector being consistent with shares from WS, section W. The original series of the rate of capital return (r) is calculated as $r = \alpha Y/K$ (in constant prices).

Distribution of National Income
(Current prices: 1941-44, million yen; 1946-70, billion yen)

Year	National income at factor cost (1)	Compensation of employees (2)	Income from unincorporated enterprises (4) + (5) (3)	Agriculture, forestry & fishing (4)	Others (5)
1941	35,834	13,845	11,394	5,137	6,257
1942	42,144	16,190	13,341	6,310	7,031
1943	48,448	20,790	12,687	6,125	6,562
1944	56,937	26,648	13,352	7,667	5,685
1945					
1946	362	111	236	123	113
1947	968	315	640	303	337
1948	1,961	828	1,091	547	544
1949	2,737	1,144	1,336	652	684
1950	3,382	1,415	1,541	772	769
1951	4,525	1,927	1,958	992	966
1952	5,007	2,384	1,992	1,028	964
1953	5,843	2,938	2,135	1,099	1,036
1954	6,566	3,246	2,371	1,290	1,081
1955	7,114	3,527	2,636	1,456	1,180
1956	7,854	4,004	2,700	1,377	1,323
1957	9,208	4,585	2,876	1,492	1,384
1958	9,562	4,991	2,817	1,446	1,371
1959	10,586	5,540	2,999	1,530	1,469
1960	12,817	6,435	3,393	1,625	1,768
1961	15,155	7,625	3,904	1,786	2,118
1962	17,349	9,091	4,278	1,907	2,371
1963	19,904	10,682	4,900	2,043	2,857
1964	22,753	12,349	5,413	2,089	3,324
1965	25,430	14,303	5,971	2,382	3,589
1966	29,341	16,416	6,614	2,710	3,904
1967	34,908	18,961	7,947	3,329	4,619
1968	41,489	22,144	9,292	3,466	5,826
1969	47,969	25,803	10,255	3,441	6,814
1970	57,170	31,073	11,356	3,571	7,785

Distribution of National Income
(Current prices: 1941–44, million yen; 1946–70, billion yen)

Income from property (7) + (8) + (9) (6)	Rent (7)	Investment (8)	Dividends (9)	Corporate transfers to households & private nonprofit institutions (10)	Direct taxes and charges on private corporations (11)	Year
6,642	2,225	3,261	1,156		1,783	1941
7,495	2,168	4,096	1,231		2,344	1942
8,958	2,454	5,168	1,336		2,951	1943
10,190	2,200	6,611	1,379		4,204	1944
14	5	8	1		4	1946
21	10	9	2		13	1947
42	17	17	8		40	1948
62	19	29	14		94	1949
104	30	41	33		109	1950
145	40	56	49		30	1951
227	89	86	52	6	251	1952
312	126	119	67	9	242	1953
371	158	154	59	10	271	1954
484	193	206	85	12	242	1955
577	233	242	102	16	291	1956
694	275	291	128	17	415	1957
810	325	354	132	15	413	1958
1,010	407	445	158	19	466	1959
1,253	491	548	214	24	648	1960
1,544	586	687	271	28	835	1961
1,830	677	806	347	30	966	1962
2,135	783	961	391	35	1,045	1963
2,513	936	1,137	440	39	1,159	1964
2,876	1,078	1,351	447	43	1,265	1965
3,462	1,391	1,601	470	46	1,333	1966
4,027	1,614	1,906	507	58	1,629	1967
4,744	1,875	2,276	593	67	2,046	1968
5,561	2,172	2,715	674	86	2,560	1969
6,633	2,553	3,277	803	101	3,224	1970

(continued)

Distribution of National Income
(Current prices: 1941–44, million yen; 1946–70, billion yen)

Year	Saving of private corporations (12)	General govt. income from property and entrepreneur-ship (13)	Less: Interest on public debt (14)	Less: Interest on consumers' debt (15)	Income from private corporations (16)	Net factor income from abroad
1941	1,781	130			4,720	259
1942	2,176	231			5,751	367
1943	2,519	195			6,806	348
1944	2,986	-608			8,569	165
1945						
1946	-1	-2			4	
1947	-4	-15			10	-1
1948	2	-41			51	-1
1949	38	64			146	-1
1950	192	23			334	-2
1951	215	50			493	-3
1952	152	33	30	8	464	
1953	214	46	42	11	531	
1954	300	56	46	13	641	
1955	222	58	51	16	561	
1956	274	66	55	19	683	
1957	555	140	53	21	1,115	
1958	443	163	63	27	1,003	
1959	478	163	61	28	1,121	
1960	956	204	63	33	1,842	
1961	1,050	274	63	42	2,184	
1962	966	297	62	47	2,309	
1963	916	330	86	53	2,387	
1964	1,163	276	90	69	2,800	
1965	955	208	106	85	2,709	
1966	1,448	264	143	99	3,523	
1967	2,289	332	211	124	4,616	
1968	3,272	379	297	158	5,962	
1969	3,724	539	367	192	7,545	
1970	4,757	689	421	242	9,048	

Sources and remarks: No reliable and consistent estimates are available for the prewar distribution of national income. Postwar: 1941–51, NIS (1962), pp. 144–45; 1952–65, revised NIS (1969), pp. 70–71; 1966–70, NIS (1972), pp. 38–39. Figures for 1945 are not available; figures for 1946–51 are for fiscal year. For 1941–51, "net factor income from abroad" is listed separately because a breakdown is not available.

Index

Index